Work, Unemployment,
and Mental Health

Work, Unemployment, and Mental Health

PETER WARR

MRC/ESRC Social and Applied Psychology Unit, University of Sheffield

CLARENDON PRESS · OXFORD

1987

Oxford University Press, Walton Street, Oxford OX2 6DP

Oxford New York Toronto
Delhi Bombay Calcutta Madras Karachi
Petaling Jaya Singapore Hong Kong Tokyo
Nairobi Dar es Salaam Cape Town
Melbourne Auckland

and associated companies in
Beirut Berlin Ibadan Nicosia

Oxford is a trademark of Oxford University Press

Published in the United States
by Oxford University Press, New York

British Library Cataloguing in Publication Data
Warr, Peter
Work, unemployment and mental health.
1. Psychology, Industrial   2. Unemployment
—Psychological aspects
I. Title
158.7   HF5548.8
ISBN 0–19–852158–8
ISBN 0–19–852159–6 Pbk

Library of Congress Cataloging-in-Publication Data
Warr, Peter B. (Peter Bryan)
Work, unemployment, and mental health.
Bibliography: p.
Includes indexes.
1. Industrial psychiatry.   2. Work—Psychological
aspects.   3. Unemployment—Psychological aspects.
I. Title. [DNLM: 1. Employment. 2. Mental Health.
3. Unemployment.   WA 400 W286w]
RC967.5.W37   1987   616.89   87–5674
ISBN 0–19–852158–8
ISBN 0–19–852159–6 (pbk.)

Processed by the Oxford Text System
Printed and bound in
Great Britain by Biddles Ltd,
Guildford and King's Lynn

Preface

In writing a book one has many purposes. The explicit goal in this case is to develop and apply a systematic conceptual framework for interpreting and investigating the impact of environments upon mental health. A model is proposed which is intended to embrace all kinds of human settings; and particularly detailed attention is given to the environments of employment and unemployment.

The book's conceptual framework is presented as the 'vitamin model', developing an analogy with the impact of vitamins upon physical health. Nine categories of environmental 'vitamins' are proposed, and the processes through which they may act upon mental health are examined. Modifying influences of personal characteristics are also addressed in each case.

Associated with the primary goal are several other purposes. For example, I have been disturbed by the fact that investigators into employment and unemployment fall into two rather separate professional groups, each largely ignorant of the other. It is important to bring the two research fields closer together, and some encouragement in that direction is attempted here.

Defining and solving problems in the everyday world requires that we draw from a range of disciplinary perspectives. Nevertheless, a primary focus from the standpoint of a single discipline usually remains desirable. In the present case, I have sought to combine the interests of psychologists, psychiatrists, sociologists, and management scientists, with a focus which is initially psychological, but which takes in many themes and references from neighbouring domains.

Another, more personal, concern has been to create time for reflecting purposively upon some difficult conceptual issues, which tend to be set aside in the course of much empirical research. Investigations tend to start from contemporary assumptions and use available methods, statistics and computer packages. That is often appropriate and sensible, but we should also seek to develop alternative frameworks and to examine the validity of orthodox perspectives.

For example, why should we assume that environmental factors are

associated with psychological responses in a linear fashion? What are the conceptual and methodological implications of a non-linear model? Are different non-linear models required for different psychological responses? In examining the impact of, say, jobs upon mental health, how should the latter be construed and measured? How can we ever demonstrate that a specific environmental feature is by itself causally important? Is 'baseline' mental health substantially modified by current situational conditions? Do environmental factors combine additively or synergistically in their impact upon people? Are the modes of combination different for different aspects of mental health? What are the consequences of building a model in terms primarily of situations rather than of persons? How can specific attributes of environments and of persons be studied in mutual interaction? What conceptual bases can be suggested for those interactions?

I have set out to reflect upon broad questions of that kind, reviewing the ideas of experienced commentators, and suggesting an account which takes a stance in each respect. The result is a conceptual framework which appears to be systematic and internally coherent. As with all broad models of the kind, it is not in overall terms 'right' or 'wrong' in a simple empirical sense. However, many specific predictions are included, and these are now open to empirical test. More generally, in evaluating the framework, assessments should particularly ask whether it is useful for the specific purposes intended; information on which to base such a judgement is presented throughout the book.

The general approach has been to follow a 'what if?' course. What do we expect to find if we choose to view the world through this particular framework? What are the implications of the perspective for research and practice? What assumptions and procedures now come under challenge? Large bodies of empirical data have been examined along the way, but they (with their inevitable contemporary limitations) have not been the final arbiter of my conclusions. In that sense I have deliberately been operating at a level somewhat detached from current factual knowledge.

However, I have also set out to provide a comprehensive review of relevant literatures. For example, the chapters on unemployment and on certain job factors are probably as exhaustive in their treatment of published research as any other available account. The book thus seeks to provide an entry into substantial sets of literature, as well as having its own distinct and systematic perspective.

Chapter 1 outlines the overall framework and introduces some objectives for later chapters. Chapters 2 and 3 present a view of mental health in Western society and an account of possible measurement approaches. The essential value-base of mental health assessment is emphasized there and in later sections. The middle part of the book (Chapters 5 to 10) deals with the vitamin model in its application to job environments, and the next two chapters apply the framework to the settings of unemployment. Individual differences and person–situation interactions are the focus of Chapters 13 and 14; and the final chapter summarizes the strengths and weaknesses of the approach. That last chapter also expands upon the fact that both jobs and joblessness can be construed in the same terms, so that employment and unemployment can in parallel ways be psychologically either 'good' or 'bad'. Possible ways to move both types of environment from 'bad' towards 'good' are considered.

In that respect the book has very practical intentions. The broad conceptual issues are first tackled in an abstract way, both because that is intrinsically necessary, but also in the hope that bringing together factual and theoretical material will suggest changes in the way particular environments can be designed. The book thus provides a 'framework', both in the sense of structured aid to perception and inquiry, and also as a basis for action. I hope that it will be used in both ways.

In the course of preparing the work, I have received assistance from many people. I am particularly grateful to colleagues at the Social and Applied Psychology Unit for their comments on earlier drafts and for being a consistently valuable source of ideas and suggestions. In addition, I am also much indebted to members of other institutions, who found time in their extremely busy professional lives to advise me on specific points or to review sections of interest to them. Particular thanks are due to my secretary, Karen Thompson, who so effectively word-processed the entire text through its many versions. Thank you all very much.

Sheffield   P.B.W.
August 1986

Contents

1. **Environmental influences upon mental health**   1

Principal features of the environment   2
   1. Opportunity for control   3
   2. Opportunity for skill use   4
   3. Externally generated goals   5
   4. Variety   6
   5. Environmental clarity   6
   6. Availability of money   6
   7. Physical security   7
   8. Opportunity for interpersonal contact   7
   9. Valued social position   8
A vitamin model of the environment and mental health   9
   The mid-range plateau   11
   Very high environmental values   13
The environment and the individual   15
   Situation-centred models   15
   Measuring the environment   17
   Individual differences   18
Some implications of the vitamin model   19
Summary and forward look   22

2. **The concept of mental health**   24

Mental health from a Western perspective   25
Affective well-being   26
Competence   29
Autonomy   30
Aspiration   31
Integrated functioning   33

Some general issues	34
Duration of episodes	34
Complex inference from several components	35
Different points of view	36
Summary	38

3. The measurement of context-free and job-related mental health — 40

Measuring affective well-being	40
Context-free well-being	41
Job-related well-being	46
Measuring competence	49
Context-free competence	49
Job-related competence	50
Measuring autonomy	51
Measuring aspiration	52
Measuring integrated functioning	53
Summary	54

4. Jobs and mental health: nine types of evidence — 56

Employment, unemployment, non-employment, and work	56
The impact of unemployment	59
Population estimates of job-related mental health	60
Qualitative evidence about particular jobs	63
Quantitative evidence about particular jobs	65
Job features which affect mental health	67
Movement between jobs	68
Evidence from the clinic	69
Employment as a support for the mentally ill	70
Spill-over or compensation	72
Summary	76

5. Job content: opportunity for control, opportunity for skill use, and variety — 78

Opportunity for control	79
Intrinsic control	80
Extrinsic control	87
Opportunity for skill use	90
Variety	94
Summary	100

6. **Interpreting research into job characteristics**   101

    Overall job complexity   101
    Results in relation to five components of mental health   105
    Four general issues   109
      Subjective measures and common-method variance   110
      Non-linear relationships   112
      Specific causal factors   113
      Reciprocal causality   114
    Summary   115

7. **Goals, workload, and the structure of tasks**   117

    Intrinsic job demands   118
      Job-related mental health   120
      Context-free mental health   121
      Conflicting demands   124
      Overview   126
    The combined effects of workload and control   128
    Task identity, traction, and flow   134
    Time demands   138
      Magnitude of time demands   139
      Pattern of time demands   141
    Summary   143

8. **Environmental clarity**   145

    Information about the consequences of behaviour   146
    Information about the future   149
    Information about required behaviour   151
    Information after a transition   153
    Review of findings about the four types of job clarity   157
    Summary   161

9. **Extrinsic job features: pay and physical conditions**   162

    Availability of money   162
      Income level   163
      Perceived fairness   165
      Adequacy and continuity   166

Physical security   168
  Temperature   170
  Noise   170
  Illumination, vibration, danger, and physical effort   171
  Equipment design   172
  Overview   173
Summary   174

10. **Extrinsic job features: interpersonal contact and social   176
     position**

Opportunity for interpersonal contact   176
  Amount of interaction   178
  Social support   180
  Privacy and personal territory   186
Valued social position   188
  Cultural evaluations   189
  Sub-cultural evaluations   190
  Personal evaluations   191
Summary   192

11. **The impact of unemployment**   194

Research findings   195
  Mental health   196
  Aggregate time-series investigations   199
  Physical health   202
  Family processes   206
Summary   207
Appendix   208

12. **The jobless environment**   210

Nine environmental features   212
  Opportunity for control   212
  Opportunity for skill use   212
  Externally generated goals   213
  Variety   215
  Environmental clarity   215
  Availability of money   217
  Physical security   220
  Opportunity for interpersonal contact   220
  Valued social position   223

Five specific applications of the model 226
  Middle-aged men 226
  Teenagers 227
  Women 229
  The long-term unemployed 231
  Unemployed people who regain a job 234
Summary 235

13. **Interactions between persons and situations** 237

Enduring personal characteristics 238
  Demographic features, abilities, and values 238
  Baseline mental health 239
Measuring the impact of personal characteristics 242
  Statistical procedures 243
  An overall framework 244
Summary 247

14. **Personal characteristics and mental health in jobs and unemployment** 248

Individual differences and job-related mental health 248
  Baseline mental health 248
  Demographic features 249
  Values 251
  Abilities 253
Personal modifiers of the impact of job conditions 253
  Matching personal characteristics 253
  Research findings 255
  Preference models of person–environment fit 265
  Overview 270
Individual differences and unemployment 271
Summary 275

15. **The vitamin model: appraisal and application** 277

The notion of mental health 277
The vitamin model 280
  Categorization of the environment 280
  Processes within the vitamin model 286
  Interactions between persons and situations 290
Good and bad jobs and good and bad unemployment 291
  Changing the work environment 292
  Changing unemployment 299
Summary 301

References	303
Subject index	345
Author index	351

1

Environmental influences upon mental health

The principal aim of this book is to propose and apply a broad-ranging model of some environmental determinants of mental health. The features to be considered may be studied in any environment, but particular attention will be paid to the settings of paid work and unemployment. It will be argued that mental health in both these settings is determined by the same environmental characteristics. The harmful features of some jobs are also those which cause deterioration in unemployment, and the factors which are beneficial in jobs can also enhance mental health during unemployment.

The framework to be developed has three major parts. The first two are what McGuire (1983) has described as 'categorical' and 'process' theories. The former 'involve chunking the innumerable variables into a manageable set of categories, perhaps five to ten, each of which can be further partitioned into several levels of more specific subcategories' (p. 33). In the present case, nine broad environmental categories will be proposed, and a number of features within each will be examined. 'Process' theories, the second type, attempt to account for the ways in which outcome variables take their particular forms. As McGuire points out, a combination of categorical and process theories can provide a particularly useful representation of a complex domain, if a categorical analysis of the primary causal variables can be joined with a process analysis of the outcome variables.

That is the aim of the first two parts of the model. But what are the 'outcome variables'? The concept of mental health is problematic in several respects, and it would be helpful to have available an account of the usage to be adopted. Chapter 2 thus describes a five-component perspective, which seeks to summarize principal aspects of mental health common to the models developed by many Western writers. It will then be possible in subsequent chapters to explore processes linking the nine environmental categories and their several subcategories to the five components of mental health.

The third part of the overall framework addresses the interaction between persons and situations. Associations between each environmental feature and the suggested components of mental health are expected to differ, according to the level of certain relatively stable personal attributes. A systematic account of individual characteristics which might act as mediating factors will be developed in Chapters 13 and 14.

The book is an attempt at 'top down' as well as 'bottom up' theorizing, combining inferences from general statements and broad assumptions with specific inductions from known facts and limited generalizations. Conceptual frameworks of this kind are never entirely supported by empirical data, because they are created relatively independently of published findings in order to shape perceptions and research activity (e.g. Warr 1980). However, it is desirable that broad perspectives are linked to the more specific models already under investigation, and connections of that kind will be made throughout the book.

This opening chapter introduces the three main parts of the framework. First is an outline of the nine features proposed as determinants of mental health in all kinds of environment. Second, the pattern through which these environmental features are thought to influence mental health is described. Third, the chapter contains an initial consideration of possible interactions between people and their environments. Finally, attention is turned to some implications of the suggested approach. If we adopt the present perspective, what are the consequences for empirical enquiry, theoretical development, and practical intervention?

Principal features of the environment

Nine features of the environment have been selected to form the basis of this book. These will first be introduced in general terms, commencing with a summary list:
1. Opportunity for control
2. Opportunity for skill use
3. Externally generated goals
4. Variety
5. Environmental clarity
6. Availability of money
7. Physical security
8. Opportunity for interpersonal contact
9. Valued social position

It is important to recognize the logical status of the presentation which follows. Some research evidence is available in respect of each of the nine features, although no comprehensive test of their overall importance has been carried out. Evidence will mainly be cited from occupational and organizational psychology, but reference will also be made to studies in clinical psychology and psychiatry, sociology, and community and social psychology. However, several important components of the model remain at this stage unvalidated assumptions. The present framework of environmental categories and causal processes will thus in a sense be imposed upon currently available findings, in order to test out its value and to provide an overarching perspective on a number of different issues.

For convenience of exposition the outline which follows tends to treat 'the environment' as separate from and independent of 'the individual'. In practice, however, the two interact in many ways, conceptually as well as behaviourally. These interactions give rise to the third component of the present model, which will be considered later in the chapter and at several other points in the book.

For the present it should be noted that those primary categories of the environment referred to as 'opportunities' may be considered at three levels. First, there is a sense in which an opportunity may exist in the environment, whether or not it is noticed. Second, this opportunity might be perceived by an individual to be present. And, third, he or she may act to take advantage of it. These three levels (present, perceived, and acted upon) will sometimes be distinguished in later discussions, but at this introductory stage will often be treated together. In general, an environment containing 'the opportunity for X' is one which promotes, encourages or facilitates X. An environment lacking that opportunity is one which prevents or inhibits X.

Perceived opportunities have in some circumstances been referred to as 'affordances' (e.g. Gibson 1979; Von Hofsten 1985). These are properties of the world which are personally significant to a perceiver or a group of perceivers; they indicate that an environment affords certain possibilities or permits certain actions which are important to the person. In Gibson's approach, affordances were viewed as natural units of perception. The present account is less concerned with perceptual processes and is in more macroscopic and social terms, but it shares with Gibson's model an emphasis upon environmental features which have important positive or negative consequences. This point will be developed later in the chapter.

The shape of the association between environmental features and mental health will also be examined later. At the heart of the model is a postulated non-linear association. However, in this introductory section it will suffice merely to consider higher and lower values of each feature; in general, low values are thought to be potentially harmful. 'Mental health' is itself left undefined at this stage, and a detailed account of the way in which the term is to be used will be provided in Chapter 2. At that point the following major components of mental health will be identified : affective well-being, competence, autonomy, aspiration, and integrated functioning. The principal focus throughout the book is upon gradations of mental health among people who are themselves healthy, those identified as not-ill in terms of conventional medical criteria.

1. Opportunity for control

The first determinant of mental health is assumed to lie in the opportunities provided by an environment for a person to control activities and events.

Such opportunities may be of a very restricted kind, giving rise to limited decisions about one's own actions, or they may extend into major discretion over other people's lives.

Mental health is expected to be enhanced by situations which promote personal control. Although the amount of control exercised by a particular individual is partly determined by his or her motivation relative to a given situation (e.g. Langer 1983), it is clear that physical environments and roles within social institutions vary in the extent to which they constrain or provide opportunities for decision-making and influence. In employment settings, for instance, jobs differ considerably in the freedom they provide for workers to choose their objectives, to schedule their tasks, and to determine the ways in which work should be undertaken.

The opportunity for control has two main elements: the opportunity to decide and act in one's chosen way, and the potential to predict the consequences of action. The former is of particular importance, and will receive primary attention under this heading. Absence of the second element gives rise to a specific form of uncontrollability, when a person has freedom of decision and action but cannot predict the outcomes of these. Not knowing the consequences of behaviour, one cannot control what will happen (e.g. Seligman 1975). That particular type of low control opportunity in the absence of information will be considered later, as a form of low 'environmental clarity'.

Opportunity for control is introduced first among the assumed foundations of mental health for an explicit reason. If the remaining eight environmental features have substantial impact upon mental health, it may be that it is through influencing the level of those that a person can most directly affect his or her mental health. Opportunity for control may thus be important in determining the level of other features as well as contributing to mental health in its own right.

2.   Opportunity for skill use

A related feature is the degree to which the environment inhibits or encourages the utilization and development of skills. Skilled performance is satisfying in its smooth and familiar aspects and for permitting effective responses to novel or complex stimuli. It is also psychologically important in assisting people to achieve targets, or to produce something useful or attractive. Restrictions on skill use may be of two kinds. First are those which prevent people from using skills which they already possess, permitting instead only behaviours which are well within routine capability. Second are restrictions on the acquisition of new skills, requiring people to remain at low levels of skilled performance despite their potential for extending into more complex activity.

This second environmental feature is often associated with the previous one, in that skill use typically implies environmental control. However, control can sometimes be present in conjunction with a low level of skill, when a person can influence the environment in ways which are simple and unskilled but nevertheless of great personal importance.

3.   *Externally generated goals*

A third feature assumed to underlie mental health is the presence or absence of goals generated by the environment. Such goals arise partly through physical deficits in the environment (for example, the absence of food in one's current location but its known presence elsewhere), but also through obligations and targets deriving from roles within formal and informal institutions. These roles introduce normative requirements to behave in certain ways, to follow certain routines, and to be in specified locations at certain times (e.g. Biddle 1979). Role-generated requirements give rise to organized sequences of actions, in which specific targets and their overall structure provide 'traction' which draws people along.

These environmental characteristics are here suggested to yield 'goals', rather than 'demands', 'requirements', 'prescriptions', or similar terms, in order to recognize that targets arising from the environment vary in the degree to which they are imposed or voluntarily accepted. In the former case the imposed targets might be referred to as environmental 'demands', 'requirements', etc., and these labels will be used in some later discussions. However, they have the disadvantage of suggesting coercion in all cases, whereas 'goal' more appropriately refers to all targets, whether they are imposed or self-selected.

Miller *et al.* (1960) have illustrated how goals give rise to plans, which structure the pattern of behaviour. People test the environment by seeking feedback in relation to their progress towards a goal, and discrepancies between the contemporary environment and a target give rise to further goals. Goals and plans are thus viewed as being generated by the nature of an environment as well as through motivational characteristics of people themselves. This perspective falls within 'action theory', a broad perspective which takes goal-oriented action to be the fundamental unit of psychology (e.g. Frese and Sabini 1985). Protagonists of this approach point out that it is through action that we come to know the world; perceptual and cognitive processes are enmeshed within sequences of actions which provide new information and feedback about previous actions. 'Action units' are defined by their goals, and goals arise both from the environment and from the person.

An environment which makes no demands upon a person sets up no objectives and encourages no activity or achievement. Conversely, a setting which gives rise to the establishment and pursuit of goals is assumed to lead to activities which both intrinsically and through their consequences may have a positive impact upon mental health. One may of course envisage situations which generate too many goals or goals which are too difficult, as well as cases in which a person chooses not to act in relation to a perceived demand. Those possibilities will be considered later, as will the fact that people differ in their tendency to establish goals themselves in the absence of environmental pressure.

4. Variety

It sometimes happens that externally generated goals and associated actions are repetitive and invariant. Required activity of a repetitive kind seems unlikely to contribute to mental health to the same degree as more diverse requirements, which introduce novelty and break up uniformity of activity and location. Hence it is important to include environmental variety as an additional feature in this framework.

A low-variety environment may be viewed as one which constrains a person in physical location and in role-related activities. Variety is increased in relation to the number of roles available, but in addition some roles carry with them greater heterogeneity than do others. For example, the job activities of a senior manager are notably more diverse than those of a worker on an assembly line. Low variety within a role or within a set of roles is here assumed in general to have a negative impact upon mental health.

5. Environmental clarity

The fifth feature thought to underlie mental health concerns the degree to which a person's environment is clear or opaque. Three aspects of this seem to be of particular significance. First is the availability of feedback about the consequences of one's actions; low predictability of these outcomes was introduced earlier as the source of one type of uncontrollability. Second is the degree to which other people and systems in the environment are pre-dictable, so that one can foresee likely responses to one's own actions and, in the longer term, develop a conception of a likely life course. And third is the clarity of role requirements and normative expectations about behaviour, the degree to which standards are explicit and generally accepted within one's environment.

It is assumed that environments which are unclear in these three respects are likely to impair mental health. Associated with this possibility is the significance of rate of change within an environment. Rapid changes may affect a range of contingencies and outcomes, and in so doing they can markedly reduce clarity of the kinds suggested here.

6. Availability of money

Money is often ignored in discussions of mental health, yet its absence can give rise to extensive psychological problems. When personal and family requirements exceed the financial resources available, small changes in either requirements or resources become particularly significant (e.g. Ashley 1983). Poverty is in several ways self-perpetuating. For example, poor people are liable to pay more than others for equivalent goods or services. Heating costs may be greater because of an inability to pay for insulation or for energy-efficient equipment; bulk purchases of household items at reduced prices are impossible because of lack of cash; a car is not available to travel to cheaper retail outlets.

More generally, shortage of money means that payment of some bills is only possible if others are left unpaid. Wilson and Herbert (1978) describe unresolved problems such as the toilet out of action for six weeks or water dripping from the ceiling for months. Household gas or electricity may be disconnected and debts may increase with no prospect of being met. Entertainment requiring expenditure is not possible, psychological threats are increased, and life is impoverished in many senses beyond the merely financial.

Poverty is likely to affect other environmental features in the present framework. For example, it reduces the opportunity for personal control, and inhibits skill use in hobby activities which require money. In some settings it is helpful to regard a low standard of living in terms of relative rather than absolute deprivation: level of poverty should then be judged in relation to the living standards of other members of the population in question (e.g. Rainwater 1974; Townsend 1974). In general, however, it seems clear that severely restricted access to money can give rise to many processes likely to impair mental health. That is not to suggest that each increase in income will increase mental health; the assumed pattern of association will be considered shortly.

7. Physical security

A seventh feature within the present framework is a physically secure living environment. Environments need to protect a person against physical threat and to provide an adequate level of physical security in respect of heating, facilities for food preparation, space for sleeping, and a private area of personal territory. They also need to be reasonably permanent, providing security of tenure in the sense that occupants can look forward to their continued presence or can predict moving to other adequate settings.

This feature tends in practice to be associated with the previous one, availability of money. However, it will be helpful in later chapters to preserve the conceptual distinction between them.

8. Opportunity for interpersonal contact

Environments also differ in the opportunity they provide for contact with other people. This is important for at least four reasons. First, such contact meets needs for friendship and reduces feelings of loneliness. The desirability of this is clear from everyday experience, and it has been incorporated in many theoretical frameworks. For example, existential psychologists such as Binswanger (1963) and May (1967) have emphasized people's attempts through personal choice and commitment to bridge the distance between themselves and others. Early drive and motivation theorists such as McDougall (1932) and Murray (1938) regularly included 'social' drives within their expositions of human psychology.

Second, it is clear that interpersonal contact can provide help of many kinds. These have often been referred to generically as 'social support' (e.g. Thoits 1982), with the suggestion that support may be 'emotional' (contributing primarily to well-being through emotional inputs) or 'instrumental' (contributing to the resolution of problems through practical help and advice). Also important is 'motivational' support, whereby people are encouraged to persist in their efforts at problem-solution, and reassured that their endeavours will ultimately be successful (e.g. Wills 1985).

A third function is in terms of social comparison. Festinger's (1954) theory asserted that people are motivated to compare their opinions and abilities with those of other people, in order better to interpret and appraise themselves. In some cases they can obtain fairly objective information about their position (for example, by athletic competition), but in most areas they have to rely on more uncertain knowledge arising from social encounters. These encounters provide opportunities for comparisons between oneself and others, and in part they are steered by participants with this in mind.

A fourth importance of interpersonal contact arises from the fact that many goals can be achieved only through the interdependent efforts of several people. Membership of formal or informal groups makes possible the establishment and attainment of goals which could not be realized by an individual alone. In this way the opportunity for interpersonal contact provided by an environment can be seen to link with those features in the present account which are concerned with goals, variety, control, and skill use.

9. Valued social position

The ninth aspect considered to be important is a position within a social structure which carries some esteem from others. In practice, a person may be a member of several social structures (for instance, a family, a manufacturing company, a local community, and society as a whole), so that he or she has the possibility of esteem from several positions.

Esteem within a social structure is generated primarily through the value attached to activities inherent in a role and the contribution these make to the institution in question. Role incumbency also provides public evidence that one has certain abilities, conforms to certain norms, and meets certain social obligations. In turn, membership of an institution may carry with it high or low esteem in the wider community. Particular role activities may of course be considered important to different degrees by different people, and external indicators of social esteem do not always coincide with the value which a person accords to his or her own contributions. Nevertheless, there is often widespread agreement about the levels of social and personal esteem which derive from particular positions.

This feature is also associated with several of the others. For example, a position and its role activities provide opportunities for social comparison, may enhance predictability and environmental clarity, and impose goals and behavioural traction. More valued positions in wider society may also carry with them larger incomes than those accorded lower status.

The conceptual and empirical overlaps between these nine features might suggest that a smaller number of categories should be identified as primary. Reducing the number of components in the model may appear convenient, but it would be at the expense of creating a less differentiated treatment of the environment. Decisions about number of elements in a model always have to balance the opposed requirements of parsimony and complexity, and are ultimately a matter of judgement which has to be assessed in the light of subsequent applications. It is in that tentative spirit that the present choice of nine components is made, rather than, say, six or twelve.

The features themselves are viewed as 'categories' within an outline categorical model of the type mentioned at the beginning of the chapter. For each one, a number of subcategories will later be introduced. These categories and subcategories are important beyond being merely static descriptors. If we are concerned to change environments in order to enhance mental health, then the model implies that the nine categories are also 'levers' which might be 'pulled' to generate beneficial change. In addition, longitudinal studies of environmental change and mental health might use the nine features as principal dimensions of comparison between previous and present settings. The impact of a transition is often thought to be a function of the magnitude of the difference between two environments; such differences may usefully be characterized in these nine terms.

A vitamin model of the environment and mental health

We turn now to the second part of the overall framework, with an initial consideration of the ways in which the primary environmental features may affect mental health. Specific processes in respect of each feature will be considered in later chapters, but these are thought to operate within a general non-linear pattern of association. Mental health is assumed to be influenced by the environment in a manner analogous to the effect of vitamins on physical health.

The availability of vitamins is important for physical health up to but not beyond a certain level. At low levels of intake, vitamin deficiency gives rise

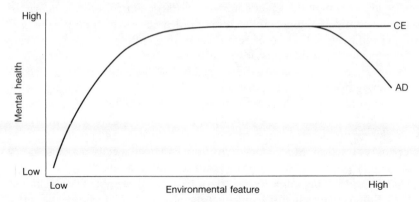

Fig. 1.1   Schematic representation of two assumed relationships between environmental features and mental health.
(CE is 'constant effect'. AD is 'additional decrement'.)

to physiological impairment and ill-health, but after attainment of specified levels there is no benefit derived from additional quantities. It is suggested that principal environmental features are important to mental health in a similar manner: their absence tends towards an impairment in mental health, but their presence beyond a required level does not yield further benefit. In addition, however, certain vitamins become harmful in very large quantities. In these infrequent cases the association between increased vitamin intake and health becomes negative after a broad range of moderate quantities.

A similar pattern is proposed here for the importance of the nine environmental features. Each is assumed to be associated with mental health in the manner summarized in Fig. 1.1, where low values are depicted as particularly harmful and those in the middle range are shown as having a constant beneficial effect on mental health. A second decrement is proposed at particularly high environmental values in certain cases (labelled as 'AD') but not in others ('CE').

This distinction between two assumed relationships to the right of Fig. 1.1 also derives from the vitamin analogy. There are no toxic consequences from very high intake of a number of vitamins; deficiency causes ill-health, but additional doses beyond the required amount have a constant effect. Vitamins of this kind include those identified as compounds C and E (Barker and Bender 1980, 1982). The label 'CE' to the right of the figure derives from that fact, and also has the virtue of being an abbreviation for 'constant effect'. On the other hand, vitamins A and D are known to be toxic at very high levels (Barker and Bender 1980, 1982). This is summarized in the second curve in the figure, where 'AD' may be read as 'additional decrement'.

The model of environmental influences upon mental health which is being developed here thus parallels the operation of chemical vitamins in two ways. In all cases, low levels of an environmental feature are considered harmful, but increases beyond a certain level confer no further benefit. And environmental features, like vitamins, are viewed as being of two kinds in their effect at very high levels. Some are harmful (as vitamins A and D, yielding an additional decrement) and others have no additional impact (as vitamins C and E, yielding a constant effect). The generic account, identifying nine principal categories and specifying a non-linear impact upon mental health, will be referred to as the 'vitamin model', and when necessary separate mention will be made of the 'vitamin AD model' and the 'vitamin CE model'.

The mid-range plateau

The assumed harmful effects of low environmental values (to the left of Fig. 1.1) probably require no further justification at this point. However, the assumptions about a plateau and a decrement in some cases at extremely high values require consideration. Both might be justified in either empirical or conceptual terms.

Empirical research in this area has typically examined relationships between aspects of environments and of people as though the two sets of variables were likely to be associated in a linear manner. Statistical interpretation has most often been based upon linear correlation coefficients or multiple regression analyses, and the possibility of the non-linear associations proposed in Fig. 1.1 has rarely been empirically examined. As a result, there is little research support for the pattern. Neither is there evidence against it, since relevant predictions have not been tested.

Empirical support is of course necessary before the proposed plateau can be firmly accepted. However, a conceptual underpinning is also required. The general rationale stems initially from a belief that the nine environmental features are inherently unlikely to be associated with mental health in a linear fashion: a straight-line function is quite implausible. Instead, increments of a certain size in, say, environmental variety or availability of money seem likely to give rise to greater increases in mental health at lower values than at moderate values. Given that conjecture, a form of non-linear model becomes essential.

But why propose a plateau, rather than a smooth curve of steadily reducing steepness as we move from left to right in Fig. 1.1? Several arguments can be presented for this, including a belief that it is helpful to view particular environments and their attributes as falling within two broad classes. In addition to those which are to varying degrees problematic, there are many settings which, despite differing between themselves in one of the features described above, have a broadly similar and beneficial impact upon mental health. The latter is influenced by a number of variables (including other aspects of the environment and previous mental health), which sustain mental health unchanged despite variation within the 'unproblematic' range of a specific environmental factor. Such a plateau of impact might also be expected in evolutionary terms. Humans have acquired the potential to cope with a wide span of environmental conditions, with problems of adaptation occurring only at relatively extreme values.

In practice, empirical research is unlikely to be able to discriminate between a plateau and a negatively accelerating curve within the left-hand and middle ranges of Fig. 1.1. Such an empirical differentiation is prevented by problems of measurement unreliability and by difficulties in determining the statistical significance of differences between curves of varying shapes. In these circumstances it appears additionally desirable to argue for the plateau, in order to emphasize more sharply the non-linear alternative and to focus attention on a strong prediction (of no association within a restricted range) which is open to empirical test.

The postulated plateau thus has some plausibility from everyday experience and appears to be heuristically preferable to a smoothly changing curve. It may also be supported through a number of arguments about how people perceive and adapt to environments of different levels of threat. The general theme of these is that differences of a given magnitude between environmental stimuli are treated as less important in the benign middle range of the horizontal axis than towards the left of the figure. Note however that these perceptual processes are considered to be additional to the actual impact of environmental factors themselves; the segmented assumption summarized in Fig. 1.1 is primarily justified by a belief that it represents the way in which environmental features actually have their psychological effect.

Among these supplementary arguments, it may first be suggested that, since moderate levels of an environmental feature are by their nature relatively unproblematic, they give rise to less affective concern than do those which are to the left of the horizontal axis in Fig. 1.1. In the latter case, initial appraisal is likely to suggest potential threat to the person. Raised anxiety, at least up to moderate levels, is expected to increase a person's level of motivated attention, yielding greater perceptual discrimination and awareness of smaller differences between gradations of a feature (e.g. Upmeyer 1981; Wachtel 1967). The same objective difference between stimuli is thus likely to be perceived as of smaller magnitude in the middle range than to the left of the figure. The resulting greater perceptual equivalence in the middle range will tend towards a plateau of the kind suggested, since affective and other responses will be influenced by objective differences to a smaller extent.

A second line of supplementary reasoning is in terms of causal attributions made to account for one's present state. There is considerable research evidence that people tend to attribute their negative states more to causal features in the environment than to aspects of themselves, and that positive states are more likely to be thought due to one's own characteristics than to the environment (e.g. Langer 1983). People located to the left of Fig. 1.1 are defined by the postulated curve as experiencing negative affect. They may thus be thought more likely to blame the environment for their negative experiences, whereas those in the middle of Fig. 1.1 (experiencing more positive states) will tend to give themselves relatively greater credit for their mental condition. This smaller cognitive emphasis on the environment in the middle of the figure is again likely to be associated with less perceptual discrimination between environments than will occur to the left of the figure.

A third supplementary argument for this plateau also derives from the fact that the middle range is indicated in the model to be associated with relatively high levels of mental health. As will be described in Chapter 2, high mental health typically implies a moderate autonomy from external influence; conversely, lower mental health tends to be accompanied by greater susceptibility to environmental pressures. It follows that persons currently located in the middle of Fig.1.1 will tend to exhibit greater autonomous stability in the face of environmental variation. People located to the left of the figure are of lower mental health, and as a result their affective states are thought to be more dependent on current environmental conditions. Differences in conditions towards the left of the figure will thus tend to have greater impact than differences of equivalent magnitude in the centre, since, associated with differences in their mental health, people are differentially open to influence at the two locations.

The arguments in the preceding paragraphs have concerned the segmented assumption of the vitamin model, particularly its suggested plateau. This has been justified on the grounds that a linear relationship between the environment and mental health is in general implausible, and that a distinction between environments which are threatening and those which are unproblematic is expected on evolutionary grounds and in terms of current behavioural effectiveness. Three supplementary arguments have been proposed, in terms of differences in perception and adaptation at different levels of an environmental feature.

Very high environmental values

Next, what of the decrement which is assumed to occur when a feature of the AD ('additional decrement') type takes on an extremely high value? This may have two bases. First, the decline is expected for intrinsic reasons, because of the impact of very high levels of a feature on its own. Illustrations will be cited shortly. Second, extremely high levels of a feature tend to have consequences for the level of certain others; for example, extremely high values of one feature may give rise to harmfully low values of another.

Let us consider the possible consequences of very high levels in respect of each of the nine features. Six may be proposed as analogues of vitamins A and D, and three seem more likely to parallel vitamins C and E. For externally generated goals and variety (numbers 3 and 4), the expectation of an additional decrement appears clear. As goals become exceptionally difficult and/or numerous, overload is predicted, with an inability to cope with environmental pressures and consequential harmful effects. Extremely high variety requires constant switching of attention, with resulting low concentration and achievement in any single task; conflict between contradictory goals may be present; and extreme diversity may prevent development and use of substantial skills. Turning to feature number 5, environments of extremely high clarity are those in which no uncertainty exists, where the future is fully predictable, and where role requirements are completely specified with no ambiguity. Such settings permit no risk, contain little variety or potential for skill development, and offer no opportunity to expand one's control over the environment. They are thus also expected in general to impair mental health, falling within the AD version of the vitamin model.

The three features identified as 'opportunities' (for control, skill use, and interpersonal contact; numbers 1, 2, and 8), also appear likely to give rise to decrements at particularly high levels. These are expected on the grounds that an 'opportunity' is liable to become an 'unavoidable requirement' at very high levels; behaviour becomes 'coerced' rather than being 'encouraged' or 'facilitated'. Environments which call for unremitting control (feature number 1) through difficult decision-making and sustained personal responsibility, or which demand continuous use of extremely complex skills (feature number 2), are expected to give rise to overload strain; in part this comes about because of a correlated shift to a particularly high level of externally generated goals. It may also happen that very high levels of successfully exercised control make the environment entirely predictable; such a large increase in feature number 5 has already been suggested to be undesirable. Extremely high levels of interpersonal contact (feature number 8) may also be thought potentially harmful, for example through overcrowding in high density environments, or through lack of personal control and reduced initiation of valued activities because of excessive demands from other people. Behavioural procedures and physical structures to prevent excessive social contact have been reported to be present in cultures of all kinds (e.g. Altman and Chemers 1980).

The remaining three environmental features seem more likely to fall within the vitamin CE ('constant effect') model. There appear to be no strong reasons to expect that a decrement in mental health will arise from extremely high availability of money, physical security, or valued social position (features 6, 7, and 9). In all cases, however, these expectations of an additional decrement or a constant effect are of course subject to empirical support or disconfirmation; research findings about this aspect of the model will be examined in later chapters.

Finally in this section it should be noted that by their nature all analogies are in part invalid. They can be useful in advancing thought and research by importing concepts and patterned relationships from another domain. We use these by proceeding as if the importation corresponded to reality, while recognizing that this is not completely so. The vitamin analogy appears to have sufficient merit to be developed in that way, but it is necessarily invalid in certain respects. Strengths and weaknesses of the overall framework will be considered throughout the book, with an overview presented in Chapter 15.

The environment and the individual

An approach of this kind gives rise to many questions about the nature of interactions between people and environments. Detailed examples of these will be considered in later chapters, but an initial overview appears desirable at this stage. The present section will first offer a general account of types of theorizing about persons and environments, and then discuss ways in which individuals shape those external features which in turn affect them. Questions of 'objective' and 'subjective' measurement will next be considered. Finally, the section will examine some principal ways in which individual differences have been incorporated within models of environmental influence.

Situation-centred models

Gergen and Gergen (1982) have suggested that any theory within the social and behavioural sciences can be described as primarily either situation-centred or person-centred. In the former case priority in explanation is given to factors outside the person, and in the second case the focus is primarily upon personal characteristics. They also propose that within each category a division may be made between accounts which are 'enabling' and those which are 'controlling'. (Gergen and Gergen use the term 'empowered' for the latter description.)

Placing together the two categorizations, they identify four principal types of theory. Those that are both situation-centred and controlling propose that people act as they are required to do by the environments to which they are exposed; radical behaviourism, with its emphasis on reinforcement contingencies, is cited as an example of this form of explanation. Theories which are both person-centred and controlling are illustrated by psychoanalytic and trait models, where little freedom of action is accorded to individuals. Cognitive theories are also said to fall under this heading, since they posit automatic processes of information storage and retrieval.

Approaches which are situation-centred and enabling offer explanations in terms of environmental influences, but include the assumption that people can mould these influences in various ways. Examples cited by Gergen and Gergen are models of conformity and attitude change and some accounts of personal development. Finally, person-centred forms of enabling explanation are illustrated through phenomenological, ethogenic, and hermeneutic models, where the emphasis is upon psychological constructs which permit the individual ultimate freedom of choice.

The present conceptual framework falls within the category of situation-centred and enabling theories. It sets out to define principal aspects of environments and to suggest ways in which these may affect people. However, individuals are viewed as having some power over their environments and over the ways in which they are influenced by those environments.

How should this type of personal power be viewed? An initial distinction may be made between people's influence upon the environment which is cognitive and that which is behavioural. In the former case, it is clear that responses to environmental features are dependent upon the way in which those features are construed and evaluated. The importance of the personal meaning attached to environmental elements has been emphasized by many theorists. For example, Lazarus and Folkman (1984) develop an account in terms of cognitive appraisal. They suggest that this 'can be most readily understood as the process of categorizing an encounter, and its various facets, with respect to its significance for well-being. . . . It is largely *evaluative*, focused on meaning or significance, and takes place continuously during waking life' (p. 31; italics in original).

Lazarus and Folkman describe several forms of environmental appraisal, including assessments in relation to potential threat and challenge, in relation to harm and loss, and in respect of possible ways of coping with difficulties. On the basis of reviews of research in several fields, they conclude that 'the way a person appraises an encounter strongly influences the coping process and how the person reacts emotionally' (p. 34). Although that generalization is supported by considerable experimental research (see also Fleming *et al.* 1984; Krantz and Manuck 1984), rather little is known about the nature and determinants of personal appraisals in the settings of everyday life: the way in which people cognitively shape the environments to which they are subject is in detail little understood.

The second type of personal power within an enabling model, people's behavioural impact upon their environment, takes two forms: choices about which environments to enter or to avoid, and behaviours which shape current environmental conditions and the process of future interaction. Although such influences are ubiquitous, there is a lack of general theorizing which can comprehend and account for them. This probably derives from the enormous diversity of types of individual agency and influence. A person's impact on an environment which is social is particularly difficult to study in other than the short term, since the ramifications of that impact in the future behaviour of others may be extremely diffuse and difficult to identify.

To summarize so far: the present conceptual framework is explicitly situation-centred and enabling; situations are influenced by the people they affect; these influences are both cognitive and behavioural, but we have some way to go before they can be specified in detail.

The distinction between situation-centred and person-centred theories is important in defining the principal focus of any model and encouraging clarity in its presentation. However, there is a sense in which each type depends upon aspects of the other. For example, the present situation-centred model points to nine features of the environment which are assumed to be psychologically important. But why are they important? Presumably because of certain characteristics of people. A situation-centred model thus inevitably contains some person-centred assumptions, but it derives its distinctiveness from taking the environment as its primary object of investigation.

This point may be developed by returning to the notion of 'affordances', introduced earlier in the chapter. These are properties of the environment identified as important for and by particular groups of perceivers.

An important fact about the affordances of the environment is that they are in a sense objective, real, and physical, unlike values and meanings, which are often supposed to be subjective, phenomenal, and mental. But, actually, an affordance is neither an objective property nor a subjective property; or it is both if you like. An affordance cuts across the dichotomy of subjective–objective and helps us to understand its inadequacy. It is equally a fact of the environment and a fact of behavior. It is both physical and psychical, yet neither. An affordance points both ways, to the environment and to the observer (Gibson 1979, p. 129).

Situation-centred models of the kind developed in this book are primarily concerned with environmental features, the 'categories' of a 'categorical theory' as introduced on page 1. However, through the identification of primary categories and the elaboration of processes within a 'process theory', such models are also concerned with the characteristics of persons. Affordances, or perceived opportunities in the environment, link together both categories and processes and also situations and persons.

Measuring the environment

How should we characterize environments in operational terms: should we seek measures which aim to be 'objective', or make use of those which are clearly 'subjective'? An 'objective' measure of an environmental feature is usually defined as one which is taken independently of the person being studied. This may be in directly measurable terms, identifying and quantifying temperature, noise, or other publicly observable characteristics. The indices here are usually of physical features, although social environments may sometimes be specified in terms of publicly-stated role requirements, and 'behaviour settings' such as a church or restaurant may be described in both physical and social terms (e.g Wicker 1981).

'Objective' assessment through direct measurement may be unacceptably coarse in some research designs, where particular environmental characteristics do not yield publicly available markers. For example, within the present framework features such as opportunity for control and environmental clarity are difficult to index in direct physical terms. Using a second approach to 'objective' measurement, researchers have therefore sometimes turned to trained observers or other people familiar with the environment, asking for their ratings of features independently of the person being studied. Such ratings are 'objective' in the sense of 'independent' (although information received by raters from the focal person cannot always be ruled out), but they are 'subjective' in that they depend on human judgements.

Ratings by other people are unlikely to provide completely accurate records of the environment as it actually impinges upon a person. This is because observers are restricted to partial information, for example about developments over time, previous personal experiences, or complex cause-effect networks, and because of the major importance of individual cognitive appraisal and the imposition of personal meaning. Such arguments suggest that it is sometimes preferable to take 'subjective' measures, directly from the focal person. In that way one might, for example, ask people about the amount of variety or opportunity for skill use which they perceive to be present in their environment.

However, when 'subjective' assessments of environmental features are studied in relation to affective or behavioural responses by the same person, the interpretation of observed correlations may become problematic. Is the association due to the effect of the environmental feature? Or has it occurred because a person's emotional condition has determined perception of the environment? Or are both processes present? There is no doubt that causal priority can sometimes be from the person to his or her ratings of the environment; depressed people illustrate this process, being less likely than others to recognize the positive attributes of their environment (e.g. Alloy and Abramson 1979).

Both 'objective' and 'subjective' measures of environmental features thus have their limitations. In practice, the former have been most used in studies of physical characteristics, with subjective ratings from the focal person more common in respect of social aspects of environments. There is evidence that careful design and application of measures yield environmental scores which are similar between the two approaches; examples of this type of enquiry will be described in Chapter 6. For the present, we may note that each type of measure has its own merit, and that 'subjective' measures often themselves incorporate some aspects of prior person–environment interaction, already reflecting the outcomes of an individual's cognitive and behavioural shaping of that environment.

Individual differences

Finally in this section, let us begin to consider how individual differences can be included within studies of environmental effects. After measuring ('objectively', 'subjectively', or both) features of the environment which are identified as of interest, how can we conceptualize and study differences between people in the impact of those features? One conventional procedure is to introduce individual difference characteristics as possible moderators of the main effect of an environmental factor. In that way one might study the moderating influence of sex, age, or particular personality attributes within an investigation which also identifies an overall effect of an environmental feature. Such an approach is useful in many research settings, but sometimes suffers from the absence of clear criteria for selecting possible moderators; in principle the number of such individual-difference variables is extremely large.

In the present framework, a 'vitamin' model which is situation-centred and enabling, some attention will be given to demographic variables and specific values and abilities as possible moderators. However, particular weight will be placed upon a person's continuing level of mental health.

Recognizing that this concept has yet to be defined, it seems clear that mental health is both relatively fixed and also open to change. For example, some aspects of affective well-being are highly stable over periods of years (e.g. Conley 1984, 1985; Costa and McRae 1980; Ormel 1983), but they are also responsive to negative life events in the recent past (e.g. Williams *et al.* 1981). It is thus appropriate to think of an individual's mental health in terms of its continuing relatively stable level and also in terms of temporary deviations from that level. Certain environmental conditions may be expected to yield changes in health, but different individuals will respond to those same conditions from different baselines.

Baseline mental health may thus be viewed as a principal potential moderator of the impact of environmental features upon current mental health. A version of this argument has already been employed in relation to the postulated plateau in Fig. 1.1: at moderate environmental levels people are predicted to exhibit better mental health than at low levels, and with better mental health they are expected to respond more autonomously to environmental variation. More generally, higher levels of baseline mental health include a greater ability to cope with current adversity and to take advantage of new opportunities. They are thus to some extent self-sustaining, as are low levels, which may be reflected in chronically poor mental health irrespective of contemporary circumstances (e.g. Depue and Monroe 1986).

The importance of baseline mental health, defined in terms of the five components to be introduced in Chapter 2, will be further examined in later chapters. An extended model of relationships between enduring personal characteristics and environmental conditions will be presented in Chapters 13 and 14. There are practical problems in this (and all other) approaches to individual differences, in that one ideally needs prior measurement of baseline mental health before studying the impact of an environment; that has rarely been achieved.

Some implications of the vitamin model

As pointed out above, the framework under development here is a combined categorical and process model. The aim is to identify principal categories of the environment and to clarify the processes through which these influence mental health. Nine environmental features have been identified, and two types of non-linear association with mental health have been proposed.

Suppose that this nine-factor model turned out to be acceptable, at least as a provisional account. What would be the consequences of that for research and practice? Eight interrelated points deserve mention.

First, in relation to the study of jobs, the model provides a more comprehensive descriptive and explanatory treatment than is usual. As will be shown later, it serves to incorporate elements from more conventional frameworks; and the subcategories to be described under the nine headings embrace a wide range of factors, which have been examined by investigators from several different backgrounds.

The model thus provides a standard framework through which all jobs can be described and compared. In addition to examination of particular individual jobs, groups of occupations may be appraised in common terms; service versus manufacturing employment, for example, new technology versus traditional jobs, or managerial versus manual work.

Beyond merely description, the approach also seeks to identify causal processes through which jobs have their impact on mental health. Associated with each environmental feature, explanations may be offered in terms of processes to be described throughout the book. These explanations are less developed in some cases than in others, but reasonably sound foundations have been laid for each of the nine categories.

Second, the model is in similar ways applicable to unemployment. The situations of individual unemployed people may be described and compared, specific groups may be examined in standard terms (unemployed teenagers, or middle-aged men, for example), and explanations of observed mental health levels may be developed in each case. Furthermore, the same features are proposed as important both in jobs and during unemployment, so that these two major roles can be treated conceptually and empirically in identical terms.

A third implication extends the previous two. Beyond jobs and unemployment, the nine-category model provides a broad and systematic framework for viewing and comparing environments of all kinds; family settings, domestic work, retirement, hospitalization, voluntary work, and indeed a person's lifespace as a whole. It also permits a comprehensive account of differences between social groups or between socio-economic levels. Studies of group or class differences have often been limited by a restriction of attention to only a small number of the nine features suggested here.

Fourth, the model can be used to predict or interpret the effects of transitions between environments. For example, both for groups and for particular individuals, we can examine in standard terms the move from one job to another, from employment to unemployment, or from employment into retirement. Other possibilities include assessment in these terms of the employment alternatives available to a woman currently engaged principally in childcare. Since transitions involve shifts between environments, and environments may be characterized in the terms proposed here, the vitamin model can help to clarify the costs and benefits of particular transitions, before or after they are made.

Turning the discussion back to jobs, a fifth implication concerns the focus of research enquiries. There is a widespread tendency to measure variables and study correlations between them in whatever sample of jobs is convenient at the time. A central thrust of the present approach is that variations between many jobs are of no psychological consequence. Variations in those occupational environments which fall in the middle range of Fig. 1.1 (page 10) are thought to be irrelevant to mental health. Rather than studying these environments, it is more important to concentrate attention upon jobs which fall at the extremes of the nine environmental dimensions, especially those with very low values. Given that research resources are expensive and limited, the vitamin model can be used to suggest where they might most effectively be deployed.

Associated with the non-linear form of the vitamin model is a related implication in terms of the development of theory. Changes in jobs are expected to have their effect on mental health only outside a broad middle range of environmental levels. If that general expectation receives empirical support, it will require the creation of segmented models based upon non-linear assumptions. Rather than suggesting that certain features are always associated with each other, the vitamin model implies that we should identify two or three ranges of environmental factors, low, moderate and (for some factors) very high, expecting different associations with mental health in each range. Despite the plausibility of this form of segmentation, it has rarely been pursued conceptually or in empirical research (c.f. Hage 1982).

Seventh, the model has clear measurement implications. Each of the nine features, and the elements within them, deserves careful measurement. Systematic procedures are available in certain cases, but there is in general scope for extensive development and standardization of new instruments. The vitamin model provides a framework into which to set that important work.

Finally, a general point may be made which derives from several of those already made. The present approach is directed towards the mental health of people in many different settings. It seeks not only to study mental health but primarily to provide a framework for its improvement. Through presenting a systematic categorical model, identifying causal processes, and suggesting measurement approaches, the approach aims to yield recommendations for enhancing mental health by changing those environments identified as harmful. That goal is shared by many different groups of practitioners, and the vitamin model might provide a broad perspective on the 'levers' of change, to be 'pulled' in the setting of concern to each group.

Summary and forward look

This chapter has introduced the three principal parts of the overall vitamin model. First is a categorization of the environment into nine broad features, each of which is thought to be important in determining mental health. The features have been labelled as opportunity for control, opportunity for skill use, externally generated goals, variety, environmental clarity, availability of money, physical security, opportunity for interpersonal contact, and valued social position. Each has been broadly described, and a number of sub-categories have been identified.

The second part of the conceptual framework concerns the processes whereby environmental features might have their effect. Specific processes are to be illustrated later in respect of each aspect of the environment, but the general pattern of their association with mental health is viewed as analogous with the relationship between vitamins and physical health. At low levels of intake, vitamin deficiency gives rise to bodily impairment, but after attainment of specified levels there is no benefit derived from additional quantities. In addition, certain vitamins become toxic in very large amounts. The nine environmental features have been proposed to be like vitamins in that respect, and two groups have been identified. Six features are thought likely to be 'toxic' at extremely high levels, giving rise to additional decrements in mental health, whereas three are suggested to generate a constant effect after a certain threshold. These hypothesized relationships have been summarized in Fig. 1.1 (page 10), which sets out what will be referred to as the 'vitamin AD' and the 'vitamin CE' models.

The third part of the framework concerns differences between people. It has been emphasized that the overall model sets out to be 'situation-centred', but it is 'enabling', in that people are assumed to be able to shape the character of their environment and to influence its impact upon them. The middle part of the chapter has presented an initial description of some ways in which these personal influences might occur.

Questions of measurement were also addressed. 'Objective' measures of the environment are taken independently of a focal person, whereas 'subjective' measures are derived from reports made by that person. It has been suggested that both approaches have their limitations, but that one strength of subjective indices is that they take immediate account of the fact that environmental features can have different meanings for different individuals.

The overall vitamin framework thus links together a categorical model, a process model, and a model of person–situation interactions. The last of these will be developed in Chapters 13 and 14, and the other two parts will be examined in the settings of paid employment in Chapters 5 to 10 and with respect to unemployment in Chapters 11 and 12.

Before reaching those substantive presentations, it is necessary to examine the manner in which mental health is to be conceptualized. A five-component account will be offered in Chapter 2, drawing upon the theories and descriptions of many Western writers. Chapter 3 will examine approaches to the measurement of each of these components, summarizing details of contemporary instruments and suggesting some needed improvements.

Chapter 4 provides a link between the broad-ranging treatment within the first three chapters, and the detailed applications of the model which follow. This chapter reviews nine types of evidence indicating the importance of jobs for mental health. It includes brief summaries of quantitative and qualitative research and evidence from clinical and psychotherapeutic studies, and it introduces aspects of 'spill-over' between jobs and other life settings.

As was indicated at the beginning of the present chapter, the vitamin model is intended to have application to any environment. Within this book it is principally applied to paid work and unemployment, seeking to examine and interpret the impact of these two environments in parallel terms. This issue is taken up finally in Chapter 15, where possible ways to improve both jobs and unemployment are considered. In that chapter also is a retrospective evaluation of the vitamin model, considering its strengths and weaknesses in both conceptual and empirical terms.

2

The concept of mental health

Throughout Chapter 1 the concept of mental health was left undefined. It is the task of the present chapter to examine this notion in more detail. Some approaches to measurement will then be described in Chapter 3.

The term 'mental health' is difficult to specify, and no universally-accepted definition is available. There are two principal reasons for this. First is the fact that psychological processes can be described and interpreted through many different conceptual filters and languages. Discrepancies between writers occur in the basic content of their models, the facts they address, and the features they describe; and also in terms of style, for example whether models are based upon detailed analyses of specific states and processes or upon person-centred approaches from a holistic perspective. It is thus rarely possible to integrate the models of mental health proposed by different authors.

A second difficulty in reaching general agreement about definition arises from the fact that the concept of mental health is to a considerable degree value-laden; one seeks to map descriptive statements onto an evaluative dimension. Processes and outcomes which are designated as healthy are typically those accepted and valued by contemporary society, often by the middle-class members of that society. Even within the middle class itself, there are many differences of opinion about which specific behaviours and experiences should be deemed 'healthy' or 'unhealthy'. A single definition of the term is thus very unlikely to be achieved.

Mental health from a Western perspective

Recognizing these difficulties, it is nevertheless important to describe the usage to be adopted throughout the book. This section will propose a view of five principal components of mental health, with particular reference to contemporary Western society. The account will draw widely from models developed by other writers, but does not aim itself to be an aetiological or developmental theory. Neither does it seek to combine the widely differing stances of individual writers to whom reference is made. The aim is to identify in a parsimonious manner those features of mental health which would be accepted as important by most Western theorists, with principal emphasis on components to be studied in relation to the vitamin model introduced in Chapter 1.

The medical profession has developed and routinely applies criteria which serve to designate individuals as either mentally 'ill' or 'not ill'. Decisions of that kind can in particular cases be complex and difficult, but three general issues are likely to be involved in each case (e.g. American Psychiatric Association 1981; Kendell 1975; Lewis 1967). The first conventional criterion of ill-health is that a person *feels* unwell. Second, he or she has one or more impaired functions—psychological, social, and/or physical. Third is the presence of a recognizable pattern or syndrome of symptoms, whether or not these are known to the person. Application of these three medical criteria does not remove all conceptual or diagnostic difficulties. For example, a person may be considered ill even though he or she does not feel ill: criteria two and three are met, but criterion one is not. Furthermore, the pattern of development of a syndrome over time may be of particular clinical importance. However, the three criteria serve widely as the bases for medical decision-making.

This book is less concerned with characterizing people as 'ill' or 'not ill' than with differences between them irrespective of their medical designation. The emphasis is upon variations in degrees of health in the population at large, whether or not they would be identified as 'ill' in a medical sense. Let us start by treating statements about mental health as statements about a person's location on a continuum. This may be said to range from very good mental health, through conditions typically considered moderately healthy, to those widely taken to be indicative of moderate and severe illness. Ill-health and health are thus both viewed in the same primary terms, although it is recognized that specific syndromes of illness may yield patterns which sometimes appear qualitatively different from those which are typical in the population. In the same way, one might seek to identify specific syndromes of outstandingly good health, which appear to set certain very healthy individuals apart from the rest.

It seems appropriate to assume a normal frequency distribution, with most people falling in the middle range of the health/ill-health continuum and only a few at each extreme. A minority of people fall below a threshold of 'illness', and a similarly small number of particularly fit people at the opposite end of the distribution may be described as 'extremely healthy'.

Within this overall perspective one may identify a number of major components of mental health, each of which may itself be treated overall as a continuum. The present description contains five such components, as follows:

1. Affective well-being
2. Competence
3. Autonomy

4.   Aspiration

5.   Integrated functioning

The first component, affective well-being, is similar to the primary medical criterion introduced above. Components two, three, and four cover aspects of a person's behaviour in relation to the environment, and may be suggested to be important in three different ways.

First, these behavioural features (competence, autonomy, and aspiration) often determine the level of a person's affective well-being. For example, an inability to cope with current difficulties (a form of low competence) may give rise to distress (an aspect of low affective well-being). Second, competence, autonomy, and aspiration tend to be valued in their own right as indicators of good mental health. For example, competence is required both in the face of current problems, as suggested above, but it is also valued in general terms, as a continuing capability whether or not it is currently in evidence. A mentally healthy person has the *potential to be* competent even in the absence of contemporary evidence.

The third sense in which these three components are important in discussions of mental health arises from the distinction between assessments which are 'objective' and those which are 'subjective'. Each component may be viewed in those two aspects. 'Objective' assessments of competence, autonomy, and aspiration are those made by other people, for example, mental health professionals, family members, job colleagues, or society more widely. On the other hand, each component may be viewed subjectively, in terms of a focal individual's perception and evaluation of his or her own competence, autonomy or aspiration. Within the present model, it is suggested that subjectively assessed levels of competence, autonomy, and aspiration are major elements of self-esteem. This notion will be discussed further in the next section.

The fifth component of mental health suggested above, integrated functioning, falls on a different level of description from the others. Statements about integrated functioning are of a more macroscopic kind, being concerned with multiple relationships between the other four components and covering issues of overall structure.

These and other points will be developed in the next six sections, one for each proposed component and one for general issues. Measurement procedures will be examined in the following chapter.

Affective well-being

The first feature is often viewed in overall terms along a single dimension, roughly from feeling good to feeling bad. However, it is preferable, on conceptual and empirical grounds, to identify two separate dimensions of affective well-being, which may be referred to as 'pleasure' and 'arousal'.

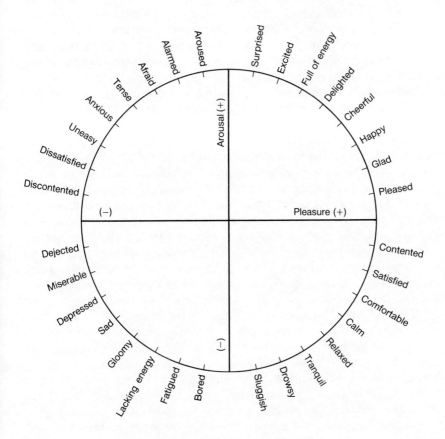

Fig. 2.1   A two-dimensional view of affective well-being.

They can be treated as independent of each other in the manner shown in Fig. 2.1.

This diagram provides a schematic representation of a model which has been empirically substantiated in many different settings (e.g. Russell 1979, 1980, 1983; Russell and Ridgeway 1983). The precise location of individual terms within the framework may vary slightly between studies, but the general structure is widely observed. We may view any affective state in terms of its location on the separate dimensions of pleasure and arousal (see also Mackay 1980; Watson and Tellegen 1985; Zevon and Tellegen 1982). A particular level of pleasure may be accompanied by high or low levels of arousal, and a particular level of arousal may be either pleasurable or un-pleasurable. The specific quality of affect derives from both dimensions, and may be summarized in terms of location relative to the midpoint of the figure. For example, depressed feelings are characterized by low scores on each dimension (being located in the bottom left-hand sector), and anxiety may be described in terms of a low score on pleasure and a high score on arousal (in the top left-hand quadrant).

This perspective also includes the possibility of degrees of each affect. For instance, although anxiety is set at a particular angle from the centre of the figure, different *amounts* of anxiety may be defined in terms of their distance from the centre. The labels in Fig. 2.1 are placed equidistant from the neutral point primarily for convenience of presentation.

Feelings of the kind set out in the figure are usually focused upon particular issues or objects. Thus one may be pleased about a certain family activity or depressed about being unemployed. Affective foci vary in their specificity, ranging from single events localized in time and space through to continuing and diffuse circumstances involving numerous people and occurrences. A particularly important set of feelings have the self as their object, and the notion of self-esteem may usefully be viewed in terms of feelings about the self within the two-dimensional framework summarized here. However, feelings about oneself are likely to be intertwined also with feelings about other aspects of a lifespace (e.g. Wessman and Ricks 1966), and within the present model it is suggested that self-evaluations of one's competence, autonomy, and aspiration (components two, three, and four) are also sig-nificant contributors to self-esteem. There are thus strong interconnections between affective well-being in general and self-esteem in particular, the latter being viewed in terms of pleasure-and-arousal feelings about the self and subjective assessments of one's competence, autonomy, and aspiration.

Although higher levels of affective well-being are in general associated with the right-hand side of Fig. 2.1, mentally healthy people can also experience feelings located in the left-hand sectors; a person as it were moves about in the two-dimensional affective space. This suggests the possibility of adding a third dimension to the figure, concerned with time, and ranging from rela-tively transient or momentary feelings to more permanent, enduring states. More generally, we can describe a person's affective well-being over a given period in terms of the proportion of time which he or she spends in each of the four principal sectors. That description may sometimes be augmented by reference to the intensity of feelings, as suggested above.

Time spent in the top left-hand quadrant (experiencing tension and related feelings) is particularly important in this form of interpretation, since tension is often a necessary prelude to affects located to the right-hand side of the figure. Movement between these quadrants may be gradual or sudden. For example, Apter's 'reversal theory' of experienced motivation stresses how a person may on different occasions seek different combinations of arousal and pleasure, sometimes switching very rapidly from one mode to another (e.g. Apter 1984). High variability of this kind is central within the theory's definition of the mentally healthy person (e.g. Murgatroyd and Apter 1984).

Affective conditions may be physiological as well as psychological. This is particularly clear in respect of low well-being, where, for example, anxiety may be reflected in muscular tension, rapid heart-rate, and increased perspiration, and depressed mood is often accompanied by sleep disturbance, fatigue, and loss of appetite. However, many positive affects are also linked to bodily states, as is illustrated through terms such as 'excited', 'full of energy', 'relaxed' and 'drowsy' to the right-hand side of Fig. 2.1.

Competence

The second feature of mental health, here referred to as competence (e.g. Smith 1968), has been widely discussed in the literature. Jahoda (1958) wrote in terms of 'environmental mastery', viewing good mental health partly in terms of an acceptable degree of success in different spheres—interpersonal relations, problem-solving, paid employment, and so on. Bradburn (1969) covered similar issues in his consideration of people's ability to cope with and transcend their 'difficulties in living'. Vaillant (1977) argued that good mental health becomes apparent only when a person faces adversity. He examined differences in competence through a hierarchical model of the mechanisms used by different people to cope with their problems.

The competent person is one who has adequate psychological resources to deal with experienced pressures. In part this is a question of having appropriate cognitive, problem-solving, or psychomotor skills, and in part it is a reflection of emotional features, such as appropriate limits upon affect-based distortion of perception, and a willingness to test out beliefs and feelings against reality. In some settings, *physical* resources may also be important in determining level of competence, at least in the sense that physical frailty can impair a person's ability to cope with his or her daily problems.

As noted above, competence may be viewed as 'objective' (what a person can actually do) or 'subjective' (his or her sense of competence). Bandura (1977) described the latter in terms of beliefs about 'self-efficacy', or 'expectations of personal mastery'. White (1959) considered that feelings of efficacy arise from successful activity driven by 'effectance' motivation. Levels of objective and subjective competence are likely to be positively inter-correlated, but they do of course sometimes differ.

It would be wrong to view all types of low competence as evidence of low mental health; everyone is incompetent in some respects. Two themes are important here, associated with the types of value attached to competence, autonomy, and aspiration which were introduced in the earlier section. First, it may be suggested that a key factor in deciding whether level of competence reflects level of mental health is its positive causal impact upon affective well-being; low competence which is not linked to negative affect would often be viewed as having no bearing upon mental health. Within this link we should include the contribution of subjective competence to level of self-esteem, itself a specific aspect of affective well-being.

The second theme values competence in its own right, irrespective of its link with affective well-being. On this basis, successful transactions with the environment and the maintenance of effective behaviour are valued for their own sake, both in respect of contemporary demands and as a reflection of an enduring characteristic which is widely viewed as desirable. Effective individual performance is often also considered important at a societal level, increasing the prospect of a society's continuity or progress (e.g. Lazarus 1975).

Autonomy

Similar points apply to the third component in the present frame-work, referred to as 'autonomy'. Many Western writers have stressed the importance of a person's ability to resist environmental influences and to determine his or her own opinions and actions. For example, Angyal (1965) argued that the tendency to strive for independence and self-regulation was a fundamental characteristic of the healthy organism. He viewed mental illness as a halt or regression in this autonomous trend. In a similar vein, Loevinger (1980) included in her account of personal development a high-level 'autonomous stage'. Other writers have viewed this aspect of mental health in terms of internal locus of control, a general tendency to feel and act on the assumption that one is influential rather than helpless in the face of life's difficulties (e.g. Lefcourt 1982; Rotter 1966; Seligman 1975).

However, too much autonomy as well as too little is often seen as un-desirable. Many writers have pointed out that it is successful interdependence, rather than extreme independence, which is a sign of good mental health. Different models contain terms such as 'social feeling' (Adler), 'belonging' (Fromm), 'union with separation' (Rank), 'intimacy' (Erikson), and 'inter-personal relations' (Sullivan); see for example Lazarus (1975). Angyal (1965) has described this as follows:

The manifestations of impairment or of distortion of the autonomous trend may appear as either a *lack* or an *excess* of autonomous striving.... When the lack of autonomy is a generalized one, a person's course seems to be determined by external happenings; he becomes a straw in the wind, a piece of driftwood carried by currents, a creature of circumstances.... Lack of self-government in interpersonal relations can take many shapes: excessive conformism, an inability to disagree with anybody, or dependence on the help of others far in excess of the objective necessity.... [On the other hand] the distortions which take the form of excessive autonomy [include] extreme resentment and rejection of any influence exercised by others...re-belliousness and intolerance...the wish to be completely independent of others and to accept no help (pp. 11–12).

It thus seems appropriate to envisage a dimension of autonomy ranging from extreme dependence to extreme counterdependence, between which are located both interdependence and independence; it is a combination of the latter two locations on the continuum which reflects good mental health of this kind. Statements about autonomy in this setting thus cover two features. First is the extent to which a person is an independent agent, acting upon the environment, relying upon his or her own judgements, and feeling responsible for his or her actions. Second is the degree to which the person is interdependent with other people in that environment, contributing to their interests as well as seeking his or her own satisfactions. In general, independence appears to be given a greater value relative to interdependence in Western than in Eastern societies.

Autonomy is linked with competence and aspiration in several ways. For example, it is often through actions to master the environment (striving to be competent) that a person gains independence; and increased autonomy often requires that an individual is personally competent to handle life's problems.

Aspiration

The mentally healthy person is often viewed as someone who has an interest in, and engages with, the environment. He or she establishes goals and makes active efforts to attain them. A raised aspiration level is reflected in motivated behaviour, alertness to new opportunities, and efforts to meet challenges that are personally significant. Conversely, low levels of aspiration are exhibited in reduced activity, and an acceptance of the present state no matter how unsatisfactory that appears to others.

Csikszentmihalyi (1975), in a review of positive experiences in a wide range of settings, has emphasized the importance of endeavours which involve 'a going beyond the known, a stretching of one's self toward new dimensions of skill and competence' (p. 33). Kornhauser (1965) was particularly concerned with the mental health of people in jobs, arguing that motivation level may sometimes be too high as well as too low:

Industrial workers, like all the rest of us, are caught on the horns of a dilemma: if they want *too much* relative to what they are prepared to strive for with some degree of success, the result is defeat and frustration; if they want *too little*, the consequence is a drab existence devoid of colour, exhilaration, and self-esteem. Good mental health demands a middle course (p. 270).

An adequate conceptualization of good mental health refers to something more than passive adjustment, contentment, 'homeostatic balance', and freedom from inner tensions. Few people would accept the healthy vegetable as a model. The more positive aspects of mental health ... surely deserve attention (p. 38).

The value attached to positive health, going beyond 'the healthy vegetable', is also evident in Herzberg's (1966) treatment. He suggested that mental health requires two kinds of development, both an adjustment to the environment so that negative states are minimized and also the occurrence of and potential for 'psychological growth'. A key feature of psychological growth was seen as the continuing motivation to expose oneself to situations which are unfamiliar and novel.

A related theme is in terms of 'self-realization', striving to fulfil one's own ideal nature in the face of environmental and personal constraints. For example, Maslow (e.g. 1943, 1973) elaborated the concept of 'self-actualization', by distinguishing between 'becoming' and 'being'. The process of movement towards our full potential, towards the actualization of what we might be, is one of 'becoming', and we are closer on some occasions than others to 'being' our true selves. Personal effort in that direction was viewed as an important aspect of the healthy personality.

The importance of raised aspiration as a feature of mental health re-emphasizes the fact that the mentally healthy person is not always free from tension or anxiety. In striving to achieve personal goals one may well face stressful situations, indeed one may *create* them through identifying and pursuing difficult targets.

The presence of active wants may be considered healthy in two ways. First, acting upon aspirations which have a moderate probability of goal attainment tends to promote feelings in the top right-hand quadrant of Fig. 2.1, active pleasure. Motivation, if translated into successful action, enhances affective well-being. Second, although wants may give rise to anxiety (the top left-hand quadrant) as a person strives to achieve goals, active striving towards personally-valued targets is often regarded in Western societies as psychologically desirable for its own sake. This is because motivated interest in the environment is itself widely taken to be healthy, and because the converse (disengagement or apathy in the face of problems) tends to be seen as intrinsically undesirable.

The importance of raised aspiration level to good mental health is particularly clear in circumstances adverse to the individual, where the desire for change is likely to be viewed as central to a healthy response. However, in a problem-free setting, the identification of high aspiration with high mental health is more a matter of personal value orientation. Contentment without perceiving a need for change might in these circumstances be viewed as healthy, but some observers are likely to see an absence of motivation as shading into apathetic ill-health.

What of very high levels of aspiration? It is clear that people can have wants which are unrealistic in relation to their competence or to constraints in their environment. Aspirations which are extremely high in this sense can give rise to chronic distress, as actions lead to failure. The contribution of aspiration to mental health is thus probably curvilinear: moderately high motivation, especially in a problematic environment, tends to exemplify better mental health than does either extreme. However, deciding when 'moderately high' aspirations become 'too high' is clearly difficult, and ultimately a function of a judge's personal values. As noted on several other occasions, broader cultural norms are likely to influence these assessments.

Writers about this fourth component often emphasize the attainment as well as the establishment of goals. This is in part a reflection of the second component (competence), in that the healthy person is also viewed as having adequate resources for goal attainment. Several aspects of mental health thus come together in the effective performance of tasks directed toward personally valued goals.

Integrated functioning

The final component of mental health, here referred to as integrated functioning, is qualitatively different from the previous features. Statements about integrated functioning refer to the person as a whole, often in respect of multiple interrelationships between the other four components; structural issues are thus of prime concern. The importance of this component arises from the fact that people who are psychologically healthy exhibit several forms of balance, harmony, and inner relatedness. Indeed, the original meaning of 'health' was 'wholeness', with 'to heal' meaning 'to make whole'.

The notion of integrated functioning is multifaceted and difficult to define. Writers tend to develop their account within the framework of a preferred theoretical approach. For example, some have written in psychoanalytic terms, examining the relationships between ego, superego, and id, and others have emphasized consistency of character, a unifying outlook on life, or the successful acceptance or resolution of mental conflicts (e.g. Jahoda 1958). Assessments may again be made by an observer, or be 'subjective', through reports from the focal person. In the latter case integrated functioning includes viewing oneself and one's experiences as a coherent pattern of processes and states, which come together to yield a sense of identity and individuality (e.g. Erikson 1950). Smooth interdependence between the three previous components to yield predominantly high levels of affective well-being would also illustrate integrated functioning.

Another approach to this component is in relation to three broad areas of social role functioning, sometimes referred to as 'love, work, and play'. These cover family relations, paid employment, and leisure, and it is clear that conflicts between them can sometimes arise. It has been suggested that the healthy person is someone who balances the importance of the three areas, avoiding for example 'workaholic' behaviour to the detriment of his or her family life (e.g. Vaillant 1977). Integrated functioning may also be considered across time, either in terms of a balance between accepting strain during difficult phases of goal attainment and relaxation during the intervening periods, or in terms of a development of the self through stages of life. In the latter case the suggestion is usually made that progression through certain defined stages leads to a mature integration which is otherwise lacking; however, the postulated nature of developmental stages varies somewhat between theorists. (For example, see the review by Lazarus 1975.)

The converse of this aspect of good mental health is disintegration and structural breakdown. For instance, in certain forms of neurotic disorder a person not only experiences very low affective well-being, but also shows marked impairment in all other respects: in subjective as well as objective competence, autonomy, and aspiration. Such a generalized collapse is accompanied by a loss of previously established coherence and mutual support between elements.

Some general issues

This account of mental health is in many respects content-free. For example, competence and aspiration are treated as major components, but specific types of competence or aspiration are not in general valued above others. The abstract notions described here adopt a wide variety of concrete expressions in different people and in different settings. For example, variations are expected through the life cycle, with autonomy and aspiration taking different forms in the later years of life (e.g. Birren and Renner 1981).

Features deemed healthy are in part determined by the nature of prevailing 'social ethics', for example in relation to the desired balance between self-serving activity and communal obligations (e.g. Yankelovich 1982). Social norms and ideologies can also be important in assessing what is an 'appropriate' amount of autonomy, a 'reasonable' aspiration level, or behaviour in keeping with 'objective necessity'. Furthermore, to describe someone as mentally ill or healthy is sometimes partly to offer suggestions about how society should respond to that person; assessments of 'reasonableness' can be closely linked to the operation of social controls (e.g. Szasz 1961, 1983). In all these respects it is clear that a person's mental health cannot be fully specified without some reference to the social setting in which he or she is located; for example, distress in a benign environment is quite different from distress in circumstances of strong adversity.

Duration of episodes

It is important to take note of the time distribution of different levels of mental health. As pointed out previously, people designated as in general mentally healthy may intermittently experience low affective well-being, for example tension and anxiety as they cope with current difficulties or pursue self-initiated goals. The inference that someone currently exhibiting low affective well-being is subject to low mental health in a more general sense may not always be warranted. It should be made only if the impairment to well-being is severe and/or if the low well-being is considerably extended in time.

Table 2.1 Four types of low affective well-being, distinguished in respect of duration and frequency

| Time category | Low affective well-being | |
	Extended in time?	Occurs frequently?
1	No	No
2	No	Yes
3	Yes	No
4	Yes	Yes

The fact that temporarily low levels of affective well-being can be associated with a high overall level of continuing mental health has often been inadequately recognized in empirical research. There is a widespread tendency to imply that an observed high level of, say, anxiety is indicative of impaired mental health. A more differentiated perspective is suggested in Table 2.1.

This draws attention to four types of low affective well-being, distinguished by their duration and frequency. In time-category one, a person experiences low well-being, but this is brief and occasional. Category two covers short but recurrent episodes; and category three contains low affective well-being which is occasional but prolonged. Finally, time-category four includes affective well-being which is chronically low.

Low affective well-being in the fourth category is unquestionably an indicator of low mental health. This can also be the case in some instances within time-categories two and three; severity of impairment usually provides a decision rule here. However, low affective well-being as described in category one does not alone justify the inference that a person is exhibiting low mental health.

Complex inference from several components

The other components of mental health typically contribute to, and draw from, affective well-being in a consistent fashion. However, certain forms of low well-being, even in extended form, do not necessarily signify low mental health. In some circumstances low well-being takes on a different meaning in conjunction with behaviour and feelings which are considered situationally 'appropriate' or 'realistic'. For example, in occupational settings high levels of motivation and risk-taking among managers may be associated with high levels of competence, autonomy, and aspiration, but also with raised anxiety. Moderate elevation of the latter, although normally suggesting impaired mental health, might here be considered appropriate within processes which overall are viewed as healthy.

Conversely, it is occasionally the case that high well-being in conjunction with a particular configuration of other factors is viewed as reflecting poor rather than good mental health. Persons described as 'manic' illustrate this possibility, where very high affective well-being (in the high-arousal and high-pleasure quadrant of Fig. 2.1) and high levels of subjective competence, autonomy, and aspiration are accompanied by markedly lower objective competence and objective autonomy. The latter perspectives take priority in an overall assessment in these circumstances.

There is also a second-order sense in which low scores on other components as well as affective well-being can sometimes be viewed as indicating a healthy state. In clearly adverse environments beyond the control of the person (a prisoner-of-war camp, for instance, or extreme poverty), negative affect as well as impaired competence, autonomy, and aspiration might be reasonable. In those adverse and uncontrollable conditions, symptoms of poor mental health are in a sense healthy, since the response is 'normal' and indicative of a properly functioning system.

Such an interpretation is 'second-order' in that it comments upon the first-order statement that a person is exhibiting low mental health. Irrespective of the validity of particular second-order statements of that kind, it is first-order assessments which are of primary concern in this book. For practical purposes, such as modifying environments or assisting people, we need first-order information in terms of mental health as it is demonstrated in a current situation.

Different points of view

Variations between the components of mental health and differences between individual perspectives have been considered by Strupp and Hadley (1977). They point out that different groups of people emphasize different elements of mental health. First are individuals reflecting upon their own health. Strupp and Hadley argue that from the standpoint of this group the principal index of level of mental health is subjective feeling of high or low well-being.

A second perspective on a particular person's mental health is taken by other people and by society as a whole. Definitions here tend to focus upon effective behaviours to meet situational requirements, predictability, and conformity to social codes. From this societal perspective, a person may be considered in good mental health despite his or her own much more negative assessment in terms of subjective well-being.

Third, Strupp and Hadley consider the perspective of mental health professionals such as clinical psychologists and psychiatrists. This group is said primarily to view mental health within the framework of one or more preferred models of personality structure. These almost always go beyond merely individual well-being and particular social behaviours, so that the professional's assessment of a person's mental health may in some cases be at variance from assessments made both by the individual and by wider society.

Strupp and Hadley point out that, if one is seeking a comprehensive assessment of a person's mental health, descriptions based on a single vantage point are inadequate. However, each perspective has its own validity in providing a partial account. In practice, almost all theory and empirical research in this field is partial in that sense. The description developed in this chapter is intended to be relatively comprehensive by its inclusion of ideas from a wide range of authors. It also aims to accommodate the framework suggested by Strupp and Hadley.

Table 2.2 on page 38 illustrates how the emphases they describe are represented within the five-component framework set out here. Strupp and Hadley's category of 'society' has been separated into 'society in general' and 'significant others'. Since the latter, comprising people who are in daily contact with the focal person, are likely often to have a particular concern over and above that shown by society in general, it seems appropriate here to consider them as a subset of the wider social category.

Table 2.2 makes the point that definitions of mental health within the present model take different forms, dependent upon the source of judgement. The summary account in the table is an oversimplification in the interest of clarity, in that judged importance is really a continuous variable rather than a dichotomous one as indicated.

Mental health defined by the focal person is likely to give primary emphasis to the components here identified as affective well-being and subjective aspects of competence, autonomy, and aspiration; in many cases integrated functioning may also be of concern. Society in general (see column two) tends to emphasize objective forms of competence, autonomy, and aspiration, with less concern for affective well-being. Significant others in a person's life also emphasize objective aspects of social role functioning, summarized in terms of competence, autonomy, and aspiration. However, these perceivers (for example, spouses or friends) are likely in addition to define a person's mental health in terms of his or her affective well-being.

Finally in the table is the perspective of mental health practitioners. Consistent with the arguments of Strupp and Hadley, this group may be said to give primary emphasis to integrated functioning, through their concern for sound personality structure defined according to their particular professional training and theoretical preference. Since statements about integrated functioning usually include information about competence, autonomy, and

Table 2.2   Definitions of mental health from four different perspectives. (Components of primary importance in each case are indicated by 'Yes')

	Perspective			
	Focal person	Society in general	Significant others	Mental health practitioners
Affective well-being	Yes		Yes	Yes
Competence				
—subjective	Yes			
—objective		Yes	Yes	Yes
Autonomy				
—subjective	Yes			
—objective		Yes	Yes	Yes
Aspiration				
—subjective	Yes			
—objective		Yes	Yes	Yes
Integrated functioning	Yes			Yes

motivation, these components (especially their objective forms) are also indicated to be important in practitioners' definitions. Affective well-being is often also of concern, both as a principal medical criterion (see the earlier section) and as a significant correlate of the three components concerned with environmental relationships.

As pointed out earlier, a comprehensive definition of mental health should cover all perspectives. In the present model this means including all the features to the left of Table 2.2, recognizing that within each of those abstract categories are many specific behaviours and experiences. However, partial definitions are in practice more common than such a comprehensive approach, and many researchers in non-clinical settings have relied almost exclusively on self-report measures of affective well-being as indicators of wider mental health. As will be clear from the preceding discussion, that is far from ideal.

Summary

This chapter has introduced the account of mental health which will be adopted throughout the book. It is drawn from theories developed by many Western writers, and seeks to specify major components which are widely recognized. Alternative models may be more appropriate in non-Western settings.

Statements about mental health refer to a person's location on a continuum from 'extremely healthy' to 'extremely unhealthy'. Only a small proportion of people are at any one time medically designated as 'ill', with the majority of the population being 'healthy' to varying degrees. The present account primarily concerns the latter group, all of whom are defined as 'not-ill'.

Five major components of mental health have been described, labelled as affective well-being, competence, autonomy, aspiration, and integrated functioning. The first of these has been considered in terms of two separate dimensions, identified as 'pleasure' and 'arousal', with the specific quality of an affect deriving from both dimensions. Feelings may be focused upon features of the environment or upon aspects of the self. The latter are viewed within the notion of 'self-esteem'.

Components two, three, and four (competence, autonomy, and aspiration) refer to a person's transactions with the environment, as perceived by oneself ('subjective competence', for example) or by an observer ('objective competence'). Subjective forms of these behavioural components are thought also to contribute to self-esteem.

The 'competent' person is one who has adequate psychological resources to deal with experienced pressures; this has sometimes been discussed in terms of 'environmental mastery' or 'efficacy'. 'Autonomy' involves a combination of moderate levels of independence from, and interdependence with, other people. And statements about 'aspiration' concern an individual's interest in and engagement with the environment; a raised aspiration level is reflected in motivated behaviour, alertness to new opportunities, and efforts to meet challenges which are personally significant.

The fifth component in the present account, integrated functioning, covers the interrelationships between other features. It is thus more concerned with structural issues than are the previous components. Writers tend to develop their treatment of integrated functioning from a particular theoretical perspective, so that descriptions and interpretations vary quite widely.

Finally, the chapter touched upon four general issues: the importance of cultural norms, the time distribution of different levels of mental health, the occasional divergence between components as indicators of overall health, and the need to distinguish views of the focal person from assessments by other people. In the last respect, Strupp and Hadley's (1977) approach was extended slightly and applied to the present five-component account.

3

The measurement of context-free and job-related mental health

Statements about mental health vary in the breadth of situations to which they refer. Many cover a wide range of settings or deal with life in general, whereas others are more focused, applying only to one particular context. The discussion so far has primarily been of the former kind, concerned with mental health which may be termed 'context-free'. Mental health which is 'context-specific' is observed within a single setting, such as a person's job or family, and relevant concepts and measures are partly determined by which particular setting is of interest. It is *job-related* mental health which is the context-specific form of greatest concern to this book.

In describing approaches to the measurement of mental health the distinction between these two levels of specificity will be retained for the first four components of the account introduced in Chapter 2. Reference will thus be made separately to affective well-being which is context-free and to that which is job-related, and different measurement instruments will be described for the two levels. Similarly, both context-free and job-related forms of competence, autonomy, and aspiration will be examined. However, the fifth component, integrated functioning, which is mainly concerned with structural aspects of mental health, appears to be best treated only at the undifferentiated context-free level.

Measuring affective well-being

The two principal dimensions of the present model of affective well-being have been described in Chapter 2 as 'pleasure' and 'arousal'. A derivative of the basic account is set out in Figure 3.1.

As previously, the pleasure axis is shown horizontally, with arousal as the vertical dimension. However, two diagonal axes are now included, and the diagram has been changed from a circular to an elongated form. The basis for the latter will be described shortly. Let us first consider the three axes identified as running from 1a, 2a, and 3a to 1b, 2b, and 3b respectively. These

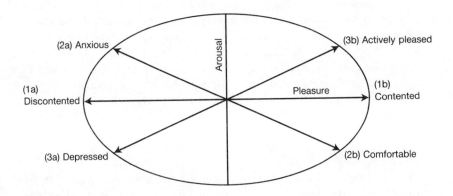

Fig. 3.1   Affective well-being: Three principal axes of measurement.

are intended to represent primary dimensions of measurement. The arousal dimension is on its own not considered an indicator of well-being and its poles are therefore left unlabelled.

Context-free well-being

Measures of self-reported well-being have been developed in respect of each of the three principal axes. They may be considered in turn, starting with context-free measures concerned with life in general. Along the first axis (from 'discontented' to 'contented') are scales which index degree of pleasure without specific reference to level of arousal. In some measures arousal is assumed to be at a moderate level, close to the horizontal axis; these may be referred to as 'narrow-band' measures. Items in other procedures cover a broader range of arousal values, including features from several distances above and below the horizontal axis. In these 'broad-band' measures, axis one is treated (not always explicitly) as a composite of axes two and three.

The simplest measures in respect of the first axis are self-ratings of happiness. For example, Bradburn and Caplovitz (1965) set out to assess 'overall sense of well-being' through the question: 'Taking all things together, how would you say things are these days? Would you say you are very happy, pretty happy, or not too happy?' A single item of that kind has also been used by Andrews and Withey (1974), Brenner (1975) and many others. Multi-item measures of happiness, yielding average or total scores across items, have been described by Bryant and Veroff (1982, 1984), Fordyce (1985), Kammann et al. (1979), Kammann and Flett (1983), and others. Examples of both single- and multi-item measures have been reviewed by Diener (1984) and Veenhoven and Jonkers (1984).

Those forms of assessment are through 'narrow-band' measures as defined above. A narrow-band approach has also been taken to the measurement of satisfaction with present life, for example through adjectival checklists or responses to descriptive or evaluative statements (e.g. Andrews and Withey 1974; Gilleard *et al.* 1981; Larsen *et al.* 1985; Warr 1978; Warr *et al.* 1979). Reported happiness and satisfaction are typically intercorrelated to a high degree, but, as suggested in Fig. 2.1 (page 27), they are ideally viewed as vectors with slightly different angles in respect of the primary pleasure axis. Campbell *et al.* (1976, p. 37) have drawn attention to a differing association with age: at least in cross-sectional studies there is a tendency for happiness to decline with age while life satisfaction increases beyond the middle years (see also Herzog *et al.* 1982).

The first dimension of affective well-being has also been studied through broad-band instruments, in the form of self-completion inventories which cover a wide range of levels of arousal. For example, Beckman's (1981) measure of 'general psychological well-being' contains items drawn from other scales covering life satisfaction, depression, morale, and social isolation. A second example is Goldberg's (1972, 1978) General Health Questionnaire. This was constructed in order to distinguish empirically between patients identified by medical practitioners as suffering from minor psychiatric disorders and those considered to be free of such disorder. The General Health Questionnaire covers a range of symptoms located in the left-hand side of Fig. 3.1, both above and below the horizontal axis. Illustrative questions ask about sleep loss through worry, feelings of strain, finding life a struggle, being unable to face up to problems, feeling depressed, worthless and hopeless, and thinking that life is not worth living. Other wide-ranging measures of negative affect have been described by Dohrenwend *et al.* (1980), Headey *et al.* (1984), Kellner and Sheffield (1973), Langner (1962), and others.

Self-report inventories have also been constructed to assess separately affective well-being on the two diagonal axes of Fig. 3.1, from 'anxious' to 'comfortable', and from 'depressed' to 'actively pleased'. Measures of context-free anxiety have been published by, among others, Spielberger *et al.* (1970), Warr *et al.* (1979), and Zung (1971). Depression inventories include those by Beck *et al.* (1961), Lubin (1965), Radloff (1977), and Zung (1965); see for example Boyle (1985). A related measure aims to assess 'tedium', defined as 'the experience of physical, emotional and mental exhaustion' (Pines *et al.* 1981). Within the California Psychological Inventory (Gough 1975), the 'sense of well-being' sub-scale appears also to emphasize feelings along the third axis, from depressed to actively pleased. For example, high scorers are described as 'energetic, enterprising, alert, ambitious, versatile, productive, active, and valuing work and effort for its own sake'.

A number of more wide-ranging questionnaires embody separate sub-scales of both anxiety and depression. Among these are the Minnesota Multiphasic Personality Inventory (e.g. Dempsey 1964), the Middlesex Hospital

Questionnaire (Crown and Crisp 1966), the Leeds Self-Assessment Scales (Snaith *et al.* 1976), a scaled version of the General Health Questionnaire (Goldberg and Hillier 1979), the Mental Health Inventory (Veit and Ware 1983), the Symptom Check List (Derogatis *et al.* 1974), and two shorter forms of the last-named: the Brief Symptom Inventory (Derogatis and Melisaratos 1983) and the Typology of Psychic Distress (Mellinger *et al.* 1983). More specific measures may of course be designed to tap separately particular features of either anxiety or depression (e.g. Berndt *et al.* 1983; Berndt *et al.* 1984; Blatt *et al.* 1976; Blatt *et al.* 1982; Delmonte and Ryan 1983).

The location of axes two and three in the elongated shape of Fig. 3.1 (at an angle less than 90 degrees) suggests that scores on measures of anxiety and depression will be empirically associated with each other. In their pure forms the affects can be viewed as clinically distinct, but in practice measured levels are usually positively intercorrelated (e.g. Dobson 1985). This comes about because the two sets of symptoms are found in many cases to co-exist, and because most depression inventories also contain items reflecting high anxiety (e.g. Watson and Clark 1984). In addition, specific forms of depression vary between those which emphasize retardation and slowness, and those which are heavily loaded with agitation and tension (e.g. Overall and Zisook 1980). In the latter case, particularly high correlations with anxiety scores are of course to be expected.

The perspective in Fig. 3.1 would require extension to cover these and other specific forms of depression and anxiety. As currently presented, it has a more general focus and content. At this general level it may be suggested that the pleasure dimension is accorded greater weight than the arousal dimension, with pleasure taking priority in determining the overall quality of affective well-being. In schematic terms this differential weighting would yield, rather than a circular diagram as implied by Fig. 2.1 (page 27), an oval shape elongated horizontally as in Fig. 3.1 (page 41). The clinical manifestations of 'mixed affective disorder' or 'generalized dysphoria' would in this framework be viewed as combining features of both high and low arousal, which all load negatively on the more heavily weighted pleasure dimension.

There is widespread agreement about the content of principal forms of low well-being, so that items are very similar from scale to scale. (Useful reviews are to be found in books edited by Pichot and Olivier-Martin 1974, and Lambert *et al.* 1983. See also Watson and Clark 1984.) However, there are some variations in the degree to which scale content extends from thoughts and feelings into physiological processes. Characteristic forms of the latter are central to specific types of low affective well-being, so that comprehensive assessment of anxiety or depression should include evidence about bodily symptoms, such as muscular tension, stomach problems, and insomnia. Self-reports of these are in practice more common in measures designed primarily for clinical than for community or occupational use, in that the former concentrate to a greater extent upon states of ill-health.

The time perspective to be adopted by persons describing themselves on inventory items also varies somewhat between measures. It ranges from 'at this moment, right now', through 'the past month' and 'recently', to 'the past year'. Some measures are identified as being intended to assess transient states (e.g. mood measures; see reviews by Howarth and Schokman-Gates 1981, and Mackay 1980), whereas others are more clearly trait or personality features (as, for example, the Depression scale of the Minnesota Multiphasic Personality Inventory, or the Neuroticism scale of the Eysenck Personality Questionnaire). Spielberger *et al.* (1970) have produced measures to assess anxiety both as a state and as a trait. The measures are similar in most respects, but differ in their temporal focus. Associations between indices of state anxiety and trait measures of neuroticism are usually found to be significantly positive (e.g. Costa and McRae 1980; Warr *et al.* 1983; Williams 1981).

Many inventories are restricted to negative features only; rather than covering the full range from very low to very high well-being, they are in effect half-range measures covering only low to moderate values. Bradburn (1969) emphasized the need additionally to assess positive feelings, presenting a scale of positive affect as well as one of negative affect. These were described as though they reflected opposed sections of a pleasure dimension (1a and 1b in Fig. 3.1). However, Bradburn reports that, rather than being strongly negatively intercorrelated, the two scales are effectively independent (see also Beiser 1974; Diener 1984; Warr 1978). Examination of his items in the terms of Fig. 3.1 (page 41) suggests one reason for this. In practice, the positive affect items appear to tap vector 3b (actively pleased), whereas the negative affect scale is made up of items straddling 2a, 1a and 3a (see also Cherlin and Reeder 1975; McDowell and Praught 1982). A strong negative correlation would be predicted if positive and negative affect items were located at opposite ends of a single dimension; in this case the fact that the two sets of items are located at an angle of less than 180 degrees indicates that a less strong association is to be expected.

This limited negative correlation is in turn reduced for reasons proposed by Warr *et al.* (1983). Bradburn required subjects to respond in terms of whether each feeling had or had not been experienced at all during the last few weeks. That form of response appears to permit the occurrence of both positive and negative feelings within the period. By contrast, with more conventional response modes, for example from 'none of the time' to 'most of the time', positive responses necessarily exclude negative ones with reference to a fixed time period. Warr and colleagues showed that an observed correlation of -0.07 between positive and negative affect using Bradburn's procedure became -0.54 when a more conventional proportion-of-time response mode was used with the same items. Bradburn's conclusions about the apparent independence of the two forms of affect are thus likely to derive largely from the particular items and response time-frame which he employed. (See also Diener and Emmons 1985.)

One aspect of affective well-being mentioned earlier concerned feelings about the self. These specific evaluations have been measured through several scales of self-esteem (e.g. Tharenou 1979), among which Rosenberg's (1965) ten-item scale is of particular interest. Whereas the positively-worded items in this inventory are ranged along the right-hand section of the first dimension of Fig. 3.1 (close to 1b, contented), the negatively-worded items appear to reflect self-denigration of a kind represented by vector 3a (depressed); the two sets of items are in fact not located at opposite ends of a single dimension. That difference may at least partly account for the fact that the positive and negative items are found either to constitute independent factors (e.g. Pearlin and Schooler 1978) or to be only moderately negatively intercorrelated; for example, coefficients between -0.24 and -0.66 were recorded in studies by Kohn and Schooler (1983) and Warr and Jackson (1983). Self-denigration items are also found in depression inventories, and the two types of scale are significantly intercorrelated (e.g. Blatt *et al.* 1982). Ratings of subjective competence, autonomy, and aspiration may also contribute to the measurement of self-esteem in ways suggested in Chapter 2.

Self-reports of affective well-being may sometimes be augmented by interpretations made by a competent observer. In clinical applications this process can be aided through the use of standardized interview questioning which leads to an observer making ratings along defined dimensions such as anxiety or depression, or in terms of clinical diagnosis (e.g. Bech *et al.* 1980; Eaton and Kessler 1985; Wing *et al.* 1974; Wittenborn 1984; Zung 1971). Such procedures have rarely been used in making assessments of affective well-being in the right-hand sections of Fig. 3.1, and there may be scope for the development of rating procedures in respect of those more positive aspects.

One specific type of information derived by observers rather than through subjective report is in terms of physiological functioning. Three sets of measures have been of particular interest: cardiac responses, and levels of secretion of corticosteroids (by the adrenal cortex), and of catecholamines (by the adrenal medulla). The first of these have been studied in terms of heart-rate and blood pressure, with elevated levels being taken to represent active coping efforts, and chronic elevation seen as leading to physical ill-health. Most often examined among the corticosteroids is cortisol and among the catecholamines adrenaline and noradrenaline. Although correlations with reported feelings are not always high, their association with external demands suggests that levels of these hormones might be taken as markers of affective well-being (e.g. Carruthers 1977; Frankenhaeuser 1981; Frankenhaeuser and Johansson 1981; Karasek *et al.* 1982). Evidence is accumulating that secretion of adrenaline is associated with anxiety and that cortisol levels are linked to depression (e.g. Lundberg and Frankenhaeuser 1980; Henry 1982; Veith-Flanigan and Sandman 1985).

There are practical difficulties in the use of physiological indices (urine or blood samples may have to be collected, for example), and unreliability may be present if controls are not introduced for systematic diurnal fluctuations and ancillary factors such as body weight, physical activity, smoking, and level of caffeine consumption. These difficulties have been considered by, among others, Baum *et al.* (1982), Fried *et al.* (1984), and Krantz and Manuck (1984). Examples of research using cardiac and hormonal measures will be cited in later chapters.

Job-related well-being

The discussion so far has dealt only with what was introduced as 'context-free' affective well-being. Let us now move on to parallel examination of one form of 'context-specific' well-being, in respect of jobs. Table 3.1 summarizes the preceding account and contains a forward look into what is to follow. The middle column refers to 'job-related' affective well-being, and contains examples of measures to tap feelings about one's job as a whole. However, some self-report inventories have dealt specifically with reactions to particular aspects of a job rather than with feelings about a job overall, and these are included in the third column, covering 'facet-specific' affective well-being.

The primary dimension of affective well-being (from discontented to contented) has been operationalized in occupational settings through measures of job satisfaction. Satisfaction in general has sometimes been tapped through single items, such as 'All in all, how satisfied are you with your job?' (e.g. McGehee and Tullar 1979), or through multi-item inventories covering a variety of evaluations which are averaged or summed. Procedures and principal types of content are by now well established, and measures of overall job satisfaction tend to be statistically reliable and to intercorrelate to a high degree. Cook *et al.* (1981) have described and evaluated 17 different inventories of this kind.

Satisfaction measures covering specific facets of jobs (in the right-hand column of Table 3.1) are of two kinds. Some inventories deal with a single facet on its own (satisfaction with pay or with colleagues, for instance), whereas others contain several sub-scales each representing a particular feature. The job facets most widely examined include the kind of work undertaken, colleagues, supervision, pay, working conditions, promotion prospects, security of employment, and the company as a whole (e.g. Smith 1976; Smith *et al.* 1969; Warr and Routledge 1969). Twenty-nine measures of this kind have been reviewed by Cook *et al.* (1981), who point out that the different facet satisfactions tend to be positively intercorrelated and that one of them (satisfaction with the kind of work undertaken) is particularly

Table 3.1 Affective well-being: Three axes of measurement and three levels of specificity, with illustrative types of index

Axis	Affective well-being		
	Context-free	Job-related	Facet-specific
1. Discontented— contented	Happiness Life satisfaction General distress Negative affect	Job satisfaction Alienation from work Job attachment Organizational commitment	Specific satisfactions (with pay, amount of responsibility etc.)
2. Anxious— comfortable	Anxiety Neuroticism	Job-related tension Resigned satisfaction	Specific feelings of job strain
3. Depressed— actively pleased	Depression Tedium Self-denigration Positive affect	Job-related depression Job-related burnout Job boredom Job-related pleasure Job involvement Morale	Specific aspects of job boredom

closely associated with other specific satisfactions and with overall job satisfaction.

A distinction is often drawn between 'intrinsic' and 'extrinsic' job satisfaction. The first of these covers satisfaction with features which are inherent in the conduct of the job itself: freedom to choose how to undertake the work, amount of responsibility, skill requirements, variety, challenge, etc. Extrinsic job satisfaction concerns aspects of a job which form the background to the task itself. It is thus viewed in terms of satisfaction with pay, conditions, hours of work, industrial relations procedures, job security, etc. Intrinsic and extrinsic satisfaction scores tend in practice to be positively intercorrelated, but the conceptual distinction is important and will recur throughout the book.

Job-related affective well-being in respect of the first axis (discontented–contented) has also been measured through scales of 'alienation from work' (e.g. Aiken and Hage 1966), 'attachment to the job' (e.g. Koch and Steers 1978) and 'organizational commitment' (e.g. Mowday *et al.* 1979). These have items whose content reflects the scale titles (although 'alienation' scales are often very similar to measures of job satisfaction; e.g. Lefkowitz and Brigando 1980), and are found to be positively correlated both with each other and with job satisfaction measures.

Turning next to the anxious–comfortable axis, several researchers have developed measures of job-related tension, tapping aspects of anxiety and experienced strain (the top left-hand quadrant of Figs. 2.1 and 3.1) brought about by working in a particular job. For example, Buck (1972), House and Rizzo (1972), Parker and DeCotiis (1983) and others include items such as 'Problems associated with my job have kept me awake at night' and 'I have felt fidgety or nervous because of my job'. Caplan *et al.* (1975), Schriesheim and Murphy (1976), van Dijkhuizen (1980), and others have amended the instructions of standard anxiety inventories to request that respondents 'think about yourself and your job nowadays' or describe 'how you usually feel on your present job'.

The positive pole of this second axis (the bottom right-hand quadrant of the figures) may be viewed as representing 'resigned satisfaction'. Many studies have suggested that employees are predominantly satisfied with their jobs (see Chapter 4), but consideration of types of satisfaction at different points on the arousal dimension has usually been lacking. It seems likely that many 'satisfied' employees (especially those who have been in their job for years) are in fact in a state of quiescent resignation; they accept their job as an unchanging and broadly tolerable aspect of life, but their aspiration level and degree of arousal are both low. This low-arousal form of job satisfaction has not been adequately investigated (cf. Bruggemann *et al.* 1975).

Negative features of this second axis of affective well-being in occupational settings have also been examined through measures which are facet-specific. For example, specific job strains (arising from high workload, rapid pacing, etc.) have been studied (see Chapters 5 and 7), as have the tensions experienced by mothers of dependent children in coping with the demands of both home and employment roles (e.g. Cooke and Rousseau 1984; Parry and Warr 1980).

Finally, what of the third axis, from depressed to actively pleased? Negative aspects of this have been tapped through measures of depressed mood applied to paid work. For example, Caplan *et al.* (1975), Quinn and Shepard (1974) and van Dijkhuizen (1980) used standard depression items under the instruction 'Check how you feel when you think about yourself and your job'. A related construct is that of job-related 'burnout', one component of which has been viewed as emotional exhaustion arising from work, especially in jobs which require the sustained provision of help to other people (e.g. Maslach and Jackson 1981, 1984; Meier 1984). Other forms of the negative pole of the third dimension have been measured through check-lists of job boredom and fatigue (e.g. Yoshitake 1978).

The positive pole of this dimension has been assessed through reports of job-related pleasure (Warr and Payne 1983a), and through scales of 'job involvement' (e.g. Lodahl and Kejner 1965). In that the latter appear to cover the two dimensions of job-related pleasure and arousal, it is not surprising that scores correlate with job satisfaction, the latter being a reflection primarily of the first dimension on its own. More generally, the actively pleased quadrant in employment settings seems to reflect notions of worker 'morale', an active, pleasurable involvement in working hard. In addition, however, morale tends to be viewed in social psychological terms of group cohesiveness and the establishment of positive group norms.

In summary, this section has built upon the two-dimensional framework introduced earlier, to examine three principal axes of affective well-being. As shown in Fig. 3.1 and Table 3.1, these have been referred to as discontented–contented, anxious–comfortable, and depressed–actively pleased. Each represents a range of values on the primary pleasure dimension of Fig. 2.1, but they differ in their placement with respect to the arousal dimension. Three principal forms of context-free measure have been illustrated (for example, inventories of life satisfaction, anxiety and depression), and it has been shown how this framework is also useful in grouping measures of affective well-being in job settings. In practice, the occupational literature has given priority to the study of job satisfaction (axis 1), and there is a need to look more closely at the other two major axes.

Measuring competence

The second aspect of mental health, competence in dealing with the environment, has received less measurement attention than the previous component. Approaches may again be examined under the headings of context-free and job-related indices. In both cases, competence may be assessed by observers or by the focal person; as noted in Chapter 2, the latter type of index is sometimes referred to as covering 'subjective competence'.

Context-free competence

Scales of context-free subjective competence have tended to emphasize the negative, an inability to cope. For example, Bryant and Veroff (1982) identified a factor covering several life domains which they described as 'personal inadequacy'; they later referred to 'evaluations of personal competence' in negative situations (Bryant and Veroff 1984). Several authors have published self-report scales of coping failures. For example, Cohen *et al.* (1983) have assessed failures through items of the kind: 'In the last month, how often have you felt difficulties were piling up so high that you could not overcome them?' Also in this vein, but less extreme and more focused, is the Cognitive Failures Questionnaire (Broadbent *et al.* 1982), with questions about minor mistakes in daily activity; for example, 'Do you read something and find you haven't been thinking about it and must read it again?' Scores on this cognitive competence measure are significantly associated with anxiety and depression levels.

Heppner and Petersen (1982) have developed a Problem Solving Inventory, which is used to obtain self-reports about behaviours and experiences indicative of effective or ineffective resolution of everyday problems. Scores on this measure of subjective competence have been found by Nezu (1985) to be significantly negatively associated with depression, anxiety, and beliefs about personal autonomy.

Research by clinical psychologists and psychiatrists has sometimes examined competence in terms of a person's 'social adjustment'. For example, the Social Adjustment Scale permits assessment of functioning in six different areas: work (paid or unpaid), social and leisure activities, relationship with extended family, spouse role, parental role, and as a member of the family unit. Information is obtained via interviews or self-report or from significant others (e.g Weissman and Bothwell 1976; Weissman *et al.* 1971). Illustrative questions about work include: 'Have you been doing your job well during the past month?' 'Have you fallen behind in your work?' 'Has anyone had to speak to you about your work?' The Social Adjustment Scale links answers to these questions directly to level of affective well-being, in that it was devised and is widely used as an indicator of depression.

Also within the clinical domain are procedures for identifying whether individuals have attained specific change targets, for example in psychotherapy. One method is Goal Attainment Scaling (Kiresuk and Sherman 1968), in which therapists and/or patients establish measurable goals relevant to behavioural problems under consideration. Illustrative competence goals include specific forms of assertiveness, changes in eating or drinking patterns, improved social interactions, and the reduction of specific phobias (e.g. Lambert *et al.* 1983). A more wide-ranging index of effectiveness is Vaillant's (1975, 1977) Adult Adjustment Scale. This permits ratings of adjustment in four principal areas: work, social, psychological, and medical.

Job-related competence

Turning to specifically job-related measures of competence, it is clear that the approaches described above may in principle be applied in occupational settings. However, there are likely to be difficulties in specifying when level of coping is a reflection of health rather than of a specific job skill. Wagner and Morse (1975) have published a 23-item measure of subjective job competence (for example, 'No-one knows this job better than I do'), and a more focused version has been described by McEnrue (1984). Jones (1986) has presented an eight-item scale to assess job-related self-efficacy, with particular reference to a person's ability to cope with new role settings. Quinn and Shepard (1974) have used a five-item scale covering self-ratings of job success, importance, knowledge, etc. Within their measure of job-related burnout, Maslach and Jackson (1981) have included a 'personal accomplishment' sub-scale, tapping subjective competence in job settings. Lack of competence has elsewhere been measured through assessments of coping inability, in which workers indicate if specific job demands are too great for them to handle.

These forms of coping difficulty in jobs may be viewed as indicators of mental health, but only in certain circumstances. For example, low job competence might yield low affective well-being as a person fails to cope with the demands of his or her job. However, there are other forms of occupational competence or incompetence which cannot be so readily mapped on to the health–ill-health continuum. For example, managers' ratings of subordinates' work performance are commonly made within companies' staff appraisal systems. Whatever their organizational merit, such ratings of competence cannot in general be viewed as a reflection of employees' mental health. That appears to be the case only when job-related competence is associated with some broader aspects of context-free functioning. When level of job competence influences or is influenced by affective well-being (for example, when inadequate job performance or failure to cope gives rise to anxiety), then job-related competence may be mapped on to the health–ill-health continuum. Similarly, low subjective job competence spilling over into generally low self-esteem may also be taken as an indicator of poor mental health. However, in cases when job competence is unrelated to wider functioning, it is inappropriate to draw inferences about mental health solely from assessments of a person's competence at work.

Measuring autonomy

A balance between interdependence and self-regulation makes up the third component of mental health. As illustrated in Chapter 2, this component (referred to as 'autonomy') is linked with competence and aspiration, since an autonomous person has often achieved that condition through motivated activity which has generated personal success. However, it is moderate rather than extremely high levels of autonomy which are typically regarded as healthy, and this curvilinear pattern gives rise to measurement difficulties.

Examples of context-free self-report inventories include the seven-item scale of Pearlin *et al.* (1981) which measures 'the extent to which people see themselves as being in control of the forces which importantly affect their lives'. Other approaches are sometimes under the heading of internal versus external control. Rotter's (1966) measure of this construct has been widely used to determine generalized expectancies that one has independent control over one's own activities and rewards, rather than beliefs that these are determined by external forces; this and other measures of subjective autonomy have been reviewed by Lefcourt (1982) and Phares (1976). Internal control appears to be seen in Western society as more desirable than external control, and external control scores tend to be significantly correlated with low affective well-being on vectors 2a and 3a of Fig. 3.1 (e.g. Archer 1979; Lefcourt 1982).

Whereas measures in the field of locus of control are based upon reports about beliefs (how much control I believe myself to have), Shostrom's (1964) Personal Orientation Inventory was designed to examine personal values. Ten sub-scales were linked under a broadly defined concept of self-actualization, and it was found that the items contributing most to differences in overall scores were those tapping autonomy, self-support and freedom from social pressures. These were grouped under the general concept of 'inner directedness'. The Personal Orientation Inventory thus provides an index of context-free autonomy in terms of a person's expressed values. (See also Tosi and Lindamood 1975.)

Another group of measures have dealt with 'powerlessness' within models of alienation (e.g. Seeman 1959; Kanungo 1979; Kohn and Schooler 1983). Powerlessness is seen as an inability to influence the course of events in one's lifespace. It clearly has context-free reference, but job-related measures have also been devised (e.g. Shepard 1972).

The instruments described so far in this section primarily assess those aspects of autonomy concerned with the extent to which a person is an independent agent. The balance with interdependence which is central to the present notion of autonomy has less often been assessed through standardized measures. Subjective and objective forms of assessment would appear to be practicable, both context-free and job-related, but there are clear methodological problems in combining scores for interdependence with those for independence to yield an index of the overall construct of autonomy.

Measuring aspiration

A raised aspiration level is reflected in motivated activity, an interest in the environment, and wanting to extend oneself in ways which are personally significant. Features of this kind are associated with elevated scores on the arousal dimension of affective well-being. Context-free inventories which tap the actively pleased vector of Fig. 3.1 may therefore contain questions bearing upon subjective aspiration level, but self-report measures or standardized interview schedules directed specifically to the aspiration component are difficult to construct. This is partly because aspirations need to be viewed relative to current environmental conditions, and also because aspirations may have their targets in many different domains; a very broad-ranging set of questions would either miss a person's active behaviours or be likely to touch upon them only in passing. However, Wadsworth and Ford (1983) have developed an interview procedure which elicits aspirations in each of six different domains (family, work and school, social life, leisure, personal growth and maintenance, material/environmental). The information so gathered can be used to examine features of goals such as their number, diversity, content, immediacy, and interrelatedness.

More specific measures have been published in the occupational domain, although they are not usually identified as health indices. As generally, the key feature is that a person voluntarily works towards challenging goals and enjoys seeking and attaining them. Conversely, if a job engages no aspirations for personal satisfaction through its performance, then the consequent feelings of apathy and non-involvement might be deemed unhealthy.

This form of job-related aspiration is often referred to as 'intrinsic motivation'. Other descriptions include Gardell's (1971) account in terms of the satisfaction of 'ego-relevant needs, i.e. desires for self-realization in the performance of work' (p. 150). An early measure of intrinsic job motivation was devised by Hackman and Lawler (1971), with self-report items of the kind 'I feel a great sense of personal satisfaction when I do my job well.' Later instruments have been published by Hackman and Oldham (1975) and Warr *et al.* (1979).

Job-related aspiration of an intrinsic kind has also been tapped through indices of 'growth-need strength' (Hackman and Oldham 1975) or 'higher-order need strength' (Warr *et al.* 1979). For example, the former measure sets out to identify the degree to which a person seeks work which is stimulating and challenging and which provides a sense of worthwhile accomplishment. In practice, the notion and measurement of growth-need strength overlap considerably with those of intrinsic job motivation, described above, although the former has typically been viewed in the literature as a more stable characteristic than the latter.

In summary, the context-free measurement of aspiration has not been developed to any high degree. Observers with close knowledge of a person can no doubt provide reasonably accurate assessments, but few self-report questionnaires or interview schedules are available. In the occupational domain some progress has been made in the identification of different levels of intrinsic job motivation and of higher-order need strength. In general, there is a need to link measured aspiration level to a focal person's contemporary environment.

Measuring integrated functioning

The final component of mental health is reflected in co-ordination or harmony of various kinds. Examples given earlier included a sense of coherence, balance between temporary strain and the satisfactions of goal attainment, and compatibility between activities and satisfactions in different life domains.

The scope and diffuseness of this concept, and the fact that it subsumes many of the preceding features and relationships between them, make it especially difficult to operationalize. The aspects of integration which might serve as criteria for measurement are clearly wide-ranging, and different issues are likely to be salient in the assessment of different individuals.

Measures in this area are usually developed within the framework of a particular theoretical approach. For example, Patton *et al.* (1982) have devised a series of rating scales from 'optimum self-cohesion' to 'severe discohesion' in terms of Kohut's psychology of the self. These cover, for example, use of abilities, tension tolerance, ambitions, goals, and differentiation from others. Other approaches have been in terms of maturity of development through hypothesized stages; see, for example, the review by Lazarus (1975).

An associated procedure is Vaillant's (1975, 1977) Maturity of Defences Scale. He identified 15 types of mechanisms used to cope with adversity, which he grouped into three levels of maturity. Defences defined as immature include projection, passive-aggressive behaviour, and acting out; mature mechanisms include suppression, anticipation, and sublimation. From extensive interviews and tests, Vaillant was able to allot to each person in his study an overall score reflecting this characteristic of their personality structure.

Integration has also been assessed through measures of 'ego-strength' derived from sources as diverse as the Rorschach projective test and the Minnesota Multiphasic Personality Inventory. For example, Barron's (1953) measure, derived from the latter, covers areas such as physiological stability, sense of reality, feelings of personal adequacy, emotional outgoingness, and spontaneity. In general, however, different indicators of ego-strength yield different results (e.g. Garfield 1978), reflecting different theoretical perspectives and problems of measurement at the level of personality structure and dynamics.

Integrated functioning is of particular concern within clinical psychology and psychiatry. It has rarely been measured in the domain covered by later chapters of this book.

Summary

This chapter has examined measurement approaches to the five components of mental health introduced in Chapter 2. 'Context-free' and 'job-related' aspects have been considered, and measures in terms of both self-report and observer ratings have been described.

Three primary axes for the assessment of affective well-being have been suggested. These are labelled from 'discontented' to 'contented', from 'anxious' to 'comfortable', and from 'depressed' to 'actively pleased'. Fig. 3.1 (page 41) illustrates their interrelationships, and some published measures of each have been cited. The need for additional indices of positive forms of well-being has been emphasized, and the potential value of physiological assessment has noted. A summary of self-report and observer-rating measures of both context-free and job-related well-being has been presented in Table 3.1 (page 47).

Other components of mental health have received less measurement attention from both clinical and occupational researchers. However, a number of scales of competence, autonomy, and aspiration have been described in the second half of the chapter, and several conceptual and operational difficulties have been considered. For example, low levels of competence indicate impaired mental health only in certain circumstances, such as when they bring about low affective well-being. However, the nature and boundaries of those limiting circumstances have yet to be specified in detail.

Finally, consideration was given to the measurement of integrated functioning. Indices have usually been developed from broad theoretical frameworks, and the complexity and diffuseness of the concept imply that simple numerical scales are unlikely to be entirely satisfactory. This fifth aspect has rarely been studied in the domain of the present book.

Measures of the other four components of mental health will be illustrated throughout the chapters which follow.

4

Jobs and mental health: nine types of evidence

It is time now for an initial examination of the impact of jobs and un-employment upon mental health. Nine research approaches will be illus-trated, with a focus upon both 'context-free' and 'job-related' outcomes. First, however, we should consider some issues of definition.

Employment, unemployment, non-employment, and work

In contemporary Western society there is a widespread normative belief that paid employment is necessary. That usually means having a single paid job at any one time, with terms and conditions summarized in an explicit or implicit contract. Employment thus typically takes the form of a contractual relationship between an individual and an employer. 'Self-employed' people are very much in the minority, for example comprising around 11 per cent of the employed population of the United Kingdom in 1984; for men and for women the proportions were fourteen and seven respectively (Creigh *et al.* 1986).

Jobs may be considered as 'socially acceptable means of earning a living' (Garraty 1978, p. 10), thus excluding activities which are defined as illegal. Those which are referred to as 'full-time' typically take up between 35 and 45 hours in a week, but travelling to and from a place of employment adds on average a further 10 per cent or thereabouts (e.g. Szalai 1972). 'Part-time' jobs may of course vary in their weekly duration, but 30 hours per week is often taken as their upper limit for statistical and survey purposes.

There are differences between men and women in Western society in their probability of being employed. Between the completion of education and the age of retirement, it is usual for men to seek to be in employment without interruption. Women are more likely to leave the labour market during their 20s and 30s for periods devoted primarily to child-care. However, in recent years there has been a growing tendency in many countries for women to return to employment after child-rearing. For example, in the United States in 1950 women comprised 29 per cent of all employees, but by 1982 this figure had risen to 43 per cent. Parallel figures for the United Kingdom are

31 per cent and 39 per cent respectively, and for Australia the values are 22 per cent and 37 per cent. Other countries show similar current figures but without much change in recent decades. For example, women accounted for 38 per cent and 39 per cent of the 1982 labour force in West Germany and Japan, but comparable figures for 1950 were already as high as 35 per cent and 38 per cent respectively (Organization for Economic Co-operation and Development 1985).

However, women's jobs are more likely than men's to be on a part-time basis. Their 1981 share of part-time employment was 70 per cent, 94 per cent, 79 per cent, 94 per cent and 67 per cent respectively in USA, UK, Australia, West Germany and Japan (Organization for Economic Co-operation and Development 1985). Part-time employment is particularly common among women who are married. For example, the percentages of married and unmarried women working part-time in the United Kingdom in 1983 were 50 and 20 (Manpower Services Commission 1984).

People defined as 'unemployed' have recently made up more than 10 per cent of the labour force in many countries. Official definitions of unemployment vary from country to country, but usually include the notion that, in order to be classed as 'unemployed', a person must not only lack a job but also be looking for one. Adults below the age of retirement who have no job and are not seeking one (those who are voluntarily caring for their children or otherwise not wanting employment) will here be referred to as 'non-employed', distinguishing this group from the unemployed in terms of their current preference with respect to a job.

What about the term 'work'? In everyday use this is often taken as equivalent to 'paid employment' or 'a job'. People who have jobs are sometimes described as being 'in work' or as 'working', and unemployed people may be referred to as 'out-of-work' or 'workless'. However, work also takes many forms outside paid employment. Examples include housework, voluntary work, repair and decorating work, and a large number of other activities not explicitly identified through their titles as work. These activities may be present during both unemployment and non-employment.

Definitions of the term have in common the assertion that work is an activity directed to valued goals beyond enjoyment of the activity itself (e.g. Anderson 1974; Jahoda 1982; Handy 1984; Kabanoff 1980; Parker 1983; Weiss and Kahn 1960). In addition, there is often a suggestion that it is required in some way; work is frequently seen as unavoidable. Furthermore, the term often connotes difficulty, a need to labour or exert oneself against the environment: the goal is to achieve something that is physically and/or psychologically difficult.

Work can vary from momentary exertion through to activity sustained over long periods of time. Sustained activity almost always takes place within a network of social roles and institutions: in paid jobs, in weekend sports teams, in voluntary welfare groups, in amateur dramatic societies, or in the family home. In these cases people when working are often operating within some form of exchange relationship, applying their strength, skills, knowledge, or other resources partly in exchange for material, psychological, or social returns.

The amount of work undertaken outside paid employment differs between men and women. A Dutch time-budget investigation recorded that of all the work performed by men, 36 per cent was outside their job, whereas for women the overall percentage was 84 (Knulst and Schoonderwoerd 1983). An earlier study of married people aged between 30 and 49 in London indicated that only 17 per cent of full-time employed men's work concerned household tasks, compared to 36 per cent for full-time employed women, 57 per cent for part-time employed women, and 100 per cent for non-employed housewives. The total number of hours worked by each of these groups was found to be 59, 63, 62, and 46 respectively (Young and Willmott 1973).

Differences in the distribution of household work between male and female partners were also found by Pahl (1984) to be associated with a woman's employment status. In households where the female partner had a full-time paid job the division of domestic labour between men and women was more equal than in those where the woman was non-employed, although differences were still present. Other factors were also found to affect the distribution of work. For example, the presence of young children in the home was linked with both female non-employment and a larger female share of household tasks.

The employment status of the male partner is also influential. For example, Warr and Payne (1983b) observed that 71 per cent of unemployed British men reported doing more household chores after losing their jobs, and 59 per cent reported that they were now more frequently preparing meals for other people.

Work thus takes many forms, and these occur within employment, unemployment, and non-employment. Themes which recur in discussions of the concept are the joint presence of obligation and choice and of benefit and cost. These are associated with widespread feelings of ambivalence. As with other salient parts of their lives, people are likely to have mixed feelings about work: they may both love it and hate it. Introducing a book of workers' descriptions of their jobs and their feelings about those jobs, Terkel (1972) stresses ambivalence in a striking manner:

This book, being about work, is, by its very nature, about violence—to the spirit as well as the body. It is about ulcers as well as accidents, about shouting matches as well as fistfights, about nervous breakdowns as well as kicking the dog around. It is, above all (or beneath all), about daily humiliations. To survive the day is triumph enough for the walking wounded among the great many of us. . . . It is about a search, too, for daily meaning as well as daily bread, for recognition as well as cash, for astonishment rather than torpor; in short for a sort of life rather than a Monday through Friday sort of dying. Perhaps immortality, too, is part of the quest. To be remembered was the wish, spoken and unspoken, of the heroes and heroines of this book (p. xi).

These comments from an unemployed man also make the point well; note that he too is describing work in terms of a paid job:

Frankly, I hate work. Of course, I could say with equal truth that I love work; that it is a supremely interesting activity; that it is often fascinating; that I wish I didn't have to do it; that I wish I had a job at which I could earn a decent wage. That makes six subjective statements about work and all of them are true to me (Fraser 1968, p. 273).

It is feelings like those which form the starting point of this chapter. Nine different types of research evidence will be summarized, in an initial examination of the mental health impact of jobs and unemployment. Subsequent chapters will explore the processes through which the observed effects occur. This will be undertaken by viewing both jobs and joblessness as environments which differ in terms of the nine categories introduced in Chapter 1.

The impact of unemployment

Research into job loss and continuing unemployment has clearly established that in general being unemployed significantly impairs mental health. Conversely, obtaining a job leads quickly to improvement. This important area deserves extended treatment, and a full review will be provided in Chapters 11 and 12. At this point, let us merely consider three illustrations. First, here are some descriptions provided by unemployed people themselves:

You feel as if your whole life is crumbling. You feel devalued out of work; you feel your age, you feel you have less and less to offer. Instead of feeling you're getting richer in experience, you feel something is being taken away from you.... You lead a sort of double life: the pointlessness of the reduced daily round, and the knowledge that you are still a feeling, thinking human being whose skills and talents are lying unused. (A British blue-collar employee) (Seabrook, 1982, pp. 122–3).

A complete crushing of self-respect and imagination.... It's as bad and has to be respected as much as someone who's lost a leg. But we don't.... I couldn't articulate the problem.... I lived in a mental shell, not talking about what the real problems are.... I was totally crushed by the whole thing. (A British manager) (Swinburne 1981, p. 49).

We were raised on work up here. I find myself even now thinking it's time to get up, and I put my feet out of bed, grab my trousers before I remember that I don't have to go. Then you get back into bed, and you're glad you're not late; till it dawns on you you'll never have to get up early ever again.... You don't realize what it means to you. I worked with three good blokes over ten years. You get to know them, you respect them, you know all about their families. You talk about the football or the horses or the telly; you know exactly where they stand, what they think. But if I see them now, there's none of them working, we haven't anything to say to each other. (A British blue-collar employee) (Seabrook 1982, p. 109).

Second, longitudinal investigations with quantitative assessments of mental health have demonstrated a substantial impact of movement into unemployment. For example, Banks and Jackson (1982) interviewed teenagers in their last year of school and during the subsequent two years. The General Health Questionnaire was used as an overall measure of context-free affective well-being (see Chapter 3). Dividing the sample in terms of their employment status after school-leaving revealed a significant increase in well-being for those who moved into jobs and a significant deterioration for those who became unemployed. No difference had been present in the two groups' General Health Questionnaire scores while previously at school. Unemployed members of the sample who later went on to obtain jobs exhibited significant improvements in affective well-being after becoming employed (Jackson *et al.* 1983).

As a third example of the value attached to having a job, consider people's expressed wish for paid work in the absence of financial need. Several studies have asked random samples of the American population the question: 'If you were to get enough money to live as comfortably as you would like for the rest of your life, would you continue to work?' In the setting of the interview, 'work' was clearly to be construed as 'paid employment', and around 70 per cent of full-time employed men in each study indicated that they would work in a job even when that was not financially necessary. This figure does not appear to have declined during the 1970s (Quinn and Staines 1979; Vecchio 1980), although the possibility of change since then has apparently not yet been tested.

In a similar study in Britain, Warr (1982) found that full-time employed women were almost as likely as full-time employed men (65 per cent against 69 per cent) to give a positive answer to a similar question. Single women were more likely than married women to exhibit this form of employment commitment, and for both men and women age and social class were significantly associated with the attitude: commitment to a job in the absence of financial need was stronger among younger people and those of higher occupational status.

Many other investigations into unemployment will be described in Chapters 11 and 12. The summary point to be made at this initial stage is that, for most people in contemporary Western society, research overwhelmingly points to the psychological importance of having a job.

Population estimates of job-related mental health

A second type of investigation is rather different. This aims to identify in quantitative form aspects of job-related mental health in the population as a whole or in specific sub-populations. Research of this kind uses survey methods to obtain subjective reports from job-holders, and has in practice concentrated upon aspects of affective well-being rather than upon other components of mental health. Studies may be grouped in terms of their focus upon each of the dimensions of job-related affective well-being identified in Chapter 3 (see Table 3.1, page 47, for a summary).

The first dimension, from discontented to contented, is exemplified through measures of job satisfaction and attachment. There have been many surveys of job satisfaction levels within the American employed population, and overall scores on multi-item scales are consistently found to be high, especially among non-manual workers (e.g. Quinn and Shepard 1974; Quinn and Staines 1979). Using a single item, it has repeatedly been found that around 50 per cent of American employees describe themselves as 'very satisfied' with their job, between 35 per cent and 40 per cent as 'somewhat satisfied', and less than 15 per cent as 'a little dissatisfied' or 'very dissatisfied' (e.g. Weaver 1980). Positive associations are found with occupational and educational levels, income, age, and being white rather than black; note that several of these factors are themselves interrelated. There appear to be no overall sex differences in response to this kind of job satisfaction question; see also Chapter 14.

The related construct of job attachment has been examined in national surveys by asking whether a person would take the same job if he or she 'had to decide all over again'. Around 65 per cent of American workers report that they would decide without hesitation to take the same job (Quinn and Staines 1979), but there is considerable variation across job level. For example, in research using a similar question 90 per cent of university professors and scientists indicated that they would choose the same job, whereas about 40 per cent of skilled manual workers and only 20 per cent of unskilled manual workers would do so (Kahn 1981).

The high overall levels of job satisfaction and attachment recorded in American studies are usually matched elsewhere, although random population surveys have less often been reported in other countries. For example, studies of particular sub-populations in the United Kingdom have revealed high job-related well-being of this kind (e.g. Warr *et al.* 1979; Young and Wilmott 1973). To some extent these positive reactions are a result of selective recruitment and retention over time, as there is naturally a tendency for very dissatisfied people to move out of a job. One might also expect processes of adaptation and rationalization to augment the levels of satisfaction revealed in this type of survey research.

What of the second dimension of affective well-being, ranging from anxious to comfortable? There have been many studies of negative forms, for example of job-related tension. Since these typically draw limited samples from specific sub-populations, it is difficult to determine overall prevalence. However, some examples are as follows.

Nerell and Wahlund (1981) carried out a postal study of around 10 000 Swedish white-collar workers, finding that 32 per cent reported their work to cause mental strain very often or quite often; members of this group were significantly more likely than those not reporting job strain to make use of sedatives and tranquillizers and to smoke more. In a study of 60 female British managers by Davidson and Cooper (1983), as many as 92 per cent indicated experiencing moderate to high strain at work.

Cherry (1984a) summarized data from more than 1000 32-year-old British men in a wide range of occupations. Forty-four per cent indicated that they were under some or severe nervous strain at work, and reports of job strain were significantly associated with sleep and stomach problems and with a greater probability of headaches. Higher rates of strain were observed at higher occupational levels. For example, 55 per cent of professional workers reported job-related strain, but only 15 per cent of semi-skilled and unskilled workers. Comparable data from samples of full-time and part-time employed women in the same age-group were presented by Cherry (1984b). Job strain defined in this way was reported by 46 per cent and 16 per cent of those sub-groups respectively.

A difficulty with many studies of job-related tension (and also of job satisfaction) is that the reference period to be used by respondents is unclear or unspecified. Information may be sought about this week, the recent past, the last year, or merely about one's job in general. Recorded prevalence of strain is likely to be higher if the reference period is broad or undefined, and there are problems of comparability between studies using different periods. With this in mind, Warr and Payne (1983a) examined job-related strain experienced on the preceding day. In a random sample of the British labour-force, 15 per cent of men reported experiencing unpleasant emotional strain sometime on the previous day which they attributed to their job. Corresponding figures for full-time and part-time employed women were 10 per cent and 4 per cent respectively. As in Cherry's (1984a) results, job-related strain was more prevalent at higher occupational levels. For example, 18 per cent of male managerial, professional and administrative workers reported job strain sometime on the previous day, but only 9 per cent of male semi-skilled and unskilled manual workers.

Excretion of catecholamines was suggested in Chapter 3 as a physiological response to environmental demands which might be associated with affective well-being. A study by Jenner *et al.* (1980) did not measure the latter directly, but revealed a consistent physiological impact of job activities. These authors examined the rate of excretion of adrenaline and noradrenaline by male workers on workdays and at weekends. Three samples were taken both on a Thursday and on a Sunday: immediately after getting up, around midday, and around 6 p.m. No differences in excretion rate between Thursday and Sunday were found for the first sample of each day (reflecting overnight rest), but significantly higher rates of adrenaline excretion were found for the midday and 6 p.m. samples on workdays in comparison with Sundays. A significant difference in the same direction was found for noradrenaline at 6 p.m., but not at midday.

The study also examined differences associated with occupational level. Comparisons between manual and non-manual workers revealed no differences in adrenaline or noradrenaline excretion overnight or throughout Sunday. However, non-manual workers exhibited significantly higher adrenaline excretion than did manual workers during the working day. Noradrenaline excretion rates were not systematically different between the two groups, but appeared to be positively related to level of physical activity in work. (See also Reynolds *et al.* 1981.)

Research appears not to have dealt specifically with the positive pole of the anxious–comfortable dimension of job-related well-being. A key construct is that of 'resigned satisfaction'. In practice it seems likely that measures of overall job satisfaction often tap this form of low-arousal reaction, and that many 'satisfied' workers are both resigned to jobs of low quality and have ceased to aspire to anything better. More focused enquiries into the prevalence of this condition would be of value.

Turning to the third dimension, from depressed to actively pleased, there have been few prevalence studies of negative forms of this kind of job-related well-being. One American national survey asked about boredom: 'on most days on your job, how often does time seem to drag for you?' Nine per cent responded often, 31 per cent sometimes, 37 per cent rarely and 23 per cent never (Quinn and Staines 1979).

A direct approach to job-related pleasure was taken by Warr and Payne (1983a). In their study of experiences on the preceding day, 21 per cent of full-time male workers reported that they had felt very pleased sometime yesterday because of their job. This experience was identified in the question posed as being 'happy, cheerful, proud, feeling full of life, feeling a sense of achievement, and so on'. Job-related pleasure on the previous day was significantly more common (25 per cent) among managerial, professional, and administrative workers than among semi-skilled and unskilled manual workers; however, 17 per cent of the latter reported active pleasure from their job on the previous day.

In summary, this second kind of research evidence confirms that job-holders report psychological consequences of their employment which are both good and bad. Positive reports (of job satisfaction, job-related pleasure, etc.) seem to be more common than negative ones (for example, job-related tension), but a substantial minority indicate that they feel under strain because of their job. The two types of feeling may co-exist, for example at higher occupational levels where both strain and pleasure from jobs are relatively common.

Qualitative evidence about particular jobs

A third kind of evidence for the impact of paid work upon mental health comes from detailed studies of particular jobs, sometimes making comparisons between jobs in the same or different settings. These studies may be grouped as either qualitative (described in this section) or quantitative (illustrated in the next section). An early qualitative study was by Whyte (1948), who investigated jobs and relationships among American restaurant workers. Pressures on cooks and waitresses arising from an unpredictably varying work-load were described, for example through detailed analysis of the problems facing waitresses who were in competition for warm plates to serve customers. The pressures were sufficiently intense that a member of staff might break down in tears and be unable to work for up to an hour following a stressful episode.

A particularly clear example of the impact of jobs can be seen in the work of hospital nurses caring for the terminally ill. Extremely high job demands, coupled with a strong commitment to patients and distress at their death, may combine to yield extensive feelings of helplessness, hopelessness, and exhaustion. These experiences have been recorded by, for example, Pines *et al.* (1981).

Other investigators have studied the first-line supervisor's job in industrial settings, detailing strains arising from its location between organized labour and management (e.g. Dalton 1959; Kahn *et al.* 1964). Trade union officials themselves are liable to overload problems: 'you sometimes feel at the end of the day as if your brain's addled—it just couldn't function any more' (Nicholson 1976, p. 23). Unskilled factory work has also been described and assessed. Kornhauser (1965, p. 80) illustrates principal themes through quotations from workers in American car factories:

Factory work is so monotonous. You are always being told where to go and what to do. It slows people up; they can't think for themselves; they are like machines or robots. A man does the same thing over and over again so many times he just doesn't care any more. It seems I just don't care any more; I am there and that's all.

It's very tiring work; it makes you nervous. I've seen men just shake after working 10 hours on the line; they get so tired they can't control it. Also they get more jumpy and they get irritated easier. I can't put my finger on it, but it brings out the nervousness in me; my stomach tightens up and my legs ache so that I get home and I can't sleep.

Shortens a man's life. The work is hard; you're working under tension all the time; must not fall behind. The men are on edge all the time so when they get home they are crabby. It took a lot of my good health.

The continuous grind, listening to growling of machines—you are broken up, shaken. You are tired, worn down at home, start arguing.

Case studies in particular settings do of course leave unanswered the question of how typical such responses are of the population as a whole. The need to complement qualitative case studies with quantitative population estimates (the second kind of evidence, above) is widely recognized. However, contrasts drawn between different jobs within a single study can be of particular value. Here are some quotations from workers in more skilled jobs in Kornhauser's enquiry:

I love mechanical work; I could eat and sleep with it; I was always interested in it since I was a kid. The work is highly skilled; I can do it and they know my work; it's good, it's always good. If ever there was a man that's in love with his job, I'm that man.

I like it; there's a chance for advancement; always a chance to learn something on that kind of a job; never a dull moment. The future looks better when you're learning a trade; you got something to look forward to. There's guys been in it 20 years and they're still learning.

It's fine; I enjoy the work, seeing that everything goes well. I have a chance to be a supervisor; I'd like that. All the workers work in harmony; there's good understanding on the job; the atmosphere is pleasant. They treat us like one big happy family. They give a man credit if he finds a better way; it's an open field; it awakens me a whole lot (Kornhauser 1965, p. 81).

Other research has studied individual workers in greater depth. Piotrkowski's (1978) conclusion about one particular hospital technician echoes themes from Chapters 1 and 2 about the sources and the components of mental health:

The sense of mastery he achieves doing his work is in itself self-enhancing. Not only is he validated in his position as provider for his family—a role he values—but he is confirmed as a masterful, competent person who maintains a sense of integrity by doing work he believes in. This confirmation comes not only from his personal sense of achievement about a job well done but also through the explicit recognition given him by the hospital administration....He is secure in his job, safe in his environment, and believes in his competence to handle the tasks at hand (p. 35).

As a final example of qualitative evidence about particular occupations, consider the job of the woman manager. This is increasingly receiving research attention, particularly in view of cultural and individual pressures which are peculiar to women in that role. Cooper and Davidson (1982, pp. 194–5) provide these reports from extreme cases:

I get very, very tired. I go to bed, but sometimes I wake up in the middle of the night and think of all the things that should have been done and which I haven't done.

When I first became a supervisor I smoked more and sometimes I would come home and bawl my eyes out. I used to say to my husband that it's too much, I can't cope.

My job has given me severe headaches and frequently crying bouts. I also find it very difficult to sleep before a big meeting or when I feel I'm being evaluated.

As in other cases, we are left unsure of the generality of responses of this kind, or whether they are in practice more common among women than men. However, the point is again firmly made from the evidence in this section that jobs can have marked effects, both positive and negative, on aspects of mental health.

Quantitative evidence about particular jobs

Quantitative investigations tend to seek less detailed and subtle information than may be available from qualitative studies, often obtaining responses to multiple-choice questions through self-completion questionnaires. Despite the limitations of this approach, it does make it more possible to compare the mental health of workers in different jobs. In practice, the research emphasis has been upon ill-health rather than on positive states.

For example, Caplan *et al.* (1975) studied 2010 American workers in 23 different occupations. Comparisons in terms of job-related anxiety, depression, irritation, and somatic complaints indicated that assemblers and machine tenders had particularly high prevalence rates, whereas university professors and physicians had low rates (see also French *et al.* 1982; Kroes 1981).

In their study of reported strain arising from white-collar work in Sweden, Nerell and Wahlund (1981) observed the highest prevalence (60 per cent reporting job-related strain very often or quite often) among class-teachers. High rates were also found among police personnel (49 per cent) and journalists (48 per cent), with lowest prevalence among archivists (4 per cent), administrators (21 per cent), and customs personnel (27 per cent). Kyriacou and Sutcliffe (1978) reported that 20 per cent of their sample of British comprehensive school teachers found their job very stressful (16 per cent) or extremely stressful (4 per cent); in addition 38 per cent described being a teacher as moderately stressful.

Colligan *et al.* (1977) examined admission records of community mental health centres in one American state, in order to determine incidence rates of diagnosed mental health disorders from 130 occupations. Comparing observed frequencies of admission with expected frequencies based on census data, they observed a particularly high probability of admission for occupations such as waiters and waitresses, factory operatives, and labourers. Recognizing limitations of this kind of data (for example, possible differential willingness to seek medical help), the findings point to varying mental health risks associated with different jobs.

Groen (1981) has reviewed occupational differences in the prevalence of peptic ulcer. The highest rates are found in white-collar workers, industrial supervisors, and skilled manual workers. In the medical profession, surgeons have a higher prevalence than other specialists.

Working within a single industry, Johansson *et al.* (1978) studied two sets of jobs in Swedish sawmills. One group of workers comprised sawyers, edgers, and graders in a mechanized plant; these were compared with a control group of repairmen and maintenance workers in the same plant. Of particular interest were differences between the two groups in feelings of irritation and being rushed. Significantly lower well-being in the former group was accompanied by a greater build-up in adrenaline during the working day. A differential ability to relax after work was also observed, with the stressed group requiring up to two hours recovery time after leaving their jobs. Employees in other jobs who have been found to require extended recovery time after work include high-workload visual display unit operators

(Johansson and Aronsson 1984) and women after a lengthy period of over-time work (Frankenhaeuser 1981).

Job features which affect mental health

Another kind of research evidence deals more specifically with those characteristics of jobs which give rise to good or bad mental health. Influential features have been identified and patterns of association with health explored. For example, studies of managers reporting job-related strain frequently point to problems associated with tight deadlines and large quantities of work (e.g. Davidson and Cooper 1983; Kiev and Kohn 1979).

It is evidence of this kind which forms the basis of Chapters 5 to 10. The nine environmental features identified in Chapter 1 will be studied in settings of paid employment, to assess their importance for mental health. At this introductory stage, however, two studies using aggregate measures of job features will serve to illustrate the approach.

The first example covers male blue-collar workers from several factories in the German metal industry (Frese 1985). A composite index of potentially harmful job features was constructed, covering time pressures, uncertainty about job requirements, risk of causing damage to materials or equipment, danger of accidents, environmental noise, dirt and smells, and problems with uneven work-flow. Each person's job was rated on this composite index, by the worker himself and (independently) by trained observers. Both forms of job rating were found to be significantly predictive of workers' reported psychosomatic complaints, the latter index being significantly associated with use of medication and visits to a doctor. The correlations between un-favourable job conditions and higher levels of psychosomatic complaints were shown to be unaffected by possible confounding factors such as income, age, availability of alternative jobs, and emotional support from one's wife.

A second example of research using an aggregate measure of job features is a study by Theorell and Floderus-Myrhed (1977), who followed up 5187 Swedish building workers to investigate the influence of job characteristics on subsequent myocardial infarction ('heart attack'). Earlier retrospective studies had suggested that premature myocardial infarction victims were often overworked, so these authors constructed a measure of 'workload'. In practice, this covered a range of job features, extending beyond merely quantity of work. Items dealt with too little as well as too much job responsibility, problems with workmates and superiors, change of job, and change of working hours; as in the previous example, the measure is best viewed as providing a broad index of unfavourable job conditions.

After responses to this measure had been obtained, enquiries were made in the subsequent two years to identify from mortality and hospital records fatal and non-fatal cases of myocardial infarction. It was then possible to examine the association between unfavourable work conditions as defined

and subsequent cardiac disease. Workers who had previously reported unfavourable job conditions were found to be significantly more likely to suffer
heart attacks in the next two years than were those whose job conditions
were less stressful.

Movement between jobs

In showing that jobs affect mental health, other kinds of longitudinal evidence
would also be desirable. For example, it would in general be expected that
movement between jobs would enhance mental health, at least in times when
unemployment is low and people move by choice rather than involuntarily.
This expectation arises because workers are likely to leave jobs which they
dislike, and also from the fact that many transitions will be promotions up the
occupational hierarchy. Cross-sectional studies, including several reviewed
above, have repeatedly found a positive association between job level and
aspects of good mental health, despite the fact that job-related strain also
appears to be more prevalent at higher levels.

Longitudinal research into job-changing is rare, but results are as expected.
For example, Aro and Hanninen (1984) used a general measure of affective
well-being and an index of somatic symptoms in a five-year longitudinal
study of employees in the Finnish metal industry. Workers changing jobs
over this period showed significantly greater improvements on both measures
than those who remained in the same job.

Karasek (1979) analysed data obtained from Swedish male workers in
both 1968 and 1974. He examined changes in reported exhaustion and depression as a function of increases or decreases in job pressure. (The measures
used are described in Chapters 5 and 7.) Workers moving to more stressful
jobs in the intervening period exhibited greater exhaustion and depression
than previously, whereas those moving to less stressful work showed the
opposite changes. Andrisani and Nestel (1976) obtained data from a sample
of middle-aged American men in 1969 and 1971. Changes in subjective
autonomy, measured through a version of Rotter's (1966) scale of internal
control, were examined as a function of several occupational variables. Particularly strong was the positive effect on internal control of a person's
occupational advancement, measured both through income and job-level
changes.

Increases in strain following promotion are expected in managerial and
professional samples, congruent with the cross-sectional association between
job-related tension and occupational level described earlier in the chapter
(see also Jamal 1985). Data supporting this expectation were obtained by
Cherry (1984a). She examined reports of 'nervous strain at work' among a
sample of men aged 26 and also when they were 32. Among those free of
strain at age 26, professional and managerial employees changing their jobs
between survey points were significantly more likely to report strain at age
32 than were those who remained in the same job.

Brett (1982) studied one particular kind of job transition, in which employees are transferred by their company to a different part of the country (USA in this case). She compared several aspects of mental health in a 'mobile' sample with data obtained from studies of employees who were more 'stable' in these geographical terms. No differences were found in respect of context-free anxiety. However, both mobile male employees and their wives exhibited greater life satisfaction and sense of subjective competence than comparison respondents. Few differences were present in terms of job attitudes, but more mobile workers showed significantly greater satisfaction with promotion, presumably associated with their more rapid progress up the organizational hierarchy.

Brett suggests that challenges associated with job transfer can make life more interesting both for male employees and their wives. In the latter case the experience of establishing and running a new household may contribute to feelings of enhanced mastery and personal effectiveness. These long-term improvements do not preclude short-term strain associated with uncertainty and overload when a person moves into a new job or geographical location. Features of that kind will be discussed again in Chapter 8.

Evidence from the clinic

Seventh, let us consider a quite different source of research evidence for the mental health impact of jobs. It is fairly common (but no one knows how common) for people to consult their doctors for help with psychological symptoms which they believe arise from their employment. In primary care settings (general practice, for example) the most probable treatment is pharmacological support, but efforts are also being directed to therapy, either through psychological or psychiatric clinics within a company's medical centre (e.g. McLean 1981) or linked to the public health service (e.g. Shapiro *et al.* 1979).

The emphasis of this psychotherapeutic approach is upon the individual rather than the work organization, so that, for example, childhood experiences might be explored in order to identify mechanisms causing difficulties in adult life (e.g. Firth 1985). One case described by Firth (1983) was a production manager, who came to the clinic in considerable distress provoked by uncertainties over the future of the firm and his position in it.

He began to suffer headaches and worried about their cause. He found his mouth would not perform correctly when he wanted to speak, and at meetings he would sit in silence and then burst into rages at what appeared to others to be trivial matters. He felt colleagues laughed at him. Needless to say, he produced no work at all. Although his marriage appeared good from without, at home he cried and felt inadequate as both husband and father. Despite some years of feeling capable and successful, his life now appeared to be in chaos. He had no understanding of the powerful emotions that were paining him and feared he was going mad. The question he most wanted answered was: 'Why me?'. Many other members in the firm suffered similar uncertainties, so what special meaning did the events have for [him] that made them so particularly painful? (pp. 13–14).

Therapy included relaxation training and other behavioural assistance. Of primary importance, however, was exploration of his childhood relationships with his parents and the echoes of these in his current need for approval from his boss.

Unrealistically high internal standards and personal aspirations are often found to impair mental health in organizational settings, especially at times of transition or promotion, when norms of acceptable performance are un-clear or feedback from others is lacking. Brewin (1980) has illustrated these themes in descriptions of managers who sought psychotherapy for help with their work problems. For example, one had recently been promoted to a position as head of department.

He worried a great deal about his work and there was no-one with whom he could now discuss his difficulties. He found it difficult to delegate and his excessive conscientiousness had the result that his workload increased beyond manageable proportions. Receiving little feedback on his performance, he became anxious that he was failing in the job. Everyday problems loomed larger and larger until the job appeared to be one long series of problems. Anxiety led to him working longer hours and trying even harder to satisfy himself that he was performing well. Work began to dominate his life and it became almost impossible to 'switch off'. The end came when some additional and more serious problems arose at work. These proved to be the last straw. He had no energy left to devote to them and yet had to take them seriously. There was no practical way out of this situation. Anxiety gave way to a period of acute depression and he needed several months off work to recover (p. 27).

The details of individual cases and their therapy are not of primary concern in the present section. Aspects of high workload are further examined in Chapter 7, and the potential of psychotherapy in occupational settings is described in Chapter 15. For the moment the cases are important primarily as examples of the seventh source of research evidence for the impact of jobs on mental health.

Employment as a support for the mentally ill

Another type of investigation has examined the value of jobs as aids to people who have been diagnosed as mentally ill, with symptoms not directly related to occupational problems. Paid employment is here viewed as a form of support or as an element in therapy. For instance, Mostow and Newberry (1975) studied rates of recovery from diagnosed depression in American women. Comparisons were made between matched samples of employed women and housewives, revealing that the former were significantly less depressed than the latter after a period of three months, despite the fact that both groups were taking antidepressant medication. In a similar study of male alcoholic outpatients in the United States, Braunstein *et al.* (1983) found that an employed group showed significantly greater improvement than an unemployed group over 12 months in respect of anxiety, depression, vigour, and fatigue; the same pattern was found for psychomotor tests of fine motor control and finger dexterity.

The causal processes in these studies are complex, in that there is presumably some self-selection into the unemployed or employed groups. To understand more fully the therapeutic value of jobs for mentally ill patients, we need to learn more about those background factors. Weiner *et al.* (1973) have emphasized this complexity in describing their experience with patients in a clinic associated with the New York clothing industry:

In the absence of a clear understanding of the causal relationship between work and mental illness, we chose, rather, to look at the world of work in terms of its positive implications for the individual with emotional difficulties. True, there were some for whom the work setting was neutral in impact, and even some for whom it exacerbated their emotional problems. For a much larger portion, however, we saw their participation in the world of work as oxygen, sustaining them in the face of emotional disorder (p. 143).

Among the examples cited by these authors is a chronic paranoid schizophrenic with a history of hospitalization. A skilled manual worker, 'he came to the project when auditory hallucinations made him sense that he might be unable to continue on the job, an activity he valued as his sole area of independent functioning. He was in treatment for two years, and, despite severe mental illness, continued to work throughout' (p. 70).

Within this section mention should also be made of 'Sunday neuroses'. Ferenzci (1926), writing at a time when Sunday was typically the only day of the week free of work, observed that removal of job obligations and disciplines was sometimes associated with neurotic and psychosomatic symptoms on that day. He viewed this in terms of an external and inner 'liberation', which permitted repressed impulses and punishment fantasies to be mobilized against the self, especially among those who were 'neurotically disposed'. Such an account is consistent with Freud's (1930) view of work as a person's strongest tie to reality, providing links with the environment which prevent one from becoming overwhelmed by fantasy and emotion.

Abraham (1950) extended the notion of Sunday neuroses to holidays and vacation periods of all kinds:

A considerable number of persons are able to protect themselves against the outbreak of serious neurotic phenomena only through intense work. Owing to the exaggerated repression of their impulses, they are in constant danger of having their excess excitation transformed into neurotic symptoms .... More or less serious and acute neurotic symptoms appear *if and when the work is interrupted by influences from without*. In this way the mental balance which has been maintained with difficulty through working is overturned for the duration of a Sunday, a holiday, or possibly even for a longer period (pp. 313–14; italics in original).

Whether or not one accepts such a psycho-analytic explanation, it does seem possible that working at a job can 'take your mind off' problems, which thus present themselves more forcibly on other days.

Spill-over or compensation

Finally in this discussion of types of evidence for the mental health impact of paid work, let us look at the rather diffuse literature sometimes identified in terms of 'work and non-work'. Many authors have analysed possible forms of interaction between those two domains of life (see, for instance, reviews by Kabanoff 1980; Near *et al.* 1980; and Staines 1980), sometimes drawing a contrast between 'spill-over' and 'compensation' hypotheses.

The first of these (also referred to as the 'generalization' or the 'carry-over' hypothesis) predicts that job conditions and attitudes carry over to affect behaviours and experiences in other aspects of life; positive correlations between job and non-job factors are thus expected. On the other hand, the compensation hypothesis predicts negative associations, as people seek out non-job activities and experiences which make up for the deficits in their paid work.

Such broad possibilities are not easily tested, but three research approaches may be illustrated. First, there have been many studies concerned with quantitative indices of affective well-being. These have examined the association between people's attitudes to their job and their affective well-being outside employment. As would be expected from the spill-over hypothesis, correlations between job satisfaction and both life satisfaction and absence of psychiatric symptoms are strongly positive (e.g. Kornhauser 1965; Rice 1984; Veenhoven and Jonkers 1984).

Kavanagh *et al.* (1981) have pointed out that such associations may sometimes be inflated through respondents completing self-report questionnaires of the two forms of well-being, often in quick succession. To avoid contamination through a bias to consistent responding, they obtained information about context-free mental health through a standardized interview carried out by a clinical psychologist. Satisfaction with work was measured separately through a self-completion questionnaire, administered through a computer video terminal.

Subjects were American air traffic controllers. Low work satisfaction was found to be significantly associated with independently assessed symptom levels in five areas: general distress, behavioural disturbance, inadequate impulse control, alcohol abuse, and problems in job functioning. Similar associations were also present for reality-testing problems, and parent-role problems, but these did not reach statistical significance because of extremely small numbers of employees exhibiting those particular symptoms.

Additional evidence comes from research comparing husbands' job-related affective well-being with wives' descriptions of at-home behaviour and experience. Jackson and Maslach (1982) observed that level of husbands' job-related emotional exhaustion was significantly associated with wives reporting that their husband comes home tense, unhappy, tired, and upset, and that he has difficulty sleeping at night. Husbands' job-related emotional exhaustion was also significantly correlated with wives reporting a low quality of family life. Billings and Moos (1982) examined stress levels in the jobs of employed wives. Higher wives' job stress was associated with husbands' lower affective well-being, although the difference did not quite reach statistical significance. However, husbands of wives who were highly stressed in their jobs did perceive significantly less cohesion in their family relationships.

A second type of study has bypassed subjective reports of well-being and focused upon the content of people's jobs and leisure activities. This research asks whether people in jobs which are, for instance, routine and unchallenging take up leisure pursuits which compensate for this lack of challenge. Kabanoff and O'Brien (1980) asked a sample of Australian workers about five attributes of their job, and investigated the links between these ratings and assessments in the same terms by independent judges of the leisure activities undertaken by each person. The attributes in question were variety, influence, skill utilization, social interaction, and pressure. A significant but low positive correlation between the two domains was found for variety and skill utilization, with no association in respect of the other types of content.

The authors note that neither principal hypothesis receives strong support from these results, and suggest that different groups of workers may exhibit different forms of relationship between work and non-work (see also Kabanoff 1980). For example, their sample contained a group of unskilled male workers with low income and low intrinsic job motivation. Their job ratings in terms of the focal attributes were consistently low, and so were the judgements made of their leisure attributes. Another group contained high-income workers with high intrinsic job motivation; in this case leisure as well as job attributes were rated highly. Data from both those groups are consistent with the spill-over hypothesis.

On the other hand, compensation processes may have occurred in a sub-sample of married women workers whose jobs received low ratings, but whose non-work activities scored particularly highly on the rated attributes. A different form of compensation was illustrated in a group of men, whose jobs placed considerable demands upon them and whose leisure attributes tended to be rated at a substantially lower level.

A single type of relationship between the content of work and of leisure is thus unlikely (see also Gadbois 1978; Kabanoff and O'Brien 1982; Karasek 1981; Staines 1980). By the same token, it may be expected that different patterns of causal priority exist. For example, correlations consistent with a compensatory relationship may sometimes reflect a purposeful reaction to job conditions through the choice of specific leisure attributes, whereas in other cases (mothers of school-children, for instance) jobs may be chosen because they are attractively different from the content of non-work life.

A third type of study has examined through observation and intensive interview the impact of husbands' jobs on family interactions. For example, Piotrkowski (1978) studied 13 working-class and lower middle-class American families, identifying three forms of spill-over between an employed husband's job and family life at home. First was 'positive carry-over', in which a husband enjoyed his job and experienced feelings of self-enhancement from successes during the working day. Such a husband came home cheerful, and was described as both 'emotionally available' and 'interpersonally available' to other family members. He introduced personal energy into family activities, laughed and joked, initiated warm and interested interactions, and responded positively to his wife and children.

Somewhat more common was 'negative carry-over', where low affective well-being at work was brought into the family system, displacing the potential for positive family interactions and requiring family members to expend their personal resources to help the husband manage his feelings of strain. In these cases, a job contained negative features, underload or overload for example, and the impact of these reduced the worker's emotional and interpersonal availability at home. Irritability, non-responsiveness and disengagement were visible, and family members had to work hard to sustain the husband's and their own affective well-being.

The third type of spill-over described by Piotrkowski was 'energy deficit'. This was widely observed, in terms of a husband's personal depletion and lack of energy after time spent on his job. These sometimes arose from physical tiredness, but also from extended low psychological arousal in boring work. Husbands described how as a result of their jobs they felt 'slowed down', 'beat', 'lifeless', 'lazy', 'worn down', 'dead', and 'disconnected from life'. This relationship between work and home was distinguished from negative carry-over, above, in that feelings about work were not brought directly into the family system. However, the effects, in terms of reduced emotional and interpersonal availability, were often very similar. Piotrkowsky points out that negative job consequences of this kind are likely to be particularly harmful at certain stages in a family life-cycle, especially when young children place considerable demands upon psychological resources.

Differences between life-cycle stages were also clear in the study of successful male managers described by Evans and Bartolome (1980). These authors reviewed several possible relationships between job and family experiences (for example, complete independence or irreconcilable conflict), observing that interdependence through positive or negative carry-over was the most common. In practice, carry-over was almost entirely from job to home, with very little influence observed in the reverse direction. It often took a negative form:

During periods of work stress, either short or protracted, the manager becomes less sensitive to what is going on in his private life. Tension dulls his awareness of his wife, children and friends. It clouds his capacity to enjoy his private life, which becomes essentially passive. The weekend is sacred only because he can recuperate— not because he can get actively involved in other pursuits. Joy, sorrow, anger, pleasure, and fun are suppressed; they simply cannot be experienced (Evans and Bartolome 1980, p. 19).

The research approaches described so far in this section have mainly concerned the intrinsic content of jobs. However, it is clear that jobs also have a major influence on people through locating them within a social structure and thereby exposing them to specific norms, values and social pressures. For instance, associated with different societal locations, the leisure activities of professional workers are quite different from those of unskilled manual workers. Similarly, there are differences in working conditions and living environments between occupational levels, with the professional worker being likely to experience greater material support and comfort in both cases.

These examples highlight the fact that there is more to a job than what happens at work. Jobs are a primary reflection, and also cause and effect, of a person's place in society. The consequences of a job for mental health arise partly from the working environment created by that job. In addition, however, the interplay between a person's occupation and wider role in society means that jobs also affect mental health in less direct ways. They strongly influence the nature and quality of other environments to which a person is exposed; and factors operative in those correlated non-job environments have their own impact upon mental health.

The relative importance of job and non-job factors in determining mental health is likely to depend upon which form of the latter is under consideration, context-free or job-related mental health. This is illustrated schematically in Fig. 4.1, where magnitude of impact is indicated by the diameter of a circle representing each type of factor. In the case of *context-free* mental health, concerned with life in general, it seems probable that non-job factors are usually of greater significance than those within a job. This is shown to the left of Fig. 4.1. Non-job factors arise from events and processes in other environments, such as one's family, local community, social groups, educational networks, leisure milieux, etc. We should also include here a person's physical health, as well as baseline mental health in ways which will be explored in Chapters 13 and 14. On the other hand, *job-related* mental health (job satisfaction and job-related anxiety, for instance) is by definition primarily determined by characteristics of the occupational environment; this is shown to the right of Fig. 4.1.

Job and non-job factors are intercorrelated and mutually interactive, as indicated by the overlap between circles in the figure. Studies which measure job factors alone are therefore likely also to reflect non-job factors to some

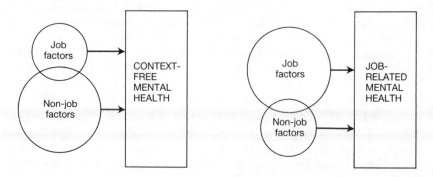

Fig. 4.1   Schematic representation of the relative importance of paid employment and other factors influencing context-free and job-related mental health.

extent, and we may be unsure about the nature and size of that unmeasured contribution.

In general, however, a difference may be expected in relation to the type of sample investigated. Job factors are likely to be particularly strong markers of associated non-job features in studies which take samples ranging broadly across occupational and social class levels. Comparisons of context-free mental health across people at widely differing occupational levels are more likely to reflect features of social position as well as job characteristics than are studies carried out within a single restricted group, unskilled factory workers for example. In the latter case, non-job factors are liable to vary less between members of the sample, leaving job features as a larger contributor to observed differences in mental health.

Variations between studies in these two respects (type of measure and breadth of sample) may sometimes give rise to inconsistent results. Nevertheless, the several types of evidence summarized in this chapter have made it clear that being employed contributes significantly to context-free as well as job-related mental health. It is the task of the following chapters to explore in more detail the environmental features and the processes which give rise to outcomes of the kind illustrated here.

Summary

This chapter has introduced the principal types of research evidence indicating that jobs affect mental health. The influence is both positive and negative, in keeping with a widespread ambivalence about paid employment. However, an overall positive impact of jobs on context-free mental health is indicated by research into the impact of unemployment. In addition, survey research into job-related mental health in the population or in sub-populations has revealed high levels of satisfaction and attachment, and suggested that around 10 per cent of workers experience occupational strain on any one day. Both strain and positive forms of well-being are more prevalent at higher occupational levels.

Qualitative evidence and case studies of particular jobs have pointed to a number of problematic occupations. Furthermore, quantitative comparisons between jobs indicate relatively high prevalence of strain among, for instance, assembly-line workers, teachers, and police personnel. Movements up the occupational hierarchy have been shown to give rise to improved mental health of several kinds, although reports of increased strain can also follow promotion.

Two other types of evidence have been drawn from clinical research. First were cases of patients whose anxiety and depression arose at least partly from current job problems. And second was research into the supportive function of being employed, suggesting that out-patients who have jobs during their treatment or recovery phase are more likely to improve than those who are out of work.

Finally, some evidence bearing upon the spill-over and compensation hypotheses has been examined. It was concluded that several different patterns of relationship between work and non-work were likely to exist, and that the overlap between the two domains could colour the results of research in either one of them. Non-work factors (for instance, differences in leisure and educational pursuits, or variations in physical health) may give rise to differences in mental health observed between occupational levels in broad population surveys, in addition to the impact of jobs themselves. However, in research at a particular occupational level, the impact of associated non-work factors on mental health is likely to be less marked.

5

Job content: opportunity for control, opportunity for skill use, and variety

The next six chapters examine those features introduced in Chapter 1 as determinants of mental health, investigating their importance in the occupational environment: how do characteristics of jobs affect the mental health of job-holders? First to be considered are features numbered earlier as 1, 2, and 4: opportunity for control, opportunity for skill use, and variety.

There is commonly an association between the organizational level of a job and the restrictions placed upon holders of that job, so that the behaviour of lower-level employees tends to be particularly governed by the demands of their organization. That is the case in both capitalist and communist societies, and arises more from organizational objectives and traditional designs than from political ideologies (e.g. Gardell 1971; Kohn and Schooler 1983; Thompson 1983). Organizational goals and procedures imposed upon lower-level employees are thus particularly likely to conflict with the bases of mental health as postulated in the three job conditions covered in this chapter. Nevertheless, even lower-level jobs may incorporate relatively less or more of each feature, and a positive association between each one's presence and good mental health is expected.

That expectation must be bounded by the non-linear associations which were postulated in Chapter 1. As summarized in Fig. 1.1 (see page 10), the present conceptual framework views the identified environmental features as important up to some moderate level. Analogous to the importance of vitamins for physical health, low values of an environmental feature are considered harmful, and a broad middle range is thought to have a relatively unchanging impact. The three factors to be examined in this chapter have been proposed as fitting the vitamin AD model (see page 10), with an additional decrement in mental health accompanying extremely high levels of each one. These decrements are thought to arise for two reasons. First, because of the deleterious impact of very high levels of a feature on its own; and second because extremely high levels of one feature tend to have harmful consequences for others within the model.

Predictions from the overall vitamin model have rarely been tested in empirical research, since it is the linear component of associations between job content and employee reactions which has usually been examined. In practice, however, many investigators have dealt only with jobs at lower organizational levels and thus within the lower range of environmental values, for instance those with limited variety or restricted opportunity for control. Studies reviewed in this chapter are mainly of that kind, so that a positive relationship is generally expected between the three features and employee mental health.

The occupational environment itself may be measured in two ways, in 'objective' or 'subjective' terms. As pointed out in Chapter 1, 'objective' measures are taken independently of a focal person's perceptions, whereas 'subjective' measures utilize assessments made by that person. The two approaches do not always yield exactly the same results, since people differ between themselves in their knowledge and interpretation of environmental features. Investigators must therefore decide which form of measurement to adopt, consistent with their model of how environmental features have their impact on mental health. This impact is usually thought likely to be through personal appraisal (e.g. Greenberger and Strasser 1986), so that it is subjective measures which are most frequently used. On that basis employees with the same job title may be found to have different perceptions of the environment, and it is these, as reported by the employees themselves, which are examined in relation to variations in mental health.

Most investigations in this and subsequent chapters are of that kind. The fact that 'subjective' assessments are being taken will be indicated through reference to job features as 'reported' or 'perceived', and the smaller number of studies using independent measures will be clearly identified as such. Possible limitations of research which takes subjective measures of both environmental features and mental health will be explored in the next chapter.

Opportunity for control

The first feature to be considered is the degree to which an occupational environment permits an individual to control activities and events. This was described in Chapter 1 as opportunity for control, but related terms in the literature include autonomy, discretion, influence, power, participation in decision-making, and decision latitude.

Strictly speaking, to say that a worker has 'control' over something entails that he or she has complete influence over what happens. In practice, however, a person is likely to have differing degrees of influence over different aspects of a job; and complete control over all one's activities is not usually possible within the constraints of organizational membership. *Variations in the amount* of control are thus likely to occur. These may take three forms: first, in the amount of influence (from none to complete) in a specific area;

second, variation in the breadth of influence across different areas; third, a combination of those two, such that a person may have complete control in some areas, limited influence in others, and no influence at all in remaining areas.

In that influence is exercised through choice from among options, variation in level of control has often been studied in the laboratory through experimental manipulation of the number of available alternatives (e.g. Langer 1983). It also requires some predictability of outcomes, so that knowledge of consequences is widely viewed as central to the process. Variations in the amount of control (seen above to be in terms of degree and extensiveness of influence) are thus likely to be associated with variations in the range of alternatives and in the predictability of outcomes.

It is helpful to distinguish between two broad aspects of control, those which are intrinsic and those which are extrinsic to the tasks undertaken. 'Intrinsic control' is a question of influence over the content of one's job, as for example tapped through the autonomy scale of the Job Diagnostic Survey (Hackman and Oldham 1975, 1980): 'the degree to which the job provides substantial freedom, independence, and discretion to the employee in scheduling the work and in determining the procedures to be used in carrying it out'. This feature, control over the immediate work process, has also been central to theoretical discussions of powerlessness within the general framework of employee alienation (e.g. Blauner 1964).

'Extrinsic control' occurs, or is lacking, in respect of other features of the working environment, such as wages, hours, canteen facilities, product and pricing decisions, and broader company policy. For example, employees (usually through their trade unions) seek and gain influence over their employers through financial and other demands which are relatively independent of their wishes for intrinsic control in individual jobs. This form of control, or its absence (powerlessness), has again been important in discussions of worker 'alienation'; and at a societal level there is considerable overlap between intrinsic and extrinsic control, in that greater power of both kinds is available to people of higher socio-economic status.

Opportunity for control is associated with other job features, both those examined in this chapter and those covered later. For example, greater control permits workers to introduce more variety into their work, and jobs with greater opportunity for control are often the ones which require greater skill utilization. The centrality of control within this network of features has sometimes led to measures labelled as control but whose content extends inappropriately beyond the boundaries of that concept on its own. These will be illustrated below.

Intrinsic control

Let us first consider intrinsic control. A large number of studies have shown that workers in jobs providing greater opportunities for this type of personal influence are more likely to exhibit high levels of job-related affective well-being.

Job-related mental health   American and British investigations with the Job Diagnostic Survey have consistently found substantial positive correlations between reported autonomy and general job satisfaction, intrinsic job satisfaction, satisfaction with work content, and intrinsic job motivation (e.g. Breaugh 1985; Hackman and Oldham 1975; Oldham and Rotchford 1983; Oldham *et al.* 1978; Wall *et al.* 1978). Specific facet satisfactions (for instance, satisfaction with the work itself or with supervision) have also been found to be significantly associated with autonomy as measured by the Job Characteristics Inventory (e.g. Sims and Szilagyi 1976; Sims *et al.* 1976). These cross-sectional findings are supported by results from longitudinal research, where increased or decreased job autonomy has been found to lead to predicted changes in overall job satisfaction, intrinsic job satisfaction and intrinsic job motivation (Bechtold *et al.* 1981; Hackman *et al.* 1978; Wall and Clegg 1981a).

Coburn (1978) used a six-item index of job control with a Canadian sample, observing significant associations of reported control with high job satisfaction and low alienation after partialling out factors such as pay, job security, and social class. Mottaz (1981) studied American employees from an alienation perspective, observing a significant relationship between powerlessness (defined as a lack of control over task activities) and self-estrangement (defined as a lack of intrinsic fulfilment in work). In an Australian study, O'Brien (1982b) employed a wide-ranging measure of reported 'influence', which extended into extrinsic aspects such as influence over arrangements for overtime and choice of supervisor. After controlling for other job content features such as variety and task pressure, reported influence exhibited a significant positive association with overall job satisfaction. In separate samples of male and female American employees, Weaver (1978a) obtained the same result: after controlling for other factors, including income and occupational prestige, worker autonomy was significantly predictive of overall job satisfaction. Also in USA, an independent job analysis procedure was used by Shaw and Riskind (1983); they recorded a strong negative association between independently assessed decision-making discretion and overall job dissatisfaction.

Loher *et al.* (1985) describe a meta-analysis of 28 American studies, with a total sample size in excess of 15 000. After correcting for unreliability in the measures, they report that the sample-weighted average correlation between employee assessments of job autonomy and overall job satisfaction was 0.46.

In research with a representative sample of the working population of Finland (N = 5471), Kauppinen-Toropainen *et al.* (1983) used a scale of work-related exhaustion, containing items falling in the bottom left-hand quadrant of affective well-being (low scores on both the pleasure and the arousal axes; see Figs. 2.1 and 3.1). Work-related exhaustion was significantly associated with reports of lower self-determination at work for both men and women, where self-determination was tapped through four autonomy items and one item assessing variety. This relationship was also present in separate analyses of blue-collar and white-collar jobs.

Relationships of these kinds with job-related well-being are to be expected from the nature and operation of personal control: people use what influence they have to improve features of the occupational environment which they dislike. In addition, therefore, it is particularly important to study associations between opportunity for control and more wide-ranging aspects of mental health.

Context-free mental health   In an American community sample, Billings and Moos (1982) recorded a significant association between self-reported low job autonomy and frequency of physical symptoms (insomnia, headaches, etc.) for both men and women; in addition, correlations with depression and anxiety were found to be significant for men but not for women. Reports of low job autonomy were also found by Pines and Kafry (1981) to be significantly associated with more tedium, measured in terms of physical, emotional, and mental exhaustion; this pattern was found for both men and women, in a sample of American professional employees. (See also Pines *et al.* 1981.) Among East German blue-collar employees, the same association has been observed in relation to anxiety (Hacker 1985), and among American hospital employees in relation to context-free general distress (Jackson 1983).

Payne and Fletcher (1983), in a study of British school-teachers, conducted multiple regression analyses of reported job discretion and work-load demands in respect of four sub-scales of the Middlesex Hospital Questionnaire: depression, free-floating anxiety, obsessionality, and somatic complaints. Job discretion was found to make a significant independent contribution beyond that of demands (see Chapter 7) in respect of depression and anxiety, but not for the other two measures. Gardell (1971) studied Swedish workers in two industrial sectors, assessing four aspects of context-free mental health: anxiety, self-esteem, general life satisfaction, and subjective competence. In each case greater intrinsic control in jobs (assessed independently by engineering and technical experts) was associated with better mental health, although for anxiety the relationship was statistically significant in only one of the sectors. Among Swedish white-collar employees Nerell and Wahlund (1981) found that 'mental strain at work' was reported much more frequently by those with less influence over the planning and conduct of their work; reported frequency of nervous complaints was also greater among that group.

Mortimer and Lorence (1979) obtained self-ratings of competence from American students at college and also nine years later when they were in jobs, mainly of a professional or managerial kind. Increases in subjective competence since leaving college were found to be significantly associated with current level of work autonomy, after controlling for income, educational attainment, and family socio-economic level. (Income was itself not associated with changes in reported competence.) In practice, the three-item scale of work autonomy included one question which instead appears to tap required skill utilization ('How much innovative thinking does your job require?'), but correlations between individual items (in Table 3 of the report) suggest that the same result would be obtained after omission of that item. A similar problem of definition occurs in the study of school-leavers described by Mortimer and Finch (1986). Five years after high school, work autonomy was found to be significantly associated with affective well-being (measured in terms of positive self-evaluations), despite controls for earnings, job level, family socio-economic status, intellectual ability, education, and prior well-being. However, the measure of job content was broader than its title might suggest, including also items about skill use and job interest.

Longitudinal changes at the level of the work-group were investigated by Wall and Clegg (1981a). Jobs within a British confectionery manufacturing company were redesigned in a way which significantly increased work-group autonomy. This involved a shift of responsibility from supervisors to teams of workers, and a reduction in the number of supervisors employed. Each team was given control over setting the pace of production, the distribution of tasks among team members, the organization of breaks and change-overs between different products, and the allocation of overtime. In addition to significant increases in overall job satisfaction and intrinsic work motivation as a result of these changes, there were also significant improvements in context-free affective well-being measured through the General Health Questionnaire.

An investigation by Kohn and Schooler (e.g. 1983) examined relationships between a wide range of variables measured on two occasions separated by 10 years. Other features of this study will be reviewed in later sections. At this point, the researchers' findings about 'closeness of supervision' are important; this characteristic was measured through items tapping, for instance, perceived freedom to make decisions and opportunity to disagree with one's supervisor. Data were obtained initially from a sample of 3101 American men, representative of those aged above 16 and employed in civilian occupations for at least 25 hours a week. The relationship between closeness of supervision and psychological functioning was examined after statistically controlling for educational differences and all other occupational characteristics which were measured (some 50 in all, including job level, degree of bureaucracy, and number of hours worked each week).

This measure of low opportunity for control was found to be significantly associated in cross-sectional analyses with high anxiety, low self-confidence, low job satisfaction, and low occupational commitment. However, these findings were not replicated in a parallel study of women (Miller *et al.* 1979), and neither enquiry recorded a significant association between closeness of supervision and 'ideational flexibility'; this latter measure will be described later (see page 96). Karasek (1979) examined reported 'job decision latitude', defined as 'the working individual's potential control over his tasks and his conduct during the working day' (pp. 289–90). He re-analysed data from male workers in two earlier national surveys, in USA and in Sweden. In the American study job decision latitude was measured through the sum of four items covering autonomy and four items tapping skill level, variety, and the need for creativity. Although the two sets of items were intercorrelated 0.48, and results are said to be similar when two separate scales are used (p. 292), the overall measure clearly extends beyond merely control. That is also the case in respect of the Swedish index of job decision latitude. This was quite different from measures of intrinsic control as viewed here, being a combination of required skill level (training beyond minimum education) and amount of job variety.

Karasek was concerned to examine the combined influence of job decision latitude and task demands upon mental and physical health. His overall model and results in respect of the two factors together will be described in Chapter 7; for the present his findings for mental health in relation to self-reports of job decision latitude will be reviewed, recognizing that decision latitude as measured does not fully correspond to opportunity for control as assessed in other studies described in this section.

In both the American and Swedish surveys there was a strong association between low job decision latitude and reports of context-free exhaustion and depression. The former aspect of mental health was measured through items about tiredness and feeling worn out, and the depression measures (differing between surveys) covered aspects of anxiety as well as core features of depression itself. In terms of the present account of affective well-being (Figs. 2.1 and 3.1) the exhaustion scale contained context-free items ranged along the third axis, and the depression index provided a broad-band context-free assessment along dimension 1. The American survey also included measures of life satisfaction (combining items about happiness and satisfaction) and job satisfaction (combining job-related depression and job attachment). Both forms of satisfaction were found to be significantly lower among workers with low job decision latitude.

Karasek's presentation of results has the advantage of going beyond linear regression coefficients to describe also the pattern of scores for separate sub-groups of workers. Observed associations between decision latitude and outcome variables were non-linear; employees with very low latitude (typically those in repetitive jobs, with minimum educational attainment) exhibited very low well-being, but there was a levelling off in well-being scores at moderate and high levels of latitude. Indeed, Karasek reported that there was typically a reversal of association at very high levels of decision latitude, when well-being was lower than in jobs of moderate latitude. For example, the probability of severe depression in groups arrayed from very low to very high decision latitude was 0.37, 0.31, 0.18, and 0.22 in the American data and 0.23, 0.13, 0.09, and 0.16 in the Swedish results (recall that the measures differed between studies). This pattern is very similar to that proposed within the vitamin AD model in Fig. 1.1 (see page 10).

A second study which tested for the presence of non-linear relationships has been described by van Dijkhuizen (1980). In a sample of Dutch manual, managerial, and professional employees, low opportunity to participate in job decisions was significantly associated with high job dissatisfaction. However, the value of *eta* (a coefficient of non-linear association) was greater than that of the linear correlation coefficient, and the pattern of association was similar to that described in the preceding paragraph. For groups ranging from low to high opportunity to participate, mean job dissatisfaction scores were 2.90, 2.41, 1.87, 1.60, and 1.73 respectively. Much the same pattern was observed for low self-esteem, although relations with job-related anxiety and depression were of a different form (and non-significant in the latter case).

Reports of signs and symptoms associated with coronary heart disease were studied in relation to job decision latitude by Karasek *et al.* (1981). Using data from the Swedish study described by Karasek (1979), low decision latitude was found to be significantly correlated with the indicator of coronary heart disease. Furthermore, in longitudinal analyses of data from workers exhibiting no evidence of heart disease in 1968, low decision latitude measured in that year was significantly predictive of the incidence of signs and symptoms of coronary heart disease in the following six years. This relationship was retained after statistical controls had been introduced for age, weight, smoking, education, and other job content variables.

A briefer time period was examined in Parkes's (1982) experimental research. She studied British student nurses as they moved between two types of hospital ward, taking self-report measures of depression, anxiety, somatic symptoms, job satisfaction, and social dysfunction. (Note that the last of these might be viewed as partial index of low context-free subjective competence.) The research design was balanced to cover moves in both directions, with job discretion being assessed through Karasek's (1979) scale. (As mentioned earlier, this extends beyond merely control to include reports of skill utilization.) There were considerable differences in the amount of discretion afforded in jobs between the two types of ward, and correlations between change scores indicated that changes in amount of discretion when a nurse moved between wards were significantly associated with changes in each mental health index except somatic symptoms. 'Since the analysis was based on within-subjects difference scores with counterbalancing in order effects, it can be unambiguously concluded that the different work settings gave rise to the effects observed' (Parkes 1982, p. 793).

Machine-pacing The studies described so far in this section have mainly concerned what was earlier labelled as opportunity for 'intrinsic' control:

discretion, influence, or autonomy in relation to the content of one's job. Studies of machine-pacing versus self-pacing may be included here, since a key feature of the former is a reduction in the potential for personal control over work pace. Some comparative studies of this kind have been reported, with varying results. For example, Kornhauser (1965) found that lower job satisfaction and lower overall mental health were associated with machine-pacing among middle-aged workers (40 to 49 years) but not among their younger colleagues (20 to 29 years). In a sample of assembly workers including both those age-ranges, Caplan *et al.* (1975) recorded significantly greater boredom, job-related anxiety, and job-related depression among those whose tasks were machine-paced. However, differences between the groups in job satisfaction, workload satisfaction, and job-related somatic complaints were not significant.

Broadbent and Gath (1981) found no differences between the two conditions in respect of job satisfaction, depression, somatic symptoms, or obsessional symptoms; however, machine-paced workers did exhibit significantly higher levels of anxiety. (See also Broadbent 1985.) In a comparison of postal workers in machine-paced and non-paced jobs, Hurrell (1985) observed that the former group exhibited significantly worse scores on five measures of mood state: tension–anxiety, depression–dejection, anger–hostility, fatigue–inertia, and vigour–activity. Other results of that kind are described by Smith (1985). However, Salvendy's (1981) review led him to conclude that 'no statistically significant, or clinically meaningful, differences exist in psychophysiological indicators of stress between machine-paced and self-paced work' (p. 5).

This diversity of findings may arise at least in part from the fact that both machine-paced and self-paced jobs differ widely among themselves. Overall comparisons between the two categories may thus often be confounded by other task differences. In addition, 'pacing' can be of several kinds and intensities. Dainoff *et al.* (1981) have distinguished between four principal types, in terms of whether or not a worker has control over the separate factors of initiation and duration of a work cycle. Complete machine-pacing occurs when a machine controls both these functions, determining both when a new cycle should commence and how fast it should be executed. In a second category, a worker may control the initiation of a cycle but then become paced by the machine; for example, picking up items from stock and feeding them into machines for processing at a predetermined speed. In a third case (illustrated by work on a telephone switchboard), the initiation of tasks may be externally determined but speed of operation be within the employee's control. In each of these cases the *rate* of machine-pacing is of course an additional important variable. A fourth category is work where an operator determines both the initiation and the duration of a task.

However, even this fourth category of work (seemingly 'self-paced') is in fact open to considerable pacing pressures. These may arise from incentive payment schemes, managers' demands, or work-group influences, sometimes yielding a lack of personal control over initiation and duration of work cycle which is as great as on some machine-paced jobs (e.g. Drury 1985). In view of these several within-category variations, it seems unlikely that machine-pacing versus self-pacing will prove to be a fruitful distinction on its own. The many configurations of each type of work might instead be viewed within the nine-category framework introduced here, describing and comparing individual jobs of both types in the same nine terms. Some machine-paced jobs will undoubtedly achieve low scores on several of the factors (low opportunity for control, low opportunity for skill use, high workload demands, etc.), as will also some self-paced jobs; other machine-paced jobs will be found to be less harmful in these nine respects. In general, however, it seems that 'complete' machine-pacing, in the sense introduced in the previous paragraph, is likely to give rise to jobs which have deleterious consequences for at least some aspects of mental health. Further specification of these effects requires research which controls for additional aspects of jobs in a more systematic manner than has been usual to date.

Second-order intrinsic control   Before leaving intrinsic forms of control, a second-order mode of operation is worth noting. Persons with substantial continuing opportunities for personal control can also determine the degree of control they exert at any one point in time. Such persons can adjust the nature of their work temporarily to increase or reduce personal control; in the latter case they might, for example, seek out challenging circumstances of possible failure and take risks in those circumstances. This form of adjustment is not open to those whose overall control opportunities are restricted; such people must work at levels of control which are both low and unchanging. More generally, high levels of control opportunity permit manipulation of other features, allowing a person to vary from time to time the level within a job of skill use, goals, variety, and environmental clarity. This second-order opportunity, when present, seems likely to contribute in important ways to an employee's mental health.

Extrinsic control

Let us turn now to 'extrinsic' control, influence over features such as wages, hours, and departmental or company policy. This requires a further distinction, between 'direct' and 'indirect' influence. The first of these is a matter of an individual employee personally influencing an aspect of his or her job or organization. 'Indirect' influence comes about through representatives (usually trade union officials) acting on behalf of individuals and groups. In practical terms there is often an overlap between extrinsic and indirect influence, where representatives negotiate over aspects of working conditions, and between intrinsic and direct influence, where individuals exert personal control over their own jobs.   It is obvious that employees value opportunities for their representatives to influence conditions and policies. In terms of the distribution of social and economic power, greater influence of this kind might be expected indirectly to enhance mental health in lower socio-economic groups. Such a long-term political process is difficult to investigate. However, its effects (if observed) would be likely to arise from the application of power to strengthen the bases of mental health set out in Chapter 1. For example, greater influence could improve working-class mental health through an enhanced standard of living, greater intrinsic job control, and increased opportunity for skill use in jobs. It is thus possible to reconstrue some aspects of social and political conflict and change within the framework of the nine environmental features described here.

The aim of the present chapter is more limited: to increase understanding at the level of employing organizations. Extrinsic control (usually indirectly through representatives) is often viewed in organizations as quite separate from intrinsic control at the level of individual workers. Gardell (1982) has emphasized how this is a mistake, made by trade unions as well as by management. He describes the development in Sweden of 'a democratic work organization where co-determination in representative forms and autonomous production groups have been united' (p. 533). Co-determination processes arose in that case from employees' presence on the company board, the financial committee, and the health and safety committee. Intrinsic job control occurred through autonomous group working, where groups of workers were responsible for their own supervision, training, job rotation, work allocation, and production assignments.

The effects of the gradual introduction of this 'participatory work environment' (Gardell 1982, p. 532) were studied over several years. At the individual level, Gardell describes increased feelings of competence, self-confidence, self-esteem, and intrinsic job satisfaction; and a lower probability in autonomous groups of tiredness or trouble relaxing after work. In addition, autonomous group working led to greater skill utilization, since each group member had the opportunity to learn all jobs within the group's domain. Greater autonomy was found to be associated with a greater interest in the trade union, both in expressed attitudes and through participation in discussion and decision-making.

An increase in shop-floor workers' desire for greater responsibility was also observed. This aspect of job motivation falls within the aspiration component of mental health as described in Chapter 2. A similar effect of increased participation has been observed by other investigators. Warr *et al.* (1978) reported that a programme to increase shop-floor employees' direct and indirect influence within a British steel works was accompanied by significant increases in desired responsibility and job motivation. And within a British confectionery factory enhanced work-group autonomy and responsibility were followed by significant increases in desire for information and desire for promotion (Wall and Clegg 1981a).

Finally in this section let us note that workers' wish to control their environment is often manifest in ways which do not fall readily within the types of behaviour illustrated so far. Several activities in opposition to the demands of management have as one of their aims the affirmation that lower-level workers are self-determining agents. Concrete expressions of this are often seen during disputes with management, where an initial disagreement (over hours of work, for example) becomes intertwined with broader issues of how far management has the right to expect workers to follow any instruction or to accept any working condition.

Other examples include workers' 'restriction of output' while on piecework payment systems. Despite the fact that higher output in these situations leads to higher take-home pay, it is quite usual for an informal work-group quota or'norm to be set and for workers to restrict their output to this quota. There are several reasons for this practice (described, for example, by Lupton 1963, Myers 1920, and Roy 1952; see also Chapter 9), one of which is employees' desire to assert their own influence in the face of management's attempts to control behaviour.

Parallel processes occur among managers. There is informal evidence that many decisions are taken and administrative procedures established in order to strengthen managers' feelings that they are in control of events for which they are held responsible. This is not merely a question of managers taking pleasure in exploiting the power granted by their position; often it is an attempt to ward off anxiety associated with potential failure in their job. Managers' desire for control is liable to be translated into a reduction in the control opportunities which are available to lower-level employees. For example, Clegg (1984) has examined the processes giving rise to the widespread 'simplification' of shop-floor jobs, noting the overriding importance of managers' search for technological and structural arrangements which afford them greatest control over what happens in the work-place.

Attempts by workers and managers to control their activities and opportunities in these ways may be viewed in both individual and collective terms. A person may seek increased power primarily for his or her own benefit, or as part of a wider process of inter-group bargaining. In the latter case the group in question can vary in size, formality, and demographic and/or geographic scope, ranging from an informal grouping of workers or managers in a single plant to a large formal organization with a national membership.

The focus of this book tends to be upon individuals and small groups, but these do of course operate within a wider political context. Some writers have examined 'worker resistance under capitalism' in terms of a class struggle in which members of the working class have the explicit objective of collectively gaining greater power at the expense of capitalists (e.g. Braverman 1974; Friedman 1977; Gorz 1976). Such a process may be partly motivated in some settings through a wider 'working-class consciousness', although it is clear that conflicts over the distribution of power also occur within middle-class superior–subordinate hierarchies and that attempts to gain personal control may often be entirely free of wider political motivation.

In overview, this section has built upon the distinction between intrinsic and extrinsic control. Results from many studies have demonstrated an association between level of intrinsic control (over job content) and a wide range of mental health indicators. Links between low levels of intrinsic control and negative job attitudes are universally found. These are of less importance to the present theme than are the widely observed relationships with context-free aspects of mental health, such as depression, anxiety and exhaustion, and low levels of self-esteem, life satisfaction, and subjective competence. Extrinsic control (over wider aspects of a job) appears to be less directly associated with mental health, although it may of course be desired on other grounds. The indirect effects of increased extrinsic control are likely to be through changes to the nine environmental features which form the basis of the present model.

Opportunity for skill use

The second environmental feature within the 'vitamin' framework concerns the utilization of skills. The latter are viewed broadly as capabilities to perform particular tasks, and it is expected that workers in jobs with greater opportunity for skill use will tend to be mentally more healthy than those in jobs with less opportunity; in part this expectation arises from the assumption that the greater the opportunity which is available the more will a person use his or her skills. As with opportunity for control, in the previous section, higher scores on this environmental variable may reflect both increased number and level of skills; in practice those two indices are likely to be intercorrelated.

Skill utilization in work settings has been studied by several investigators. For example, in Kornhauser's (1965) study of American car-workers, a particularly strong predictor of context-free mental health was a person's response to the question 'would you say your job gives you a chance to use your abilities?' Mental health was measured in this study through a wide-ranging interview, which covered freedom from anxiety, self-esteem, freedom from hostility, sociability, life satisfaction, and personal morale. The significant relationship with opportunity for skill use was present among young and middle-aged workers (between 20 and 29 years, and 40 and 49 years respectively) and among workers in both semi-skilled and skilled jobs. For example, 53 per cent of the middle-aged semi-skilled men who reported no opportunity for skill use were categorized as having low mental health, compared with only 18 per cent of those indicating that their job gave them a chance to use their abilities. Corresponding figures for young semi-skilled workers were 45 per cent and 10 per cent. A strong association with job satisfaction was also found.

In a study of American men in 23 different occupations, opportunity for skill use was measured through a three-item self-report scale. Scores were found to be strongly positively correlated with job satisfaction and negatively with boredom; and low opportunity was also significantly predictive of dissatisfaction with workload, job-related anxiety, job-related depression, and job-related somatic complaints such as insomnia, dizziness, and feeling short of breath when resting (Caplan *et al.* 1975; French *et al.* 1982; Kroes 1981; LaRocco *et al.* 1980). In a related study of five groups of US navy enlisted men, French *et al.* (1983) recorded a median correlation between opportunity for skill use and overall job satisfaction of 0.37. This feature was also significantly associated with low context-free anxiety and depression, and high context-free subjective competence; however, it was not correlated with context-free somatic complaints.

Similar measures were used by Wilkes *et al.* (1981) in a study of American poultry inspectors; perceived opportunity for skill use was correlated 0.49 with overall job satisfaction. In Gavin and Axelrod's (1977) research with American mining managers, the corresponding value was 0.42. In addition, opportunity for skill use was found to be correlated -0.22 with somatic symptoms and -0.60 with a combined index of job-related anxiety, depression, and irritation. In Donaldson's (1975) study of female Scottish assembly workers, overall job satisfaction was correlated 0.34 with the degree to which 'this job enables me to make use of my abilities'. Hall and Schneider (1973) asked American priests about use of their 'most important skills and abilities', finding that reported opportunity for skill use was correlated 0.53 with intrinsic job satisfaction. In a six-nation study of senior managers, Heller and Wilpert (1981) recorded a correlation with overall job satisfaction of 0.26.

The importance of skill utilization has been emphasized in two projects reported by O'Brien. In multiple regression analyses of data from 1383 employed Australian men and women, he found that opportunity for skill use was more strongly associated with overall job satisfaction than were features such as opportunity for control and job variety (O'Brien 1982b). In a second investigation, opportunity for skill use was again found to be more important than control and variety, as well as several other job characteristics, in this case in relation to satisfaction with work undertaken and overall job satisfaction (O'Brien 1983).

O'Brien's first project also included two context-free measures of mental health. One was an index of overall strain, covering sleeplessness, tiredness, indigestion, depression, anxiety, etc. Strain scores were found to be significantly higher among workers with lower opportunity for skill use (O'Brien 1980). The second context-free measure was Rotter's (1966) locus of control scale, which may be viewed as tapping the subjective autonomy component of mental health. Internal locus of control score was found to be significantly positively correlated with opportunity for skill use in one's job. Using two-stage least-squares analysis, O'Brien (1984a) claimed that locus of control and opportunity for skill use in a job are reciprocally determined: people exhibiting internal control are more likely to attain jobs which afford high skill use, and those whose jobs permit considerable use of skills are in turn likely to develop internal control beliefs.

All analyses described so far in this section have made use of linear co-efficients of correlation. In a study of Dutch manual, managerial and professional employees, van Dijkhuizen (1980) asked whether associations with opportunity for skill use were in fact non-linear. For several measures of affective well-being this turned out to be the case, with very low skill use being linked to low well-being but a plateau occurring at higher levels of the job feature. For groups arrayed from low to high opportunity for skill use, mean job dissatisfaction scores were 2.69, 2.07, 1.89, 1.65, and 1.71 respectively. Values for job-related psychosomatic complaints were 1.41, 1.28, 1.31, 1.23, and 1.25; and for low self-esteem they were 3.36, 2.67, 2.60, 2.40, and 2.37 (p <0.001 in each case). Significant non-linear associations were also found for job-related anxiety and depression, but these took on different patterns and were not readily interpretable.

Skill use and occupational level   Opportunity for skill use is likely to vary systematically with occupational level, educational qualifications and social class. A correlation of 0.31 with occupational level was found by O'Brien (1982b; 1984a), and coefficients of 0.44 and 0.60 in respect of education level and social class were reported by LaRocco et al. (1980); see also Shaw and Riskind (1983). These associations raise the possibility that the major factor influencing mental health is not opportunity for skill use within a job but a broader range of environmental features associated with a person's position in society.

Features of the latter kind are undoubtedly important determinants of mental health (see Chapters 4 and 10). However, there are two grounds for rejecting the argument that they entirely account for the findings described above, leaving opportunity for skill use as merely a proxy measure of social position. First, partialling out social position within multiple regression analyses leaves the independent effect of opportunity for skill use almost unchanged. O'Brien (1982b) has shown this in respect of social class indexed through income and education level; and calculation of partial correlations from values provided by LaRocco et al. (1980, Appendix A) reveals that opportunity for skill use remains significantly associated with job-related anxiety, job-related depression, and somatic symptoms after controlling separately for socio-economic status and education level.

Second, investigations with homogeneous groups of employees have also recorded strong associations between this job feature and aspects of mental health. Results have been described above from separate studies of naval enlisted men, poultry inspectors, mining managers, assembly workers, and priests, each indicating the importance of this characteristic. O'Brien (1982b) has also split his large sample into seven occupational categories (professional, clerical, retail, etc.), and has found opportunity for skill use to be the primary independent predictor of overall job satisfaction in each category. The association between this feature and high mental health of the kinds illustrated here is thus likely to be a valid one.

What is known about the prevalence of low opportunity for skill use? Surveys have revealed that a high proportion of workers report too little opportunity to use their abilities. For example, Quinn and Staines (1979) describe how 36 per cent of American workers responded affirmatively to the question 'Do you have some skills from your experience and training that you would like to be using in your work but can't use on your present job?' In O'Brien's (1980) Australian survey, 39 per cent of workers desired more skill utilization than they were currently experiencing. These figures, coming from random population samples, cover all occupational levels. Since there is an association between higher job level and greater opportunity for skill use, the proportion of lower-level workers reporting underutilization will of course be much greater. For instance, in Kornhauser's (1965) study as many as 55 per cent of semi-skilled workers reported that their job failed to permit them to use their abilities.

On the other hand, some employees have too few skills for the requirements of their job. Thirteen per cent of O'Brien's (1980) sample wanted less skill utilization. Job demands beyond the ability of a worker will be discussed in Chapter 7. For the present we may note that jobs which require too great an input of skill would be located at the right-hand side of the vitamin AD model in Fig. 1.1: at particularly high levels of this environmental feature, mental health is predicted to be lower than in the moderate range.

Finally, it is of interest to consider relationships between this job feature and opportunity for control. The latter was described earlier as either intrinsic to the job (within job activities themselves) or extrinsic and often exercised by trade union or other representatives. Opportunity for intrinsic control is sometimes associated with opportunity for skill use, in that certain control actions require high levels of skill. However, the overlap is far from complete, since many other forms of control activity are simple and unskilled. It thus seems likely that, whereas *low* opportunity for intrinsic control will be associated with low opportunity for skill use, *high* opportunity for intrinsic control may be associated with either high or low opportunity for skill use.

What about extrinsic control? Skilled workers often have considerable bargaining power because of the relative scarcity of their skill. This is important to them because it provides greater influence, through their trade union for example, over terms and conditions of employment. It is also important because management cannot easily locate substitute labour if a group of employees chooses to strike or otherwise impair productivity. Trade unions therefore often seek to obtain a monopoly over skills required for particular jobs, because that increases their ability to influence management decisions. Conversely, management may seek to reduce the opportunity for skill use in a job because that restricts employees' opportunity for both intrinsic and extrinsic control.

Variety

We turn now to the third feature to be examined in this chapter, the amount of variety in a job. In general, statements about variety concern novelty or change in a physical, social, or institutional environment, and it is again helpful to distinguish between features that are intrinsic and those which are extrinsic to prescribed tasks. 'Intrinsic' variety is usually taken to be a question of the number of different operations performed, but it may also be viewed in terms of variety within each of the other 'intrinsic' features of the present model. These are opportunity for control, opportunity for skill use, externally generated goals, and environmental clarity. For example, opportunity for skill use in a job may be fixed and unchanging, or it may vary in its level during a period of work. The psychological impact of jobs with low average opportunity for skill use may be thought to differ as a function of this feature's variability across time; greater variability around a low average may be desirable in its own right and also because shifts in the direction of greater skill utilization are themselves desirable.

'Extrinsic' variety concerns features outside the content of a job itself. These may involve changes in location, or physical variation of other kinds, such as changes in noise, lighting, background music, or opportunity to look outside the work-place. We may also think in terms of variations within each of the 'extrinsic' features of the present model. For example, differences across time in the opportunity for interpersonal contact or variations in physical security may be welcomed for their own sake, irrespective of the average level of these features.

The importance of variety became clear in studies during the 1920s by the Industrial Fatigue Research Board. These early investigations involved intensive observation of small groups of British workers engaged in highly repetitive jobs such as packaging, wrapping, folding, weighing, and assembly-work. The performance and attitudes of employees were recorded under standard conditions and also after changes had been introduced to increase job variety. The results suggested that some increase in variety improved output, although too much had adverse effects since it disturbed operators' work rhythm. However, employees responded favourably to the increased variety. As Wyatt *et al.* (1928, p. 25) reported, 'operatives who have had experience of both uniform and varied conditions of work generally prefer the latter'.

Walker and Guest (1952) investigated the relationship between American car workers' job attitudes and intrinsic variety (number of operations performed) in assembly-line jobs. A strong association was recorded between variety and interest in the work. Similar findings have been obtained in many other studies, using a wide range of well-being measures.

In a study of male Canadian workers, Coburn (1978) used a two-item index of reported job variety. He found that scores on this were significantly predictive of low alienation and high satisfaction (the latter variables being intercorrelated -0.60), after statistically controlling for other factors such as pay, job security, and social class. Variety and overall job satisfaction were also found to be significantly positively associated in Donaldson's (1975) study of female Scottish assembly workers.

Kornhauser's (1965) analyses of data from American car workers included comparisons between semi-skilled employees in repetitive and non-repetitive jobs; the former showed significantly lower overall job satisfaction (p. 159). The study also permitted comparisons between these two groups on a wide-ranging interview measure of context-free mental health, described in the previous section. Semi-skilled workers in non-repetitive jobs exhibited considerably better mental health than did semi-skilled workers in repetitive jobs (p. 57). Broadbent and Gath (1981) reported similar comparisons for two samples of British car workers. Job satisfaction was again found to be significantly lower among those in repetitive jobs, but in this study differences in respect of anxiety, depression, somatic symptoms, and obsessional symptoms failed to reach statistical significance.

The Job Diagnostic Survey (JDS) (Hackman and Oldham 1975 1980) contains a measure of 'skill variety': 'the degree to which a job requires a variety of different activities in carrying out the work, which involve the use of a number of different skills and talents of the employee'. This construct is similar to intrinsic variety as defined here (see also Cooper 1973), and scores on reported skill variety are consistently found to be significantly related to employees' general job satisfaction, intrinsic job satisfaction, and intrinsic work motivation (e.g. Oldham *et al.* 1978). Unfortunately, inspection of the three JDS items tapping skill variety indicates that one is more appropriately viewed as an indicator of level rather than variety of skill ('the job requires me to use a number of complex or high-level skills'). This is reflected in a factor structure which fails to exhibit the named factors (Dunham 1976; O'Brien 1982a), and casts doubt upon findings from this instrument in respect of variety.

However, a similar instrument, the Job Characteristics Inventory (Sims *et al.* 1976) also contains a scale of skill variety. This is defined as 'the degree to which a job requires employees to perform a wide range of operations in their work and/or the degree to which employees must use a variety of equipment and procedures in their work'. Items in the Job Characteristics Inventory tap variety in a more direct fashion and yield a clearer factor structure (e.g. Pierce and Dunham 1978). Observed significant correlations with intrinsic and overall job satisfaction (e.g. Brief and Aldag 1978) and with specific facet satisfactions (e.g. Sims and Szilagyi 1976) are thus likely to be valid indicators of the importance of intrinsic variety for job-related well-being. A longitudinal study by Bechtold *et al.* (1981) has confirmed that increases or decreases in variety are accompanied by changes in the same direction in satisfaction with work content.

Two studies have taken measures of job variety independently of workers whose well-being is being assessed. In research with Swedish manual employees, Johansson *et al.* (1978) obtained expert ratings, finding that low levels of variety in a job were associated with workers' reports of more irritation and less calmness. Excretion of both adrenaline and noradrenaline (see page 45) was also greater in low-variety jobs. In an American study, independent job analysis assessments of variety were found by Shaw and Riskind (1983) to be significantly negatively associated with job-related anxiety and depression, and job dissatisfaction.

In the investigation by Kohn and Schooler (e.g. 1983), described earlier, 'routinization' was measured in terms of job-holders' reports of repetitiveness and cycle-time. After statistical controls, as summarized above, routinization of work was found to be significantly negatively associated with overall job satisfaction and with commitment to one's occupation (Kohn and Schooler 1973). It was also significantly positively associated with authoritarian conservatism, an index of what respondents find socially acceptable, ranging from rigid adherence to authority to more open value systems and tolerance of non-conformity.

Central to the investigation was a measure of 'ideational flexibility', evidenced by performance in handling cognitive problems that require both sides of an issue to be considered. In the present setting this may be viewed as an aspect of context-free competence, the second component of mental health described earlier. Members of the sample were required to offer answers to two questions, concerning the optimal location of a food stand and the arguments for and against cigarette advertising on television. Their answers were subsequently rated for adequacy, and scores were combined with an intelligence rating by the interviewer and the frequency of 'agree' responses during the interview. Weights given to these four variables were 0.26, 0.40, 0.65, and -0.44 in the initial set of data (e.g. Kohn and Schooler 1983, p. 113; the strong contribution of interviewers' rating of intelligence (0.65) in this measure might be considered problematic).

Routinization of work was found to be significantly negatively associated with ideational flexibility in the initial study, after controlling for other variables (Kohn and Schooler 1973). Furthermore, job routinization had a significant negative lagged effect on ideational flexibility measured ten years later, again controlling for background variables (Kohn and Schooler 1982). However, these analyses revealed no significant effects of routinization upon affective well-being, in terms of anxiety and self-esteem. A similar pattern of findings was reported in a cross-sectional study of 269 employed women by Miller *et al.* (1979): a negative association with ideational flexibility, a positive association with authoritarian conservatism, and no relationship with self-esteem or anxiety.

Risk of heart attack was found to be associated with reported job monotony in a study by Alfredsson *et al.* (1982). All cases of fatal and non-fatal myocardial infarction in men aged 40 to 64 in the Greater Stockholm area between 1974 and 1976 were recorded, together with details of jobs held. For each case at least two matched controls without infarction were selected randomly from parish registers. From interviews with a separate sample of 3876 working men, the 'psychosocial characteristics' of 118 different jobs were determined. The risk of mycardial infarction in jobs with different characteristics was then calculated from the three sets of data. Job monotony emerged as the strongest single predictor of this type of heart attack for the group as a whole. Within that overall finding, however, there was evidence for one sub-group (men aged between 40 and 54) that low educational level and the need for much heavy lifting may have been confounding factors in the relationship; see Alfredsson and Theorell (1983).

Although the studies reviewed so far have primarily concerned what was earlier termed 'intrinsic' variety, the number of different operations performed, they are likely also to have tapped aspects of extrinsic variety. Specific types of the latter have sometimes been investigated in relation to boredom at work. For example, Fox (1983) and Shackleton (1981) have summarized studies suggesting that background music can reduce boredom, at least for a high proportion of workers.

Enhancing variety   Roy (1960) illustrated how a small group of American employees informally brought variation into their work by ritual non-work activities. These occurred at known times of the day, and involved a routine interaction between specified members. For example, 'banana time' occurred at the same period each day, when one man would surreptitiously steal another's banana, and the latter would protest and denounce him. Other members of the group would join in the protests and denunciations. These interactions were additional to formal progress points such as coffee or lunch time, and together they served to provide variety in an otherwise unchanging environment.

As phases of the daily series, they occurred almost hourly, and so short were they in duration that they disrupted work activity only slightly. Their significance lay not so much in their function as rest pauses, although it cannot be denied that physical refreshment was involved . . . The physical interplay which momentarily halted work activity would initiate verbal exchanges and thought processes to occupy group members until the next interruption. The group interactions thus not only marked off the time; they gave it content and hurried it along (Roy 1960, pp. 161–2).

In other ways too employees mark off time, give it content and hurry it along, even in jobs with little intrinsic variety. Roy (1960) also described the importance of setting personal schedules, so that (for example) a worker processed 1000 items of one colour then 500 of another, according to a self-determined plan for the day. Such a procedure (introducing 'batch traction', described in Chapter 7) yielded 'a continuous sequence of short-range production goals with achievement rewards in the form of activity change' (p. 161). In a study of British car workers, Broadbent (1981) described how 'a number of the men reported using methods of occupying their minds while doing parts of the work which needed no thought. This of course meant that a physical action must be infrequent; suitable activities are crossword puzzles, and the playing of games such as chess. Each of these allowed a movement to be made in a moment of rest, while allowing thought about the next problem during return to the monotonous job' (p. 48). It seems likely that workers in all repetitive jobs create limited variety in ways such as these (see also Fraser 1968, pp. 97–8; Turner and Miclette 1962). Note that the strategy embraces other features covered in this chapter: personal control is exercised, and in some cases skills are used for non-job purposes.

Variety is also increased by programmes of job rotation, where employees change jobs with others in the same wage grade, either within a period of work or between periods. Such programmes may be formally introduced by management, or may arise informally to meet the wishes of employees. Systematic evidence about the impact of rotation on well-being is limited, but it seems likely to be particularly appropriate in relieving workers from extremely low-variety tasks. In jobs which individually have moderate variety, rotation carries possible disadvantages in the form of interruptions to batch traction and to interpersonal networks.

More generally, it may be suggested that extremely high levels of variety are themselves harmful, as proposed in the vitamin AD model of Fig. 1.1 (page 10). Having a very wide range of tasks to undertake requires a person to shift concentration and attention with a frequency which can yield discomfort and inefficiency. The resulting inefficiency may itself give rise to distress and feelings of low competence. In addition, extremely high levels of job variety may give rise to correlated harmful changes in other environmental features. For example, the number of externally generated goals (feature number 3) may become excessive. Conflict between these goals may also arise, with difficulties in choosing between diverse but approximately equal priorities; and very frequent shifts between activities may interrupt the smooth flow of any one activity, reducing the satisfactions which can arise from work traction (see Chapter 7).

All this seems possible; but there appears to be no systematic research evidence to support or deny the possibilities. In practice, the effect may be mediated by other features within the present model. For example, if the workload demanded in a job is particularly high (see Chapter 7, covering externally generated goals), then extremely high variety is especially likely to be harmful in the ways suggested. But, if task demands are themselves low, then very high variety may have no negative consequences on mental health.

Cycle-time Finally in this section, what is known about the impact of cycle-time? Jobs in which the duration of each activity cycle is extremely short embody very little intrinsic variety, in that the number of different operations within a cycle is inevitably small. We might thus expect to find an association of cycle-time with low mental health. In fact, however, the two variables appear not to be related in that manner, at least in studies examining jobs whose content is otherwise similar.

Kornhauser (1965) compared holders of three groups of repetitive jobs, with cycle-times of less than a minute, one to three minutes, and more than three minutes; no difference was found in overall mental health scores. Broadbent and Gath (1981) also failed to find an effect of cycle-time on job satisfaction or indices of anxiety, depression, somatic symptoms, and obsessional symptoms. In the study by Birchall and Wild (1977), longer cycle-time was *negatively* associated with overall job satisfaction ($r = -0.45$), although the authors offer no explanation for that surprising relationship.

These findings of a negative or a zero correlation may arise in part from the fact that other types of variety and other aspects of job content may operate favourably in some short cycle-time jobs. For example, spatial and interpersonal variety do not necessarily covary with duration of work cycle; and employees may be required to carry out short cycle-time activities for only a part of their working period. Forms of traction (described in Chapter 7) may also be more influential in relatively short cycle-time jobs.

In addition, it is likely that frequent repetition of relatively simple tasks leads to their becoming automatic, without the need for careful attention from the worker. Psychological 'automatization' of that kind can reduce the demands from jobs with both short- and medium-length cycles, raising instead the importance of quite different job features, which may be uncorrelated with cycle-time itself. Furthermore, in jobs which are partly or completely self-paced (see page 86), workers' freedom to control their own work-rate through pauses between cycles is potentially greater in short cycle-time jobs, in that more opportunities for between-cycle pauses present themselves. An alternative explanation of the seeming unimportance of cycle-time is methodological; it is possible that an inadequate range of times has been studied within any single investigation. Additional studies, perhaps with more comprehensive examination of extrinsic as well as intrinsic variety, would clearly be of value.

For the present, however, it is appropriate to conclude that an unremitting requirement for a person to work on a short cycle-time task which is also rapidly paced is likely to be mentally injurious. In the terms of the present model, such work combines low variety with low opportunity for control as well as low opportunity for skill use—the first three environmental features in the suggested categorization.

In review of this section, the evidence makes it clear that low variety in a job gives rise to low affective well-being at work, and that workers are likely to take steps to introduce variation when that is possible. There is less evidence that low job variety induces low context-free well-being, or that it is associated with reduced competence, autonomy, or aspiration. However, an impact on 'ideational flexibility' has been demonstrated. No empirical tests have been reported of the proposals from the vitamin AD model that, although low variety is harmful, increases in variety beyond a moderate level do not provide further benefit, and that very high variety is associated with an additional decrement in mental health.

Summary

This chapter has brought together a large number of investigations into three aspects of the occupational environment: opportunity for control, opportunity for skill use, and variety. These are features numbered 1, 2, and 4 in the nine-vitamin model introduced in Chapter 1.

Results consistently point to the psychological importance of these three job characteristics. More specific aspects of each ('subcategories' in the language of Chapter 1) have also been identified and investigated. For example, opportunity for 'intrinsic' control appears to have a strong effect on certain forms of job-related mental health, whereas 'extrinsic' control seems likely to have a more general influence upon context-free mental health. A negative impact of machine-pacing (a subcategory of opportunity for control) has not been consistently found, perhaps because research designs have failed to exclude confounding influences from other factors.

Opportunity for skill use in a job covaries with socio-economic status and education level. The latter might thus be thought to be responsible for the observed importance of this job characteristic. However, it has been shown that opportunity for skill use remains associated with employee well-being after statistically or empirically controlling for occupational or educational level.

Subcategories of variety in a job include intrinsic and extrinsic variety; the former has been most studied, with a clear impact upon job-related well-being. Low cycle-time (one form of low intrinsic variety) has not been consistently found to impair employee mental health, possibly because of inadequate research designs.

The investigations described in this chapter were naturally conducted independently of the five-component account of mental health presented in Chapter 2. There remains a need to map published findings more closely on to that account. This task will be undertaken, with others, in the course of Chapter 6.

6

Interpreting research into job characteristics

This chapter seeks to expand and reflect upon the material in Chapter 5. A central section will interpret that material systematically in terms of the present account of mental health. That will be followed by an examination of four issues which can be problematic in any research into the impact of environmental features. These issues bear upon the findings described in the previous chapter, but also need to be considered when interpreting studies to be described later in the book. For that reason they are introduced at this intermediate stage.

First, however, we should examine research which has taken together the three factors examined so far. Consider this description by a spot-welder working some years ago in an American car assembly plant:

I stand in one spot, about two- or three-feet area, all night. The only time a person stops is when the line stops. We do about thirty-two jobs per car, per unit. Forty-eight units an hour, eight hours a day. Thirty-two times forty-eight times eight. Figure it out. That's how many times I push that button. . . . Repetition is such that if you were to think about the job itself, you'd slowly go out of your mind. . . . You pretty much stay to yourself. You get involved with yourself. You dream, you think of things you've done. I drift back continuously to when I was a kid and what me and my brothers did. . . . Lots of times I worked from the time I started to the time of the break and never realized I had even worked. When you dream you reduce the chances of friction with the foreman or the next guy (Terkel 1972, pp. 159–60).

That job clearly contained little opportunity for control or for skill use and also had extremely limited variety. In addition to examining those three features individually, it is also appropriate to consider the complexity of a job as a whole, viewing this primarily in terms of a combination of the factors discussed so far.

Overall job complexity

Many investigators have approached jobs in that way. For example, users of the Job Diagnostic Survey have sometimes calculated a job's 'motivating potential score' (MPS) in terms of a weighted combination of autonomy, feedback, skill variety, task identity, and task significance. Scores on this overall measure are strongly positively associated with overall job satisfaction, intrinsic job satisfaction, and intrinsic work motivation (e.g. Dunham 1976; Oldham *et al.* 1978; Wall *et al.* 1978; see also meta-analyses by Loher *et al.* 1985, and Spector, 1985). Such results are of course to be expected from the pattern of positive findings in relation to each specific job feature on its own.

Longitudinal research has shown that increases or decreases in 'motivating potential score' are accompanied by significant changes in overall job satisfaction, intrinsic job satisfaction and intrinsic work motivation (Hackman *et al.* 1978). Longitudinal studies with other measures of job complexity have replicated these findings in respect of intrinsic job satisfaction (Bechtold *et al.* 1981) and general job satisfaction (Kirjonen and Hanninen 1986). And an experimental study of part-time employees has confirmed that job content is of causal (rather than merely correlational) importance in these relationships (Griffeth 1985).

Motivating potential scores have also been examined in relation to context-free measures of mental health. For example, Wiener *et al.* (1981) studied American professional employees, reporting that greater job complexity was significantly associated with lower depression, higher self-esteem, and greater life satisfaction. Strong associations with overall job satisfaction, job involvement, and career satisfaction were also found, although the negative correlation with anxiety failed to reach significance. Tharenou and Harker (1982, 1984), in research with Australian apprentice electricians, observed substantial correlations between motivating potential score and scores on Wagner and Morse's (1975) measure of subjective job competence (see Chapter 3); however, motivating potential score was found to be unrelated to context-free self-esteem.

Gardell (1971) measured job complexity through combined ratings made by independent observers of variety, control, skill required, responsibility, and required social interaction, finding significant associations in two Swedish blue-collar samples with measures of self-esteem. In a study of American factory workers, House *et al.* (1979) assessed the degree to which jobs contained variety and interest and permitted personal control and skill utilization; they labelled these features 'intrinsic rewards'. Controlling for educational level and other variables, it was found that perceived low levels of intrinsic rewards were significantly associated with higher scores on a wide-ranging measure of neurotic symptoms.

Kemp *et al.* (1983) studied British shop-floor workers, assessing the degree to which jobs contained intrinsic job characteristics and embodied complex group activities. Reported levels of intrinsic job characteristics and group work complexity were significantly associated with overall job satisfaction, intrinsic job motivation, organizational commitment, and trust in management, and also with context-free affective well-being assessed through the

General Health Questionnaire. Comparing one sub-group whose jobs had been designed specifically to enhance work complexity with three control groups in conventional jobs revealed significantly greater job satisfaction in the complex jobs. This was also the case in respect of the other measures of well-being, both job-related and context-free, in comparisons with a control group also working on day-shifts; however, comparisons with evening-shift control groups were not usually significant.

This study was extended longitudinally, with further measurements being taken after one and two years (Wall *et al.* 1986). In the course of this period, the jobs of one of the original control groups were redesigned to increase their complexity. A significant increase was observed to follow in intrinsic job satisfaction, but not in intrinsic job motivation, organizational commitment, or context-free affective well-being. Productivity increases followed the change, through a reduction in indirect labour costs rather than through increases in individual performance.

Wall and Clegg's (1981a) change study in a different company has already been described in Chapter 5. In addition to specific job content measures, increases in overall complexity of group working were also examined. These were followed by significant increases in job satisfaction, intrinsic job motivation, growth-need strength, and context-free affective well-being measured through the General Health Questionnaire. Significantly increased desires for information and for promotion were also recorded; these are here viewed within the notion of job-related aspiration.

Algera (1983) examined jobs in the Dutch steel industry, obtaining ratings of 24 specific job characteristics both from job-holders and also from their supervisors and personnel officers. He calculated multiple correlations between these job characteristics and 17 outcome variables, reporting significant associations of both sets of ratings ('independent' as well as 'subjective') with aspects of mental health such as job satisfaction, intrinsic work motivation, job involvement, anxiety, and irritability. Significant associations were also found with measures of general health complaints and unspecified 'coronary ailments'.

Campion and Thayer (1985) obtained independent ratings of the content of American wood product workers' jobs, including opportunity for control, opportunity for skill use, and variety. Combining these ratings with assessments of other intrinsic characteristics, they observed that overall job content scores were significantly associated with responses on a composite job satisfaction and job involvement scale. However, both job content and affective well-being were separately associated with skill level, and after statistical control of that variable the correlation between job content and well-being was no longer significant.

In an American community survey, Seeman and Anderson (1983) assessed the 'substantive complexity' of jobs in terms of scores available from the census classification of occupational titles. Those scores are intended to reflect four principal dimensions: the complexity of tasks in dealing with people, data, and things; abstract and creative versus routine and concrete activities; high general educational development and specific vocational preparation; and work not involving repetitive or continuous processes. Substantive complexity measured in this way was found to be significantly associated with intrinsic job satisfaction, but was unrelated to several measures of excessive alcohol consumption. In practice, the complexity score was correlated 0.81 with socio-economic status, thus strongly reflecting occupational level. However, after partialling out the effect of socio-economic status (from values presented in the authors' Table 1) the correlation between job complexity and satisfaction remains significant.

A similar measure was employed in an examination of longitudinal data by Kohn and Schooler (e.g. 1983). As described in Chapter 5, their study investigated relationships between a wide range of variables measured on two occasions separated by 10 years in a sample of more than 3 000 American men. In addition to the factors described previously, Kohn and Schooler also assessed the 'substantive complexity' of each person's job. This was achieved by rating detailed interview information in terms of the complexity and duration of work with people, data, and things. After statistically controlling for background features such as education, race, age, region, parents' education, and father's and grandfathers' occupational level, and also controlling for other job factors, substantive complexity was found to have a significant independent impact upon 'ideational flexibility' (see page 96 for the definition and measurement of this concept).

Significant negative associations with self-deprecation and authoritarian conservatism were also found, although anxiety was unrelated to substantive complexity of jobs (Kohn and Schooler 1978, 1982). Earlier analyses of part of the data-set (also controlling for other variables) had revealed a significant effect of substantive complexity on job satisfaction and occupational commitment (Kohn and Schooler 1973). In a parallel study of women's jobs (Miller *et al.* 1979), substantive complexity was again found to have an independent effect on ideational flexibility, although links with authoritarian conservatism and self-deprecation were in this case less strong.

Substantive complexity as assessed by Kohn and Schooler was closely correlated with occupational level, with a sharp break in scores occurring between blue-collar and white-collar workers. For example, average deviation from the overall mean complexity score was -1.26 for blue-collar workers, 0.51 for junior white-collar workers, and 1.23 for managers and employers (1983, p. 184). Substantive complexity scores for individual people's jobs were also found to be strongly correlated (0.78) with overall dictionary values for job titles of the kind used in Seeman and Anderson's study described above (Kohn and Schooler 1983, p. 67).

Changes in job content were studied by Kirjonen and Hanninen (1986), as Finnish metal industry employees moved between positions across a five-year period. Increases or decreases in job complexity were significantly associated with reductions or increases in context-free distress for both white-collar and blue-collar workers. This relationship was present despite controls for a range of other changes in job characteristics and in pay satisfaction.

A longitudinal investigation by Brousseau (1978) examined the association of current job content with changes in several aspects of mental health over the preceding six-year period. A form of the motivating potential score from the Job Diagnostic Survey was found to be significantly associated with changes over this period in the direction of lower depression scores and a more active orientation. The longitudinal patterns observed by Mortimer and Lorence (1979) and Mortimer and Finch (1986), in which level of current work autonomy was associated with previous increases in subjective competence and in affective well-being, were described in Chapter 5. At that point it was noted that the measures of job content labelled as 'autonomy' in fact extended more broadly; those studies may thus also be classified under the present heading of overall job complexity. Karasek's (1979) findings in respect of 'job decision latitude' should also be cited here; as noted earlier, his measures in practice extended beyond that particular construct.

All the studies cited above, except that of Karasek, have considered predictions in terms of a linear association between job complexity and affective well-being. One other investigator (Champoux 1978, 1980) has emphasized that complexity is likely to be less influential at moderate to high levels than at low levels, when it is in effect absent. To examine this possibility, he included a non-linear term in regression analyses of overall job satisfaction and intrinsic job satisfaction. Consistent with the vitamin analogy described in Chapter 1, a significant tendency towards a plateau at medium and high levels of job complexity was observed in three out of four organizations. There was, however, no indication that very high complexity was associated with an additional decrement in satisfaction, possibly because the samples included very few employees with jobs of that extreme kind. Further investigations of possible non-linear relationships are required.

Results in relation to five components of mental health

Let us turn now to a summary assessment of the importance of the specific job features considered so far. This is attempted in Table 6.1 (page 107), in respect of the five components of mental health which were introduced earlier. A reminder about each of these would perhaps be helpful.

Affective well-being has been characterized in terms of three principal axes in two-dimensional space. The primary axis, from discontented to contented, covers a range of feelings along the pleasure dimension (horizontal in Figs. 2.1 and 3.1; see page 27 and page 41), without regard to location on the arousal dimension (vertical in the figures). The second and third axes are between opposite quadrants of the model, such that axis two ranges from anxious to comfortable, and axis three extends from depressed to actively pleased.

As described earlier (see Table 3.1, page 47, for a summary), each dimension may be viewed in 'job-related' or 'context-free' terms. Job-related forms of the first axis are seen in measures of job satisfaction, work alienation, etc.; and context-free measures cover life satisfaction, happiness, general distress, and overall self-esteem. The second axis covers, for example, anxiety and neuroticism (context-free) and job-related tension or resigned job satisfaction (job-related). The third axis includes depression or positive affect (context-free) and job-related depression or job involvement (job-related).

The next three components (competence, autonomy, and aspiration) cover aspects of a person's transactions with the environment, and may be treated in both 'subjective' and 'objective' terms. Subjective assessments are derived through reports from the focal person, and the latter are obtained through independent observations. In each case 'job-related' or 'context-free' measures may be taken.

Competence is viewed in terms of an ability to handle day-to-day problems; autonomy is a question of moderate independence and self-regulation; and aspiration covers active efforts to attain goals and to extend oneself through motivated behaviour. Finally, integrated functioning is an overarching feature reflected in balance or harmony of various kinds; in view of its diffuseness, it seems appropriate to leave this aspect of mental health without differentiation into job-related or context-free aspects.

Table 6.1 contains assessments of the probability, in the light of currently available evidence, that each of the three job features influences each aspect of mental health. In addition, studies of overall job complexity defined primarily in terms of these features are summarized in the right-hand column. In some cases no evidence has been found, and these are identified by 'ndl' (no data located). Certain other relationships are present by definition (identified as 'by def'). In all other cases an assessment of probability has been made, in the terms summarized below the table. Note that these assessments are sometimes based on limited published evidence, so that a particular probability statement may require revision in the light of future research. Indeed, one purpose of this summary is to point out issues in need of investigation.

Studies reviewed throughout Chapter 5 were mainly cross-sectional, comparing groups with differing job content or correlating job content with well-being. However, a number of longitudinal investigations and change studies at the work-place were also described, and it is these which permit causal statements to be made. Of course, affirmation of a causal link from job content to mental health does not preclude the existence of a reverse

Table 6.1 Assessment of causal relationships between four job features and major aspects of mental health, based upon currently available evidence

	Job feature			
	Opportunity for control	Opportunity for skill use	Variety	Overall complexity
AFFECTIVE WELL-BEING				
Job-related				
1. Discontented–contented	+++	+++	+++	+++
2. Anxious–comfortable	ndl	+	+	ndl
3. Depressed–actively pleased	+	++	+	++
Context-free				
1. Discontented–contented	+++	+++	+	++
2. Anxious–comfortable	++	++	?	?
3. Depressed–actively pleased	++	++	?	+
COMPETENCE				
Job-related, subjective	by def	by def	ndl	by def
Job-related, objective	ndl	ndl	ndl	ndl
Context-free, subjective	++	+	ndl	+
Context-free, objective	ndl	ndl	+	+
AUTONOMY				
Job-related, subjective	by def	by def	ndl	by def
Job-related, objective	ndl	ndl	ndl	ndl
Context-free, subjective	ndl	+	ndl	ndl
Context-free, objective	ndl	ndl	ndl	ndl
ASPIRATION				
Job-related, subjective	++	ndl	ndl	++
Job-related, objective	+	ndl	ndl	ndl
Context-free, subjective	ndl	ndl	ndl	ndl
Context-free, objective	ndl	ndl	ndl	ndl
INTEGRATED FUNCTIONING	ndl	ndl	ndl	ndl

Abbreviations are as follows:

ndl: no data located
by def: by definition
?: results ambiguous

+ : probably a causal link from this job feature to this aspect of mental health
++: very probably such a causal link
+++: almost certainly such a causal link

causal process. This possibility will be taken up again later, as will the pattern of the recorded relationships, linear or non-linear for example.

First in Table 6.1 is job-related affective well-being in respect of the discontented–contented dimension. Studies have mainly concerned overall or specific job satisfaction, and the pattern is clear and consistent. There is no doubt that workers are more satisfied with and feel more contented in those jobs which exhibit higher levels of the three features. The next row of the table indicates a shortage of data about the anxious–comfortable axis of job-related affective well-being. The third row suggests that we may be confident about an effect on the depressed–actively pleased axis of the opportunity for skill use, and that the other two specific job features are probably also influential to a significant degree.

Turning to the three axes of context-free affective well-being, the evidence is strong in each case for effects of opportunity for control and opportunity for skill use. Higher levels of these features give rise to greater life satisfaction and self-esteem and lower levels of general distress, anxiety, exhaustion, and depression outside the job setting. The impact of job variety has however not been so clearly demonstrated.

Both subjective forms of the second aspect of mental health, competence, are suggested in Table 6.1 to be affected by the first two job factors and by overall job complexity. In part the empirical association in relation to *job-related* subjective competence arises from the definitional link between both control and skill use and that particular outcome: people controlling their own job activities and using skills are necessarily sustaining or extending their feelings of competence at work. These relationships are shown as 'by def' in Table 6.1. However, the results summarized in the table suggest that opportunity for control in a job also increases a person's subjective competence in a *context-free* sense. Very little evidence has been located for objective measures of competence, either job-related or context-free.

Table 6.1 also contains a low-probability assertion that context-free subjective autonomy is affected by opportunity for skill use; and somewhat stronger evidence is present for links between control opportunity and job-related aspiration feelings. Neither component has been much studied in 'objective' terms. It is not known empirically whether integrated functioning is affected by the job features examined here. However, there is a sense in which an extremely alienated worker, hating a job which takes up a large part of life, is failing to achieve a balance in the triad of 'love, work, and play'. And a carry-over from job activities, interests, and skills into a wider competence and pattern of aspirations (see Chapter 4) represents an aspect of integrated functioning, one which appears to be more probable at higher levels of job control and skill use.

The overall pattern of evidence reviewed in the previous chapter thus points strongly to the causal impact of the three job features upon certain aspects of mental health. Furthermore, opportunity for skill use and opportunity for control emerge as more influential than the presence of variety.

What other statements can be made which differentiate between the impact of the three features in Table 6.1? Fifty-seven relationships are summarized there, 19 for each feature, excluding overall complexity. Taking one extreme view, we might simply postulate that all of these are likely to be statistically significant and causally important. This would result in the provisional inclusion of ' + + +' at each of the 57 intersections.

However, such an undifferentiated perspective would be inappropriate, for at least three reasons. First is the fact that, despite their statistical and conceptual overlap, the several mental health components are substantially different in their nature and likely consequences. For example, even within job-related affective well-being, the experiences of dissatisfaction and tension (axes 1 and 2 in Fig. 3.1) are quite different from each other; and, whereas chronic job-related tension predicts subsequent mortality, that is not the case for job dissatisfaction (House *et al.* 1986). Second, different job features are likely to have varying profiles of influence upon the 19 outcomes. For example, job variety may have limited impact upon context-free anxiety but a substantial effect upon job-related autonomy; the pattern may be reversed in respect of opportunity for skill use.

The third reason for expecting a differentiated pattern of associations concerns the processes whereby each job feature has its impact. The vitamin model being developed in this book was introduced in Chapter 1 as combining 'categorical' and 'process' theories. The evidence that each job feature in Table 6.1 influences some aspects of mental health bears upon the categorical part of the model: each of the three categories of the environment is thereby shown to be important in certain respects. However, little has been said so far about the processes whereby different consequences occur. Indeed, quantitative studies are often completely silent on this point. A different style of research may be needed to explore processes, especially those extended in time within complex organizations; the emphasis often needs to be more qualitative than in the studies reviewed so far. With such a focus we would expect different processes to occur within different cells of the matrix in Table 6.1. Complete differentiation (57 varieties of process) is unlikely, but some differences are certain.

Four general issues

These issues will be taken up at several points later in the book. At this stage, four other questions deserve examination. How far has common-method variance inflated the associations which have been observed? Are non-linear relationships present? How far can specific job features be identified as individual causal agents? And to what extent are causal relationships likely to be reciprocal rather than unidirectional? These will be considered in turn.

Subjective measures and common-method variance

It is often suggested that the widespread procedure of assessing job content through the reports of job-holders is liable to inflate correlations with affective well-being scores obtained from those same people (e.g. Aldag *et al.* 1981, Roberts and Glick 1981). This may arise because perceptions of the job are themselves influenced by a person's affective state, or because both values are determined by a third factor, for instance a work-group norm of perception and affect. This possibility was considered in Chapter 1 in respect of subjective assessments of the environment more generally, and it is important to examine whether results in job settings are thereby distorted.

One approach is to investigate the similarity between job-holders' ratings of job characteristics and those made by other people. The two sets of scores are typically found to be significantly intercorrelated. Hackman and Lawler (1971), Hackman and Oldham (1975) and Algera (1983) cite median correlations between job-holders' and supervisors' ratings of 0.57, 0.52, and 0.54 respectively. Stone and Porter (1975) present coefficients of concordance for eight different ratings of 16 jobs made by incumbents, supervisors and co-workers. The median coefficient was found to be 0.75. Dean and Brass (1985) examined the similarity between employees' ratings of five job characteristics and the ratings made independently by a researcher; the median correlation was 0.65.

Taber *et al.* (1985) recorded a correlation of 0.54 between independent job evaluation ratings of 'judgment and initiative' and self-reported opportunity for skill use. Dunham (1977) found that a composite measure of perceived job complexity was correlated 0.40 with a standardized job evaluation grading based upon the Position Analysis Questionnaire. In this case gradings were derived from information provided by job incumbents, but, as the author points out, research has revealed very similar job analysis responses to this instrument from job holders, supervisors, and independent analysts.

Using the motivating potential score from the Job Diagnostic Survey, Oldham *et al.* (1976) recorded a correlation of 0.85 between job-holders' and supervisors' ratings. Frese (1985) describes how, after only 90 minutes observation of blue-collar jobs, independent assessments of psychological job stressors correlated on average 0.36 with job holders' perceptions. However, in the study by Brief and Aldag (1978) the median correlation between supervisors' and job-holders' ratings was only 0.16; the authors suggest that this low value arose from the fact that their sample of jobs was particularly homogeneous (all employees were nurses with the same job title).

A second approach, which bypasses the potential problem of common-method variance, is to examine correlations between employees' mental health and independent measures of job content, assessing the latter through observers other than job-holders. Common-method variance would have its impact upon associations of job-holders' affective well-being with their own assessments of content, but not in respect of other people's ratings of content. Among studies reviewed in the previous chapter, significant associations of employee well-being with independently measured job content were described by Algera (1983), Gardell (1971), Seeman and Anderson (1983), and Shaw and Riskind (1983). Kiggundu (1980) has shown that correlations between job features measured through the Job Diagnostic Survey and job satisfaction and intrinsic motivation remain significant when ratings are made by supervisors or by other workers, but that the magnitude of association tends to be reduced. For example, correlations between ratings of overall job complexity and workers' job satisfaction were 0.54, 0.20, and 0.34 for job-holders, supervisors, and other workers respectively.

Algera (1983) also calculated coefficients separately from job-holders' and non job-holders' ratings of job characteristics. The latter judges were supervisors and personnel officers, and use of their ratings again reduced associations between job content and employees' mental health scores. However, correlations between job content and mental health almost always remained statistically significant when the two sets of data were obtained from different people. For example, multiple correlations with overall job satisfaction were 0.80 and 0.69 from job-holders' and non job-holders' ratings of content. Corresponding values for anxiety were 0.51 and 0.44, for irritability 0.36 and 0.33, and for job involvement 0.59 in both cases.

Independent ratings alone were taken in the study by Johansson *et al.* (1978); experts' assessments of job variety were found to be positively associated with workers' reported well-being. In two studies reported by Frese (1985), the observed average association with employees' psychosomatic complaints was 0.35 for job-holders' reports of psychological stressors and 0.19 for assessments of these stressors made by independent raters after 90 minutes observation ($p < 0.01$ in all cases).

It thus seems appropriate to conclude that common-method variance does indeed increase some observed relationships with employees' mental health, but that these relationships are in general likely to remain significant when independent measures of job content are used. That conclusion is reinforced by results from quasi-experimental studies, where observers' views of changes in job content are typically consistent with job-holders' ratings and can in principle be used as interchangeable indices.

However, it should be noted that assessments by other people are not necessarily preferable to those made by job-holders themselves. The former are often relatively crude, since supervisors or other external raters have only limited contact with the detailed activities and experiences involved in a job. Furthermore, it may sometimes happen that these raters use information provided in discussions with job-holders; the independence of their ratings may on occasions thus be questionable.

On conceptual grounds, too, there may be reason to prefer subjective assessments of the environment. As pointed out in Chapter 1, environmental features are likely to have their impact primarily through the appraisal made by a focal person; it may thus be desirable to measure the environment as appraised by the focal person rather than the environment irrespective of his or her appraisal. This is particularly so for features such as opportunity for control and opportunity for skill use, since there may be wide differences between people in their tendency to recognize opportunities within the same external environment

Non-linear relationships

The possibility of non-linear associations between job content and mental health is central to the vitamin analogy described in Chapter 1. It was postulated there that low levels of an environmental factor have a sharp negative effect on mental health, but that across moderate levels mental health remains unchanged; at very high levels of six factors (including the three examined in the previous chapter), a decline is predicted. The rationale for this expectation was presented in Chapter 1 (page 11), and both the plateau and the high-level decrement appear plausible in respect of opportunity for control, opportunity for skill use, and variety..

However, the vast majority of studies described in Chapter 5 have presented results in terms of linear correlation coefficients, so that the possibility has not yet been adequately tested. Some positive evidence is found in studies by Champoux (1978, 1980), Karasek (1979) and van Dijkhuizen (1980) (see pages 85 and 105), but further empirical examination of the prediction is clearly needed. This will require the application of other forms of statistical analysis beyond those based upon linear correlation. In addition, there is need for more qualitative research, to explore dynamic processes across time which may underpin (or fail to underpin) the postulated non-linear pattern.

Within the general 'vitamin' expectation, we should also consider the possibility of a difference between the two broad categories of mental health, context-free, and job-related. Do we expect the same pattern of association in each case, or is the plateau of the vitamin model more appropriate in one case than the other?

Context-free mental health is potentially influenced by a range of different factors, within the person as well as in the environment, so that it is unlikely to be affected by changes which do not extend beyond the unproblematic range of any one local environmental feature. The arguments presented in Chapter 1 for the assumption of a plateau (see page 11) thus appear particularly strong in relation to mental health which is context-free.

However, it does seem likely that aspects of *job-related* mental health are reactive to job conditions over a wider range of environmental values. For example, although increases in opportunity for control in a job may give rise to increased life satisfaction (context-free) only up to a given level, additional increases in this environmental variable may continue to enhance job-related mental health (job satisfaction, for instance) up to a higher level, before the plateau is reached.

It thus seems appropriate in respect of occupational environments to predict a broader plateau for context-free mental health than for job-related mental health. In general terms, we should expect a family of curves within the overall framework of Fig. 1.1 (page 10), with particular outcomes related to given environmental factors in similar but slightly different ways. However, there is at present no empirical data on which to base such a structure; it serves as an important objective for the future.

Specific causal factors

The third issue concerns the identification of individual causal agents. In cases where a particular job feature, variety for instance, has been shown to be significantly associated with an aspect of mental health, how can we determine whether it is that feature rather than a correlated (and possibly unmeasured) factor which has major explanatory importance? This difficulty faces researchers in many fields, and there appears to be no entirely satisfactory procedure for identifying the causal importance of single variables in any naturally occurring environment.

Consider first studies which are correlational, leaving aside their limitation in respect of possible non-linear associations. The minimum evidence required for inferring a causal association between an environmental feature and an aspect of mental health is a significant correlation between those two variables. Many such bivariate correlations have been summarized above. However, it is possible that they sometimes reflect the primary importance of another feature, within the job or elsewhere, with which the measured variable is correlated and for which it stands as a proxy.

It is thus desirable to supplement single bivariate correlations with multivariate analyses which permit statistical control of other features. Multiple regression procedures are often used for this purpose, providing assessments of the magnitude of the independent contributions made by each variable within an analysis. For example, the study by Payne and Fletcher (1983) was in Chapter 5 reported to have demonstrated a significant positive association between perceived job discretion and context-free anxiety after controlling for level of job demands. Several other instances of this form of statistical control have been cited.

Results generally support the belief that, over and above the impact of other measured variables, the three factors examined here are significant independent contributors to variations in mental health. However, multiple correlation procedures are not without their problems. For example, the recorded importance of a single variable in part depends on which other factors are included in the analysis. There are few guidelines for choosing a set of variables for inclusion, and the basis in many cases appears to have been opportunistic rather than conceptually justified.

Other problems include multicollinearity, when high intercorrelations between predictor variables may render unreliable an observed pattern of regression weights. A specific limitation of multiple regression analysis in tests of the vitamin model proposed here should also be noted. The model proposes that at low levels of an environmental feature there will be a positive association between environmental values and aspects of mental health; but at moderate to high levels that correlation is not expected. The observed regression weight of one particular feature, opportunity for control for instance, will thus differ according to its own average level, but also be determined by the average level of other environmental features in the analysis, since their correlation with mental health is thought to be dependent upon how low or high are their average values.

We should thus expect some variability in the results of multiple regression analyses in respect of a single environmental feature, depending upon other characteristics of the research setting. Statistically controlling the effect of other specific factors is essential in this research area, and confidence about the importance of individual features can be built up only through the conduct of a range of different enquiries. In general, this confidence increases in proportion to the number of other variables which have been accounted for in multiple regressions demonstrating a significant independent contribution of the focal variable on its own.

Similar arguments apply to longitudinal or quasi-experimental studies, where the impact of a single measured variable may be difficult to separate from the overlapping effects of other features. Problems of this kind confront investigators in any non-artificial environment, and reflect the natural interdependence of variables. As such the problems cannot be 'solved' in any fundamental sense; they must be minimized through careful and cumulative inquiry.

Reciprocal causality

Finally, let us turn to the fourth issue of interpretation raised earlier: what can be said about the direction of causation in the research examined in this and the previous chapter? Although most studies have been cross-sectional, there is enough longitudinal and quasi-experimental evidence to support the conclusion that the three features of the occupational environment considered here do themselves influence aspects of employees' mental health. In addition, however, a person's mental health may also influence the kind of job into which he or she moves, the content of that job, and the way it is perceived.

Let us first consider the third of those effects, in terms of subjective measurement of environmental features. We have seen that job characteristics are often assessed through job-holders' perceptions, and that certain subjective assessments are significantly associated with affective well-being. These associations have been interpreted above as reflecting a causal impact of perceptions (and hence, it is assumed, the environment) upon affective responses. However, we should also bear in mind that the latter may themselves influence perceptions.

This point was addressed by James and Tetrick (1986) in a two-stage least-squares analysis of job perceptions and job satisfaction. Through comparisons between several alternative causal models, they concluded that perceptions and satisfaction influenced each other reciprocally rather than unidirectionally. Furthermore, their evidence suggested that, within this reciprocal relationship, job satisfaction tended to occur after job perceptions, rather than the process being initiated in the reverse sequence.

Over and above this intra-personal issue, a reciprocal pattern is inherent in more substantive terms within the 'enabling' nature of the present 'situation-centred' model. This has been a central concern in Kohn and Schooler's ten-year study of American men, and their conclusion is worth quoting:

We now have strong evidence that job conditions actually do affect personality, and also that personality affects job conditions. . . . Jobs that facilitate occupational self-direction increase men's ideational flexibility and promote a self-directed orientation to self and to society; jobs that limit occupational self-direction decrease men's ideational flexibility and promote a conformist orientation to self and to society. . . . The longitudinal analysis also provides evidence of other job-to-personality effects, the most important being that oppressive work conditions produce a sense of distress. Implicit in all these findings is the consistent implication that the principal process by which a job affects personality is one of straightforward generalization from the lessons of the job to life off the job. . . .

The longitudinal analysis demonstrates also that, over time, personality has important consequences for the individual's place in the job structure. Both ideational flexibility and a self-directed orientation lead, in time, to more responsible jobs that allow greater latitude for occupational self-direction. Feelings of distress lead to actual or perceived time pressure and uncertainty. . . . Over a long enough time, many men either modify their jobs or move to other jobs more consonant with their personalities. Thus the long-term effects of personality on job conditions are considerable. The process of job affecting man and man affecting job is truly reciprocal throughout adult life (Kohn and Schooler 1982, pp. 1281–2).

Summary

This chapter has provided an opportunity to reflect upon the findings presented in Chapter 5, and also to introduce some general issues which bear upon the vitamin model and its empirical investigation. These general issues will be taken up again later in the book.

The first section noted that many researchers have taken measures of job content which combine opportunity for control, opportunity for skill use, and variety. These were described as measures of 'job complexity', and cross-sectional and longitudinal studies were cited which indicate that level of complexity significantly affects several forms of mental health.

A summary assessment of current evidence in relation to job complexity and the three constituent elements examined in the previous chapter was presented in Table 6.1. Causal influences were widely demonstrated, but it was argued that we should look for differentiated patterns and processes of association between separate job features and individual aspects of mental health.

Other general issues were considered in the final section. It was shown that observed relationships between job content and mental health remain significant when job attributes are measured through assessments made by independent observers, rather than through self-reports from workers themselves. The non-linear assumption of the vitamin model was indicated to remain in need of empirical support; and the possibility of different patterns of relationships for job-related and for context-free mental health was raised. Multiple regression procedures to assist in the identification of specific causal agents were considered next, and, despite their undoubted value, some difficulties in their use were outlined. Finally, it was emphasized that observed associations between job features and mental health were likely to reflect cyclical processes across time: jobs affect people's mental health, and mental health affects the jobs which people enter and those in which they stay.

Goals, workload, and the structure of tasks

This chapter examines research into the third environmental feature introduced in Chapter 1: externally generated goals. It was pointed out in that chapter that goals arise from the environment partly through physical deficits (the absence of food but its known presence elsewhere, for example), but primarily through obligations deriving from institutional roles. The latter (including roles in paid employment) carry with them requirements to behave in certain ways and to follow certain routines within specified times

Like all goals, those within jobs can of course vary in the degree to which they are attractive. They have also been examined in respect of their diversity, clarity, difficulty, and number. The first of these has been discussed in Chapter 5, where research into variety was summarized. Goal clarity (the degree to which requirements are explicit and definite) will be considered in Chapter 8, where several other aspects of environmental clarity will also be discussed. Goal difficulty has sometimes been investigated under the heading of 'qualitative workload', with the number of goals which have to be met in a limited time being referred to as 'quantitative workload'. These two features, difficulty and number of goals, form the principal subject-matter of the present chapter. Although they are conceptually distinct, in practice they tend to be positively intercorrelated, and a single index, sometimes described as being of 'job demands', is often taken.

The vitamin AD model introduced in Chapter 1 proposes that demands which are either low or very high will have negative effects upon mental health, but that level of workload will be unrelated to mental health in the broad middle range. These possibilities will be explored in the first part of the chapter. The second section will examine possible interactions between job demands and a worker's power to control his or her task activities. This latter feature was one of the job characteristics shown in Chapter 5 to influence mental health; opportunity for control will here be examined as a possible mediator of the impact of high workload. An additional characteristic will then be introduced. Goals also vary in the extent to which they give rise to a coherent structure of activities, with clear task identity and a smooth rhythm of goal-oriented activity. The concepts of 'traction' and 'flow' will be described at that point.

Individual research studies have typically focused upon only one pole of the workload continuum, with few comprehensive attempts to map out the impact of all possible levels of job demand. It will be helpful initially to follow that convention, examining separately research into low and high workload. In the latter case a distinction will be made between intrinsic and extrinsic high demands. As previously, the former are viewed as arising from the content of a job itself, whereas extrinsic demands derive from the context in which paid work is set. The latter demands are mainly due to the need to cope with job requirements in the context of those from domestic and leisure life; such cumulative time demands from home and employment and the time requirements of shiftwork will be considered in the final section.

Throughout the chapter the terms 'workload', 'goals', and 'demands' will be used as interconnected in meaning. 'Workload' is the amount and/or difficulty of work required to achieve goals. Goals themselves vary in the degree to which they are voluntary or imposed, but commitment to an overarching goal (to work in a particular job, for instance) itself entails other more specific goals, some of which are experienced as relatively unavoidable 'demands'. 'Demands' are thus viewed as a sub-set of 'goals', both of which give rise to 'workload'.

Extremes of workload are sometimes described as 'underload' or 'overload', indicating through the label that demands are considered by an employee or an observer to be excessively low or excessively high. That may be appropriate when a harmful departure from an acceptable level is clearly present. However, the terms should be used cautiously. Having both environmental and individual reference, they mix descriptive information about environmental demand with evaluative assertions about the undesirability of that demand.

Intrinsic job demands

An extreme example of low environmental demand was studied during the 1950s in laboratory investigations of 'sensory deprivation'. Subjects who were required to spend their time lying unoccupied in a soundproof room soon developed hallucinations, delusions, and anxiety symptoms. Perceptual and cognitive functions rapidly became impaired. Less extreme forms of low workload have been found in laboratory research to give rise to physiological changes (for instance, in adrenal hormone secretion and in cortical activity) as well as to psychological and motivational impairment (e.g. Frankenhaeuser and Johansson 1981).

Studies of people in paid employment have approached low task demands in several ways. Research into limited diversity was examined in Chapter 5 in terms of low variety, and studies of low overall complexity summarized in Chapter 6 may also be viewed as covering jobs with goals of limited difficulty. Research in a different tradition, examining the effects of goal-setting on work performance, has shown that relatively difficult tasks lead to higher performance than those in which goals are easy or indeterminate (e.g. Campbell 1982; Locke *et al.* 1981). This feature was studied many years ago by Lewin *et al.* (1944), who examined success and expected success in moderately difficult situations of practical problem-solving or sensori-motor skill. A recurrent theme was that success at a task leads to raised aspiration level, where that is defined in terms of how high to set the goal on the next attempt. This fact is usually interpreted in terms of a tendency to set higher and higher goals until success becomes uncertain: in general, people like to undertake moderately difficult tasks, and, since practice makes these easier through the enhancement of skill, aspirations tend to increase with increases in skill.

Kohn and Schooler's investigation into job content and psychological functioning in a sample of men was cited on several occasions in Chapters 5 and 6. An important outcome of that study was the observed value of moderate job demands:

Our findings emphasize the psychological importance of the structural imperatives of the job—those aspects of the job that impinge upon a man most directly, insistently, and demandingly.... Men thrive in meeting occupational challenges.... A man's job affects his perceptions, values and thinking processes primarily because it confronts him with demands he must try to meet (Kohn and Schooler 1983, p. 81).

Aspects of low intrinsic demand may be summarized through the comment of a factory worker that 'in the industry in which I work the worker's role is becoming more and more that of an onlooker and less that of a participant' (Fraser 1968, p. 16). This movement of workers from 'participant' to 'onlooker' appears to be continuing in many sectors of manufacturing and process industry.

For other workers, the problems are quite different. Consider the demands in this textile worker's job:

Watching the cones, checking the fabric, attending the machines which constantly break down, you're on the go all the time. If a machine stops, it must be started, and when it is going the cones are running out and have to be replaced. Hour after hour without break, from one machine to another and back, putting up ends, changing cones, starting the machines and trying to watch the fabric.... Usually an operative has three machines with a total of 150 cones, many of which you can't see immediately because they're on the other side of the machines; you have to memorize which cones are going to run out. With bad yarn the machines snag constantly; it's gruelling keeping everything running (Fraser 1969, pp. 88–9).

Having too much work to do in a limited time is by definition (as 'too' much) liable to have negative psychological consequences. Despite the existence of an overall tautological relationship of that kind, interesting empirical questions about high workload remain to be investigated. For example, how strong are the associations between different types of job demands and particular aspects of mental health? Which aspects of mental health are most responsive to reductions in work overload? What processes enable people to cope with continuing high levels of demand? Unfortunately, differentiated issues of this kind have rarely been studied, and research in the area has largely been restricted to rather simple examination of overall statistical patterns. Indices of workload have been used which often combine goal number and difficulty, and measures of mental health are typically chosen without a clear theoretical rationale. Furthermore, almost all investigations have been cross-sectional, correlating workload and mental health at one point in time.

Studies will be reviewed in respect of the principal features of mental health outlined in Chapter 2. First, however, what is known about the prevalence of overload? In Quinn and Staines's (1979) survey of the American employed population, 13 per cent strongly agreed and a further 30 per cent agreed that 'I never seem to have enough time to get everything done in my job'. An earlier American study revealed that 45 per cent of male employees indicated being disturbed that they had too heavy a workload, one that they could not possibly finish during an ordinary working day (Kahn *et al.* 1964, p. 59). Research into occupational stress among managerial and professional workers has consistently identified heavy workload, severe time pressures, and tight deadlines as primary stressors (e.g. Cooper and Davidson 1982; Fimian 1984; Kiev and Kohn 1979; Kyriacou and Sutcliffe 1978). Overload appears less likely to be cited as a source of stress among blue-collar workers in general, although, as the quotation at the beginning of this section illustrates, demands in particular jobs can undoubtedly be considerable. Twenty-four per cent of blue-collar factory workers in 16 American industries reported that their job made them 'work too fast most of the time' (Blauner 1964).

Job-related mental health

In respect of the first dimension of job-related affective well-being (from discontented to contented), several investigators have reported significant associations between high demand and low job satisfaction. For example, in a study of American managers, Buck (1972, p. 159) obtained correlations of self-reported job demands with satisfaction items whose median was -0.34; in a similar sample the correlation was found to be -0.30 (Berger-Gross and Kraut 1984). Research with American school-teachers has yielded coefficients of -0.24 (Cooke and Rousseau, 1984) and -0.34 (Sutton 1984), and significant associations of high demands with low satisfaction have been retained after statistically controlling for other variables in analyses by Karasek (1979), Kohn and Schooler (1973), O'Brien (1982b) and others. Caplan *et al.* (1975) obtained information about dissatisfaction with workload, recording a correlation of 0.35 between this index and a measure of perceived quantitative workload among American employees in 23 jobs. However, the association with overall job satisfaction was almost zero, as it was in a second study using the same measures (Gavin and Axelrod 1977). Mean job satisfaction scores for each of the 23 jobs were examined by Shaw and Riskind (1983), in relation to job analysis assessments of task demands in other, similar jobs. The correlation between this independent measure of demands and low job satisfaction was found to average 0.61 (calculated from their Table 2).

Associations between high workload and the second dimension of job-related affective well-being (anxious–comfortable) are less often reported. However, in their study of 'mental strain at work' among Swedish white-collar workers, Nerell and Wahlund (1981) recorded more frequent job strain in situations of high load. In a study of British 32-year-olds Cherry (1984a, b) measured a single aspect of workload, the number of people supervised. Supervisory responsibility was found to be strongly linked to experienced strain at work. For example, 67 per cent of men supervising eight or more people reported 'some' or 'severe' work strain, compared with only 29 per cent of those with no supervisory responsibility; this pattern was found in both manual (53 per cent and 20 per cent) and in non-manual male workers (71 per cent and 46 per cent), and also among full-time women workers (77 per cent and 35 per cent; separate figures for manual and non-manual female employees were not cited). Qualitative workload in nursing was studied by Vredenburgh and Trinkaus (1983), who recorded in an American sample a significant positive association between complexity of patient conditions and job-related tension. However, in the study of 23 different American jobs (not including nurses) described by Caplan *et al.* (1975) neither quantitative workload nor responsibility for persons was linearly correlated with job-related anxiety.

Job-related depression (the third dimension of affective well-being in employment settings) was also unrelated to workload in the investigation by Caplan and colleagues; one possibility is that the jobs studied ranged from underload through acceptable demands to conditions of overload, so that a significant linear correlation would not be expected. Kauppinen-Toropainen *et al.* (1983) measured job-related exhaustion in a sample which was representative of the working population of Finland, finding significant correlations between exhaustion and time pressures at work. Using other measures of high workload with American samples, Maslach and Jackson (1981, 1984) also reported significant associations with job-related exhaustion.

Context-free mental health

Of greater interest than studies merely linking job pressure with negative job feelings are investigations into context-free affective well-being, not restricted to the job setting. Several researchers have found significant negative associations between workload and scores on the first dimension (discontented–contented). These have been recorded for life satisfaction by Cooke and Rousseau (1984) and Sutton (1984), for general distress by Fimian (1984), and for broad measures of affective well-being by Buck (1972) and Martin (1984); the last-named also recorded a significant association with high levels of somatic symptoms such as upset stomach and sleep difficulties. House *et al.* (1979) observed significantly more neurotic symptoms among employees with high workload than among their colleagues with lower workload. Fraser (1947) described psychiatric interviews with more than 3000 British engineering workers below the rank of foreman, aiming to identify factors associated with diagnosed neurosis. Jobs demanding high levels of concentration (requiring visual attention and preventing conversation for over 50 per cent of the operation cycle) were found to be associated with a higher incidence of recent minor neurosis, defined as covering states of anxiety, depression, obsessionality, and hysteria.

High job demands have also been found to be significantly correlated with raised levels of context-free anxiety (e.g. Billings and Moos 1982; Caplan and Jones 1975; Kohn and Schooler 1973; LaRocco *et al.* 1980; Payne and Fletcher 1983; Sorensen *et al.* 1985). Parallel results have been obtained for measures of context-free exhaustion (Etzion 1984; Pines *et al.* 1981) and depression (Billings and Moos 1982; Caplan and Jones 1975; Karasek 1979; Payne and Fletcher 1983). (In practice, Karasek's measure, although labelled as 'depression', also covered aspects of anxiety and nervousness.) Caplan and Jones's study differed from the others in that data were gathered on two separate occasions, the first of greater workload than the second. Context-free anxiety and depression both declined significantly between measurement occasions. Changes in individual persons' reported quantitative workload were significantly correlated with changes in anxiety between occasions; however, the correlation between changes in reported workload and changes in depression was not significant.

Conway *et al.* (1981) measured reported workload on 14 different days, examining within-person correlations between a day's workload and cigarette smoking and coffee drinking; significant positive covariation with workload was recorded for both behaviours. Eden (1982) also adopted a longitudinal design, measuring a range of variables on five occasions over a six-month period. Student nurses were studied before and after two 'critical job events', their first episode of comprehensive patient care and their final examination. Both events were associated with significant increases and subsequent decreases in anxiety, systolic blood pressure, and pulse rate. In addition, the final examination (which was perceived by the nurses as the more stressful event) was associated with significant increases and subsequent decreases in depression, psychosomatic complaints, and diastolic blood pressure; self-esteem was negatively affected in the same way.

Other research has examined catecholamine excretion from the adrenal medulla as a function of workload. For example, Frankenhaeuser and Johansson (1976) observed that raised task demands in a laboratory experiment were accompanied by a significant increase in the production of adrenaline, but not of noradrenaline. In job settings, groups with higher workload have also been found to excrete significantly more adrenaline, but differences in nonadrenaline are less often found (Frankenhaeuser 1981; Johansson and Aronsson 1984; Johansson *et al.* 1978). These studies have also shown that hormonal responses to high task demands may extend into subsequent time periods (evenings after a daytime job, for example), in that many employees require an extended duration to 'unwind'. Nevertheless, it is not known whether increased adrenaline excretion, even over long periods, has a significant harmful effect on health (e.g. Krantz and Manuck 1984).

Reynolds *et al.* (1981) described a community investigation of male employees' adrenaline and noradrenaline excretion in relation to several characteristics of work and lifestyle. They observed that men describing their jobs on the day of measurement as stressful, under frequent time pressure, or mentally tiring had significantly raised adrenaline levels. Those whose workday was described as boring or physically tiring exhibited significantly lower rates of adrenaline excretion. A similar pattern, but less marked, was found for noradrenaline. Among female respondents the associations were generally less strong (Harrison *et al.* 1981).

Payne and Rick (1985) studied cortisol levels (reflecting excretion from the adrenal cortex) in heart surgeons and anaesthetists, finding both groups to be significantly above normal levels. Furthermore, the surgeons exhibited significantly higher values than the anaesthetists, consistent with their greater workload. Following changes in allocations of responsibility within the team of surgeons, it was found that cortisol excretion increased significantly for two staff promoted to positions of greater responsibility. Conversely, cortisol level declined for the senior consultant, whose duties had become more shared with the others at the time of the second measurement.

More direct indices of ill-health have also been examined in relation to level of workload. Chronically high job demands have been found to be significantly associated with somatic symptoms (Cooke and Rousseau 1984; Payne and Fletcher 1983; van Dijkhuizen 1980, 1981), hypertension (House *et al.* 1979; Weyer and Hodapp 1979), gastric complaints and nervous trouble (Nerell and Wahlund 1981), headaches and slight nervous disturbances (Johansson *et al.* 1978), physical and mental ill-health (Sutton 1984), and increased consumption of tranquillizers and sleeping tablets (Karasek 1979). Having to undertake complex and responsible tasks was found by Johansson and Aronsson (1984) to be significantly associated with gastric complaints among Swedish white-collar workers. Cobb and Rose (1973) examined the health of American air traffic controllers in centres of high and low traffic density. Greater workload was associated with a significantly higher probability of peptic ulcers and hypertension.

Coronary heart disease has also been found to be more prevalent among high workload employees. In a Swedish national survey, Karasek *et al.* (1981) used a self-report index of signs and symptoms of this form of illness, finding a significant cross-sectional association with high job demands. Furthermore, reported level of job demands was significantly predictive of the incidence of signs and symptoms of coronary heart disease in the subsequent six years, after controlling statistically for age, weight, smoking, education, and amount of control over one's job. A smaller case-control comparison by the same authors revealed that high job demands were also significantly associated with increased probability of death from cardiovascular illness.

Physiological processes linking overload strain to heart disease might include repeated increases in serum lipids such as cholesterol, raised blood pressure, acceleration of damage to coronary arteries, increased coagulability of blood, and induction of cardiac arrhythmias (e.g. Glass 1981; Karasek *et al.* 1982). Nevertheless, understanding of the physiological mechanisms underlying cardiac functioning is far from complete (e.g. Krantz and Manuck 1984), and evidence about the impact of job overload on heart disease is not entirely consistent. For instance, Alfredsson *et al.* (1982) failed to find an association of deaths from myocardial infarction with reports of hectic work. However, they did observe a significant effect of high work demands in conjunction with low personal control; this combinatorial possibility will be examined later in the chapter.

Research into some interpersonal correlates of quantitative workload has been reported by Burke *et al.* (1980). These authors obtained data from 85 Canadian administrators and also from their wives. Aspects of wives' affective well-being were examined in relation to husbands' reported workload. Husbands' high quantitative workload was found to be significantly associated with wives' low marital satisfaction and with low scores on an overall index of wives' affective well-being. High workload was also significantly correlated with wives reporting that their husbands' jobs were adversely affecting their home life. However, the correlation with wives' self-esteem was non-significant.

Conflicting demands

Finally, research into demands which conflict with each other should be examined in this section. Kahn *et al.* (1964) investigated the psychological and organizational correlates of role conflict, which they defined as 'the simultaneous occurrence of two (or more) sets of pressures such that compliance with one would make more difficult compliance with the other' (p. 19). They noted that in some cases role conflict is the same as overload, when the multiple demands upon a person cannot be met in the time available, and also drew attention to three specific types of conflict.

First is 'inter-sender' conflict, when incompatible pressures arise from two or more different people. Second, 'intra-sender' conflict occurs when the same person makes demands which are mutually contradictory. And, third, 'person-role' conflict is present when the requirements of a person's role violate his or her moral values or personal preferences.

Kahn and colleagues set out to measure inter-sender conflict in a study of American managers and supervisors. Each of these ('focal persons') identified a number of 'role senders', the people with whom they mainly interacted at work. Role senders were independently interviewed to obtain their views about desirable changes in the focal person's behaviour, and an overall index of change desired by others was taken as a measure of inter-sender conflict. It was found that higher levels of conflict measured in this way were significantly associated with greater job-related tension and job dissatisfaction in the focal person. The investigators point out that behavioural responses to conflict include withdrawal from or avoidance of those seen to be exerting pressure for change.

Despite the strong attraction of this study's separate measurement of focal persons' affective well-being and pressure from role senders, it should be noted that the procedure adopted does not necessarily assess conflict between senders (Warr and Wall 1975). It could happen that all role senders indicated that the focal person should change in the same direction; the measure would then be of consistent demands rather than of conflict between demands.

Other studies of role conflict have usually been restricted to self-reports of both perceived conflict and affective well-being obtained from the same person. Most investigators have employed the eight-item index of role conflict presented by Rizzo *et al.* (1970). This covers inter-sender conflict through items of the kind: 'I receive incompatible requests from two or more people'; 'I do things that are apt to be accepted by one person and not accepted by others'. Person–role conflict is tapped through these items: 'I work on unnecessary things'; 'I have to do things that should be done differently'. (See House *et al.* (1983) for a revision of this scale.)

Correlates of role conflict measured in this way or through the self-report scale of inter-sender conflict described by Caplan *et al.* (1975) include the following: job dissatisfaction (e.g. Brief and Aldag 1976; Caplan *et al.* 1975; House and Rizzo 1972; Miles 1975; Schuler *et al.* 1977), job-related anxiety and tension (e.g. Brief and Aldag 1976; Caplan *et al.* 1975; House and Rizzo 1972; Miles 1975; Parker and DeCotiis 1983), fatigue (House and Rizzo 1972), job-related depression (Caplan *et al.* 1975), neurotic symptoms (House *et al.* 1979), somatic complaints (e.g. Caplan *et al.* 1975; House and Rizzo 1972; Nicholson 1976), and hypertension (House *et al.* 1979). Fisher and Gitelson (1983) have reviewed data from 59 different samples, among which the mean correlations of perceived role conflict with job dissatisfaction, job-related tension, and low job involvement were 0.35, 0.28, and 0.15 respectively. In a later but overlapping review, Jackson and Schuler (1985) included corrections for restriction of range and unreliability of measurement. Corrected mean correlations with job dissatisfaction, job-related tension and low job involvement were 0.48, 0.43, and 0.26 respectively.

There is thus considerable evidence that self-reported role conflict in a job is associated with lower affective well-being, both job-related and context-free.

Information about other components of mental health appears to be lacking, although behavioural and subjective consequences of raised anxiety levels associated with chronic conflict may be anticipated. We should note, however, that the study by Burke *et al.* (1980) of husbands' job conditions and wives' mental health, described earlier in this section, recorded no significant correlates of role conflict in the reports obtained from employees' wives.

Berger-Gross and Kraut (1984) examined one specific form of conflict, disagreement between managers and their immediate superiors. Three types of information were obtained: managers' own views, their perceptions of views held by their superior, and the latter persons' views. This allowed investigation of the correlates of both 'subjective disagreement' (conflict between managers' own views and what they perceived to be their superiors' views) and 'objective disagreement' (conflict between views as expressed independently by the two people). In general, subjective disagreement was more strongly associated with outcome measures than was objective disagreement, but Berger-Gross and Kraut suggest that neither form of conflict is itself central to the observed effects.

Conflict was measured directly in terms of the difference between one's own view and an index of others' views. Difference scores of all kinds are naturally subject to the influence of each component score on its own; and the use of difference values rather than the values of separate components is potentially misleading and inaccurate, in that main effects of components rather than differences between components are often of primary importance (Cronbach and Furby 1970; Wall and Payne 1973). Berger-Gross and Kraut therefore examined the correlates of individual persons' views as well as indices of disagreement ('conflict') between those views. They found that it was managers' perception of their superiors' views which was independently predictive of job satisfaction scores; difference-score indices of conflict of the traditional kind were not significantly predictive in these analyses.

This finding reflects the interpretation offered earlier of the study by Kahn *et al.* (1964). It may be that demands from particular others are the primary direct source of experiences which have often been said to arise indirectly from inter-sender conflict. That this form of role conflict exists in some circumstances cannot be doubted, but investigators' reliance on an aggregate measure of perceived conflicts of varying and rather unspecific kinds has hampered research progress (see also Dougherty and Pritchard 1985). There is need now to focus on more specific demands and the ways in which they combine together or contradict each other.

Overview

In overall review of this section, it is clear that high job demands are consistently associated with certain forms of low affective well-being. The association of job 'overload' with low job-related affective well-being may be viewed as tautological, but findings in respect of context-free measures and indicators of physical ill-health suggest extensive spill-over effects into other domains. However, most studies have been correlational at one point in time, so that causal interpretation requires care. It is also unclear from research to date at what degree of load the demands of a job become harmful. As argued earlier, goals of some moderate difficulty are desirable for both extrinsic and intrinsic reasons, and overload for short periods is often unavoidable. It would thus be wrong to infer from the results described here that high workload always impairs mental health.

This caution brings us back to the need to study relations between the environment and mental health in terms other than the linear correlations which are so often cited. A step in this direction was made by Karasek (1979). In the American survey described earlier (see page 84), he examined four levels of job demand. Results indicated that both job dissatisfaction and life dissatisfaction (representing the first dimension of well-being in Fig. 3.1) tended to be curvilinearly associated with workload. The percentages of each sub-sample identified as dissatisfied with their job were 24, 17, 22, and 28 from very low to very high job demands. For dissatisfaction with life the corresponding values were 9, 5, 6, and 11. However, for measures of exhaustion and depression (covering the third axis) the pattern was non-linear but not curvilinear: 10 per cent, 13 per cent, 12 per cent, and 26 per cent for exhaustion, and 22 per cent, 30 per cent, 20 per cent, and 34 per cent for depression.

A strong negative impact of very high workload in conjunction with relative constancy at moderate values was also recorded by van Dikjhuizen (1980), in a study of Dutch manual, managerial, and professional employees. For example, the mean score on an index of job-related psychosomatic complaints for the sub-sample with highest workload was found to be 1.44; for three groups with progressively lower job demands the values were 1.26, 1.25, and 1.25 respectively. A similar non-linear pattern, with unusually poor health among employees with particularly high workload, was observed for self-reported symptoms of cardiac disorder and also for job-related anxiety and depression. Recognizing that these outcome measures are to some extent overlapping, the several findings may be taken as support for the right-hand section of the vitamin AD model introduced in Fig. 1.1 (page 10): a plateau of affective well-being is observed across moderate levels of goal demand, with an additional decrement (high scores on these negative indices) occurring at very high levels. Unfortunately, van Dijkhuizen's sample contained no jobs recorded as imposing very low demands, so that his findings contain no information relevant to the left-hand section of Fig. 1.1.

Finally, comment should be made about the limited range of components of mental health investigated in this area of research. Almost without exception studies have examined affective well-being. Previous chapters have drawn attention to the importance also of competence, autonomy, and aspiration. In so far as high workload causes depression or anxiety beyond the job setting, one may expect these other features to be influenced, but information about that possibility appears to be lacking.

The combined effects of workload and control

Despite the fact that high workload is associated with low affective well-being, some people experiencing very high demands also exhibit high levels of mental health. This raises the question: what factors might moderate the observed negative effects of high workload? Individual differences in motives and ability are undoubtedly important (see Chapters 13 and 14), but in addition several authors have argued for the central mediating influence of level of personal control. Opportunity for control was introduced in Chapter 1 as the primary environmental influence upon mental health, partly because higher control opportunities permit changes in other environmental features. Opportunity for control was itself shown in Chapter 5 to be a significant influence upon several aspects of job-related and context-free mental health; let us now consider its impact in conjunction with different levels of job demand.

The two variables were examined together by Karasek (1979), in secondary analyses of data previously collected from male workers in USA and in Sweden. (See also Chapter 5, page 84.) Table 7.1 presents data from the study which illustrate the association of different combinations of the two job features with two aspects of affective well-being.

The first part of the table contains results for job dissatisfaction. Regression analyses (using the full set of scores rather than the grouped values shown in the table) indicated that job demands and control were each significantly predictive of dissatisfaction, as were certain forms of statistical interaction between them. The lower part of the table contains results for depression. The two job features were individually found to be significant predictors of this form of affective well-being, but the interaction between them was not significant.

In both sets of data it is clear that lowest mental health occurs in the top right-hand cell, high job demands with low control. Karasek demonstrates that this is also the case for exhaustion and life satisfaction in the American sample, and that the American pattern for depression and exhaustion is replicated in the Swedish survey.

A second Swedish study by Karasek *et al.* (1981) (also of male workers) revealed a similar pattern for signs and symptoms of coronary heart disease. For example, 20 per cent of the sub-group reporting high job demands and low control were classified as exhibiting these signs and symptoms (the highest percentage in any cell), whereas no member of the low demands/high control sub-group was classified in that way. The authors also describe a

Table 7.1 Mental health as a function of workload and control; data for American male workers from Karasek (1979)

1. Percentage defined as dissatisfied with their job

	Job demands				
	Low	Medium-low	Medium-high	High	(All)
Control					
Low	41	26	43	55	(40)
Medium-low	22	20	13	27	(20)
Medium-high	9	11	24	24	(16)
High	19	11	14	14	(14)
(All)	(24)	(17)	(22)	(28)	(22)

2. Percentage defined as severely depressed

	Job demands				
	Low	Medium-low	Medium-high	High	(All)
Control					
Low	28	38	38	51	(37)
Medium-low	29	36	22	33	(31)
Medium-high	9	21	15	28	(18)
High	11	29	12	27	(22)
(All)	(22)	(30)	(20)	(34)	(27)

small case-control study of deaths from cardiovascular disease in the six years following the interview. Data about reported job characteristics from each of the 22 men who subsequently died from this type of disease were compared with material from three other men matched for age, tobacco smoking, education, and self-reported CHD symptoms at the time of interview. As noted in the previous section, level of job demands was significantly predictive of this form of mortality. Job discretion was itself not predictive of death, but the combined impact of high demands and low discretion was statistically significant.

A third study examined all cases of fatal and non-fatal myocardial infarction in men aged 40 to 64 in the Greater Stockholm area between 1974 and 1976 (Alfredsson *et al.* 1982; see page 97 for additional details). Although reports of 'hectic work' were themselves not significantly associated with this type of heart attack, reported hectic work in conjunction with low influence over work tempo was found to be significantly correlated. This relationship was particularly strong for men aged between 40 and 50, and was maintained despite the introduction of statistical controls for education, smoking, heavy lifting, and immigration from another country (Alfredsson and Theorell 1983).

These findings and the associated theorizing are of considerable importance. However, a number of operational and conceptual problems remain. For example, Karasek's (1979) measure is labelled 'job decision latitude', in keeping with his theoretical account of employees' control over the demands of their jobs. In practice, however, the index is made up of two sets of four items: one set covers skill level, variety and the need for learning and creativity, and the other deals more directly with job control. As noted in Chapter 5, the overall content of the scale is thus wider than its label suggests.

Furthermore, job decision latitude measured in this way is strongly correlated with occupational and educational levels. Since the affective well-being data examined by Karasek (1979) were from people in widely varying jobs, conclusions from that study might in fact reflect social class differences rather than job content features. This point was noted by Payne and Fletcher (1983), who studied a more homogeneous sample of British teachers. Although job demands and control both had independent effects upon affective well-being, as described previously, no evidence was found for the interactive influence of the two variables.

Indeed, the findings presented by Karasek (1979) do not always contain statistically significant interactions; neither do other data sometimes thought to support his model (e.g. Kauppinen-Toropainen *et al.* 1983). The nature of the possible combined influence thus deserves careful consideration. Karasek *et al.* (1981, pp. 694–5) 'propose a model which postulates that psychological strain, and subsequent physiological illness, result ... from the interaction of two types of job characteristics. Strain results from the joint effects of the demands of the work situation (stressors) and environmental moderators of stress, particularly the range of decision-making freedom (control) available to the worker facing those demands'. But what is the intended meaning of 'interaction' and 'joint effects'? The latter could be a simple additive or subtractive process, in which separate influences are combined with equal weight. In the case of two variables both associated with an outcome, an additive combination rule (including subtractions as the addition of a negative value) would itself generate a pattern broadly as illustrated in Table 7.1, with highest values in the top right-hand corner. An additive model of that kind is supported by data from all the studies cited here.

However, the initial account (Karasek 1979) was in terms of a non-additive interaction, where the two factors were predicted to combine synergistically:

compounds of very high demands and very low control were expected to be significantly more influential than would be predicted from an unweighted addition of the two values themselves. Karasek (1979) points out that conventional analyses of variance and tests of multiplicative interaction do not yield significant findings in his data, and he examines the value of several less conventional tests. These exhibit significant interactions in only a proportion of cases, and a simple subtraction (job demands minus discretion) is suggested as an adequate approximation (see also Karasek *et al.* 1982).

Analysis and interpretation are complicated by the fact that both job features are themselves non-linearly associated with affective well-being. This gives rise to secondary peaks, for example in the bottom left-hand cell of the job dissatisfaction section of Table 7.1 (low demands coupled with high control). It thus remains unclear whether the combined effect of demands and control on affective well-being is additive or synergistic. Karasek's model appears to predict the latter, but no direct confirmation of a synergistic interaction has been published. In examining the complexity of this issue, Karasek *et al.* (1982) conclude that the exact mathematical formulation of the combined effect has yet to be determined.

Cohen (1980) has reviewed parallel laboratory research in which stressors are examined in conjunction with different levels of personal control. He shows that stressors such as noise have effects on cognitive performance which continue after removal of the stressor, but that these after-effects are typically absent when a subject feels he or she has control over the presence or level of the stressor, even when that control is not in fact exercised. However, as in the case of organizational research, Cohen concludes that a synergistic interaction between stress and control has not yet been unequivocally demonstrated.

It may be preferable to set aside the search for a universally valid pattern of interaction, and to recognize that the form of the combined influence may vary as a function of the outcome variable under investigation. For instance, there may be different modes of combination in respect of job satisfaction, context-free anxiety, subjective competence, and risk of cardiac disorder.

Associated with this differentiated possibility, a major question remains: what is the nature of the process through which workload and control are thought to have their combined effects? Two broad possibilities may be suggested, a compensatory reaction and a process of mutual influence. In the latter case, a worker might use high control in several ways to ward off the effects of very high workload. For example, he or she might use the permitted discretion actively to reduce the level of demands, to take time off from the demands, to create defences against them, to extend deadlines, or to recruit support of various forms.

On the other hand, the relationship may be entirely without direct influence between the variables. Workers with very high workload and also high opportunity for control may benefit from the latter, merely as a factor which is independently attractive and in effect cancels out but does not reduce the detrimental effects of high workload. It seems likely that both types of relationship may occur, sometimes together, and a requirement now is for more careful investigation and conceptualization of the processes of interaction in practical rather than statistical terms.

Note, incidentally, that the possibility of a compensatory process raises difficulties for research into the combination of opportunity for control with other job features. It must be assumed that, at the point of measurement, control has already been exercised to reduce, say, job demands as far as an employee considers practicable or desirable. Measured demands under conditions of high control may thus be lower than they 'truly' are, before a compensatory influence of personal control has been exercised.

For the present, it may be concluded that the two features of job demands and employee control do combine to influence affective well-being, at least in an additive or subtractive fashion. However, the specific nature of the combination and the processes giving rise to it have not yet been fully determined. It seems possible that the combinations which are observed will vary according to which component of mental health is being measured, but this possibility has not yet been examined in detail.

The issues raised in this section are important beyond the specific combination of two variables which has been discussed. The model introduced in Chapter 1 proposed that nine environmental features were determinants of mental health, and that the association between each one and health outcomes was non-linear. What does the model say about the way in which these postulated non-linear influences combine with each other? It is in this area that all comprehensive theories are at their weakest, since the conceptual and statistical difficulties of dealing with huge numbers of potential combinations have so far proved impossible to handle.

A general statement of interaction processes for each combination of environmental features would thus be overambitious and unsatisfactory. However, it is important to generalize beyond the particular combination studied by Karasek and colleagues. A descriptive account of the impact upon one component of mental health of possible combinations of two job characteristics, each with the same non-linear individual pattern, is presented in Table 7.2. This merely sets out the implications of specific values attached to each factor, within the basic 'additional decrement' model presented visually in Fig. 1.1 (page 10).

The number of levels of each job characteristic has been arbitrarily set at 15, with numerical indices of each level's impact upon mental health ranging from -5 to +2 in keeping with the vitamin AD pattern proposed in Fig. 1.1. In combining the two features (identified as X and Y), the values of each have been given equal weighting. The table is identified as an 'idealized'

Table 7.2 An idealized description of the impact upon one component of mental health of possible combinations of two environmental features

	Feature X (e.g. job demands)														
Level:	1	2	3	4	5	6	7	8	9	10	11	12	13	14	15
Impact:	−5	−4	−3	−2	−1	0	+1	+2	+2	+2	+1	0	−1	−2	−3

Feature Y (e.g. opportunity for control)

1	−5	−10	−9	−8	−7	−6	−5	−4	−3	−3	−3	−4	−5	−6	−7	−8
2	−4	−9	−8	−7	−6	−5	−4	−3	−2	−2	−2	−3	−4	−5	−6	−7
3	−3	−8	−7	−6	−5	−4	−3	−2	−1	−1	−1	−2	−3	−4	−5	−6
4	−2	−7	−6	−5	−4	−3	−2	−1	0	0	0	−1	−2	−3	−4	−5
5	−1	−6	−5	−4	−3	−2	−1	0	+1	+1	+1	0	−1	−2	−3	−4
6	0	−5	−4	−3	−2	−1	0	+1	+2	+2	+2	+1	0	−1	−2	−3
7	+1	−4	−3	−2	−1	0	+1	+2	+3	+3	+3	+2	+1	0	−1	−2
8	+2	−3	−2	−1	0	+1	+2	+3	+4	+4	+4	+3	+2	+1	0	−1
9	+2	−3	−2	−1	0	+1	+2	+3	+4	+4	+4	+3	+2	+1	0	−1
10	+2	−3	−2	−1	0	+1	+2	+3	+4	+4	+4	+3	+2	+1	0	−1
11	+1	−4	−3	−2	−1	0	+1	+2	+3	+3	+3	+2	+1	0	−1	−2
12	0	−5	−4	−3	−2	−1	0	+1	+2	+2	+2	+1	0	−1	−2	−3
13	−1	−6	−5	−4	−3	−2	−1	0	+1	+1	+1	0	−1	−2	−3	−4
14	−2	−7	−6	−5	−4	−3	−2	−1	0	0	0	−1·	−2	−3	−4	−5
15	−3	−8	−7	−6	−5	−4	−3	−2	−1	−1	−1	−2	−3	−4	−5	−6

description, since not all combinations of values may occur in reality and since the cited values have no real meaning in practice.

Consider an example in respect of the features examined earlier in this section. Let Feature X be job demands and Feature Y be opportunity for control. Circumstances of very high demands and very low control might then be indicated by values of 15 on Feature X and 1 on Feature Y. These levels give rise to individual impacts on mental health of -3 and -5 respectively, with a summed impact of -8 (the top right-hand entry in the table). As control (Feature Y) increases, holding constant demands (Feature X) at a value of 15 (down the right-hand column), mental health values become relatively stable, before again becoming more negative at very high levels of control.

Such an account is of course entirely mechanical in respect of the assumptions made. On that basis no differential weighting has been permitted in Table 7.2. However, several more complex possibilities do of course exist. One might double the weight assigned to extremely negative environmental features (converting -5 and -4 to -10 and -8, for instance), yielding a synergistic combination of the kind initially proposed by Karasek. Alternatively, one might give greater weight to all values of a single feature, for example, doubling the weights attached to Feature Y throughout.

The actual decisions made within a framework such as this must ultimately depend upon detailed empirical evidence about appropriate weights. It seems very likely that these will differ between job features and between individual components of mental health, and no decisions are required here. A principal intention has been to demonstrate the very substantial limitations of currently orthodox research strategies. It is conventional merely to compute linear correlations and standard multiplicative interactions without regard for the level of each job variable and without examining possible non-linear associations. Such an approach cannot do justice to a model of the kind proposed in this book

Task identity, traction, and flow

Goals may also have an impact upon employee well-being through the nature of a task-goal structure. For example, work activities differ in the degree to which they form a coherent, organized whole. Some tasks are linked together in ways which tend to give rise to goal-attainment smoothly as a result of the structure of the activities themselves. This notion is central to the concept of a 'Gestalt' in perception and action. For example, Cooper (1973) has summarized studies suggesting that 'Gestalt tasks' are more resistant to interruption than are less organized tasks; the former 'have a relatively definite internal structure, a sort of symmetry, and a clearly defined ending which is more or less dictated by the earlier steps in the task' (p. 403).

This feature has been tapped in occupational research through measures of 'task identity'. Hackman and Oldham (1975, 1980) define that as 'the degree to which a job requires completion of a 'whole' and identifiable piece of work, that is, doing a job from beginning to end with a visible outcome'. A similar definition by Sims *et al.* (1976) is: 'the extent to which employees do an entire or whole piece of work and can clearly identify the results of their efforts'. Both definitions link task identity to feedback, which will be considered in Chapter 8, and in practice measures of the two constructs are positively intercorrelated.

Cross-sectional studies have regularly found that workers whose jobs have greater reported task identity exhibit higher general and intrinsic job satisfaction and greater intrinsic motivation (e.g. Hackman and Oldham 1975; Oldham and Rotchford 1983; Oldham *et al.* 1978). Loher and colleagues' (1985) meta-analysis of results from 28 studies yielded an average sample-weighted correlation with overall job satisfaction of 0.32, after correcting for unreliability in the measures.

In a study of American employees moving between jobs over an eighteen-month period, Bechtold *et al.* (1981) found that increases or decreases in task identity were accompanied by parallel changes in intrinsic job satisfaction. In a British study, Wall and Clegg (1981a) redesigned shop-floor jobs to increase group interdependence, particularly in respect of group task identity and group autonomy. Changes in these job characteristics were followed by significant increases in general job satisfaction and intrinsic work motivation, and also in context-free affective well-being assessed through the General

Health Questionnaire. Longitudinal research by Brousseau and Prince (1981) indicated that task identity in current job was significantly related to previous changes in personality scale across an average of seven years. For example, high current task identity was associated with significant increases in 'general activity' and 'emotional stability'.

These several types of evidence indicate that work with a coherent internal structure is psychologically desirable. Other investigators have approached this question by emphasizing the importance of rhythm in one's work, pointing out that smoothness of goal attainment can itself be pleasant, even in tasks which are repetitive and simple. Baldamus (1961) examined the 'relative satisfactions' obtained from even very monotonous work in British factories. He focused particularly upon 'traction' inherent in work tasks:

[Traction] is a feeling of being pulled along by the inertia inherent in a particular activity. The experience is pleasant and may therefore function as a relief from tedium. It usually appears to be associated ... with a feeling of reduced effort, relative to actual or imagined situations where it is difficult to maintain continuity of performance (p.59).

Baldamus saw traction as similar to the 'rhythm', 'swing', or 'pull' of work, and described several different forms. Primary among these was 'object traction' which is in practice equivalent to an overall wish for goal and sub-goal attainment. Four more specific types of traction were described as follows.

Batch traction: 'connected with a desire to complete a batch of articles .... The feeling of traction is stronger when the completion of the batch is approaching' (Baldamus 1961, p. 62).

Process traction: 'is experienced in operations where the tempo and sequence of the motions are determined by the chemical or physical nature of the production process ... There is usually a distinctly pleasant sensation in being guided or pulled along by the process in completing a given work cycle' (p. 63).

Machine traction: 'Operations on machines which are constantly running produce in the operator the feeling of being drawn along.... He [or she] feels inclined to keep going with repeated cycles while the machine is running' (p. 63).

Line traction: 'Modern methods of flow production are characterized by the same object passing through a series of operations which are carried out by different workers, with or without the help of a conveyor belt. Usually a strong movement of traction is inherent in such methods of production' (p. 63).

The thrust of Baldamus's treatment was that traction is only a 'relative satisfaction': 'feelings that arise as a relief from fundamentally disliked situations' (p. 64). He stressed that interruptions to the smooth flow of work take away that relative satisfaction by destroying the traction which is inherent in even very simple work.

Traction in jobs has rarely been investigated since the time of Baldamus's inquiries. However, two American reports are available. Turner and Miclette (1962) described motivational processes in a setting where workers appeared to be aware of the importance of traction within their repetitive jobs. Smith and Lem (1955) drew upon an earlier publication by Baldamus to investigate batch traction as a function of the size of a batch or 'lot'. They predicted that batch traction effects should 'be greatest when the lots are large enough to constitute an easily grasped psychological unit, and they should reduce as lots become so large that the worker has the end of a lot in sight for only a small percentage of the time. Reduction of very large lot sizes should, then, increase the effects of batch traction' (p. 330). This possibility was explored by varying lot sizes (for example, introducing lots requiring about 240, 48, and 24 minutes of work) and observing how often workers chose to pause during periods of work on each lot. Frequency of voluntary pauses was found to be greater among the larger lot sizes, providing some support for the traction hypothesis.

It seems appropriate to apply the concept of traction to work of many other kinds, in addition to the simple industrial jobs which Baldamus considered. For example, workers interacting with a computer through a keyboard and visual display unit develop their own work rhythm. In some jobs this rhythm is intermittently broken by a long computer processing time, and such pauses tend to be experienced as disturbing rather than as opportunities for relaxation (e.g. Johansson and Aronsson 1984). In general, we may conclude that the types of traction which Baldamus described are widely present as sources of satisfaction, and that interruption of the smooth flow of work in any job can itself generate dissatisfaction and tension.

A similar concept from a quite different domain can shed further light on this possibility. Csikszentmihalyi (1975) set out to examine the nature of play, and the intrinsic rewards associated with play activities. He studied rock climbers, chess players, music composers, dancers and basketball players, in order to analyse and interpret the experience of enjoyment. These enquiries led him to recognize the central importance of what he termed 'flow'.

In the flow state, action follows upon action according to an internal logic that seems to need no conscious intervention by the actor. He experiences it as a unified flowing from one moment to the next, in which he is in control of his actions, and in which there is little distinction between self and environment.... One may experience flow in any activity, even in some activities that seem least designed to give enjoyment— on the battlefront, on a factory assembly line, or in a concentration camp (Csikszentmihalyi 1975, p. 36).

Csikszentmihalyi argued that the flow experience is itself a goal; people are motivated to achieve this experience over and above any potential extrinsic rewards. He suggested six elements of flow.

First is the merging of action and awareness. By paying undivided attention to the task, one cannot reflect on the act of awareness itself. During a flow experience one cannot ask how well one is doing or why one is undertaking the task. 'When awareness becomes split, so that one perceives the activity from 'outside', flow is interrupted. Therefore, flow is difficult to maintain for any length of time without at least momentary interruptions' (p. 38). In terms used earlier in this chapter, flow requires a person to be a participant rather than an onlooker.

A second feature is the focusing of attention on a limited stimulus field. This arises primarily from the structure of the task, which defines a part of environment as salient and specifies a range of possible behaviours. However, personal involvement and restriction of attention may be increased for reasons both of intrinsic interest and of extrinsic reward. For example, rock climbing takes place in a very restricted setting, in which attention is sharpened by the possibility of accident: 'the remainder of the human repertoire is rendered irrelevant and irritant, and is screened out from this simplified, manageable stimulus field' (p. 81). 'Heightened concentration and enforcement of the attention boundaries is achieved through the addition of risk to the intellectually engaging aspects of the activity' (p. 82).

Associated with the first two features is a tendency towards self-forgetfulness, loss of self-consciousness, and a sense of fusion with the immediate environment; see also Privette (1983). These feelings arise in part from the fourth characteristic, which is particularly important in the present discussion. A person in flow is in control of his or her actions, feeling competent, and able to perform successfully. This comes about not because the activities are easy for the person, but because opportunities for action are perceived as being evenly matched to one's capabilities. 'A flow activity is one which provides optimal challenge in relation to the actor's skills' (p. 50). 'Flow in chess, as in other activities, depends on a very delicate balance between being in control and being overwhelmed. It is this tension that forces the player to attend to the game, with the resulting high pitch of concentration and involvement' (p. 64).

A balance between demands and control was central to Karasek's model of job strain introduced in the previous section. His discussion was at a more macroscopic level than Csikszentimihalyi's microscopic analysis of feelings of enjoyment. However, the parallels between the two approaches lend support in both directions. In addition, Csikszentimihalyi's account of this source of enjoyment in activities of all kinds provides an underpinning for those studies of skill utilization in jobs which were reviewed in Chapter 5.

A fifth quality of flow experience is that 'it usually contains coherent, noncontradictory demands for action, and provides clear, unambiguous feedback to a person's actions.... In the artificially reduced reality of a flow episode... goals and means are logically ordered' (p. 46). 'In other words, the flow experience differs from awareness in everyday reality because it contains ordered rules which make action and the evaluation of action automatic and hence unproblematic' (p. 47). This description is very similar to part of Baldamus's account of traction, despite the fact that the latter was analysing small deviations from predominantly negative experiences in simple industrial jobs.

A final characteristic of flow experience has already been mentioned: it appears to need no goals or rewards external to itself. Csikszentmihalyi quotes a rock-climber:

The justification of climbing is climbing, like the justification of poetry is writing. . . . The act of writing justifies poetry. Climbing is the same: recognizing that you are a flow. The purpose of the flow is to keep on flowing, not looking for a peak or utopia but staying in the flow. It is not a moving up but a continuous flowing; you move up only to keep the flow going (p. 47).

It is a far cry from rock climbing to almost any job, but this characterization of the process of flow is important in the present book for two reasons. First, it provides a detailed analysis of concepts which in organizational research have been presented in rather different terms. From theoretical bases which are respectively psychological and sociological have come the notions of intrinsic motivation and self-estranged alienation. Central to each of these are processes of the kind described by Csikszentmihalyi as flow. For example, 'non-alienated activity consists of immersion in the present; it is involvement. . . . In non-alienated activity the rewards are in the activity itself' (Blauner 1964, p. 27). Jobs which are described as intrinsically motivating or non-alienating may now be viewed as containing some or all of the six features described here.

Second, Csikszentmihalyi's style of research and interpretation draws attention to the complex interweaving of simultaneous interactions between person and environment. Such a dynamic perspective is important to balance the emphasis of much of the research reviewed elsewhere in the book, where a single environmental category is studied at a single time through predetermined forms of numerical measurement. Research of that kind sometimes presents an excessively mechanistic view of what is a fluid process of multiple and mutual influence. As pointed out in Chapter 1, it is essential to develop approaches which contribute to understanding at both 'categorical' and 'process' levels.

Time demands

In addition to the intrinsic job demands considered so far, we must also examine demands which are extrinsic, arising from the context in which a job is set. This has usually been done in terms of the time which people are required to devote to their paid work. Jobs defined as 'full-time' in contemporary Western society typically take up between 35 and 45 hours per week, with travelling to and from work requiring on average a further three to five hours. Part-time jobs vary considerably in their time requirement, from less than 10 hours per week to whatever number is defined as the lower limit of full-time work; in Britain at present that is often taken as 30 hours.

How do variations in time demands affect employees' mental health? It seems likely that number of hours of required employment is not itself associated with differences in mental health across a range of working times conventionally viewed as 'normal' (between 30 and 40 hours in a full-time job per week, for example), but that a requirement to work considerably more than that might in some circumstances be expected to impair health. However, detailed empirical evidence about that possibility is apparently not available.

The time demands of a job should be viewed in relation to other activities and obligations. Most frequently studied are family commitments, although we might also investigate non-family leisure activities in their competition for a person's time. Several forms of 'spill-over' between job and home were reviewed in Chapter 4, where the general point was made that job experiences are in several ways likely to colour well-being and relationships within the family. In this section we will examine the more restricted question: how do time demands from a job over and above those from one's family affect aspects of mental health? Among a representative sample of the American workforce, 34 per cent of employed husbands indicated that the demands of their job and family interfered with each other 'somewhat' or 'a lot' (Pleck *et al.* 1980; Quinn and Staines 1979). For employed wives the figure was almost the same, 37 per cent. In both cases number of job hours was significantly associated with reports of interference, and interference was most marked when the respondent had young dependent children. (See Keith and Schafer 1980, for a parallel result.)

High time demands from one's job were found to be significantly correlated with low job satisfaction and low life satisfaction (Pleck *et al.* 1980). Similar findings have been reported by Kopelman *et al.* (1983), Parry and Warr (1980), Sekaran (1985), and Sutton (1984). Significant associations have also been found with low job satisfaction by Cooke and Rousseau (1984) and Shamir (1983), with frequency of somatic symptoms by Cooke and Rousseau (1984) and Sutton (1984), with frequency of neurotic symptoms by House *et al.* (1979), and with low positive affect and high negative affect by Parry and Warr (1980).

Two forms of time demand will be considered separately in the remainder of this section. First, the *amount* of time at work will be examined (number of hours required, for example), and later we will turn to *pattern* of time (for instance, day-work, rotating shifts, or night-work).

Magnitude of time demands

Number of hours worked was investigated by Staines and Pleck (1983, 1984), who carried out further analysis of the American workforce data cited above.

They studied number of hours in relation to several measures of family activity and adjustment. It was found that a greater time in paid work was associated with less time devoted to child care and to housework, but no association was present between number of job hours and satisfaction with marriage and family life. However, Sorensen *et al.* (1985) reported that number of hours in paid work was significantly associated with context-free anxiety, for both men and women, after controlling for age, education, and marital status.

Long job hours can arise from paid overtime, in which case financial benefits may sometimes be thought to compensate for the time commitment. However, time demands can also take the form of non-paid intrusion into home life, when for example managers take work home in the evening. Firm evidence about the effects of this kind of additional load is lacking, but personal control is likely to be an important mediating factor. If a manager feels that he or she has no option but to undertake these extra tasks in order to cope with high job demands, then their negative effect may be greater than when the work at home is voluntarily initiated, possibly as a source of pleasure.

Managers may also be subject to time overload in respect of business travel, during the week or for longer periods. For example, Renshaw's (1976) interviews with American managers and their wives revealed negative consequences of business travel on the family, which included disconnected relationships, quantitative and qualitative overload for both parties, and guilt feelings in the husband for the strain experienced by his wife (see also Evans and Bartolome 1980). Within the husband's organization, problems arose from disrupted communications, backlogs of work, and increased fatigue. Time demands also occur in respect of business entertainment during evenings and weekends. Such demands, from travel and from entertaining, are presumably harmful only beyond a certain point and if their frequency and timing are personally uncontrollable, but systematic evidence about these moderating factors is lacking.

In Young and Willmott's (1973) study, 53 per cent of British professional and managerial married male employees felt that the demands of their job interfered with the requirements of home and family; among a sub-sample of managing directors the figure rose to 65 per cent. However, among semi-skilled and unskilled workers only 25 per cent reported this kind of interference. A similar difference between job levels was found among married women workers: 58 per cent and 22 per cent for professional and managerial workers and manual workers respectively.

Spill-over demands range from those that are probably harmless or even beneficial to those which are clearly intrusive, as these quotations from managers illustrate (Young and Willmott 1973):

I think about work continually when I'm at home. If you are digging a flower-bed for a couple of hours, you can have a marvellous think about some deep problems of organization (p. 166).

I get calls at night from the works.... Sometimes a telex message comes in after I've left, but they telephone me and I phone someone in the States or Scotland or wherever it might be to try and answer the question (p. 167).

I never know where I am going to be on any given evening, so we can never go anywhere socially during the week.... During the week you are a lodger in the house. The kids are in bed at night when you get home and wives feel neglected (p. 254).

The impact of such a workload on the wives of busy managers is made more negative by the simultaneous lack of practical and emotional support arising from their husband's unavailability. Here is one woman's view:

Having got used to the loneliness, it's just the fact of having to be responsible for running a family and a home. And having to be totally healthy, totally responsible all the time—never being able to relax, to be drearily exhausted. To get the flu and not being able to flop down and enjoy it—just having to be superhuman. Because I think if you are married to a man who has this sort of executive responsibility, then the women has to take on many of the tasks that the man really should do at home (Evans and Bartolome 1980, p. 80).

Time demands of jobs might be thought particularly troublesome for married women workers, since they usually spend more time on housework and child care activities than their male counterparts (e.g. Martin and Roberts 1984) and thus are more liable to experience cumulative overload from the two roles (e.g. Davidson 1987; Sekaran 1985). In the study described earlier, Staines and Pleck (1983, 1984) found that among two-earner couples the number of hours worked had a significantly stronger negative effect on time spent on child care and housework for wives than for husbands. It is clear that in general time demands from job and home are increased when both members of a couple are in paid employment; the associated problems have been examined by many writers (e.g. Hall and Hall 1980; Rapoport and Rapoport 1978). Tension associated with overload from both roles appears to be greatest among couples with children, and among those where both partners are strongly committed to their job and/or career.

Pattern of time demands

Turning to the pattern of time demands, Staines and Pleck (1983, 1984) have shown that regular weekend work reduces the amount of time spent on child care and housework, but in their study weekend work was not associated with lower family and marital satisfaction. Working afternoon, or night or rotating shifts (in comparison with day-working), was also found to be uncorrelated with family and marital satisfaction; and shiftwork schedules were accompanied by an increase (rather than the expected decrease) in time spent on housework. Shift-working was also associated with more frequent reports of interference between job and family demands. Shamir's (1983) data emphasize that afternoon shifts (e.g. between 3 p.m. and 11 p.m.) are particularly problematic in this respect.

Other research into shift-working has drawn attention to disadvantages such as sleeping problems and limited social life, and to advantages such as shift bonus payments and more free time (e.g. Drenth *et al.* 1976; Folkard and Monk 1985; Thierry and Jansen 1984; Tilley *et al.* 1982). In general, the negative consequences of shift-working appear to be somewhat less serious than might be expected, especially when workers are able to select their preferred schedule and/or when schedules are such that a person can predict time demands over the next few weeks. Sleep deficits may be restored through extended sleep during non-work days or when on afternoon shifts; and short naps may be taken during the day (Akerstedt 1984). However, feelings of tiredness and problems in sleeping are reported more often by shift-workers than non shift-workers (e.g. Frese and Harwich 1984). Note that a pervasive tendency to self-selection is likely to reduce observed negative consequences of shift-working, as people who find it particularly unpleasant tend to move to day-work jobs.

One type of shift-work appears particularly likely to impair health; this is when periods of work vary rapidly between day and night. For example, Cherry (1984a) examined reports of 'nervous strain' at work in a sample of British 32-year-old men, finding that this form of strain was especially common (70 per cent) among those whose job schedules required them to work one or two (but not more) consecutive nights. Among men working three or more consecutive nights only 35 per cent reported strain, and among day-workers the figure was 43 per cent.

Theorell and Akerstedt (1976) have studied changes in catecholamine excretion among employees moving between day- and night-shift working; a significant increase in adrenaline excretion was observed immediately after the change. Possible longer-term consequences of continuously changing day and night work schedules were identified by Alfredsson *et al.* (1982). They examined occupational factors predictive of elevated risk of myocardial infarction (see page 97 and page 130 for further details), and found continuously changing shift-work between day and night to be significantly associated with increased risk. This pattern was retained after the introduction of statistical controls for differences in age, but the data contained some suggestion that heavy smoking might be an intervening causal agent (Alfredsson and Theorell 1983).

Another approach to varying the pattern of time demands has been to introduce some flexibility of starting and finishing times as chosen by each employee. Such 'flexitime' schedules are usually welcomed, for example for their contribution to helping a person meet both job and family demands (e.g. Kanter 1977), but they seem in general to have only limited impact upon context-free mental health (e.g. Greenhaus and Beutel 1985). Staines and Pleck (1984) conclude from their review of prior research that flexitime 'may benefit workers with modest family responsibilities and minor logistical problems; but for groups having far greater complexities in combining work and family life (e.g. employed mothers) a restricted program ... does little to reduce work/family stress' (p. 23). However, as they point out, systematic research evidence is still very limited.

Summary

This chapter has examined research into some aspects of the goals generated by an occupational environment. Particular attention has been paid to the number and difficulty of job demands, and the association between chronically high workload and affective well-being.

Studies have been grouped according to their focus upon job-related or context-free well-being, and in respect of each of the three principal measurement axes suggested in Chapter 3. High levels of intrinsic job demands have been shown to be associated with lower well-being on each axis of job-related well-being (discontented–contented, anxious–comfortable, and depressed–actively pleased). Such findings may be thought to reflect an unsurprising impact on noxious conditions on feelings about those same conditions. Of greater interest are results in respect of context-free well-being, where it is found that high job demands give rise to low well-being which generalizes beyond merely the job setting. Each of the three measurement axes reveals this pattern, and research has extended into the effects of high demands on psychosomatic problems and on the increased use of tranquillizers.

'Role conflict' has been considered within the broader category of conditions of high intrinsic demand. Widespread associations of high conflict with low well-being have been summarized, but some doubt was cast upon the measurement of role conflict through conventional self-report measures.

Results were described from two investigations into the possible non-linear nature of the association between high workload and low well-being. Both studies suggested that very high demands have a disproportionately negative impact, but that varying levels of moderate to high demands have a constant, less severe, effect. These findings were taken as support for the plateau and additional decrement assumed within the vitamin AD model introduced in Chapter 1. However, additional enquiries are clearly needed, as are studies of other components of mental health: competence, autonomy, and aspiration.

The chapter then turned to the possible modes of combination of several environmental features. It was concluded that evidence in respect of the combined influence of externally generated goals and opportunity for control did not permit the inference of a synergistic interaction. Current evidence suggests a straightforward additive combination of the two features. However, the nature of this process (rather then merely the statistical pattern of its outcome) remains largely unexamined.

The concepts of task identity, traction and flow were also considered. Although deriving from different research domains, these may be viewed together in their contribution to an understanding of intrinsic motivation and self-estranged alienation. They also cast light on possible processes which may underpin observed statistical relationships.

Finally, studies of extrinsic demands have been reviewed, in terms of employees' need to meet family commitments as well as those arising from paid work. Two forms of time demands have been considered: those deriving from the amount of time required by a job, and those arising from the distribution of that time through the week. High levels of both forms of demand have been found to be significantly correlated with low affective well-being, but information about the specific pattern of this association remains to be gathered.

8

Environmental clarity

We turn next to the fifth characteristic introduced in Chapter 1, the degree to which an environment is experienced as clear and comprehensible. This chapter will review the impact of variations in clarity in job settings upon aspects of job-related and context-free mental health.

'Clarity' is used as a broad designation for a range of perceived environmental features which make it possible for someone to understand what is the case, what will happen, and what is required. Environments which are both stable and familiar are often likely to be most transparent in these senses. Conversely, rapid changes are likely to reduce both environmental clarity and affective well-being. This pattern has been documented for general life circumstances by several investigators. For instance, Myers *et al.* (1972) found that rate of change in life events was positively associated with a high level of psychiatric symptoms (a broad-band index along the first axis of context-free well-being as shown in Fig. 3.1, page 41). A similar pattern has been reported for anxiety (the second axis in Fig. 3.1) by, for example, Lauer and Thomas (1976).

In occupational research, Burke *et al.* (1980) examined the relationship between husbands' reported rate of change in their jobs and aspects of their wives' mental health. Among several positive findings were significant associations between rate of husbands' job change and high levels of wives' anxiety, depression, and psychosomatic symptoms. Interpretation of results from this kind of study is not entirely straightforward, since there are conceptual difficulties in separating as possible sources of low well-being change itself and undesirable components within that change. This issue is taken up again later.

The chapter is divided into four principal sections, each covering one aspect of environmental clarity. First is the degree to which an environment is informative about the consequences of one's actions; issues here include behavioural feedback and response uncertainty. Second is the degree to which an environment is predictable in more general terms, such that people can foresee events and plan within their understanding of the future. Third is the degree to which an environment is normatively transparent, in the sense that requirements from tasks and other people are clear and unambiguous. Fourth, the chapter will consider the degree to which an environment is clear or uncertain after a transition between jobs. The presentation is concluded by an integration of the four sections within the vitamin model.

Information about the consequences of behaviour

Information about the effects of behaviour is essential for mental health in a number of ways. Several of these are linked with the environmental features studied in previous chapters. For example, feedback about action outcomes is a minimum requirement for the establishment and maintenance of personal control and for the development and utilization of skills. In general, it would be impossible to interact successfully with the environment if the latter failed to provide information about the appropriateness or otherwise of one's actions.

Within occupational settings the importance of clear information about consequences of job behaviours has been examined in several ways. For example, task feedback is one of the characteristics assessed by the Job Diagnostic Survey (Hackman and Oldham, 1975, 1980). It is there defined as 'the degree to which carrying out the work activities required by the job provides the individual with direct and clear information about the effectiveness of his or her performance'.

Cross-sectional research in the United States and United Kingdom has frequently shown that workers in jobs which they describe as providing feedback of this kind are significantly more likely than others to exhibit high overall and intrinsic job satisfaction and intrinsic motivation (e.g. Oldham *et al.* 1978; Wall *et al.* 1978), as well as low job-related emotional exhaustion (Maslach and Jackson 1981). In the meta-analysis of results from 28 studies described by Loher *et al.* (1985), the average sample-weighted correlation with job satisfaction was 0.41 after correcting for unreliability of measures. Furthermore, longitudinal research has found that increases or decreases in task feedback are accompanied by significant changes in the predicted direction in overall job satisfaction, intrinsic job satisfaction and intrinsic motivation (Bechtold *et al.* 1981; Hackman *et al.* 1978).

Brousseau (1978) obtained Job Diagnostic Survey information about task feedback (and other job characteristics) from a sample of American engineers, scientists, and managers. He also had available personality scale responses separated by an average of almost six years; the first set of data was obtained at the time of hire and the second a few months after employees had completed the Job Diagnostic Survey. Brousseau was thus able to examine whether self-descriptions changed systematically as a function of the feedback provided in people's present job.

He regrouped the personality items into scales of 'freedom from depression', 'active orientation', 'philosophical orientation', and 'self-confidence'.

The first of these appears to tap affective well-being in the actively pleased quadrant of the present Fig. 3.1. Scores were correlated 0.34 with the measure of 'active orientation', a more diffuse construct associated with optimistic risk-taking and the assumption of personal responsibility.

Partial correlations were computed between current scores on the four personality indices and characteristics of respondents' present job, holding constant earlier scores on the personality measure. Such an analysis is formally equivalent to the examination of personality change scores adjusted for differences at the first measurement occasion. The partial correlations revealed that higher levels of current job feedback were significantly associated with changes in the direction of greater freedom from depression and a more active orientation. Furthermore, this pattern was significantly stronger for those with longer tenure in their current job, the one for which feedback had been assessed. The other two measures (of philosophical orientation and self-confidence) were unrelated to job content.

Brousseau and Prince (1981) extended the analysis to look at average job characteristic scores from a larger sample (including the earlier respondents) in respect of other sub-scales from the personality measure. Job feedback was significantly associated (in partial correlation, as before) with increases in 'emotional stability', an index correlated 0.77 with the earlier index of freedom from depression. Although deriving from what was labelled as a 'personality' scale, it is clear that both of these indices may be viewed as reflections of mental health.

In addition to feedback, other job characteristics were found in this study to be significantly associated with changes in scale scores. (Results have been summarized in Chapters 6 and 7.) Since the characteristics measured by the Job Diagnostic Survey tend to be positively intercorrelated, it is not certain from Brousseau's results how far task feedback itself, rather than another feature such as variety, or a combination of job content features, is responsible for the observed changes. Nevertheless, we might conclude from his research that jobs with higher levels of task feedback (and also with other correlated features) do tend to be associated with changes over time in the direction of better mental health.

Feedback of the kind examined in the preceding paragraphs may be viewed as 'intrinsic', being provided by the task itself. In addition we should consider 'extrinsic' feedback, supplied by other people. For example, Oldham and Brass (1979) observed significant associations of overall job satisfaction and intrinsic job motivation with higher levels of feedback from one's supervisor. Informational benefits of feedback may of course be supplemented by the desirable attributes of specific information. Thus performance feedback from one's boss may be desired for its own sake, but be particularly valued if it is likely to contain a favourable assessment. In a similar way, piecework payment systems are often appreciated by workers for the feedback they provide about job performance, but also because high performance is associated with increased income and provides evidence of successful goal attainment (e.g. Turner and Miclette 1962). Ilgen *et al.* (1979) have summarized findings and debates about a range of different forms of feedback; and Herold and Parsons (1985) have proposed the measurement of 15 dimensions, covering both positive and negative feedback from self, task, supervisor, others, and formal organizational procedures.

Learning promptly about immediate outcomes is also important for the generation of pleasant feelings of traction within work (see page 135), permitting rhythm to be built up to a desired level. Such a process of intrinsic feedback and traction is widespread in simple manual jobs, but is also observed in other types of work. For example, effective interaction with a computer system requires clear information about the state of the system after one's most recent input. Feedback delays which are long, especially those which are intermittently or unpredictably long, can increase employees' feelings of tension. In Johansson and Aronsson's (1984) study of Swedish visual display unit operators, the average response time of the computer system was just over one second, but delays ranged up to half a minute. The intermittent long delays were found to add considerably to operators' discomfort. As the authors point out, 'it is interesting to note how technical development can affect attitudes and expectations. In the days before the computer system it was not uncommon to have delays lasting several minutes while information was retrieved from paper files. Seen in this light it may seem remarkable that 63 per cent of the subjects would prefer not to have to wait more than five seconds for an answer from the computer' (p. 178).

What about the possibility that extremely high levels of feedback might have harmful consequences, as proposed by the vitamin AD model? Formal empirical evidence on this point is lacking, but it seems probable that outstandingly clear and frequent intrinsic or extrinsic feedback would reduce uncertainty to an undesirable extent. In these risk-free and perfectly predictable circumstances, a person would have no opportunity to deploy skills or to exercise personal control; mental health would thus be expected to suffer.

In summary of this section, it may be concluded from cross-sectional and longitudinal studies that clear information about the outcomes of job behaviour gives rise to higher scores on the first and third dimensions of both job-related and context-free affective well-being, from discontented to contented and from depressed to actively pleased. No evidence has been located in relation to the anxious–comfortable dimension for context-free mental health, although there are some suggestions that job-related anxiety is increased by the absence of feedback. Feedback is in general essential for successful personal control of an environment. It thus seems likely to be crucial to the development of competence, the second component of mental health, although links between feedback in a job and competence which is context-free are not easily demonstrated. Job-related subjective aspiration has been tapped in terms of intrinsic work motivation, and there is some evidence that this may be enhanced by feedback. Studies of other mental health components have not been found, nor has information about the linearity or non-linearity of associations.

Information about the future

A second aspect of environmental clarity is the degree to which it is possible to forecast what is likely to happen, irrespective of one's own behaviour. Such predictability is valued because anticipation of the nature and timing of potentially aversive events permits possible coping responses. These may be overt, in the form of evasive action or seeking information about possible contingencies; or they may be mental processes associated with planning, anticipatory problem-solving, and defences such as re-evaluation of alternatives and acceptance of the unavoidable. Uncertainty about whether or not undesirable events are likely to occur inhibits these preparatory responses, and has been widely shown in laboratory and field investigations to give rise to anxiety and other forms of low affective well-being (e.g. Miller 1981).

This relationship has also been documented in occupational research. For example, Caplan *et al.* (1975) developed a measure of 'job future ambiguity', covering a worker's degree of uncertainty about future career developments and future value of job skills. In their study of 23 jobs in the United States of America, this form of uncertainty was found to be significantly associated with high levels of job dissatisfaction, job boredom, job-related depression, and job-related anxiety. Using similar measures, van Dijkhuizen (1980) obtained identical findings from a sample of Dutch manual, managerial, and professional employees. In addition, low self-esteem was found to be associated with high ambiguity, and there was evidence of a non-linear pattern, with particularly harmful effects at very high levels of ambiguity. Kohn and Schooler (1983) examined American male workers' uncertainty about retaining their job in the next year. Statistically controlling for other possibly influential variables, they observed significant correlations with job dissatisfaction, context-free anxiety, and low self-esteem.

Job insecurity and possible job loss have been found in many other studies to be primary sources of tension and distress (e.g. Evans and Bartolome 1980; Henderson *et al.* 1981; Kiev and Kohn 1979). This is particularly likely to be the case when a company is in financial difficulties. For example, in an American study of plant closure and employee lay-off, Cobb and Kasl (1977) reported a strong 'anticipation effect' prior to closure, in terms of increased depression and feelings of insecurity. A similar Swedish investigation revealed particularly low affective well-being and sleep quality a month before a scheduled plant closure, together with elevated levels of cortisol excretion (Levi *et al.* 1984). Raised tension levels have also been shown in other companies in financial difficulty (e.g. Buss and Redburn 1983; Erikssen *et al.*

1979; Wall and Clegg 1981b). It seems likely that reduced affective well-being is to be found both among managers faced with difficult decisions in a context of uncertainty and also among subordinate workers who see their future as insecure.

The central element here is the degree to which people believe that continuity is or is not assured. As Greenhalgh and Rosenblatt (1984) have pointed out, job insecurity ('a potential loss of continuity in the job situation') is not restricted to loss of a job, but also extends into uncertainties for people who are likely to remain employed. In the latter case there may be uncertainty about career progress, income level, status, autonomy, resources, or loss of community with familiar colleagues. In respect of the first three of these, Berger-Gross and Kraut (1984) have reported a significant association between American managers' promotional uncertainty and low overall job satisfaction. A similar pattern has been reported by Gavin and Axelrod (1977) in respect of uncertainty about career, advancement possibilities, responsibilities, and the value of current skills.

As noted previously, the affective consequences of each type of potential discontinuity depend both on the perceived probability of its occurrence and also on its degree of undesirability. In the present section we are concerned with moderate probabilities of a discontinuity, since very low and very high values are by definition associated with clarity about the future. Although a moderately uncertain future may give rise to negative feelings, a future which is both moderately uncertain and also potentially threatening is expected to yield particularly low levels of affective well-being. There are of course great difficulties in empirically separating uncertainty itself from the desirability or undesirability of possible outcomes; the two features are in research practice often confounded.

Another mediating factor is likely to be degree of controllability, in that a potential undesirable discontinuity over which one has no possible influence is liable to be particularly disturbing (e.g. Lefcourt 1982; Miller 1981). Conversely, some uncertainty about events and their controllability, especially those which may be attractive, is often desired. As described in Chapter 5, novelty has its own value, and targets whose attainment is not guaranteed are often preferred over those where success is certain. However, despite the apparent plausibility of these interconnections between uncertainty, undesirability, and uncontrollability, no systematic research evidence about their combined operation in job settings appears to be available.

In seeking to give further substance to the notion of unpredictability, it may be useful to link this feature with the other eight environmental characteristics examined in this book. In considering low environmental clarity of this type, we would then investigate uncertainty about the future in respect of: opportunity for control, opportunity for skill use, externally generated goals, job variety, availability of money, physical security, opportunity for interpersonal contact, and valued social position. Lack of clarity about the future is likely to be undesirable in a generic sense, but particular uncertainties within this framework may be more undesirable than others.

Information about required behaviour

Chapter 7 considered jobs in terms of the goals they generate and the demands they make upon a job holder. The emphasis there was on the number and difficulty of those demands. In this section we will consider a different aspect: the degree to which a job setting provides clear information about what behaviours and levels of attainment are required.

Research into this form of clarity in occupational settings was greatly stimulated by the research of Kahn *et al.* (1964) into role ambiguity. They introduced their investigation in this way:

Certain information is required for adequate role performance, that is, in order for a person to conform to the role expectations held by members of his role set. First of all, he must know what these expectations are: the rights, duties, and responsibilities of his office. Second, he must know something about what activities on his part will fulfil the responsibilities of office, and how these activities can best be performed. In other words, he requires various sorts of means-ends knowledge. He wants also to know the potential consequences of his role performance or non-performance for himself, his role senders, and the organization in general.

Certain information is required for personal comfort and psychological return. In general, one needs to know what kinds of behavior will be rewarded or punished, the nature of rewards and punishments, and the likelihood of their occurrence.... Ambiguity—the lack of clear, consistent information—... may result either because information is nonexistent or because existing information is inadequately communicated (pp. 22-3).

Information about opportunities for advancement, about respect and acceptance by others, about which behaviors lead to rewards and which to punishment, is required for most of us to be personally comfortable in our jobs (p. 23).

That suggestion has been empirically supported in a large number of studies. In their initial inquiry, Kahn *et al.* (1964) examined workers' ratings of other people in their 'role set', those with whom they principally interact at work. Information was obtained about each of these 'role senders', who were identified and interviewed individually, in respect of how clearly they indicated their expectations of the focal person's work. Greater ambiguity in respect of work expectations (an 'independent' measure in the terms of Chapter 1 and Chapter 6) was found to be significantly associated with low job satisfaction, high job-related tension, and low subjective job-related competence. A separate index of perceived ambiguity in respect of job requirements and authority limits (a 'subjective' measure, with no reference to specific role senders) was also significantly associated with the same pattern of outcomes.

Later research has typically employed a six-item perceived role ambiguity scale introduced by Rizzo *et al.* (1970). This contains items like: 'I know exactly what is expected of me'; 'I know what my responsibilities are'; 'clear, planned goals and objectives exist for my job'. (See House *et al.* 1983, for a development of this scale.) Among the significant correlates of high ambiguity measured in this way, or through extremely similar scales (e.g. Caplan *et al.*, 1975), are job dissatisfaction (e.g. Brief and Aldag 1976; Berger-Gross and Kraut 1984; Caplan *et al.* 1975; Dougherty and Pritchard 1985; House and Rizzo 1972; Miles 1975; Schuler *et al.* 1977; Sutton 1984), job-related anxiety (e.g. Brief and Aldag 1976; Caplan and Jones 1975; Caplan *et al.* 1975; Dougherty and Pritchard 1985; House and Rizzo 1972; Miles 1975), fatigue (House and Rizzo 1972), job-related emotional exhaustion (Maslach and Jackson 1984), job-related depression (Caplan *et al.* 1975), job-related somatic complaints (Caplan *et al.* 1975), and context-free somatic complaints (Sutton 1984).

Fisher and Gitelson (1983) have reviewed data from 59 different samples, among which the mean linear correlation of work-role ambiguity with job-related tension or anxiety was 0.19. The mean correlation with job involvement (considered here to tap the third axis of job-related affective well-being in Fig. 3.1) was -0.26, and that with overall job satisfaction (the first axis in Fig. 3.1) was -0.25. Analysing results from a later but overlapping series of studies, Jackson and Schuler (1985) quote mean values of 0.30, -0.28, and -0.30 respectively; after correction for restriction of range and unreliability of measurement, these mean correlations are raised to 0.47, -0.44, and -0.46. Among facet-specific satisfactions, both investigations found the strongest associations to be with satisfaction with supervisor and the work itself, the weakest with satisfaction with pay; corrected mean values cited by Jackson and Schuler were -0.53, -0.52, and -0.26 respectively.

Turning to context-free measures, these authors recorded a mean corrected correlation of role ambiguity with self-esteem of -0.34. Using a separate measure of work-role ambiguity, Billings and Moos (1982) reported significant associations with context-free anxiety for both men and women. Context-free depression was significantly associated with work-role ambiguity only for women; and low self-confidence (similar to low subjective autonomy in the present framework) was significantly predicted only for men. A negative finding emerged in the study by Burke *et al.* (1980) of husbands' job conditions and wives' mental health; role ambiguity in a husband's job was unrelated to any measured aspect of his wife's affective well-being.

In summary of these studies, we may conclude that higher work-role ambiguity is significantly associated with low scores on measures of the three principal axes of job-related affective well-being. Some associations have also been found with context-free affective well-being, although much less attention has been devoted to this relationship. One study has suggested a link with reduced subjective job-related competence, but other components of mental health appear not to have been investigated.

Research in this field is almost entirely based upon cross-sectional correlations, and the question of causal direction has rarely been explored empirically. However, Miles (1975) investigated possible causal priority through measurements taken at two points in time. The pattern of dynamic and cross-lagged correlations in his results suggested that low environmental clarity of this kind did indeed cause low job satisfaction, but this causal inference could not be made in respect of job-related tension.

As for the shape of the observed correlation (linear or non-linear), evidence appears to be available only from van Dikjhuizen's (1980) investigation. Results from his sample of Dutch employees indicated that *eta* coefficients of non-linear association were consistently larger than corresponding Pearson coefficients of linear correlation. High levels of role ambiguity (low levels of clarity in the present terms) were associated with particularly low well-being, with well-being levelling off at higher values of clarity. For example, for sub-groups ranging from low to high clarity, mean job-related depression scores were found to be 1.98, 1.37, 1.21, and 1.21; for job-related anxiety the means were 2.27, 1.82, 1.60, and 1.54; and for job-related psychosomatic complaints they were 1.83, 1.32, 1.25, and 1.26.

This pattern corresponds to that proposed in the left-hand section of the vitamin model of Fig. 1.1 (page 10). However, the findings quoted do not support the prediction of an additional decrement at very high levels of clarity. An indication of this was present in relation to job dissatisfaction, where mean values were found to be 2.40, 1.93, 1.76, and 1.87 from low to high clarity. However, additional empirical information is clearly required before the prediction can be considered to be adequately tested.

Information after a transition

A transition between jobs is likely to reduce the clarity of a physical and institutional environment in terms of each of the types of information considered so far: information about the consequences of actions, about the future, and about required behaviour. These three informational changes are likely often to combine to yield a marked increase in uncertainty after movement between jobs.

Job transitions typically include the acquisition of a new job title (or a new employer while retaining the same title) as well as new responsibilities. However, substantial role changes may sometimes occur within a job which retains the same title. Movement between jobs and major changes in job content should thus both be included within the concept (e.g. Frese 1984; Nicholson 1984). As with other features, the characteristics of transitions may be treated 'objectively' (as visible to an observer) or 'subjectively' (in terms of the person's perceptions of what is taking place); of these two it is subjective aspects of change which have been studied more frequently.

Five principal types of work-role transition have been described by Louis (1980b). First is entry into the labour force, from school or other educational setting. Second is transition within the same employing organization, either vertically (almost always upwards, through promotion) or horizontally in terms of a similar hierarchical location. Third and fourth are intercompany and interprofession transitions, which also may be either vertical or horizontal. Finally, one may examine departures from the labour force, for example into retirement, involuntary unemployment, or a child-care role at home.

Among the features common to these different transitions is a process of prior consideration of the new role and possible responses to it. This has been referred to as 'anticipatory socialization' (Merton 1957), occurring as people subjectively commence their move before it takes place in an objective form. Through this process it is possible that personal changes arise more before than after a transition. On the other hand, the development of unrealistic expectations and inappropriate anticipatory coping may give rise to particularly difficult transitions, in cases where reality turns out to be very different from what was expected (e.g. Louis 1980a; Wanous 1977).

Also common to different forms of occupational transition is a process of adaptation by both the employee and his or her organization. In the former case, a person adjusts to the new role and its institutional setting, learns new skills and appropriate behaviours, copes with surprises and shocks, and possibly adjusts to a new occupational identity; previous behaviours and values are relinquished, and new sources of reliable information are sought and found (e.g. Frese 1984; Louis 1980a, b, 1982; Nicholson 1984). At the same time, the organization in general or specific individuals within it may have to respond to requirements established by the person in his or her new role (e.g. Feldman and Brett, 1983).

Nicholson (1984) has examined four possible combinations of personal change and role change initiated by a person after a transition. The first of these is 'replication', where very little change occurs in either the person or the role: the employee performs in much the same manner as in previous jobs and also in much the same manner as earlier occupants. The second type of transition is 'absorption', where the person changes substantially to meet the requirements of the new role without altering that role to any substantial degree. The converse of that is 'determination', where the person remains unchanged but actively determines the shape of the new role. Finally, 'exploration' is said to occur when there is change both in the person and in the role.

In terms of the components of mental health previously described as competence, autonomy, and aspiration, it is clear that successful determination and exploration (both representing a strong personal impact upon the new role) are likely to be more beneficial than replication, in which no changes occur in either the person or the role. However, transitions characterized as absorption may also enhance these forms of mental health if the new role calls for increased personal control and skill utilization.

The four types of transition may also be thought likely to influence affective well-being, with outcomes again depending upon the circumstances. Replication and absorption may give rise to high or to low well-being, according to the characteristics of the new job. Within the current framework, of particular importance is the degree to which a new job contains the nine environmental features outlined in Chapter 1. The affective consequences of determination and exploration also depend on job content in this way, but in addition are more likely within the current model to be accompanied by high arousal (see Fig. 2.1, page 27).

There has been very little empirical research into the immediate impact on mental health of transitions between jobs. In one study it was found that uncertainty about whether one's skills were adequate was significantly associated with psychosomatic distress symptoms one month after moving into a new job (Werbel 1983). However, this pattern was not present two months later. Mansfield (1972) interviewed graduate management trainees two months after they had started work with a British company. Level of uncertainty about placement after training was strongly associated with low overall job satisfaction. Latack (1984), in a study of American managerial and professional workers, found that perceived role ambiguity after a transition was significantly associated with job-related anxiety.

In some cases, upward transitions require a person to meet demands or uncertainties which he or she finds unbearable (e.g. Levinson 1964). Associated with this, clinical case histories have sometimes drawn attention to problems arising when promotion involves taking the place of a respected colleague. For example, 'in a number of clients, this experience of 'stepping into the shoes' of a valued superior has brought them in touch with an earlier unresolved loss, often caused by a parent's death or separation from the family home. Despite being previously quite capable of taking on the work involved, they have found themselves increasingly distressed and unable to do the job' (Firth 1985, p. 145).

There is a need for more research into short-term, acute effects of job transitions. In a review of one type of move, transfer to another job within the same company but in a different geographical location, Brett (1980) could locate no studies of the impact of this form of transfer on male workers' mental health. However, she did find some evidence for reduced affective well-being in wives arising from transfer of the family with a husband's job move. Renshaw (1976) studied a particularly extreme form of job transfer, from the United States to another country, noting wives' problems of adjustment to different cultural norms and to unfamiliar arrangements for shopping and schooling. Pinder (1981) emphasized how overall evaluation of the new geographical location is a major predictor of successful adjustment after job transfer to another area.

In a study of British managers' most recent job move (usually a promotion), Alban-Metcalfe and Nicholson (1984) asked about experiences in the first few months after the transition. New jobs during that period were reported as more stressful than preceding jobs by 54 per cent of the sample; 24 per cent reported reduced stress after the move, and 22 per cent no change. In addition, the first few months were perceived as offering greater challenge (by 79 per cent) and more satisfaction and fulfilment (by 71 per cent). Sorensen *et al.* (1985) found no evidence that upward mobility in the past three years was associated with symptoms of strain in an American community sample; they suggest that the positive aspects of such transitions are likely to outweigh negative features.

It is generally assumed that the psychological impact of a transition is a function of the degree of dissimilarity between prior and present roles. This raises the question: which dimensions of similarity-dissimilarity are important in determining the impact? One answer is in terms of particular job requirements, specified organizational norms, or identified cultural features associated with particular geographical locations. That emphasis upon concrete characteristics of old and new roles has clear merit, but in the present setting an approach in terms of the vitamin model may be advocated. The magnitude and impact of a job transition can usefully be characterized in terms of changes in the nine environmental categories set out in Chapter 1 as the foundations of mental health.

For example, this chapter has emphasized variations in environmental clarity (feature number 5). When a new role is currently more unclear than the previous one in these terms, a decrement in affective well-being may in principle be expected; conversely an increase from a very low level of clarity may yield an improvement in well-being. Other features likely to be particularly important in this form of analysis of transitions include number 1 (opportunity for control) and number 9 (valued social position). If personal control is substantially reduced in a new environment, then changes in affective well-being may be expected along the lines described in Chapter 5. In respect of feature number 9 (to be considered later in the book), transitions which take the form of promotion or demotion carry with them clear changes in social position. These shifts in status and their associated personal and social re-evaluations are important in their own right, and also because they often serve to augment or reduce the impact of changes in other features.

However, shifts in the nine environmental characteristics are considered to be non-linear in their effects, with a broad middle range of each feature thought likely to yield a relatively constant impact upon mental health. It follows that transitions between jobs which do not move a person outside that benign middle range are expected to have no overall impact. Only when levels of clarity, opportunity for control, valued social position, etc. move outside the middle range (for instance, being substantially reduced) should we expect a work-role transition to influence affective well-being and other aspects of mental health.

Furthermore, the nine features are expected to combine together. A reduction in clarity of the kind often reported after work-role transitions may sometimes be accompanied by increases in positive features, such as opportunity for skill use, availability of money, or variety. These gains can in practice outweigh the negative effects of reduced clarity, so that job transitions may sometimes have only minor impact upon immediately ensuing mental health, despite marked initial uncertainty in the new role.

Finally, another application of the vitamin model may be noted. In addition to examining individual instances of work-role transition in terms of changes in each of the nine environmental features, one might analyse different categories of transition from the same perspective. Common types of transition include promotion from shop-floor to supervisor, promotion from junior to middle management, transfer between departments, movement from technical to general management, and re-entry into paid work after unemployment. Each of these might be characterized and re-interpreted in terms of the nine central elements of the vitamin model. An illustration of that possibility is presented in Chapter 12, when the transition out of unemployment is considered in terms of the nine categories.

Review of findings about the four types of job clarity

The preceding sections have illustrated some difficulties of research into this job feature. Although clarity is conceptually distinct from other aspects of a situation, for instance the desirability or controllability of events, it is rarely possible to measure or experimentally manipulate it independently of those other attributes. This difficulty is particularly pronounced for one of the four aspects identified here, information about the future. The meaning of this differs markedly according to the desirability of the events in question. Uncertainty about the occurrence of one of several attractive outcomes is very different from uncertainty in respect of negative possibilities, for example whether one is about to lose one's job or to be demoted. This means that research should separately investigate low clarity of both evaluative kinds, examining whether a significant interaction is present between level of clarity and level of desirability; this has not yet been achieved.

A related empirical difficulty arises in respect of information after transitions. Movement between jobs involves so many changes that increases or reductions in clarity alone are difficult to separate from changes in respect of other features. Although some research has examined the short-term impact of particular work-role transitions as a totality, there is no evidence directly concerned with the impact of a reduction in clarity on its own.

Recognizing these difficulties, Table 8.1 aims to summarize research findings about the four aspects covered in this chapter. The structure and content of this table are the same as for Table 6.1, in which investigations into opportunity for control, opportunity for skill use, and job variety were summarized (see page 107). Both tables contain assessments of the probability, in the light of currently available evidence, that each of the features identified has a causal influence on each aspect of mental health.

It can be seen that, although the evidence in respect of job-related affective well-being permits quite strong inferences about the consequences of variations in clarity, and although some conclusions may be drawn about context-free well-being, there is a general lack of information about the other components of mental health. Greater attention to these is now essential.

Two comments should be made about the basis of assessments in Table 8.1. Research into uncertainty about the future has primarily examined undesirable events, in terms of job insecurity of several kinds, and it is thus low predictability in respect of undesirable outcomes which has been shown to cause lowered affective well-being; the effect of uncertainty about desirable outcomes is not known. Second, there is no research evidence concerned explicitly with the mental health effects after work-role transitions of lack of information on its own (the right-hand column of the table). However, a transition which yields a reduction in information does this by reducing some or all of the three other types of clarity in the table. The suggested impact of lack of information after transitions on job-related affective well-being has thus been inferred from assessments in the first three columns.

As indicated throughout the chapter, almost all research in this area has been cross-sectional, examining correlations between job features (usually as perceived by the job-holder) and affective well-being. We must of course be careful about inferring causal direction from such correlations, but the nature of this particular set of variables appears to permit causal inference of the kinds indicated in the table. In addition, a reverse influence may be envisaged in some cases (for example, as a person who is anxious causes his or her supervisor to avoid specifying difficult job requirements), and low affective well-being undoubtedly can colour perception of environmental features. However, the pattern of associations which is summarized in Table 8.1 would not arise without some causal influence from the job to the person.

What of the vitamin model: do we have any evidence that those associations recorded in the table are non-linear according to the pattern suggested in Fig. 1.1? Evidence from a single study (van Dijkhuizen 1980) has been cited as supportive of the model, in that very low clarity was shown to be unusually harmful and higher levels of clarity were found to have a broadly constant effect. However, further studies are clearly required. Unfortunately, researchers' inadequate reporting of findings precludes secondary analyses of published results. For example, Fisher and Gitelson (1983) have examined

Table 8.1 Assessment of causal relationships between four types of environmental clarity and major aspects of mental health, based upon currently available evidence

	Clarity of the occupational environment			
	Feedback about behaviour	Certainty about the future	Clarity of role requirements	Information after a transition
AFFECTIVE WELL-BEING				
Job-related				
1. Discontented–contented	+++	+++	+++	+++
2. Anxious–comfortable	+	++	+++	+++
3. Depressed–actively pleased	+	+	++	+
Context-free				
1. Discontented–contented	+	++	+	+
2. Anxious–comfortable	ndl	++	+	+
3. Depressed–actively pleased	+	+	?	+
COMPETENCE				
Job-related, subjective	by def	ndl	+	ndl
Job-related, objective	ndl	ndl	ndl	ndl
Context-free, subjective	ndl	ndl	ndl	ndl
Context-free, objective	ndl	ndl	ndl	ndl
AUTONOMY				
Job-related, subjective	ndl	ndl	ndl	ndl
Job-related, objective	ndl	ndl	ndl	ndl
Context-free, subjective	ndl	ndl	ndl	ndl
Context-free, objective	ndl	ndl	ndl	ndl
ASPIRATION				
Job-related, subjective	+	ndl	ndl	ndl
Job-related, objective	ndl	ndl	ndl	ndl
Context-free, subjective	ndl	ndl	ndl	ndl
Context-free, objective	ndl	ndl	ndl	ndl
INTEGRATED FUNCTIONING	ndl	ndl	ndl	ndl

Abbreviations are as follows:

ndl: no data located	+: probably a causal link from this job feature to this aspect of mental health
by def: by definition	
?: results ambiguous	++: very probably such a causal link
	+++: almost certainly such a causal link

a large number of studies investigating the association between ambiguity and job dissatisfaction, and their review might be thought to permit a test of the predicted pattern. However, they point out that very few investigators have cited mean scores. Analyses of published data to test predictions about non-linearity are thus not possible.

The expectation from the vitamin AD model that extremely high levels of this environmental feature are less beneficial to the individual than moderate levels raises the question: what is meant by an 'extremely clear' occupational environment? This appears to be one in which no uncertainty exists at all, where feedback is clear, consistent, continuous, and complete, where the future is fully predictable, and where role requirements are completely specified with no ambiguity. Settings of such extreme clarity appear likely to be harmful in their own right. In addition however, as pointed out in Chapter 1, extremely high levels of an environmental feature may have negative effects through their impact on other features within the nine-component model. For example, extremely high clarity is likely to be accompanied by very low levels of variety, opportunity for skill use, and opportunity for control, shown in Chapter 5 themselves to be liable to impair certain aspects of mental health.

In a similar manner, levels of environmental clarity which are moderate might be thought desirable partly for their associated levels of other features. For example, a certain amount of ambiguity and uncertainty is inherent in environments which permit personal control or the use of skill. Levels of clarity which are very low (that is, very high levels of ambiguity) have repeatedly been shown to be associated with reduced affective well-being. This relationship is again likely to emerge both because of the impact of ambiguity itself and also from the influence of correlated environmental features, low opportunity for control, for example.

In general, these considerations emphasize once again the implausibility of expecting a linear correlation between environmental clarity and mental health. Yet that expectation has implicitly guided most research in the field. Futhermore, research into differences in the clarity of occupational environments has concentrated to an excessive degree upon their impact upon job-related affective well-being. It is important now to obtain more substantial information about context-free well-being and the other aspects of mental health listed in Table 8.1.

Finally, the general importance of duration of environmental conditions and of psychological state should be re-emphasized. As pointed out in Chapter 2 (for example, in Table 2.1, page 35), it is incorrect to infer from a low level of well-being on its own that mental health is itself impaired. Affective well-being which is chronically low is likely to indicate impaired mental health, but brief or occasional episodes of low well-being may have quite different significance.

Duration of current psychological state has been ignored by most researchers in this field. It appears to be assumed that measured well-being which is found to be low is in fact chronically low; but that is not always the case. In a similar vein we may question researchers' tendency to assume that information they gather about environmental conditions is indicative of long-standing and unchanging characteristics. These assumptions about temporal stability require to be more carefully checked in future investigations.

Summary

The fifth environmental category in the present model has been studied in job settings in three principal forms. First, investigations have examined the clarity and promptness of the feedback which is provided about one's own performance. Second, there have been studies of employees' uncertainty or certainty about the future, irrespective of their own immediate actions. Most research has examined future ambiguity in terms of possible job loss, thus making it difficult to isolate the effects of low clarity independent of low desirability of an outcome. The third sub-category has concerned the degree to which a job setting provides clear information about what behaviours and achievements are required. Low levels of this feature have elsewhere been referred to as 'role ambiguity'.

The chapter has reviewed research into these three forms of job clarity, showing each to be associated with job-related well-being. Some evidence is also available for their impact on context-free well-being. Current knowledge has been summarized in Table 8.1, which also demonstrates the need for research into the competence, autonomy, and aspiration components of mental health.

A fourth type of uncertainty was also considered, that associated with transitions between jobs. Low clarity during a transition was expected to derive from the three primary forms of uncertainty, and inferences about those in the context of transitions have also been summarized in Table 8.1. More generally, the psychological impact of a transition is likely to depend upon the degree of dissimilarity between present and prior roles. It was suggested that the nine features of the vitamin model can usefully serve as a basis for comparing two roles and for analysing a transition between them.

9

Extrinsic job features: pay and physical conditions

The previous four chapters have examined five of the environmental categories which make up the present conceptual framework: opportunity for control, opportunity for skill use, externally generated goals, variety, and environmental clarity. These features may be described as 'intrinsic', in that they largely concern conditions and processes which are inherent in the conduct of the job itself.

We turn now to the remaining four characteristics. These are often viewed as 'extrinsic', in that they are principally concerned with the context of task activities rather than with their content. In the sequence in which they will be considered, they are availability of money (number 6), physical security (number 7), opportunity for interpersonal contact (number 8), and valued social position (number 9). The mental health impact of these in job settings has been less frequently investigated than that of the five intrinsic features. Research into the first two will be examined in this chapter, with opportunity for interpersonal contact and valued social position reviewed in Chapter 10.

Availability of money

Money buys membership in industrial society.... Money does not just buy food and clothing and housing and appliances, cars and children and vacations. The purchase of all of these commodities, in turn, allows the achievement and day-to-day living out of an identity as an at least 'average American' or average Briton or average Italian or average Japanese. When people are not protected from this inexorable dynamic of money economies by some local cultural enclave, they cannot fail to define themselves most basically in terms of their access to all that money can buy (Rainwater 1974, p.xi).

A positive relationship between standard of living and mental health has been recorded in research conducted in many different countries. Most commonly this is shown in relation to broad-based measures of the first dimension of affective well-being (e.g. Diener 1984; Veenhoven and Jonkers 1984), but a significant association with the third axis (from depressed to actively pleased) has also been observed (e.g. Ross and Huber 1985). Low living standards are particularly likely to be found among unemployed people, but there are also many jobs which provide only a meagre income. We thus need to consider both unemployed and employed people's standard of living. The focus of the present chapter is upon the latter group, and Chapters 12 and 13 will consider in greater detail the financial problems which may accompany unemployment.

As with other features discussed throughout the book, there are some problems in the measurement of a person's standard of living. An apparently straightforward, objective approach is to define this in terms of income received, but that is not wholly satisfactory. Apart from difficulties in deciding which income(s) to include within an index (money received by one person or by a complete household, for example), it should be recognized that standard of living is determined by factors other than income on its own. Also important are necessary outgoings, the cost of providing for family members, and for one's own needs. These requirements vary between individuals, even among those with the same level of income. An accurate measure of living standard needs to take into account the relationship between the two factors, income and necessary outgoings.

The meaning of a particular income level is also relative in a second sense. Absolute level of income may be less a determinant of mental health than income relative to that of others in the same community. Individuals tend to adjust their aspirations, so that their ability to purchase goods and services is appraised relative to that ability in people around them. This process is illustrated in nationwide studies over time: as real income increases within a country, average levels of affective well-being do not necessarily increase in the way which would be expected from cross-sectional correlations (e.g. Diener 1984).

It is therefore sometimes desirable to take subjective measures of living standard. In employed samples these will be based upon information not about amount of pay received but about its reported adequacy or fairness. Studies using that type of index are described later. Initially, however, let us consider some investigations into the correlates of income level itself.

Income level

Several studies of employed people, (e.g. Dyer and Theriault 1976; Goodman 1974; Schwab and Wallace 1974; Smith *et al.* 1969) have reported significant associations between amount of pay received and satisfaction with pay. That is hardly surprising, but more interesting significant correlations have been recorded with overall job satisfaction (e.g. Caplan, *et al.* 1975; Smith *et al.* 1969), satisfaction with work, supervision and co-workers (Smith *et al.* 1969), and (negatively) with job-related psychosomatic symptoms (Caplan *et al.*

1975). However, a major interpretative difficulty arises in that amount of pay received is itself a reflection of occupational level, and the latter is known to be positively related to many aspects of job-related mental health: which of the two overlapping factors is causally prior in determining job-related well-being?

A similar problem arises with context-free measures of mental health. However, research with relatively homogeneous samples (controlling occupational level to some degree) has also found that amount of pay is significantly associated with aspects of mental health. In Gardell's (1971) study of two groups of Swedish blue-collar employees (of whom only around 10 per cent had proceeded beyond elementary education), low pay was significantly associated with greater frequency of reported psychosomatic symptoms and higher anxiety, as well as with lower context-free subjective competence.

Kornhauser (1965) observed a significant correlation of income level with his broad interview measure of mental health (see page 90). This study also had the advantage of being restricted to blue-collar employees, and within that range Kornhauser considered possible differences between members of the same skill category who were receiving different amounts of pay. He found some evidence that even in a single grade (semi-skilled employees, for example) income level was positively related to mental health.

Kornhauser's conclusion that 'income differences help account for the poorer mental health of the lowest occupational groups' (p. 124) was supported by qualitative evidence such as these interview statements:

We meet the bills and that is about all. Right now it is terrible; the kids need money for school, they need to go to the dentist, our furniture is falling apart. We just live from pay to pay (p.125).

Wife working and I'm working two jobs; the working-man has to work very hard to have ends meet.... Rough going; I'd like to give my kids more; I have only one suit, yet I'm working 12 to 15 hours a day, Saturday too and Sunday sometimes. I can't even get the necessities of life now. Losing my health because of hard work (p.126).

It seems clear that in situations such as these low pay can contribute to low context-free mental health. It is less clear, however, that differences in pay at higher levels, after more basic requirements have been met, are themselves influences upon mental health. A clearer understanding of this possibility requires investigations which include income as one factor among others in multivariate analyses, in order to determine whether this variable makes an independent contribution over and above the influence of other features.

Few studies of this kind have been conducted with samples all of whose members are in paid work. In one case, O'Brien (1984a) investigated locus of control (an index of context-free subjective autonomy) among a broad sample of Australian employees. After controlling for other factors such as opportunity for control and opportunity for skill use, as well as occupational and educational level, he found that income retained its significant independent contribution to level of internal control. This pattern was present in the overall sample and among males, but was absent in a separate analysis of data from women only. In Kohn and Schooler's (1982) study of ideational flexibility among American male employees (see page 96), income level was also found to make a significant independent contribution to flexibility (here taken as a possible measure of context-free objective competence), after controls had been introduced for a range of job and personal attributes.

There is thus reason to believe that amount of pay is itself an independent contributor to mental health, but the evidence is somewhat patchy. A particular need remains for multivariate investigations using a range of indicators of context-free health.

Perceived fairness

Let us turn next to research which uses subjective measures of the fairness of one's pay. Studies in this area are often based on a version of equity theory (Adams 1963; Adams and Freedman 1976) or derive from Homans's (1961) notion of distributive justice. The latter assumes a general 'norm of reciprocity', such that rewards are desired and expected to be distributed among people in relation to the magnitude of their contribution to a group or to wider society. Homans suggested that expectations about the fair distribution of rewards are developed through comparisons between ratios of inputs and rewards: people expect that the ratio of their rewards relative to their inputs should be about the same as other people's ratios.

This general notion is potentially applicable to all kinds of activities and rewards in social settings. For example, the status allotted to members of an informal group relative to each other (a 'reward' in this context) might be thought to be a function of each person's contribution to the attainment of group goals (their 'input'). In respect of pay, equity theory proposes that employees compare the ratios of their pay levels relative to their inputs against the comparable ratios for other people. 'Inputs' in this case are likely to be defined in terms of skill, effort, qualifications, working conditions, hours of work, and so on. Persons who compare themselves unfavourably with others in these ratios are expected to feel negatively about the level of their pay.

Two questions are particularly important here: what are these negative feelings which follow unfavourable comparisons; and with whom are the comparisons made? In respect of the first question, research has mainly been conducted by industrial and occupational psychologists concerned with the operation of pay systems, and their primary outcome variable has been satisfaction with pay. That is a very restricted focus, and observed associations between felt inequity and dissatisfaction with pay might be viewed as tautologous. A wider research perspective is now required.

In respect of the second question, Goodman (1974) has drawn attention to a range of possible referents in pay comparisons. Principal among these are people inside or outside one's own organization, and Goodman has shown that unfavourable comparisons relative to both groups are accompanied by significantly reduced pay satisfaction. The choice of specific individuals to use as referents is partly determined by information available at the time, but seems also to embody a process of showing that one's own contribution is undervalued. Comparisons are thus widely made with people who are in some sense thought to be getting more than they deserve (Lawler 1965, 1971); their inputs may be low, their pay high, or both factors may be present.

Caplan *et al.* (1975) obtained assessments of the fairness of one's pay relative to colleagues and non-colleagues (separate items, which were summed), but found no significant correlations between perceived inequity of this kind and overall job satisfaction or job-related anxiety, depression, or somatic complaints. Other enquiries into mental health components as possible correlates of perceived inequity of pay would be valuable.

Adequacy and continuity

Perhaps perceived inadequacy of pay is more important than its perceived inequity. The former takes greater account of people's personal and family financial requirements. Deficiencies in comparisons between actual pay and pay needed for one's family were found by Goodman (1974) to be significantly associated with low pay satisfaction, but parallel information in relation to other aspects of job-related or context-free well-being appears not to be available.

A related issue concerns a person's need to maintain his or her income level in order to meet family or other commitments. A feeling that continuity of income is essential in this way was found by Liff (1981) to be significantly associated among British women employees with reduced affective well-being measured through the General Health Questionnaire (see page 42). Women who reported this sense of dependence on their wages were likely to need their pay to meet essential expenses on rent, food, fuel, and clothing. Martin and Roberts (1984) have also observed that women who have taken a paid job mainly because they 'need money for basic essentials' are likely to exhibit greater context-free distress than those whose financial motivation is less pressing. In these cases neither the specific level of pay nor feelings of inequity were identified as being of concern; at issue was the need for continuity of income at about its present level.

Desire for continuity is also of wider importance, for example in respect of piecework schemes. A 'straight' piecework scheme, where payment is directly proportional to items produced, is often unattractive to employees on the grounds that day-to-day variations can lead to fluctuating and unpredictable income. A 'flatter' scheme, with a basic payment and smaller increments for additional items produced, is often preferred in order to enhance stability of amounts received.

Piecework schemes of some kind are very common. For example, about a third of all employees in the United Kingdom are paid in this way, with a higher proportion, almost a half, of those at shop-floor level (e.g. Grayson 1984). An extensive network of piecework schemes can create problems and interpersonal frictions within an organization, as bargaining about standard performance and job evaluation levels is inevitably greater than in timework situations. Problems are particularly common where 'loose' rates (permitting relatively easy high earnings) accompany others which are 'tight', so that competition develops between workers to gain tasks of the former kind.

Piecework schemes are designed on the assumption that output will exceed that on timework. Not surprisingly, therefore, there is a tendency for piece-work jobs to make greater demands on employees (e.g. Wells 1982). In many situations there is likely to be some restriction of output, as employees adjust their work to produce no more than an informally agreed quota. Among the reasons typically given for this are fear of rate cutting if output is too high, avoidance of fatigue, the need to protect slower workers, and a desire to avoid competition between colleagues. Other motives derive from the control which employees gain over their own performance levels, and a desire to avoid explicit manipulation by management (e.g. Hickson 1961; Lupton 1963; Millward 1972; Myers 1920; Roy 1952; Sykes 1976). Despite the prevalence of these processes, the ability to attain targets on a piecework scheme can provide non-financial as well as financial benefit:

Usually 'making money' [by performing well on piecework] was by no means important for the sake of money alone. Incentive earnings, in most cases, seemed to be mainly significant as the basis on which a girl proved her competence as a mount operator to herself and to others. Considerable informal prestige in the department was associated with being on a money-making team (Turner and Miclette 1962, pp. 229–30).

Finally in this consideration of availability of money and the mental health of people in jobs, we should note the importance of setting current income and current financial requirements in the context of previous and expected values. A sudden drop in income or sharp increase in outgoings can have much greater impact upon an employee than would be understood within a cross-sectional enquiry alone. Gradual reductions in financial need as a person becomes older and dependent children leave home can give a different meaning to a fixed level of income. Expectations about the future are also important, both in respect of anticipated continuity or discontinuity, and also in respect of possible improvements in living standards in times to come. The latter can sometimes make possible an acceptance of a current situation which would otherwise be intolerable.

It was suggested in Chapter 1 that availability of money was likely to fall within the 'constant effect' vitamin model, with a negative impact on mental health at low values and a plateau at all higher levels. There is some evidence, cited above, that very low pay is associated with impaired mental health, but additional studies are clearly required to broaden our knowledge of this relationship. Particularly important are investigations into pay which extend beyond measuring merely satisfaction with that pay; more fundamental aspects of mental health urgently require attention. In conducting those studies, the horizontal axis of Fig. 1.1, reflecting variations in the availability of money, will need to take several different forms. The feature appears to be best operationalized through assessments of either inequity or inadequacy; as in the case of other environmental features within the model, these assessments may derive either from subjective self-reports or be obtained from independent sources.

Physical security

Environments in general need to protect people against physical threat and to provide an adequate level of physical security. In job environments, this component of the model may be examined in terms of physical working conditions, contrasting those with the features described in earlier chapters, which are sometimes referred to as 'psychosocial' conditions (e.g. Karasek 1979; Nerell and Wahlund 1981).

Consider this account of some American textile mills at the beginning of the 1960s:

Lack of free movement is made even more oppressive by the unpleasant atmosphere of the mills. During the summer, humidity is unusually high, and the temperature is often above 100 degrees. In addition, the air in many rooms becomes saturated with lint. Faintness and physical weakness are common, particularly among women who often have full household responsibilities in addition to their employment.... Because of the physical atmosphere and the lack of freedom, mill hands refer to the mill as 'the prison'; they also call it the 'sweatshop' and the 'death hole' (Blauner 1964, p.69).

Such conditions are likely to affect employees at four levels. First, they may impair performance, for example through inhibiting effort or increasing errors. Second, they are likely to give rise to feelings of discomfort and fatigue, with associated negative attitudes towards the job. Third, these feelings may carry over to non-job settings, influencing context-free mental health. And fourth, the harmful effects may include physical injury or chronic impairment to physical health. Research by industrial and occupational psychologists, human factors specialists, and ergonomists has tended to emphasize the first two levels, being restricted to task performance or job-related affect. Effects on injury and physical health (the fourth level) have sometimes been examined by epidemiologists, but context-free mental health consequences of physical working conditions have rarely been studied.

Physical work conditions might influence context-free mental health in two ways. First, negative affect might be carried over from job environments to life outside work; this general possibility has been illustrated in several earlier chapters. Second, an indirect influence on mental health may occur through job-related deterioration in physical health. Consider a worker who has a chronic back complaint arising from continuous heavy lifting, or one who is recovering from a crushed leg as a result of an industrial accident. These people clearly illustrate negative physical consequences from their paid work, but they may also exhibit linked impairment in aspects of their mental health.

Many studies have revealed a significant cross-sectional association between levels of physical and mental health (e.g. Hendrie 1981). Such a correlation might arise from several sources, and overall causal interpretation is difficult. However, there are several reasons for expecting reduced mental health to follow from physical impairment. These include chronic pain, restriction of mobility, sleeping or eating problems, reduced ability to cope with work and other demands, uncertainty about the future, and possibly reduced standard of living.

Aneshensel *et al.* (1984) have examined this possibility in a longitudinal community survey in Los Angeles. They analysed physical illnesses and level of depression as reported four times in the course of a year. Illnesses were mainly minor ones, including musculoskeletal problems, pain in arms, legs or back, and colds or flu. After statistically controlling for age, sex and socio-economic status, they observed that illness was significantly associated with depression measured at the same time, and that raised depression levels were predictive of illness in the subsequent months. A causal sequence was inferred, in which episodes of minor physical illness were seen to increase levels of depression; the latter in turn resulted in more negative experiences of physical illness.

It thus appears that physical illness and depression can be mutually reinforcing. This possibility is central to the following discussion of working conditions. Research has most often addressed the physical consequences of poor conditions, providing empirical evidence and plausible inference of negative physical effects. Levels of mental health associated with these physical effects have rarely been examined, but it appears likely that indirect psychological deterioration will in many cases accompany the direct physical consequences.

Environmental features to be covered in this section include heat and cold, noise, illumination level, and vibration, as well as those which give rise to physical danger or require considerable physical effort. In addition, brief consideration will be given to aspects of equipment design. In all cases the perspective will be that of the vitamin model: working conditions are thought to be important at levels representing low physical security, but increases beyond a moderate level are expected not to lead to further increases in mental health. The possible effects of extremely high levels of physical security (the right-hand side of Fig. 1.1, page 10) will be discussed at the end of the section. As emphasized in Chapter 2, the impact of environmental features is thought to be associated with duration of exposure; brief or intermittent work in poor physical conditions is unlikely to have a substantial effect upon mental health.

Temperature

Let us first consider research into the impact of work-place temperature levels. Persons continuously exchange heat with the environment, and this exchange is influenced by bodily factors (such as performance of physical work, which generates additional heat) and by four principal environmental variables. These are air temperature, humidity, air movement velocity, and radiant temperature. Several indices have been devised to predict thermal comfort from these four factors, and their impact upon comfort or discomfort is fairly well established (e.g. Kantowitz and Sorkin 1983; Kobrick and Fine 1983; Poulton, 1978; Ramsey 1983).

However, relationships with job-related mental health, for example overall or facet-specific job satisfaction, appear not to have been studied in detail. Perhaps it is considered self-evident that long periods of work in very high or very low temperatures will give rise to negative feelings about that work. In a similar way, there seems to be no published information about the impact of chronically high or low working temperatures on context-free mental health. Such an impact might be expected through the generalized influence of negative job-related well-being or through the indirect psychological influence of ill-health which is primarily physical.

Noise

Research into noise levels has also been extensive, although studies of job-related or context-free mental health are again difficult to locate. Important variables are the intensity and frequency of sound levels, as well as intermittency or continuity and in some cases whether sound derives from mechanical impact or explosive discharge. The importance of these factors in determining work performance has been illustrated in terms of problems arising from the masking of speech or of important auditory cues, and in respect of reduced speed and accuracy in several forms of psychomotor or cognitive task. Noise-induced deafness has also been much investigated, as have hormonal changes and reductions in peripheral blood supply. It is not clear whether the latter have a cumulative impact on physical health, although brief after-effects of several kinds have been reported to follow termination of the noise. (Research supporting these conclusions has been reviewed by, for example, Cohen and Weinstein 1982; Jones 1983; Kantowitz and Sorkin 1983; and Michael and Bienvenue 1983.)

There have been suggestions that operator errors are increased by high noise intensity (e.g Broadbent and Little 1960), and that accidents are also more frequent in noisy areas, especially for less experienced workers (e.g.

Cohen 1976). However, the generality of these findings, and of possible correlated effects on affective well-being and competence, has not yet been established. In this area as in others throughout the book, it is necessary to overcome the general problem that particular job factors are often associated with other, possibly unmeasured, variables, which may in practice be of greater causal importance than the factor under investigation.

Illumination, vibration, danger, and physical effort

A third physical feature of the work environment which has been much studied is level of illumination. Aspects of brightness, contrast, and glare have been shown to affect performance and comfort, and guidelines for good practice are well established (e.g. Grandjean 1984; Kantowitz and Sorkin 1983; Megaw and Bellamy 1983). As with the preceding two features, it seems clear that extended periods of work in poor lighting conditions can affect both performance and comfort levels; however, the impact of poor lighting on context-free mental health appears not to have been investigated.

The same point may be made about vibration. However, in this case, in addition to evidence about performance and comfort effects, research has also identified consequences for physical health. For example, work which requires the regular operation of vehicles over rough ground has been shown to give rise in the longer term to structural damage to the spine; intense vibration from hand tools can also harm peripheral circulatory and nervous systems, giving rise to intermittent loss of muscular control (e.g. Oborne 1983).

Central to this discussion is a fifth aspect of physical security, the degree to which job environments are physically dangerous. Two points may be noted. First, it is clear that some environments (building sites, coal-mines, battle-fields, etc.) contain generally higher levels of threat than do others. Perceived hazards within these environments may give rise to intermittent or continuing high levels of anxiety, sometimes accompanied by deterioration in task performance (e.g. Idzikowski and Baddeley 1983). Second, the raised danger levels in these environments may cause accidents, resulting in injury and subsequent ill-health. In these cases an indirect effect upon mental health may be expected, in view of the interconnections between physical and mental states which were considered above.

Associated with level of physical danger is the degree to which jobs require intense or sustained physical effort. Many jobs involve lifting, turning, reaching, bending, and other actions which can lead to fatigue or muscular strain. Whereas the consequences of such requirements are likely to be primarily physical, an indirect psychological impact is also to be expected, for reasons described earlier. Furthermore, jobs with high effort requirements tend to be those in which accidents are more frequent. For example, Liles *et al.* (1984) constructed a 'Job Severity Index', to measure physical stress levels associated with manual materials handling. Jobs were assessed in terms of features such as maximum required weight of lift, height, centre of gravity, and time spent lifting. The investigators found that injury rates (and associated costs) were substantially greater in work environments which scored more highly on this scale.

Equipment design

A seventh aspect of physical working conditions overlaps with some of those already introduced. This concerns the design of equipment to meet ergonomic or human factors criteria. For example, extensive anthropometric inform- ation has been gathered about the frequency distribution of variables such as overall height, eye height, forward reach, and the strength of particular muscle groups (e.g. Ayoub 1973; Kroemer 1983). Considerable attention has been paid to the design of physical displays such as pointers, scales, counters, diagrams, and charts, and to processes of control through knobs, levers, switches, dials, or keyboards (e.g. Chapanis 1976; Grandjean 1984; Kantowitz and Sorkin 1983). Despite that, equipment often requires a distorted posture, gives rise to unacceptable physical demands, or is designed in ways which cause errors and associated difficulties in coping with task demands and in building up a smooth work rhythm.

Issues of this kind may be of particular concern to the increasing number of office employees whose work requires sustained interaction with computer-based visual display units (VDUs). For example, Smith *et al.* (1981) compared a group of American VDU operators with employees carrying out similar clerical work without use of VDUs. The former group reported significantly more eye strain, blurred vision, burning eyes, back pain, sore shoulders and other physical complaints. Similar results were observed in a Swiss study by Laubli *et al.* (1980). These investigators also examined relationships between visual complaints and features of the equipment, find- ing that rate of oscillation of luminance of characters on the screen was of particular significance.

Grandjean (1980) has summarized evidence about this and other features which can cause problems to VDU operators, particularly emphasizing the constrained postures which are typically required. Operators may be forced to keep their head and hands more or less permanently in a fixed position, often having inadequate seating and lacking a suitable support for docu- ments. Extreme forms of muscular impairment arising from these deficiences of equipment design have sometimes been reported, for example under the label 'repetition strain injury' (e.g. Williams 1985). Guidelines for the design and operation of VDUs are gradually being established (e.g. Health and Safety Executive 1983), and it is in principle possible to avoid many of these technical and ergonomic problems.

However, all the authors cited here emphasize that continuous work with visual display units may have harmful effects unconnected with the design of the equipment itself. They point out that VDU jobs can require adherence to rigid work procedures with very little opportunity to control one's own tasks; performance demands tend to be very high; and variation in task and physical location is often very low. In the present terms, many computer-based office jobs may be harmful in respect of environmental feature number 7 (physical security), but also in respect of features 1, 3, and 4: opportunity for control, externally generated goals, and variety. This point will be taken up again in Chapter 15.

Overview

Returning to consideration of jobs in general, a study of Finnish employees changing jobs over a five-year period is of particular interest. This investigation (described by Kirjonen and Hanninen 1986) included at both measurement points an index of working conditions in terms of the presence or absence of physical, chemical, and ergonomic hazards. Increases or decreases in physical security so measured were found to be accompanied by parallel changes across the period in both job-related and context-free well-being. These longitudinal associations were present despite controls for changes in other job characteristics, relations with colleagues, and satisfaction with pay.

However, it remains true that the environmental characteristics examined in this section have been inadequately studied in relation to mental health. For example, very few measures of job satisfaction include items to tap feelings about physical working conditions. Scales tend instead to concentrate on intrinsic features and aspects such as co-workers, pay and promotion prospects (Cook *et al.* 1981). Taber *et al.* (1985) have noted a similar omission in studies which measure job attributes. Conventional procedures almost always exclude consideration of job hazards and other physical working conditions:

This omission is consistent with the bias in modern theories to classify working conditions arbitrarily as 'extrinsic' to the job and then to ignore them. It is quite possible that many workers consider such things as heat, fumes, oils and greases, and noise in the work place to be intrinsic characteristics of their jobs. Early studies of industrial psychology focussed on the importance of working conditions, but they play almost no role in modern social science theories of work (Taber *et al.* 1985, p.42).

The importance of studying these aspects of the job environment has also been stressed by Stone and Gueutal (1985). In investigating primary dimensions underlying people's perceptions of jobs, these authors drew attention to the presence of a major axis which they labelled as 'physical demand'. They point out that standard measures of job characteristics, such as the Job Diagnostic Survey or the Job Characteristics Index, fail to tap that principal dimension.

One recent exception to the bias away from physical working conditions is a study by Campion and Thayer (1985). These authors developed a composite scale in terms of features such as noise, tool design, lifting and postural requirements, vibration, and safety levels. The correlation between independently obtained job ratings on this scale and employees' reports of physical discomfort and health complaints was found to be 0.50.

Physical conditions are important within the present framework as one component of the vitamin CE model. This proposes that physical security is particularly important in its absence, and that variations in security beyond a moderate level have little impact on employees' mental health. For example, very high noise levels represent low physical security and are predicted to be harmful; but variation in noise across a broad range of medium and low values is thought to be unrelated to mental health. A similar non-linear relationship is proposed for vibration, physical danger, and sustained physical effort: high levels are harmful, in terms of low physical security, but medium and low levels are represented by the benign plateau incorporated in Fig. 1.1. For temperature and illumination, it is very high and very low levels which are defined as low physical security, with medium levels considered to be acceptable. The evidence reviewed in this section about these non-linear possibilities has been suggestive and indirect, but appears to be consistent with the proposed vitamin CE model.

Finally, we should note some possible combinations of physical security with other environmental features within the model. In general, it may be expected that poor physical working conditions will tend to add to the negative impact of harmful 'psychosocial' conditions discussed elsewhere in the book; as pointed out above, this possibility has largely been overlooked in recent theories. Conversely, poor physical conditions may be ameliorated by high values of opportunity for control (feature number 1); that primary environmental characteristic is important throughout the model for its potential to curb negative influences arising from the other eight features.

Summary

This chapter has examined environmental categories numbered 6 and 7 within the vitamin model: availability of money and physical security. In both cases research into their impact on employee mental health has been found to be limited.

The importance of money as a source of social identity as well as a means to meet basic needs was emphasized. It was seen necessary to consider a person's income in relation to his or her necessary outgoings, and also in relation to the perceived income of other people. The need for measures in terms of relative adequacy or judged fairness was therefore stressed. Some investigations were found to suggest a link between those measures and job-related mental health, but research in this field was seen to be generally inadequate. Particularly required are studies which consider context-free mental health, especially through multivariate analysis.

The general category of 'physical security' in job settings was examined in terms of physical working conditions. Attention was mainly directed at variations in temperature, noise, illumination level, vibration, danger, and required physical effort. Negative forms of each of these sub-categories were considered, and it was suggested that they are likely to affect mental as well as physical health through a process of carry-over from one to the other. However, research enquiries into mental health impacts were shown to be rare.

The fact that poor physical working conditions are particularly likely to be found in jobs which are deficient in other terms was illustrated through studies of VDU operators. Although visual and muscular problems can result from work on this type of equipment, impairments also arise in part from a job content which lacks opportunity for personal control, contains little variety, and makes heavy work demands. Echoing the theme developed in other parts of the book, the chapter concluded with a plea for research which examines physical working conditions in conjunction with other environmental categories.

10

Extrinsic job features: interpersonal contact and social position

This chapter will consider the final two environmental categories within the present model: opportunity for interpersonal contact, and valued social position. The importance of these within jobs will be examined, before we turn in the next two chapters to review all nine features in the settings of unemployment.

Opportunity for interpersonal contact

The possibility that social relationships at work influence employee mental health is captured in the eighth feature of the present framework. As in other cases, investigations have mainly concerned affective well-being, but additional components of mental health will be introduced where appropriate.

The section will initially examine the intrinsic value of social interaction, and then consider particular consequences of interaction, for example in relation to task-related versus social-emotional gains or losses. Research into the amount of interaction required in a job or encouraged by building design will then be examined, leading into a review of investigations concerned with the quality of 'social support' in the work-place. Finally, some issues will be raised about the combination of social support with other environmental features, and about the possible effects of extremely high levels of inter-personal contact associated with restricted privacy and the invasion of personal territory.

The intrinsic importance of contact with other people has been expressed in many theories of motivation and psychological functioning. As pointed out in Chapter 1, existential psychologists have emphasized the central experience of aloneness and people's efforts to bridge the gap between themselves and others. Early drive theorists regularly included 'social' motives within their general framework (e.g. McDougall 1932; Murray 1938). Research into interpersonal judgement has drawn attention to the fact that people tend to like others more than they dislike them (e.g. Boucher and

Osgood 1969), and social psychological studies have illustrated how physical proximity tends in general to give rise to some degree of interpersonal attraction (e.g. Lott and Lott 1965).

Of course, social contact may also be unpleasant in certain cases. Nevertheless, there are sufficient conceptual and empirical grounds for asserting that in overall terms contact with other people tends to be intrinsically enjoyable and important for the maintenance of good mental health.

What of the *consequential* importance of interpersonal contact, particularly that occurring in job settings? Interactions with other people generate outcomes which may be referred to as either 'task-related' or 'social-emotional'. In the first category, interaction with other people may assist problem-solution through the provision of information, advice, or practical help. Discussions about problems with work colleagues tend to focus upon difficulties in prescribed tasks, but they also extend into help with family, financial and personal difficulties (e.g. Burke *et al.* 1976; Kaplan and Cowan 1981).

In the second category are consequences of social contact in terms of friendships and additional pleasant experiences. For example, the Job Characteristics Inventory contains a scale to tap 'friendship opportunities'. This is made up of items of the kind: 'How much opportunity is there to meet individuals whom you would like to develop friendships with?' Reported friendship opportunities in a job, measured in this way or through the earlier index of Hackman and Lawler (1971), have been found to be significantly associated with overall and facet-specific job satisfaction (e.g. Hackman and Lawler 1971; Oldham and Brass 1979; Sims and Szilagyi 1976; Stone and Porter 1975), and also with intrinsic job motivation (Oldham and Brass 1979).

Henderson and Argyle (1985) asked employees about the presence or absence of four types of person within their immediate work-group. First were 'people at work who you get on very well with, who you see socially outside of work, and whom you would call good friends'. Second were 'people at work who you get on well with and spend time with socially at work (at lunch and coffee times) but whom you do not see as friends outside work'. The third group were 'people at work you get on reasonably well with, but just as a workmate, not someone you spend much social time with either at work or outside work'. And fourth were 'people at work you don't get on very well with'. Current feelings of job stress were at a significantly lower level for those employees reporting at least one person in the first category, but no differences were associated with presence or absence of the other three types of co-worker. However, overall job satisfaction was unrelated to the presence or absence of any of the four categories.

Another perspective on benefits arising from interpersonal contact in job settings is in terms of the nine-category framework of the vitamin model. The consequences of varying levels of interpersonal contact may be considered in respect of each of the other eight features. For example, environmental variety (feature number 4) can be partly in terms of interpersonal contact. Jobs which provide very little contact with other people are in an important respect limited in variety; conversely, jobs with moderate levels of interpersonal contact are often attractive through the variety this brings, even when intrinsic task aspects are themselves fixed and unchanging.

Interpersonal contact in a job may also be reflected in greater environmental clarity (feature number 5). Through discussions with other people one can gather and interpret information about the work environment and about changes which may possibly occur. Chapter 8 suggested that clarity may be described in terms of feedback, predictability, and normative transparency; each of these can be enhanced through interpersonal contact.

Another environmental feature which is sometimes linked to opportunity for interpersonal contact is the presence of externally generated goals (feature number 3). In addition to the fact that information about required job behaviour is usually transmitted through other people, co-workers as well as bosses, interpersonal contact may provide 'role models' to be emulated, and information about other jobs which may be sought through promotion or transfer. On an informal level, co-workers may encourage and sustain hobby activities which generate new goals outside the work-place.

As a final example of links between interpersonal contact and other aspects of the present framework, consider opportunity for control (feature number 1). Discussions which aid problem-solving have already been considered, but in addition membership of a larger group is important in making possible some collective control over the environment. Group goals are not only those prescribed by an employing organization ('task-related' in the sense used above), but may also include protection or improvement of the position of the group in question. Explicit examples of collective action for the benefit of members may be seen in the work of trade unions, but many other groupings of a similar type, possibly informal and temporary, are to be found in most employing organizations. Increased opportunity for interpersonal contact may sometimes promote increased influence of this collective kind.

Amount of interaction

There are thus several reasons for expecting that job environments which promote contact with other people will benefit employees more than will those which offer little opportunity for contact. In practice, however, there are few published studies addressed to this possibility. One exception is the investigation by Moch (1980), who examined the degree to which employees of an American assembly plant worked closely with others. He separated 'isolates' (those reporting no close links with others) from 'non-isolates', and examined levels of intrinsic job motivation in the two groups; as suggested in Chapter 3, this variable may be viewed as an aspect of subjective job-related aspiration. Controlling for other job characteristics such as reported variety and opportunity for control, he found that isolates had significantly lower intrinsic job motivation than those who worked with colleagues. Reported opportunity for social interaction was measured directly by Gardell (1971). In separate analyses of data from two groups of blue-collar Swedish employees, this variable was found to be significantly positively associated with overall job satisfaction, life satisfaction and context-free subjective competence, and significantly negatively correlated with job-related tension and context-free anxiety.

Some studies have examined interpersonal contact through the 'dealing with others' scale of the Job Diagnostic Survey. This obtains reports of the extent to which one's job requires close working with other people, either colleagues or clients. Scores have been found to be significantly associated with overall job satisfaction, intrinsic job satisfaction, and intrinsic job motivation (e.g. Hackman and Oldham 1975; Oldham *et al.* 1978). A similar measure of 'dealing with others' within the Job Characteristics Inventory has been found to yield scores which are significantly associated with satisfaction with the work itself, with colleagues, and with supervision (Sims and Szilagyi 1976).

Another group of studies has investigated aspects of building design which promote or inhibit interpersonal contact at work. For example, Szilagyi and Holland (1980) monitored a move between buildings made by professional employees in an American company. As a result of this move, the 'social density' of working environments decreased for some individuals and increased for others.

Social density was measured for each person as the number of colleagues within a 50-foot walking distance, and the investigators identified three approximately equal-sized groups: those showing a substantial increase in density, those with a substantial decrease, and those with no great change in density. Significant differences in the pattern of change in overall job satisfaction were observed in relation to that classification, with increases in social density giving rise to enhanced satisfaction, and reductions in density being associated with reduced satisfaction.

Beneficial task-related consequences were also found to accompany increased density: significantly greater feedback (see Chapter 8), reduced role conflict (Chapter 7), and reduced role ambiguity (Chapter 8). In addition, one negative task-related change was observed, in that autonomy was reported to have declined by employees whose social density had increased. Turning to socio-emotional consequences, Szilagyi and Holland observed that perceived friendship opportunities increased in the sub-group experiencing increased density and declined in the sub-group whose density had been reduced. The authors emphasize that this group of employees required a high degree of interaction and information flow between them in order to perform their work successfully. This task attribute seems likely in general to mediate results of studies into physical layout, and is considered again later in the chapter.

Social support

The investigations described so far have mainly concerned the *quantity* of interpersonal contact, using objective measures of social density or subjective reports about the degree to which employees are required to work closely with others. Another research approach has focused upon subjective assessments of the *quality* of interpersonal contact rather than its quantity. Studies of this kind will be reviewed next.

The degree to which relationships are evaluated as good or bad has been examined by several investigators. For example, Etzion (1984) and Pines and Kafry (1981) described significant associations between reported quality of job relationships and physical, mental, and emotional exhaustion, in analyses of data from Israeli and American professional workers respectively. Van Dijkhuizen's (1981) study of Dutch managers indicated that reports of poor relations with others were significantly associated with low job satisfaction, high job-related anxiety, and more frequent job-related psychosomatic problems. In research with United States military personnel, Hendrix *et al.* (1985) observed a significant relationship between good relationships with co-workers and low job-related tension, after controlling for a range of other job features and individual difference variables.

Results of this kind from studies using broad measures of self-reported quality of interaction are not surprising, especially those in relation to job-related well-being. Other people are clearly a major part of the job environment, and feelings about them naturally contribute to job-related affect more widely. In addition, 'poor relationships' may arise through features and processes indicated earlier to be harmful: other people's restrictions on one's personal discretion, overload from supervisors or colleagues, role ambiguity, and so on.

Slightly more focused studies have been carried out into the importance of what has been referred to as 'social support'. Although this term is variously defined in the literature, it is usually taken to mean the availability of help from other people (e.g. House 1981) or the degree to which basic social needs are met through interaction with others (e.g. Thoits 1982). The feature has often been investigated in community and family settings. For example, in a longitudinal study within a single American state, Lin and Ensel (1984) recorded significant covariation over a one-year period between changes in level of support and changes in depression: increased social support was accompanied by a reduction in depression, and *vice versa*.

Significant associations have frequently been observed in occupational settings between social support and high levels of job satisfaction and context-free well-being (e.g. Jackson 1983; Payne and Jones 1986). In a longitudinal project, Parkes (1982) studied British student nurses as they moved between two types of hospital ward. Changes in reported social support were significantly associated positively with changes in overall job satisfaction and negatively with changes in context-free anxiety and depression. Support changes were also negatively correlated with changes in self-reported social dysfunction, which may be taken as a partial index of low context-free subjective competence: as support in the work setting increased so did subjective competence, and *vice versa*.

A distinction is sometimes drawn between support which arises from different sources. For example, in occupational research it may be helpful to ·distinguish between support received from colleagues at approximately one's own level in the organization and that provided by people at higher levels; these have been termed 'co-worker support' and 'boss support' respectively.

In addition, there may sometimes be advantage in studying support received from specific sub-groups within each category, a trade union branch for example, although that has not been done within the research tradition being described. More common is an interest in groups outside the job setting, for example a worker's family or friends (e.g. Blau 1981; French *et al.* 1983; Kobasa and Pucetti 1983; LaRocco *et al.* 1980; Seers *et al.* 1983). In all cases, support may be available (or absent) in respect of occupational problems (coping with current job demands, for instance) and also in respect of problems arising in other domains (family difficulties, or how to repair one's car, for example). These two problem-contexts have rarely been distinguished in empirical research.

Several investigators have examined co-worker support in relation to affective well-being. Measures may be illustrated by the scale of Caplan *et al.* (1975), used also by Blau (1981), LaRocco *et al.* (1980), and Seers *et al.* (1983). This contains four items, asking whether people at work other than one's boss 'make your work life easier', are 'easy to talk with', can 'be relied on when things get tough', and are 'willing to listen to your personal problems'. (The first three of these items were used by French *et al.* 1983.) More general measures of co-worker support include that by LaRocco and Jones (1978), who measured 'the perceived quality of work-group relationships in terms of the amount of co-operative effort among co-workers, work-group *esprit de corps*, the level of friendliness, warmth, open communication, and trust among members of the work group, as well as shared pride in the work group' (p. 630). Such a broad concept appears to have much in common with work-group morale.

Reported co-worker support has been found to be significantly associated with overall job satisfaction (e.g. Blau 1981; Ganster *et al.* 1986; House 1981; LaRocco and Jones 1978; Mottaz 1986; LaRocco *et al.* 1980) and intrinsic satisfaction (e.g. Abdel-Halim 1982). Seers *et al.* (1983) recorded significant correlations in respect of satisfaction with the work itself and satisfaction with supervisor, but non-significant associations were obtained with overall job satisfaction, satisfaction with pay, and satisfaction with promotion opportunities. Job-related anxiety has been found to be significantly negatively associated with co-worker support by Abdel-Halim (1982), LaRocco *et al.* (1980), van Dijkhuizen (1980), and Winnubst *et al.* (1982); but a non-significant association was recorded by Parker and DeCotiis (1983). Ganster *et al.* (1986), LaRocco *et al.* (1980), van Dijkhuizen (1980) and Winnubst *et al.* (1982) also observed significant negative correlations with job-related depression and job-related somatic symptoms.

Turning to context-free affective well-being, Billings and Moos (1982) found that supportive and friendly peer relationships were significantly associated with low anxiety, low depression, and few somatic symptoms among men; however the association was significant for women only in respect of depression. These authors included among their measures an index of self-confidence, which appears to cover what in Chapter 2 was described as context-free subjective autonomy. This variable was found to be significantly associated with co-worker support for men but not for women. Finally, LaRocco and Jones (1978) observed a significant correlation (also in a male sample) with a measure of self-esteem which in the present framework appears to tap context-free subjective competence.

Several of these investigators have also examined support from one's boss. This was sometimes measured in terms which parallel the measurement of co-worker support; for example, Blau (1981), Ganster *et al.* (1986), LaRocco *et al.* (1980) and Seers *et al.* (1983) used the four items cited above with separate reference to one's supervisor as well as to co-workers. However, as in the case of co-worker support, some indices are rather more broad. For example, Abdel-Halim (1982) used as a measure of boss support the 'consideration' scale of the Leader Behavior Description Questionnaire (Stogdill 1963). This covers aspects such as the degree to which one's boss is 'friendly and approachable', 'looks out for the personal welfare of group members', and 'does little things which make it pleasant to be a member of the group'.

Measures of co-worker support and boss support are typically positively intercorrelated, for example, 0.39 in the analysis by LaRocco *et al.* (1980) of the data gathered by Caplan *et al.* (1975), and 0.46 and 0.30 in the studies described by Abdel-Halim (1982) and House (1981) respectively. Not surprisingly, therefore, associations with mental health indicators are similar for the two types of support.

Significant correlations of boss support with overall job satisfaction have been reported by Blau (1981), French *et al.* (1983), Ganster *et al.* (1986), House (1981), LaRocco and Jones (1978), LaRocco *et al.* (1980), Mottaz (1986), and van Dijkhuizen (1980); however, Seers *et al.* (1983) failed to observe a significant correlation, as they had done in respect of co-worker support. Seers and colleagues also reported non-significant associations in respect of satisfaction with the work itself, satisfaction with pay, and satisfaction with promotion opportunities, but they found a very strong correlation (0.66) in respect of satisfaction with supervisor; that may be thought to be tautologous, arising from an overlap between two measures of what is effectively the same construct. Intrinsic job satisfaction was observed by Abdel-Halim (1982) to be a significant correlate of boss support. He also found that low boss support was significantly associated with high job-related anxiety. LaRocco *et al.* (1980), van Dijkuizen (1980) and Winnubst *et al.* (1982) found significant associations in respect of job-related anxiety and depression, and also with job-related somatic symptoms.

Context-free measures of somatic complaints were used by Billings and Moos (1982), Ganster *et al.* (1986) and Kobasa and Pucetti (1983). Scores were significantly negatively associated with boss support, except in Billings and Moos's female sample. These last authors also recorded significant associations for men but not for women with context-free anxiety and depression. Significant correlations with anxiety and depression were also present in the study of men described by French *et al.* (1983); however, this investigation revealed generally non-significant associations with somatic complaints.

Context-free subjective autonomy was found by Billings and Moos (1982) to be significantly associated with boss support in their male sample, but not among females. However, the measure of context-free subjective competence used by French *et al.* (1983) and LaRocco and Jones (1978) was unrelated to their measures of boss support.

Another group of studies has distinguished further between forms of social support. In addition to separately considering different *sources* (boss versus co-workers, for example), one may also examine differences in the *type* of support. One conceptual distinction which has often been drawn is between 'emotional' and 'instrumental' social support. The former includes the expression of sympathy and understanding, acceptance, affection, and esteem; the latter is seen in the provision of advice, information or practical help (e.g. Wills 1985). The investigations described so far did not distinguish in their measurement procedures between these two forms of support, but a smaller number of other studies have done so.

Jayaratne and Chess (1984) concentrated on emotional support ('the provision of empathy, caring, trust, and concern') in a study of American social workers. Emotional support from co-workers was found to be significantly associated with high overall job satisfaction, low job-related emotional exhaustion, and low context-free somatic complaints; however, it was unrelated to context-free anxiety and depression. The same pattern was observed in relation to emotional support from boss.

Karasek *et al.* (1982) employed separate measures of emotional and instrumental support supplied by co-workers and by one's boss. In a further analysis of data from the American study described by Karasek (1979) (see

Chapters 5 and 7), they had available information about job satisfaction, job-related depression, context-free depression, and life satisfaction. Significant correlations were observed between level of support in each of the four categories and each of these indicators of affective well-being, both before and after the introduction of statistical controls for task demands and decision latitude. In general, emotional co-worker support was the form least predictive of well-being. This may have been because the three items tapping this construct were inappropriate, asking about contacts with co-workers outside the workplace rather than within the job (see the authors' Table 5).

The studies of social support reviewed here have covered a wide range of employee groups, although it is notable that almost all were American. Each investigation had purposes beyond those identified here, but they make it clear with respect to the present theme that job-related affective well-being is significantly associated with level of social support at work. Conceptual distinctions between separate sources of support (e.g. co-worker versus boss) and between different types of support (e.g. emotional versus instrumental) are not reflected in varying empirical findings: similar associations with affective well-being are found in each case.

These correlations are not surprising, in view of the studies' overlapping measurement of affective responses; both job-related social support and job-related well-being cover evaluations of occupational conditions. Particularly high associations are found in respect of evaluations which are conceptually most closely linked. For example, correlations between boss support and satisfaction with boss are larger than those between boss support and satisfaction with pay. These higher correlations are especially likely to reflect a common item content: both sets of measures, of support and job-related well-being, are tapping evaluations of the same job feature.

The finding that lower reported social support in a job setting is associated with lower *context-free* well-being (for example, raised anxiety or more frequent psychosomatic symptoms) is of greater importance, suggesting that low social support may have carry-over effects into other domains of life. More detailed investigations into these associations, their linear or non-linear pattern, and their underlying processes would now be helpful.

However, there remains a general problem which pervades all research identified as covering 'social support'. It may be the case that measures of this concept are primarily tapping other environmental features, which themselves affect mental health. Consistent with this possibility are significant negative correlations between levels of support and several features discussed in earlier chapters. For example, high boss support is regularly reported in the papers cited above to be significantly associated with low role conflict, low role ambiguity, low opportunity for skill use, and high opportunity for personal control. A similar pattern of significant correlations is present in respect of co-worker support, although values are in that case slightly lower. It is possible, therefore, that social support as measured is largely a reflection of the degree to which the social environment contains (or lacks) features which have been shown to be important under different research traditions. As such it might be viewed principally as a 'proxy' variable standing for a set of other components within the vitamin model.

This possibility is particularly troublesome in investigations into the combined impact of social support and other aspects of the environment. There have been many studies of what has become known as the 'buffering hypothesis' of social support. This states that social support 'buffers' the effect of 'stress', in that it is important at high stress levels but not at low stress levels. Support is thus predicted to combine synergistically rather than additively with features such as role ambiguity or negative life events. An additive model would predict that social support and role ambiguity combine together with unchanging weights no matter how high or low each of them is. On the other hand, the buffering hypothesis suggests that low social support is disproportionately harmful (takes on a particularly large weight) when role ambiguity (or another negative environmental feature) is high.

This hypothesis has often been tested by examining in analysis of variance for the presence of a significant multiplicative interaction between level of social support and level of, say, role ambiguity, with both of these variables being measured at the same point in time. The buffering hypothesis is viewed as predicting a significant interaction, such that the impact of social support on affective well-being is significantly greater in conditions of high role ambiguity than in conditions of low ambiguity. Similar predictions are made in respect of high or low values of other potentially harmful environmental features. The buffering hypothesis has frequently been investigated in occupational settings. A number of studies have obtained results consistent with its predictions, but many others have not. For example, significant interaction terms in analysis of variance were reported in respect of role conflict and social support by Abdel-Halim (1982), LaRocco et al. (1980) (in five out of 14 analyses of overlapping data), and Seers et al. (1983). However, the same interaction terms were not significant in studies by French et al. (1983), Ganster et al. (1986), Gavin and Axelrod (1977), Jayaratne and Chess (1984) and LaRocco and Jones (1978). House (1981) describes evidence indicative of a buffering effect upon role conflict of boss support but not co-worker support. Positive results in relation to role ambiguity were obtained by Abdel-Halim (1982), but not by Ganster et al. (1986), Gavin and Axelrod (1977), Jayaratne and Chess (1984), LaRocco and Jones (1978), LaRocco et al. (1980) (in respect of future ambiguity), and Seers et al. (1983).

Using general measures of negative job features, Karasek et al. (1982) and Kobasa and Pucetti (1983) found evidence for a buffering effect, but Blau (1981) did not. Etzion's (1984) results were positive for men but not for women. Results obtained by French et al. (1983) were particularly difficult to interpret, with only a few significant interactions, a third of which (7 of 23 in respect of job factors and boss support; see their Appendix E) were opposite in direction to that predicted.

In general, therefore, it appears appropriate to conclude that research evidence does not support the proposition that social support combines with other features in job settings in a synergistic manner (see also Kasl and Wells 1985). As with other features described throughout the book, the balance of evidence is that an additive combination rule is in general to be expected.

Privacy and personal territory

Turning from these studies of the reported quality of interpersonal contact in job settings to look again at research into quantity, there appear to be no investigations explicitly concerned with how different amounts of contact combine with other environmental factors. For the present, we may surmise that the mode of combination is an additive one, yielding a pattern of summations of the kind illustrated in Table 7.2 (page 133).

In keeping with the vitamin AD model, it is assumed that very high levels of interpersonal contact tend to be harmful. This assumption can be supported on both theoretical and empirical grounds. In the former case discussions of privacy and personal territories are important. For example, Altman (1975) and Altman and Chemers (1980) have developed a model of people's attempts to regulate the degree to which they are open to interaction with others, arguing that accessibility is controlled both by behavioural processes and environmental structures. Privacy is seen as important for separate personal development (aspects of autonomy in the present framework) and also for the effective management of tasks on either an individual or a group basis. In regulating their privacy, people seek on the one hand to avoid isolation, and on the other hand to escape crowding, a feeling of having too little space. The latter experience is assumed to arise from high levels of density (a physical characteristic of the environment), and both isolation and high density are considered to be psychologically harmful.

One form of privacy regulation is the establishment of a personal territory, for oneself or for one's small group. Boundaries are created in social networks of all kinds, being valued for the potential they provide for separate existence of individuals and groups and for the effective management of tasks without external interference. Environments which give rise to an extremely high level of interpersonal contact often frustrate their occupants' concern for privacy and bring about crowding to an extent that can be disruptive. Within occupational settings this process may be illustrated through studies in which workplace layout demands interpersonal contact to a very high degree.

In an investigation of clerical employees (93 per cent women) in 19 offices at an American university, Oldham and Rotchford (1983) examined the density of each office, in terms of total area divided by the number of occupants. This value was reverse-scored, so that higher density levels reflected less space per employee. Results indicated that higher density was significantly associated with low overall job satisfaction, low satisfaction with colleagues, low satisfaction with the office, and reduced amount of feedback about performance received from supervisors or co-workers.

Lack of privacy was particularly emphasized by Oldham and Brass (1979) in their study of a move from separate conventional offices into a single large open-plan office. The latter had no interior walls and no partitions or cabinets more than three feet high. Employees participating in the study held non-supervisory jobs in an American newspaper company, and included reporters, receptionists, copy editors, clerks, and salespersons. This sample seems likely to have had a task-related need for interaction which could be described as approximately average for office workers.

The move into the open-plan office gave rise to significant decreases in overall job satisfaction and satisfaction with colleagues, as well as in intrinsic job motivation. Task-related decrements were observed in respect of reduced ability to concentrate, reduced feelings of task identity (see Chapter 7), and reduced feedback from supervisors. The authors discuss feedback in these terms:

The physical boundaries present in conventional offices provide the private space often desirable if evaluative feedback is to be offered. Open-plan offices, on the other hand, provide virtually no private space. In short, every evaluation is subject to the evaluation of others, which is likely to create discomfort among supervisors and peers and a net reduction in feedback (Oldham and Brass 1979, p. 271).

Social–emotional consequences were also undesirable, in that reported friendship opportunities were found to have declined significantly after moving into the open-plan environment. This decline was associated with employees' concern that they could not have separate discussions with colleagues without being overheard by the larger group.

The importance of this form of privacy (sometimes termed 'acoustical privacy'; e.g. Wineman 1982) has frequently been demonstrated. For example, Brookes and Kaplan (1972) described a move into an open-plan office by employees of an American retail firm. Quantitative perceptual data and open-ended comments were obtained both before the move and nine months later. Employees were concerned over their inability to talk privately in the new setting, and they also reported difficulties arising from the noise of other people's conversation intruding into their own work-space. (However, this latter feature was also reported as a problem in the previous office layout; it is clearly not confined to open-plan settings.)

The development and consequences of territorial behaviour were investigated by Altman *et al.* (1971), in research with American sailors who volunteered to live and work in socially isolated pairs for eight-day periods. Their environment, a 12-foot square cubicle, contained beds, a table, two chairs, task equipment, and basic living facilities. Territorial behaviour was defined in terms of exclusive use of a single bed area, and it was found that individuals who established territories early in their period together were able to work more effectively and exhibited fewer symptoms of strain than did those who failed to establish territories in this way. Throughout the experiment there was very little privacy, but creating bounded territories served to enhance individuality and improve task performance.

How do the results of these studies fit within the vitamin AD model of the present book? This proposes that across a broad middle range of values of opportunity for interpersonal contact variations in this feature have no impact on mental health. However, at low levels (restricted opportunity for contact) mental health is expected to be impaired, and a further decrement is predicted when contact levels are extremely high. Investigations described earlier in the chapter tend to support the prediction that low opportunity for interpersonal contact in a job will be associated with low mental health. The four studies described in the immediately preceding paragraphs are concerned more with the consequences of very high values.

Bringing together their results within the theoretical framework described by Altman and Chemers, we may conclude that job environments which demand very close interpersonal contact are likely to have negative effects upon aspects of mental health. This conclusion is similar to Altman's (1975) interpretation of non-occupational environments, where high 'physical density increases the probability that interpersonal contact will occur to an extent that may interfere with various boundary-control mechanisms' (p. 157). However, as with most other categories in the present framework, there has been too little research into the nature of the possible effects of very high levels of this feature. For example, a more differentiated approach to the measurement of the components of mental health in high density settings is required; and different forms of raised contact levels deserve separate investigation, in terms of number of people, duration of their presence, and degree of intrusiveness, as well as the temporal distribution of contacts relative to an employee's changing needs for concentration and relaxation.

Finally, one unusual negative consequence of interpersonal contact in the work-place may be noted. From time to time within work settings there is a sudden and widespread occurrence of physical illness for which no physical cause can be found. Colligan and Murphy (1979) describe cases within manufacturing plants where large proportions of a work-force were suddenly affected by dizziness, nausea, fainting, headaches, and related symptoms. In the absence of an identifiable pathogen, such occurrences have been referred to as 'mass psychogenic illness'. Although certain individual and organizational features have been implicated in the initiation and spread of these conditions, there is strong evidence that they depend upon quite close interpersonal contact (see also Colligan *et al.* 1982).

Valued social position

We turn now to the final feature in the present framework, to consider the importance of different levels of esteem attached to occupational positions.

Esteem within a social structure is generated primarily through the value attached to activities in particular roles.

This process has been approached from several theoretical standpoints. For example, Thoits (1983) considered a person's valued roles in symbolic interactionist terms, arguing that role incumbency is essential for healthy development and that an accumulation of identities through role enactment is important for mental health. She suggested that the more valued a position, the greater will be the psychological impact of its loss or gain. In an American community survey, she investigated whether or not respondents held the positions of spouse, parent, employee, student, organizational member, church member, neighbour, and friend. A significant negative association was found between number of positions held and frequency of psychosomatic symptoms. In addition, parallel associations between change scores over a two-year period were observed: people taking on additional valued roles exhibited reductions in symptoms, and *vice versa*.

In the present chapter it is social position deriving from one's job which is of interest: are differences in the value attached to jobs associated with variations in aspects of mental health? To examine this question it will be helpful to distinguish between three levels of enquiry, although in practice they overlap in many ways. The levels cover evaluations in terms which can be referred to as cultural, sub-cultural, and personal.

Cultural evaluations

Statements about differences in evaluation at the cultural level refer to rankings about which there is widespread agreement within a society as a whole. Two principal sets of rankings will be considered here, in terms of social stratification and in terms of occupational prestige.

Many investigators have examined the correlates of social-stratification position, measuring this through indices of social class or socio-economic status. These indices are typically based upon information about one or more of the variables of income, education, and occupational level. Although these three are positively intercorrelated, different combinations yield slightly different patterns of findings (e.g. Kohn and Schooler 1983; Rainwater 1974). Nevertheless, it is clear that statements about social stratification almost always contain some reference to differences between jobs. Furthermore, jobs are compared within a hierarchy which is broadly accepted among members of a particular society, with 'upper-class' or 'middle-class' jobs being ranked above those which are 'lower-class' or 'working-class'.

However, each social-stratification position embraces a wide range of individual and social conditions which extend beyond merely occupational features. It would therefore be inappropriate to place great emphasis in the present book on observed differences between the mental health of members at different class levels. Such differences have been widely reported, with poorer health and increased prevalence of diagnosed disorders being con-sistently observed at lower class levels (e.g. Kessler and Cleary 1980; Liem and Liem 1978; Veenhoven and Jonkers 1984).

More directly relevant to our present concern are studies of occupational prestige, the second form of ranking at the cultural level. Several measures have been developed which aim to rank job titles according to the prestige generally accorded to them within a society. Prestige rankings naturally overlap with assessments of occupational level, but they make some addi-tional discriminations. For example, Bradburn (1969) distinguished be-tween jobs within two separate levels (white-collar and blue-collar) according to their prestige rankings. He found that among male principal wage-earners context-free well-being was in each case greater in jobs with higher prestige. Similar correlations between aspects of context-free mental health and occu-pational prestige have been found elsewhere (e.g. Veenhoven and Jonkers 1984).

Studies of both social-stratification position and occupational prestige are based upon a rather gross categorization of jobs, initially in terms of their titles, and a subsequent assessment of each job category in terms of a broad societal consensus. The outcome of such a process is sometimes only tenu-ously linked to the conditions of a particular employee's job. The second level of enquiry mentioned above, into sub-cultural sources of esteem, may yield links with individual jobs which are rather more strong.

Sub-cultural evaluations

At this level we are concerned with esteem within a particular community or network. For example, within a neighbourhood particular jobs such as shop-keeper or postman may be accorded special esteem over and above that expected in general from social-stratification rankings. Or within a network of professional employees spread across the country, one particular role may carry unusually high or low prestige.

It seems clear that the sub-cultural esteem attaching to one's job can influence affective well-being, although this possibility has not been re-searched in any systematic way. Bradburn (1969) approached the question by asking whether 'the people you know think of you as having a good job, an average job, or not too good a job', finding significantly greater positive affect among male principal wage earners who reported higher esteem of this kind. In general, it seems probable that esteem associated with a job is especially likely to bear upon mental health when it takes on a particularly low value. This has sometimes been considered in terms of 'social alienation' in particular jobs (e.g. Blauner 1964). Problems of inferring causal direction from observed cross-sectional correlations are of course particularly trouble-some in this area.

Personal evaluations

At the third level of enquiry we are concerned with personal assessments which employees make of their jobs. These evaluations do of course overlap with the ones made at other levels, but they give greater emphasis to idiosyncratic personal meanings. Their widespread importance may be illustrated through these quotations:

When I tell people at a party I work for a bank, most of them get interested. They say, 'What do you do?' I say, 'I'm a teller'. They say, 'Oh, hmm, Okay', and walk away.... My job doesn't have prestige. It's a service job.... You are there to serve them. They are not there to serve you. Like a housemaid or a servant (Terkel 1972, p. 262).

Right from my first day there, it was made clear to me that toolmakers were craftsmen, and as such inherently superior to all the other workers except for a few other small and highly skilled trades. The ethos which has been graphically described as the 'aristocracy of labour' was very present (Fraser 1969, p. 26).

I was fine until there was a press party. We were having a fairly intelligent conversation. Then they asked me what I did. When I told them [a receptionist], they turned around to find other people with name tags. I wasn't worth bothering with. I wasn't being rejected because of what I had said or the way I talked, but simply because of my function (Terkel 1972, p. 29).

In addition to an awareness of the esteem attaching to particular job functions, employees may also evaluate the product they are making or selling. It is apparent that an individual working on a product or service which contravenes his or her moral or political values will make assessments of personal and social worth which are lower than those made in the absence of such a mismatch. Once again systematic research into this kind of individual job meaning appears to be lacking; and positions which are stigmatized in this way (rather than being broadly acceptable) appear particularly likely to have an impact upon job-holders' mental health.

Esteem at this personal level has been addressed by the 'task significance' scale of the Job Diagnostic Survey (JDS) (Hackman and Oldham 1975, 1980). This is a rather simple two-item index of an employee's assessment of the importance of his or her job. Scores have been found in cross-sectional research to be significantly correlated with overall job satisfaction, intrinsic satisfaction, and intrinsic job motivation (e.g. Hackman and Oldham 1975; Oldham *et al.* 1978; Wall *et al.* 1978); and these associations have been replicated longitudinally by Hackman *et al.* (1978). In a meta-analysis of results from 28 cross-sectional studies, Loher *et al.* (1985) found an average sample-weighted correlation with overall job satisfaction of 0.38, after correcting for measurement unreliability. Moch (1980) showed that the relationship with intrinsic motivation remained significant after statistically controlling for other job characteristics measured by the JDS. However, task significance was unrelated to context-free affective well-being (General Health Questionnaire scores) in the findings reported by Wall and colleagues.

The studies reviewed in this section contribute only a little to an understanding of the impact of valued social position on the mental health of people in jobs. More detailed investigations are needed, with particular attention being paid to low-prestige jobs and the simultaneous measurement of other job factors as well as evaluations of each position. It is also desirable to explore further the possible causal connections between this feature and other environmental factors within the present conceptual framework; social positions which are more highly valued may yield access to other environmental determinants of mental health. For example, it seems likely that greater esteem attached to a job at the cultural level is associated with a greater availability of money (feature number 6) and greater opportunity for control (number 1).

Summary

The first part of this chapter reviewed investigations into the degree to which jobs provide opportunities for interpersonal contact. This was considered in terms of its quantity, how much social interaction was required or possible, and its quality, how good or poor relationships are reported to be. The latter was examined primarily through studies of social support received from one's boss and one's colleagues.

Jobs which provide supportive and friendly relationships were found to yield higher job-related well-being. That was viewed as unsurprising, since feelings about important people in a job setting are expected to contribute to job-related affect more widely. However, significant associations have also been described in relation to context-free well-being, as well as subjective competence and autonomy. The shape of those associations, linear or non-linear, has not yet been investigated.

In terms of *quantity* of interaction, there is evidence that very low and very high levels of contact in a job are both harmful, as suggested by theories of personal territory and people's need for a balance between privacy and social interaction. However, broad-ranging tests of this possibility which might bear more directly upon the vitamin AD model have yet to be carried out.

The second part of the chapter examined the model's ninth environmental category, labelled as 'valued social position'. Three levels of description were suggested, in terms of cultural, sub-cultural, and personal evaluations. At the first level, studies of social class and occupational prestige were outlined. The second level concerned more local assessments of the value of specific jobs, for example within a single community. And the third level brought in evaluations by employees themselves of the personal significance of their own jobs.

Esteem at this personal level has sometimes been studied through the task significance scale of the Job Diagnostic Survey, and some associations of that scale with job-related well-being have been described. Nevertheless, there is a general lack of systematic research into this environmental feature. More studies are required, not only of a quantitative kind, but also in order to uncover the processes through which this feature has its particular impact.

11

The impact of unemployment

Environments of all kinds may be studied in terms of the nine features which make up the framework of this book. The environments of paid employment have been examined in this manner throughout Chapters 5 to 10, and we may now consider the situation of people who are unemployed. The present chapter will summarize research into the mental health outcomes of unemployment, and Chapter 12 will then apply the nine-component framework to interpret results from a wide range of studies.

It is important throughout these discussions to bear in mind the widespread feelings of ambivalence which exist in relation to both employment and unemployment. Most people have a strong wish to work in an employed role, but they also desire to relax and be free from responsibility (e.g. Garraty 1978). Unemployment may in general be harmful, but paid work can also be damaging.

That point was emphasized in Chapter 4, where it was also observed that official definitions of unemployment typically include the notion that an unemployed person not only lacks a job but is also looking for one, or at least would like one. Precise specification of that motivational feature is of course far from easy, especially in view of the widespread existence of ambivalent feelings. A person may both want a job and also want to remain unemployed. Another person may strongly want one particular kind of job but decline all others. A third individual may be actively seeking paid work in the immediate neighbourhood but refuse to consider opportunities five miles away. In general, however, despite the problems of practical measurement, it is useful to retain a conceptual distinction between people who are 'unemployed' and those who are 'non-employed', the latter being without a paid job by their own choice. For example, married women caring for their children without wanting paid work are among the members of the latter category.

Official procedures for the measurement of unemployment rates vary between nations. Many European countries count only those people who have formally registered as unemployed, leaving out specific jobless groups for whom there may be no advantage in registering. Others, such as the United

Kingdom, record only those claiming particular welfare benefits, omitting people ineligible for those benefits who nevertheless are seeking a job. A third group of countries assess the number of their unemployed people through random population surveys, including only those people without employment who have made specific efforts to find a job in the recent past; this procedure is adopted in the United States, for instance.

In all cases, it seems clear that official definitions are relatively restrictive, so that the number of people officially designated as unemployed will be less than that implied by some other definitions. Official figures in the mid-1980s, suggesting that between 8 per cent and 15 per cent of many Western countries' labour forces are unemployed, are thus likely to be conservative estimates. The overall figures are also subject to wide variations between groups or regions. Teenage workers, those who are older, unskilled, or previously employed in declining manufacturing industries are particularly likely to be without jobs, as are members of ethnic minorities and disabled people.

Research findings

Research into unemployment and health has often been cross-sectional, comparing a group of people who at the time are unemployed with similar people who are in paid work. Such comparisons regularly show that employed people are on average more healthy than those out of paid work, but they leave unclear the pattern of causal influence. The difference may arise from prior characteristics independent of current employment status (e.g. Feather and O'Brien 1986; Vaillant and Vaillant 1981), or it may indicate a causal impact of unemployment itself. Both processes are likely, but with differing relative importance according to the prevailing economic climate. The former interpretation is particularly plausible during periods of very low unemployment, when the small number of unemployed people failing to obtain a job in an easy labour market might be thought to have some personal attributes which impede job-getting (e.g. Goodwin 1972; Tiffany et al. 1970; Warr 1984b). However, when unemployment rates are high, and entire work-groups lose their job through plant closure or large-scale lay-off, it is more likely that the observed difference arises primarily from decrements in health occurring after job loss (e.g. White 1983).

This point was examined by Spruit et al. (1985). In a Dutch unemployed sample, they identified persons who reported prior health problems of a kind which the investigators considered might have led to their dismissal or resignation from employment. This sub-group (34 per cent of the sample) was excluded from data analysis, leaving only unemployed people who apparently had been in good health when in jobs. An employed sample served as a comparison group, and members of this group with earlier health difficulties (10 per cent of the sample) were again excluded.

It was thus possible to compare the mental and physical health of samples of currently unemployed and employed people, with reasonable confidence that the former group had not become unemployed because of their prior characteristics. Despite that control, significant differences were found between mental health in the two groups, with unemployed respondents exhibiting more psychosomatic complaints and greater negative affect. However, no differences were found in respect of physical ill-health or consumption of medicines.

Mental health

Longitudinal studies of individuals moving between employment and unemployment can make particularly clear the causal impact of being involuntarily without a job. Table 11.1 summarizes both the cross-sectional and the longitudinal evidence available in respect of the three principal axes of affective well-being suggested in Chapter 3. Source details of the investigations giving rise to this summary are provided in the Appendix to this chapter (page 208). Most of the studies concerned men or unmarried women. The position of other women will be considered separately in Chapter 12.

As an illustration of cross-sectional research which covered the first axis of well-being, consider the investigation described by Hepworth (1980). She used the General Health Questionnaire measure of general distress (see page 42) in order to compare samples of employed and unemployed British men. Scores for the employed group were generally low relative to published norms, but the mean score for unemployed men was greater by a factor of almost six. Other cross-sectional comparisons listed in the Appendix have obtained very similar results with this and other measures.

Longitudinal studies indicate that the differences are at least in part caused by changes in environmental conditions. For example, significant deterioration in affective well-being after job loss has been reported by Cobb and Kasl (1977), Cohn (1978), and Linn *et al.* (1985). Significant improvements after re-entry into employment have been described by Jackson *et al.* (1983), Payne and Jones (1987) and Warr and Jackson (1985). Several other investigations cited in the Appendix to this chapter (page 208) have shown that teenagers moving from school into unemployment are likely to experience a significant drop in well-being, whereas those entering paid work are likely to exhibit improvement; see also Chapter 4 (page 60) and Chapter 12 (page 227). However, results may sometimes be complicated for this group, since the transition out of school can itself affect mental health, irrespective of whether a school-leaver becomes employed or unemployed (e.g. Winefield and Tiggemann 1985).

What of the other components of mental health? Subjective competence is expected to decline as a result of unemployment, for example in terms of loss of skills which might be applied in future jobs. Layton (1986), in a longitudinal study of male British school-leavers, observed that those respon-

Table 11.1 Affective well-being in employment and unemployment: Summary of evidence about the negative impact of unemployment. References are provided in the Appendix to Chapter 11.

Aspect of well-being	Type of evidence	
1. Contented–discontented		
Happiness	CS	L
Pleasure	CS	
Life satisfaction	CS	L
Negative affect	CS	
Negative self-esteem	CS	L
General distress	CS	L
2. Anxious–comfortable		
Anxiety	CS	L
Strain	CS	
3. Depressed–actively pleased		
Depressed mood	CS	L
Positive affect	CS	

CS: cross-sectional comparisons
L: longitudinal comparisons

dents moving into unemployment showed a significant deterioration in self-confidence. A similar change in a measure of perceived competence was described among Australian school-leavers by Feather and O'Brien (1986). Slowing-down of cognitive and problem-solving activity has also been reported. For example, 37 per cent of unemployed men in a British study indicated that they were now taking longer to do things than they previously did, and 30 per cent that they were getting 'rusty' at things they used to do well (Fryer and Warr 1984).

The financial and other constraints of unemployment might be thought likely also to give rise to a generalized reduction in subjective autonomy. Locus of control scores provide an indication of belief in personal self-direction, and a cross-sectional difference in locus of control scores has been reported in an Australian study by O'Brien and Kabanoff (1979), with greater externality among the unemployed. This difference remained significant when age, education, health, work values, leisure quality, and other variables were statistically controlled (O'Brien 1984b). A longitudinal study of Australian school-leavers revealed a significant increase in external locus of control for teenagers moving into unemployment and a decrease for those gaining a job (Patton and Noller 1984).

However, another Australian investigation with the same design (Tiggemann and Winefield 1984; Winefield and Tiggemann 1985) observed a decrease in externality of about the same amount for school-leavers, whether they became employed or unemployed. And the study by Linn *et al.* (1985) of American middle-aged men unemployed for periods less than six months found no longitudinal change in locus of control scores after job loss. Feather and O'Brien (1986) found no effect of unemployment on locus of control scores one year after school-leaving; however, externality became significantly greater one year later among those who remained without a job.

O'Brien (1985) points out that unemployed people's responses in the direction of external control would in many cases be indicative of a realistic recognition of their social impotence. It is now desirable to measure subjective autonomy in terms also of more specific feelings of dependence or independence in the situations of daily life. Additional longitudinal studies, embracing older workers as well as school-leavers, are also needed before a firm conclusion about unemployment and autonomy can be drawn.

In relation to the fourth component of mental health, the fact that unemployment reduces level of aspiration has been documented in several studies. The process was examined in a classic investigation within the Austrian community of Marienthal (Jahoda *et al.* 1933). In a foreword to the 1971 edition of that report, Lazarsfeld emphasizes 'the vicious cycle between reduced opportunities and reduced level of aspiration', in which 'prolonged unemployment leads to a state of apathy in which the victims do not utilize any longer even the few opportunities left to them' (p. vii). Marienthal was a particularly deprived environment, but reduced motivation and interest in one's wider surroundings have been described in other investigations (e.g. Binns and Mars 1984; Fagin and Little 1984; Seabrook 1982).

Fleming *et al.* (1984) set out to measure persistence and motivation to solve items in a laboratory task, comparing an unemployed group with a group of people in jobs. The latter solved significantly more problems and tended (non-significantly) to persevere with items for longer durations than the unemployed group. On arrival at the laboratory, the unemployed people also exhibited significantly higher levels of both adrenaline and noradrenaline, suggestive of raised levels of strain. Differences associated with unemployment duration were also found (Baum *et al.* 1986); these are summarized in the next chapter (page 232).

Turning from mental health in the population as a whole to those people diagnosed by the medical profession as 'ill', there is cross-sectional evidence that the prevalence of identified neurosis is significantly greater among unemployed than employed people. For example, standardized psychiatric interviews conducted in a British urban community revealed a prevalence of neurotic disorder among unemployed men which was more than double that among men in paid work (14 per cent against 6 per cent) (Bebbington *et al.* 1981). Roy (1981) reported a similar difference in a study of depressed patients in Canada. In their psychiatric examination of unemployed young Australian workers, Finlay-Jones and Eckhardt (1981) enquired about date of onset whenever a disorder was diagnosed. They concluded that in 43 per cent of neurotic cases (mainly of depression), onset had followed un-employment in the absence of any other apparent provoking condition. In a Danish study of psychiatric patients (primarily neurotics and drug abusers), it was estimated that for 41 per cent of cases unemployment had played a significant part in provoking the illness (Fruensgaard *et al.* 1983); however, other factors such as interpersonal and family problems were more com-monly implicated.

There is less evidence available about psychotic disorder in relation to unemployment. Cross-sectional comparisons have indicated that psychoses are disproportionately more likely among unemployed people (e.g. Jaco 1960), but causal interpretation is unusually difficult. Psychotic conditions seem particularly likely to lead to unemployment, whether or not they are in some cases caused by it.

Finally, some studies have sought retrospective information, obtaining a crude indication of the personal impact of unemployment by asking un-employed people whether their health has changed at all since job loss. Research by Fröhlich (1983a), Klausen and Iversen (1981), Payne *et al.* (1984), and Warr and Jackson (1984) has shown that between 20 per cent and 30 per cent of unemployed men are likely to report a deterioration in their health since job loss. In respect of psychological health, changes are typically described in terms of increased anxiety, depression, insomnia, irritability, lack of confidence, listlessness, and general nervousness. Un-employed people may also describe a worsening in psychosomatic conditions such as dermatitis, eczema, headaches, high blood pressure, and ulcers.

However, around 10 per cent of men in these studies report an im-provement in their health since becoming unemployed. In some cases this is in respect of physical illnesses which had been exacerbated by working conditions (bronchitis, back problems, and so on), but it is also found that a small number report improved psychological health, usually because they are now free from negative aspects of their jobs. Health improvements are particularly likely to be reported by those who have only recently become unemployed (Schwefel *et al.* 1984; Warr and Jackson 1984).

Aggregate time-series investigations

Another approach to the impact of unemployment has been in terms of aggregate time-series analysis, examining overall data about diagnosed illness from communities or nations as a whole over a period of years. Investigations of this kind into mental illness will be reviewed here, with aggregate studies of mortality and suicide considered in the next section.

Brenner (1973a) examined first admissions to New York state public mental hospitals between 1914 and 1967, reporting a significant lagged relationship with changes in the state's manufacturing employment index: as unemployment went up, so did the rate of subsequent admissions. This finding has been questioned on a number of grounds, such as the omission of data from private mental hospitals and state general hospitals, variations between years and sub-samples, and possible failure in matching community areas for economic and psychiatric variables (e.g. Marshall and Funch 1979, 1980; Ratcliff 1980). A similar study of admissions (including readmissions) to mental hospitals in England and Wales between 1950 and 1976 revealed no synchronous or lagged association with unemployment rate, although synchronous correlations for two age-groups of women were found to be statistically significant (Stokes and Cochrane, 1984a).

Some American investigators have examined more short-term changes, on a month-by-month basis. In general there are some hints of a relationship between unemployment rate and admissions, but results are inconsistent between studies and across patient groups: male or female, inpatient or outpatient, first admission or readmission, public or private hospital (e.g. Ahr *et al.* 1981; Barling and Handal 1980; Catalano *et al.* 1981; Frank 1981).

Catalano *et al.* (1985) analysed quarterly data between 1966 and 1975 from a single American county. They were able to separate information about public hospitals from overall data (concerning both public and private facilities), and also to distinguish between first admissions and readmissions. They observed that decreased employment in local manufacturing industry was significantly associated with a raised level of overall admissions (public and private, admissions and readmissions). This was the case for men of all ages (in the following quarter) and for women aged above 40 years (in the synchronous quarter). However, no associations were found in respect of new admissions to public facilities, and the overall pattern appeared to arise from readmission of people who had received treatment at some earlier time.

The authors believe that an 'uncovering' explanation is as plausible an account of their data as an interpretation in terms of unemployment 'provoking' new episodes of ill-health. Health service facilities may become more accessible or attractive to people when they are unemployed, or high unemployment may reduce a community's ability to cope with illness at home; in both cases observed increases in hospital admissions may be due to an uncovering of previous illness more than reflecting new illness caused by unemployment. The empirical evidence about health service utilization does not at present permit a clear choice between these two interpretations. (See also Ahr *et al.* 1981, Catalano and Dooley 1979, Catalano *et al.* 1981, and Dooley and Catalano 1984a; the possibility of 'reprovocation' is considered in Chapter 14.)

Furthermore, processes at the level of the individual cannot be inferred from aggregate-level findings. Even if a significant aggregate-level association were observed, we would not be able to conclude that individual unemployed people were more likely than their counterparts in jobs to be admitted to a mental hospital; the pattern could equally be due to year-by-year variations among employed people. In practice, however, there is reason to suppose that raised unemployment levels might reduce rather than increase the call made by employed people on health service facilities. People in jobs might be more reluctant in these periods to present themselves for treatment, fearing that absence from work might place their employment at risk (see also Markham 1985, for a similar suggestion about job absenteeism).

Catalano and Dooley (1977) set out to link together information from both the aggregate level and the individual level. They studied associations within an American city population between local unemployment levels and self-reports of depressed mood over a 16-month period. Significant associations were found after a two-month lag. However, a second investigation in a non-metropolitan community failed to replicate the result (Dooley *et al.* 1981).

A further cross-level study was carried out across 16 quarterly periods in Los Angeles county. Aggregate-level variations in unemployment rate were found to be significantly associated with individual-level measures of both general distress and physical illness or injury in the subsequent two months. The association with symptoms of distress was present only for members of the working population (not for retired people, housewives, and students) (Dooley and Catalano 1984b); and the link with physical illness or injury was most pronounced for middle-class respondents (Catalano and Dooley 1983).

This investigation also examined the combined influence upon distress symptoms of local unemployment rate (an aggregate-level measure) and recently experienced undesirable job and financial events (an individual-level factor). The index of the latter contained 15 items referring to unemployment, financial loss, job demotion, and problems with debt. It was found that, for members of the working population, changes in both these factors made an independent contribution to variations in distress. Not only did individually-experienced life events affect distress (the pattern revealed in studies cited earlier), but local unemployment rate had its own *additional* influence upon distress. Changes in the local economic climate are thus shown to influence level of affective well-being, whether or not people have themselves experienced negative job events.

The authors point out that an increased unemployment rate affects mental health in the population partly because it causes individual job loss, but also for its more extended consequences:

Job loss is an acute event which occurs to a relatively small proportion of the population. . . . But the impact of such an aggregate economic change can affect very many more people in more subtle and more gradual ways. For example, the spouses and children of job-losers may pay a price in conflict or abuse. Workers dislocated from one job may immediately find reemployment in another but at a psychological cost of physical relocation or of retraining and may well slip down the status ladder. People who have not themselves lost a job may suffer anxiety anticipating job loss and may remain in unsatisfactory working conditions because no alternate jobs can be found. Organized labor has learned that its bargaining position for better wages and working conditions is undermined by high unemployment rates. Cuts in government revenues during recession are...translated into cuts in social services which help many people not themselves in the work force. In short, an economic indicator such as unemployment rate can be understood as reflecting adverse changes throughout the population (Dooley and Catalano 1984, p. 396).

Physical health

What about those illnesses which are primarily physical with no psychological causes, or at least with very little psychological input? Bronchitis, the cancers, or pneumonia might be taken as examples of such primarily physical illnesses. If unemployment is to bring about illness of that kind, the causal mechanisms are presumably different from those yielding poor mental health. Most probable is an increase in poverty, leading to deficiencies in food intake, heating, clothing or sanitation, or to some otherwise harmful change in lifestyle. More extended time-lags are also to be expected, with these forms of physical ill-health developing over longer periods.

It is known from cross-sectional studies that in general unemployed people have poorer physical health than those who are in jobs (e.g. Cook *et al.* 1982; D'Arcy and Siddique 1985; Verbrugge 1983; Wilder 1980). However, it is not possible from the cross-sectional results to distinguish between physical ill-health leading to unemployment and unemployment causing ill-health.

A longitudinal investigation of American men has been described by Kasl *et al.* (1975) and Kasl and Cobb (1980). This found no evidence of significant decrements in physical health associated with the transition from employment to unemployment. However, the durations studied were brief, up to 15 weeks unemployment in the subsequent two years. Linn *et al.* (1985) studied American middle-aged men who had been unemployed for up to six months. Significant increases subsequent to job loss were found in visits to the doctor, number of medications, and number of sickness days in bed. However, there was no change in the number of diagnoses made.

Similar results were obtained in a longitudinal British study of factory closure by Beale and Nethercott (1985). Analysing medical records (rather than obtaining data directly from focal persons) they found that job loss was not followed by an increase in illness episodes. However, it did give rise to more frequent medical consultations (in general practice and as a hospital outpatient), both among sample members and among their families. The effects were in general more pronounced for women ex-employees than for men. Beale and Nethercott also observed that consultation frequency increased two years before job loss, at the time when closure was first threatened. A similar 'anticipation' effect was obtained in the study by Kasl and colleagues described in the previous paragraph, and in other studies cited in the discussion of job insecurity in Chapter 8 (page 149).

Narendranathan *et al.* (1982) obtained retrospective reports from 17 707 British men for the period 1965 to 1975, examining the relationship between periods of unemployment and of sickness which lasted at least three months. Although a clear cross-sectional relationship linked to occupational level was found (unskilled men were most likely to have periods both of sickness and of unemployment), no longitudinal association was present: there was no indication that unemployment spells raised the probability of subsequent sickness lasting three months or more.

Another longitudinal investigation at the individual level has been described by Moser *et al.* (1984). (See also Fox and Goldblatt 1982, and Moser *et al.* 1986.) These authors analysed mortality data for the years 1971 to 1981 according to characteristics previously recorded in the 1971 England and Wales census. Among males aged 15 to 64 the standardized mortality ratio in the subsequent period was considerably greater for people who had been unemployed and seeking work on the date of the census than for those in jobs on that date. Analyses showed that some but not all of this difference in subsequent mortality could be accounted for by differences in age and social class, factors which were found to be associated with both mortality and unemployment rates. However, after controlling for those two variables, unemployed men remained significantly more likely to die in the course of the following decade; the differential probability was particularly marked for death by suicide or lung cancer.

In respect of this last finding, a risk factor prior to 1971 must probably be invoked, since lung cancer develops slowly over a number of years. However, it is interesting that research by other investigators has suggested that unemployment may be accompanied by an increase in smoking, at least among working-class men (Anon 1983b; Bradshaw *et al.* 1983; Cook *et al.* 1982; Warr 1984c; Warr and Payne 1983; Westcott 1985). More detailed enquiries into this possibility are now required, as are studies of other health-related behaviours.

Investigations into alcohol consumption have yielded varying results, but the pattern for the unemployed population as a whole seems to be one of no change or reduced consumption after job loss. For example, Cook *et al.* (1982) found no significant difference in the proportion of heavy drinkers (those reporting more than six drinks a day) between employed and unemployed men, after standardizing for age, social class, and town of residence. Unemployed people have been found to spend less on alcohol than those in jobs (Anon 1983b), although that finding may arise from the differential social-class composition of the two groups, with fewer unemployed people in the middle class. However, other studies have suggested that consumption is in general likely to decline after becoming unemployed (Iversen and Klausen 1986; Smart 1979; Warr 1984c; Warr and Payne 1983), probably as a result of increased financial constraints.

Bachman *et al.* (1984) found that, although episodes of heavy drinking among male American teenagers increased somewhat as they moved from school into unemployment, this increase was slightly smaller than that found among teenagers entering a job. For females, employed and unemployed members of the sample reduced their drinking by the same small amount after they had left school. Plant *et al.* (1985) examined alcohol consumption reported in the past week by employed and unemployed Scottish teenagers; no significant difference was present.

In a cross-sectional study of employed and unemployed British men, Crawford *et al.* (1987) also obtained reports of drinking behaviour in the preceding week. No differences were present between the two groups in the amount of alcohol consumed or in time spent drinking. However, the results indicated that a person's *style* of drinking was significantly associated with employment status. Unemployed men were likely to consume greater amounts in a single session and to drink more rapidly than employed men (although overall weekly quantity did not differ between the groups). These differences were associated with a greater probability of intermittent and short-term drunkenness among the unemployed respondents.

It is possible that unemployment is associated with a 'polarized' pattern of alcohol consumption. Heavy drinkers, or those people who already have serious drinking problems, may consume increased amounts of alcohol when faced with the difficulties of unemployment (e.g. Fruensgaard *et al.* 1983), whereas moderate or light drinkers may reduce consumption as part of a general cut-back in non-essential expenditure (Armor *et al.* 1978; Crawford *et al.* 1987; Smart 1979). For example, surveys of the British male population have suggested that, although there is a higher proportion of 'heavy' drinkers among the unemployed than the employed, there are also relatively more unemployed people who abstain or are only 'occasional' drinkers (Anon 1983a).

However, there remains a need in this field for more rigorous control of possibly confounding variables, such as age and social class. And longitudinal research to test the 'polarization' hypothesis is greatly needed.

Another set of studies has examined mortality data at the aggregate level, investigating changes in national death rates as a function of changes in unemployment levels over a number of years. For example, Brenner (e.g. 1980a) studied the relationship between overall mortality rates and several economic variables, including unemployment, for the United States between 1909 and 1976. He reported that, after controlling for other factors, national mortality rates were significantly associated with earlier unemployment levels; unemployment was said to have a lagged effect (greatest at between two and five years) upon United States overall death rates. He reached a similar conclusion from his analysis of mortality data from England and Wales between 1936 and 1976 (Brenner 1979, 1980b), and (using a more complex model) for England and Wales and for Scotland between 1954 and 1976 (Brenner 1983).

Evidence of this kind (see also Brenner 1971, 1973b; Brenner and Mooney 1982, 1983) has sometimes been taken to indicate that economic recession causes death rates to rise, or more precisely retards the long-term improvement. However, conflicting results have been reported (e.g. Forbes and McGregor 1984; Gravelle *et al.* 1981; John, 1983, 1985; Schwefel *et al.* 1984), and several criticisms of these studies' methodology and interpretation have been made (e.g. Eyer 1977; Kasl 1979b, 1982; Spruit 1982; Warr 1985; Winter 1983). These are not central to our present concerns, but should be considered sufficiently serious for caution to be exercised in interpreting aggregate time-series investigations of unemployment and mortality rates.

A related question is whether suicide is significantly associated with employment status. Individual cross-sectional studies indicate that people committing suicide are disproportionately likely to be unemployed (e.g. Platt 1984), but it is apparent that over time the same personal and environmental factors may have operated to yield both unemployment and suicide (e.g. Shepherd and Barraclough 1980). Aggregate time-series investigations in the United States regularly find a positive association across years between suicide frequency and undesirable economic change (for example, as shown in high unemployment rates), but the evidence from European studies is more conflicting (Platt 1984; John 1985; Schwefel *et al.* 1984; Stack 1981; Stack and Haas 1984).

A possible explanation for the lack of an aggregate positive correlation over recent years in the United Kingdom was considered by Kreitman and Platt (1984). They noted that during the 1960s the carbon monoxide content of domestic gas was gradually removed from different parts of the country, so that household gas was decreasingly available as a poison for would-be suicides. Associated with this change, overall suicide rates showed a decline over the period, whereas unemployment was gradually rising. The correlation between the two variables was thus negative, rather than positive, as found in the United States. However, examination of suicides by all other methods in the same period (excluding deaths by carbon monoxide poisoning) revealed a strong positive correlation with the national unemployment rate.

Research has also examined parasuicide ('attempted suicide' or 'deliberate self-harm') as a function of unemployment. Individual-level studies again reveal a particularly high probability of parasuicide among the unemployed, especially among those without a job for more than a year (Hawton and Rose 1986; Platt and Kreitman 1985). However, many unemployed people attempting suicide have previous histories of psychiatric treatment and/or alcoholism, and it is not clear whether these earlier factors are more responsible for parasuicide than is current unemployment. Furthermore, interviews with people who have survived parasuicide rarely point to unemployment as a major precipitating factor. Some form of interpersonal relationship problem is most often seen as the main proximal cause (Platt 1984). Nevertheless, unemployment might exacerbate relationship difficulties, and findings are at least compatible with the view that unemployment (especially when prolonged) is causally related to parasuicide.

Family processes

Finally, it should be noted that a husband's unemployment is clearly liable to cause increased strain within the family (e.g. Fagin and Little 1984; Grayson 1985; Leventman 1981; Madge 1983; Moen, 1979; Schlozman and Verba 1979; Thomas *et al*. 1980). Relationship problems arising from financial difficulties during unemployment have been particularly emphasized by Binns and Mars (1984), Liker and Elder (1983), and McKee and Bell (1985). (See also Chapter 12, page 219.) Husbands' unemployment was found by Cochrane and Stopes-Roe (1981) to be associated with higher levels of anxiety and depression among wives. However, in an American study Margolis and Farran (1984) observed no differences in the number of illness symptoms and behaviour problems in children of fathers who were employed and those who had recently lost their jobs. They consider it possible that differences would emerge with longer duration of unemployment.

The covariation between divorce and unemployment rates has been investigated by South (1985), in an aggregate time-series analysis of United States data between 1948 and 1979. After controlling for other variables, such as changes in age distribution, a significant positive contribution was recorded over time from unemployment level to the frequency of divorce in the following year: divorce rate was found to increase in periods of economic recession and to fall (or rise more slowly) during economic expansion. As with other time-series analyses described in this chapter, these findings should not be extrapolated to the level of individuals. They do not demonstrate that individual persons are more likely to become divorced after losing their job.

Child neglect and child abuse may be thought to be particularly probable in families with unemployed fathers. Such associations are indeed found in cross-sectional comparisons (e.g. Gil 1971), but causal interpretation is difficult in view of significant correlations between maltreatment and a wide range of indices of social deprivation in addition to unemployment. Furthermore, reports to official agencies are likely to be unreliable estimates of true prevalence.

Steinberg *et al*. (1981) adopted an aggregate time-series approach, relating overall levels of reported child neglect and abuse in two US counties to local economic conditions over a 30-month period. No evidence was found for a lagged relationship between economic conditions and child neglect, although the authors claim support for a link with the second variable, child abuse: in both counties there was a significant negative relationship between reported abuse and size of the work-force two months previously. However, three out of six reported lagged relationships were (non-significantly) in the opposite direction, and interpretation of this data-set is somewhat difficult.

In general, however, the findings presented in this chapter leave no doubt that unemployment has substantial harmful effects upon many individuals and their families. Furthermore, the consequences are likely in practice to be more serious than is revealed in most survey investigations. Survey researchers typically have difficulty in obtaining access to unemployed people, with large numbers of those approached preferring not to be interviewed. It is not known whether unemployed people who decline to take part differ substantially from those who do, but it seems very likely that they will in general be of poorer mental health in the terms considered in this book. Particularly low levels of affective well-being and unusually large impairments in subjective competence, aspiration, and autonomy are expected to discourage acceptance of an invitation to be interviewed. This sampling bias means that average findings from published survey investigations are likely to underestimate the true impact of unemployment.

Another source of bias in the same direction comes from the fact that unemployed people who become psychiatrically or physically impaired to a considerable degree are likely to be officially defined as 'sick' rather than 'unemployed'. Those individuals become excluded from investigations whose sample is drawn from the population formally designated as 'unemployed'. As a result, the observed amount of ill-health among jobless people is liable to be under-recorded.

Summary

This chapter has examined research into the health effects of unemployment. Studies at the individual level have mainly been cross-sectional, but longitudinal investigations are becoming more common. Significant effects of unemployment have been recorded for the three principal axes of affective well-being, and limited evidence is available in respect of competence, autonomy, and aspiration. Unemployment is in general seen to impair mental health, although this effect is not universal; indeed, a small minority of people show gains in mental health after losing their job.

Studies at the aggregate level have examined changes in communities and nations over a series of years. Aggregate time-series research into the relationship between unemployment level and mental hospital admission is generally inconclusive. Parallel studies of mortality rates have also yielded results which vary between investigators, although a growing body of research argues for a lagged relationship between unemployment and aggregate mortality, at least in certain countries.

A longitudinal investigation of mortality at the individual level has suggested a disproportionate probability of death in the ten years following a period of unemployment. Other research has linked suicide to unemployment, at least in cross-sectional and aggregate analyses. Parasuicide has been found to be particularly common among people unemployed for long periods. In terms of health-related behaviours, it seems likely that smoking increases somewhat after job loss, whereas alcohol consumption remains on average unchanged. However, previously heavy drinkers may increase consumption after they have become unemployed.

Research has shown that family strain is likely to increase as a result of a husband's unemployment, but findings in respect of child neglect and abuse are not yet clear. Divorce and unemployment levels have been found to be interrelated in one aggregate time-series investigation.

In all these areas there is a need for additional and more careful research. Particularly required are longitudinal studies of individuals moving from employment into unemployment, drawing samples and introducing controls which permit specific hypotheses to be convincingly tested.

Appendix to Chapter 11

Table 11.1 (page 197) summarizes available evidence about the impact of unemployment on ten separate indices of affective well-being. That summary is based upon findings described in the following publications. In each case affective well-being is found to be lower during unemployment than in employment. Cross-sectional studies are indicated by 'CS', and longitudinal studies by 'L'.

1. Contented—discontented

Happiness
    CS: Bradburn 1969; Bradburn and Caplovitz 1965; D'Arcy and Siddique 1985; Tiggemann and Winefield 1980, 1984.
    L: Tiggemann and Winefield 1980, 1984; Winefield and Tiggemann 1985.

Pleasure
    CS: Warr and Payne 1982.

Life satisfaction
    CS: Campbell *et al.* 1976; Cohn 1978; Donovan and Oddy 1982; Gaskell and Smith 1981; Hepworth 1980; Miles 1983; Schlozman and Verba 1979; Warr 1978.
    L: Cohn 1978; Feather and O'Brien 1986; Tiggemann and Winefield 1980.

Negative affect
    CS: Bradburn 1969; Spruit *et al.* 1985; Warr 1978.

Negative self-esteem
   CS: Feather and Bond 1983; Lawlis 1971; Patton and Noller 1984; Stokes and Cochrane 1984b; Warr and Jackson 1983.
   L: Patton and Noller 1984; Warr and Jackson 1983.

General distress
   CS: Banks and Jackson 1982; Brinkmann 1984; Cochrane and Stopes-Roe 1980; D'Arcy and Siddique 1985; Doherty and Davies 1984; Donovan and Oddy 1982; Estes and Wilensky 1978; Fineman, 1983; Finlay-Jones and Eckhardt 1984; Grayson 1985; Hepworth 1980; Hobbs *et al.* 1985; McPherson and Hall 1983; Melville *et al.* 1985; Miles 1983; Pearlin and Lieberman 1979; Stokes and Cochrane 1984b; Spruit *et al.* 1985; Thoits and Hannan 1979; Westcott 1985.
   L: Banks and Jackson 1982; Jackson *et al.* 1983; Layton 1985; Linn *et al.* 1985; Warr and Jackson 1985.

2. Anxious—comfortable

Anxiety
   CS: Cobb and Kasl 1977; Donovan and Oddy 1982; Fineman 1983; Kasl 1979a; Lawlis 1971; Margolis and Farran 1984; Viney 1985; Warr 1978.
   L: Cobb and Kasl 1977; Kasl 1979a; Linn *et al.* 1985.

Strain
   CS: Warr and Payne 1982.

3. Depressed—actively pleased

Depressed mood
   CS: Cobb and Kasl 1977; Doherty and Davies 1984; Donovan and Oddy 1982; Feather 1982; Feather and Bond 1983; Kasl 1979a; Margolis and Farran 1984; Melville *et al.* 1985; Patton and Noller 1984; Radloff 1975; Tiggemann and Winefield 1984.
   L: Cobb and Kasl 1977; Feather and O'Brien 1986; Frese 1979; Kasl 1979a; Linn *et al.* 1985; Patton and Noller 1984; Tiggemann and Winefield 1980, 1984.

Positive affect
   CS: Bradburn 1969; Warr 1978.

12

The jobless environment

Let us turn now to processes which may give rise to the outcomes recorded in Chapter 11. The nine environmental elements of the present vitamin model will be suggested as principal causes of the decrements in mental health which typically accompany unemployment. Two types of evidence will be examined. First, overall differences between the environments of employed and un- employed groups will be considered. Second, within samples of unemployed people themselves, variations in mental health will be interpreted in terms of differences in level of the nine environmental features.

There are clear difficulties in identifying particular causal agents in any non-artificial environment. In the earlier discussion of differences between jobs, problems in specifying the causal impact of any single environmental feature were frequently noted. Even in cases where a feature has been shown to be statistically associated with mental health, we cannot readily determine whether it is that aspect of the environment which has major causal import- ance or whether it is a correlated (and possibly unmeasured) component which is principally influential.

In practice it is likely that a combination of factors is important, so that multivariate investigations are required, in addition to those which examine relationships between a single environmental feature and one possible out- come variable. However, as pointed out in Chapter 6 (page 113), multivariate analyses are not without their problems: there may be excessively high inter- correlations between predictor variables, or results may be capriciously dependent upon which other factors are included in an equation.

These difficulties are compounded when we turn to examine multivariate patterns of change across time, for instance studying members of a sample as they move from employment to unemployment, and seeking to identify the configuration of causally important factors. It is not surprising, therefore, that research into the specific processes determining mental health during unemployment is somewhat undeveloped. Statistical difficulties are severe, and no single study can be sufficiently all-embracing to permit the un- equivocal conclusion that a particular factor or group of factors is primarily responsible for observed levels of mental health.

One can more easily falsify hypotheses about possibly important environmental features. At the simplest level, if there is no cross-sectional association between a given feature and a measured aspect of mental health, then that element is unlikely to be causally important in respect of that particular outcome. The development of research into environments of all kinds involves the gradual exclusion (through falsification of explicit or implicit hypotheses) of certain variables which might have been found to be important, and the compilation of a list of features which are suggested but not proven by empirical enquiry to be causally involved.

Research into the importance of particular environmental features during unemployment is still largely at the stage of list-compilation, and individual studies have tended to examine only one or two variables from the putative list, omitting other possibly influential factors. An important conceptual contribution has been the 'latent functions' model of Jahoda (e.g. 1981, 1982). She construes the psychological value of paid work in terms of its manifest and latent functions, and argues that joblessness is harmful in that it reduces the availability of these features.

Given that earning a living is taken for granted as the manifest consequence of employment, what are its latent consequences? Tentatively, I suggest the following. First, employment imposes a time structure on the waking day; second, employment implies regularly shared experiences and contacts with people outside the nuclear family; third, employment links people to goals and purposes that transcend their own; fourth, employment defines aspects of personal status and identity; and finally, employment enforces activity (Jahoda 1981, p. 188).

The nine-component framework of this book draws upon Jahoda's theorizing, in that her second and fourth latent functions appear as environmental features eight and nine in the present model (opportunity for interpersonal contact and valued social position). However, her other three latent functions are here subsumed within feature number three, externally generated goals, and a range of additional environmental characteristics has been introduced. These arise both from research into paid employment, reviewed in previous chapters, and from the recognition that people seek in all environments to exercise some personal influence and also to understand, interpret, and predict future events and the consequences of their own actions. Variations in the latter are characterized in terms respectively of opportunity for control and environmental clarity. In passing, it may be noted that such an increased breadth may not be incompatible with Jahoda's perspective, since she observes (without follow-up) that 'the five broad categories do not cover all the available research on employment. There are other latent by-products' (1981, p. 189).

The present framework is also distinguished by its assumption of a non-linear relationship between environmental features and mental health. Three aspects of this assumption are important to the present discussion. First, the unemployed person's environment is typically one which contains only limited amounts of each feature. Being to the left of Fig. 1.1 (page 10) in respect of each component, mental health is predicted to be substantially impaired. Second, despite this overall negative trend, the transition from a job to unemployment can sometimes be beneficial in the terms of the 'additional decrements' in Fig. 1.1. This occurs if a person moves from a relatively low level of mental health at the right-hand side up to the assumed plateau in the middle range of the horizontal axis. And third, this plateau represents the possibility that for some people there may be no overall difference between the two environments. The aggregation of different changes in respect of the nine factors can in some cases leave the general quality of environment (and thus of mental health) more or less unaltered.

Nine environmental features

Opportunity for control

Considering the nine features in turn, let us start with opportunity for control. It is clear that in general unemployed people have less chance than those in jobs to decide and act in their chosen ways. Lack of success in job-seeking, inability to influence employers, and increased dependence upon welfare bureaucracies all contribute to a reduction in people's ability to control what happens to them. Furthermore, shortage of money and an absence of means to increase income are constraints which themselves have wide-ranging consequences.

Previous chapters have drawn attention to the fact that higher control opportunities permit influence in respect of the other eight environmental features. Conversely, lack of control implies an inability to remedy deficiencies in those respects. Low opportunity for control is thus likely to be harmful to the unemployed person both in its own right and also because it entails powerlessness in respect of other conditions which are themselves damaging.

The contribution of this feature to low mental health during unemployment appears obvious. Perhaps for that reason empirical research has not systematically examined differences between levels and types of control opportunity in the situations of employed and unemployed people. Detailed enquiries into the nature of changes in opportunity for control as people move into unemployment would be very worthwhile.

Opportunity for skill use

The second environmental feature, opportunity for skill use, is also likely to be reduced during unemployment. Restrictions are of two kinds: those which prevent people from using skills which they already possess, and those which prevent the acquisition of new skills. Specifically occupational skills are by definition unused during unemployment, although there are of course opportunities to use certain abilities in domestic, hobby, or repair work. A small number of unemployed people may sustain their skills by providing help to neighbours and friends, for example through household electrical or plumbing work, or through administrative and managerial work in clubs or societies. The potential for acquisition of new skills which is present in some jobs may in principle also be available during unemployment, for example through education or training courses or through the development of active leisure pursuits. In practice, however, these opportunities are taken up by only a small minority of unemployed people (e.g. Fryer and Payne 1983; Stokes 1983).

The magnitude of a reduction in opportunity for skill use which accompanies job loss will depend in part on the level of that feature in a person's prior job. People becoming unemployed from jobs which have demanded a high level of skill are likely to suffer a greater reduction in this feature than people whose previous employment required only limited skill. However, the magnitude of the change naturally also depends on the opportunity for skill use in the two groups' jobless environments, and research into actual changes in this feature would be of value.

Externally generated goals

Turning to the third component, it again seems clear that unemployment brings about a sharp environmental change; a person who makes the transition from paid work into joblessness in effect moves towards the left-hand end of the horizontal axis in Fig. 1.1 (page 10). Fewer demands are made, objectives are reduced, and purposeful activity is less encouraged by the environment. Routines and cycles of behaviour are less often set in motion, and opportunities for 'traction' and 'flow' (see Chapter 7) may be limited. With fewer goals, one can less look forward to their successful attainment, so that a person's experience may come to lack positive tone as well as being homogeneous in its limited challenge.

There are also important consequences of reduced goals upon a person's sense and use of time. An absence of demands can produce an excess of time, and remove the need to choose between activities or to allocate fixed amounts of time to individual tasks. Since external demands are often linked to particular points (such as family meal-times or the start of a working day), a general reduction in demands is often accompanied by a loss of temporal differentiation. Time-markers which break up the day or week and indicate one's position in it are no longer as frequent or as urgent. There is thus likely to be a prolonged sense of waiting, for the next time-marker, or (rarely) for something unexpected to occur.

The demands of job-seeking and contact with official agencies are of course present during unemployment, but these take up only a small amount of time, especially after many months, when active job-search may have been abandoned. A number of investigators have confirmed that many unemployed people have difficulty filling their days, with long periods spent without activity, merely sitting around, sleeping, or watching television (e.g. Fagin and Little 1984; Fröhlich 1983b; Kilpatrick and Trew 1982, 1985; Knulst and Schoonderwoerd 1983; Miles 1983; Miles *et al*. 1984; Warr 1984c; Warr and Payne 1983).

Inactivity is made more probable by an unemployed person's shortage of money. He or she is likely to conserve both activity and money for specific points in the week, perhaps shopping on one particular day or visiting a social club on a single evening. Other periods are punctuated only by routine domestic demands, such as preparing meals, or through links with family members' time schedules. For example, children may need to be met from school at a certain time each day. Otherwise, however, an unemployed person has long periods when activity, if it is to occur, has to be self-generated.

Given that unemployment is known to promote depression and a slowing-down of activities (as described in the previous chapter), we might expect a person's potential for self-generated activity also to be impaired by a period without a job. However, there are undoubtedly individual differences in this form of personal agency, and a minority of unemployed people are able to identify and pursue targets of considerable personal significance (e.g. Fryer and Payne 1984, 1986).

In contrast to research within occupational environments (reviewed in Chapter 7), there have been no quantitative investigations which seek directly to relate level of externally generated goals to a person's mental health during unemployment. Instead, an indirect approach has often been taken, asking people how easy or difficult it is for them to fill the time. Responses to such a question have been shown to be associated with affective well-being, in that reported difficulty in filling the time is significantly correlated with general distress (Hepworth 1980; Miles *et al*. 1984; Warr *et al*. 1985), depression (Feather and Bond 1983), and negative self-esteem (Feather and Bond 1983). A related approach has enquired into the amount of time spent inactive in the home (sitting around, watching television, having a sleep during the day, etc.). The magnitude of reported increase since job loss in such methods of passing the time is significantly associated with lower well-being (e.g. Warr 1984c; Warr and Payne 1983b); and groups of unemployed men differing in level of activity (measured through time-diary records) show parallel differences in general distress (Kilpatrick and Trew 1985).

Since these measures of the use of time tap both a person's own level of agency or resourcefulness as well as the goals presented by his or her environment, the findings do not provide strong evidence for an exclusive impact of this environmental feature. However, everyday observation and extrapolation from research described in Chapter 7 strongly suggest its importance. So do qualitative studies of unemployment, such as the early American investigation by Komarovsky (1940):

'I am going crazy with so much time on my hands and nothing to do.' Such was the most usual reaction to the loss of daily routine. There was not a single man among the 59 [members of the sample] who welcomed freedom from the lifelong routine of work, to whom this freedom was a compensation, however slight, for the curse of unemployment.... Apparently the very formlessness of the day and the week, the absence of any required tasks, caused a letdown and weakened the drive for any activity (pp. 80–1).

Variety

A fourth environmental feature likely to be negatively affected by un-employment is variety. This is associated with the reduction in externally generated goals, being partly a question of less often having to leave the house, and also arising from a loss of contrast between job and non-job activities. Homogeneity of experience is also increased through the activity reductions which follow an unemployed person's drop in income. Further-more, those domestic and other demands which do impinge on the person are likely to be similar and unchanging from day to day, with standard routines and an absence of novelty. Martin and Wallace (1985) observed that to a large extent unemployed British women 'simply spent more time when unemployed doing the things they had previously done during their non-work hours' (pp. 419–20). 'Most women filled most of the hours left free by not going out to work by expanding their existing role of housewife, rather than branching out into new activities' (p. 418).

Differences between the amount of variety in unemployed teenagers' lives have been studied by Warr *et al.* (1985). They observed that lower levels of reported variety were significantly correlated with anxiety, depression, and general distress. Furthermore, variety retained its independent contribution to those forms of low well-being after statistical controls had been introduced for a range of labour market attitudes and job-seeking behaviours.

Environmental clarity

Environmental clarity (feature number five) is also likely to be reduced during unemployment. As discussed in Chapter 8, this concerns information about the consequences of behaviour and information about the future. Availability of such information permits appropriate decisions and actions, allows planning within predictable time schedules, and reduces the anxiety which is typically generated by uncertainty.

The unemployed person's environment is unclear in all these respects. He or she is likely to be unsure what behaviours or attributes would lead to the offer of a job (or even an interview for a job), and planning for the future is difficult in view of uncertainty about one's occupational or financial position in the months to come (e.g. Warr 1984a). In the study by Payne *et al.* (1984) of British men unemployed for between six and eleven months, some 60 per cent reported that they were troubled by 'not knowing what is going to happen to me in the future'.

Fryer and McKenna (1987) examined the importance of this form of temporal uncertainty in a comparison of two groups of men, both lacking paid work but the members of one knowing when they would be reemployed. This group comprised men laid off for a predetermined period of seven weeks, as a result of a union–management agreement that instead of making a number of employees compulsorily redundant all would voluntarily accept periods of temporary and fixed-term lay-off. During these seven-week periods, the men signed on as unemployed, claimed welfare benefits, and otherwise experienced the life of unemployed people. However, their environment differed in one principal way from that of fully unemployed people: its level of clarity was much greater, in that the future was predictable and they could plan their affairs within a defined span of time.

Fryer and McKenna compared the experiences of this sample of men with those of a similar group, all of whom had been made unemployed. The latter were found to exhibit low levels of affective well-being, similar to those observed in other unemployed samples; however, the scores of the temporarily laid-off men indicated significantly better mental health. These men experienced time to be passing much more quickly than did the unemployed group, and they were generally more likely to exhibit self-initiated goal-directed activity. Detailed enquiries into use of time by the two groups indicated that the unemployed sample experienced greater difficulties than those men who were laid off for a predetermined period.

Since the environments of the two groups were very similar except in feature number five, environmental clarity, this study demonstrates the importance of that single feature more effectively than is usually possible in a real-life environment. However, consistent with the difficulty of controlling all important factors in non-artificial settings, the authors point out that the groups also differed in one other respect, here referred to as valued social position (feature number nine). The unemployed group suffered a greater deterioration in this respect, and that may account in part for the results obtained.

Environmental clarity within the present model may also be viewed in terms of the eight other components. In appraising the certainty or uncertainty surrounding a particular unemployed person, we might therefore examine clarity in respect of, say, opportunity for skill use, physical security, or opportunity for interpersonal contact. Variations in clarity in the eight respects are expected to be significantly associated with indices of low mental health.

Availability of money

Payment for work undertaken is at the heart of any contract of employment, and the standard of living of almost all adults below retirement age is principally determined by income received from a job. Unemployment removes that income, and in almost all cases has a serious and wide-ranging impact on the availability of money. This is the sixth environmental category in the present model.

Studies of unemployed people consistently indicate that shortage of money is viewed as the greatest source of personal and family problems (e.g. Smith 1980). Poverty bears down not only upon basic needs for food and physical protection, but also prevents activity and reduces one's sense of personal control. The breadth of its impact is captured by this unemployed British man:

My wife has known nothing but debt and poverty ever since we've been married. I know I ought to feel glad, being able to spend so much time with my kids while they're young. But what can I give them? I just feel empty. I'm ashamed I can't provide them with everything they need. What kind of father is that? We have no life together, even though we're never apart (Seabrook 1982, p. 3).

The extent to which income is reduced after unemployment naturally varies between individuals, within and between countries. In the United Kingdom, welfare benefits are paid according to a number of criteria of need, size of family for example. Studies to identify the extent of financial deterioration after job loss suggest that unemployed people receive on average between 45 and 60 per cent of their employed income (Anon 1983b; Bradshaw *et al.* 1983; Davies *et al.* 1982; Payne *et al.* 1984; Smith 1980; Warr and Jackson 1984). This proportion does of course depend in part upon the level of a person's income while in a job, and for many unemployed people (previously in unskilled jobs) income was already low. The joint presence of previously low wages and benefits paid for high family needs does however make it possible for a small number of unemployed people (perhaps 3 per cent to 5 per cent) to earn slightly more than they did in their last job.

Levels of family income associated with unemployment in a range of countries have been reviewed by the Organization for Economic Co-operation and Development (1984). The general trend is clear: unemployed people are likely to be around or below the officially designated 'poverty line' in all the countries studied.

A substantially impaired standard of living means that many unemployed people have to borrow money to meet pressing needs. In a sample of British working-class men unemployed between six and eleven months, 55 per cent had needed to borrow money since becoming unemployed (Payne *et al.* 1984). In Brinkmann's (1984) German sample, the figure was 23 per cent after 18 months of unemployment, and two-thirds of the Australian sample studied by Finlay-Jones and Eckhardt (1984) were in debt after an average of ten months without a job. White (1985) has shown that debts during un-employment are particularly common among married men with dependent children.

The cost of maintaining and repaying debts is typically greater for un-employed people than for people whose living standard is higher. For exam-ple, interest rates payable to money-lenders, pawnbrokers, and through trading vouchers are substantially greater than rates on money borrowed by more 'credit-worthy' applicants through banks and insurance companies. Inability to sustain regular repayments may lead impoverished debtors to borrow more, thus increasing their weekly demands. Simultaneously they increase the probability of overcommitment, leading to arrears on housing rents or to the sale of items of furniture and other possessions in partial payment of the debt. Forty-one per cent of Payne and colleagues' working-class sample had had to sell possessions as a result of being unemployed.

Instances of unemployed people's hardship cited by Smith (1980) include inability to keep up repayments (about half the sample) and having one's fuel supply cut off because of debt (8 per cent). In addition, shortage of money during unemployment is known to be associated with reduced social contact (e.g. Fröhlich 1983b), and people may incur additional expenditure through the very fact that they are unemployed. For example, additional home heating and lighting may be required, and job-seeking activities depend upon money for postage, travel, and effective self-presentation at interviews.

Given the extensiveness of these difficulties, it is not surprising that finan-cial anxiety is typically high during unemployment (e.g. Daniel 1974; Estes and Wilensky 1978), and that low levels of affective well-being are significantly associated with worries about money (e.g. Payne *et al.* 1984; Smith 1980) and being in debt (e.g. Finlay-Jones and Eckhardt 1984). Jackson and Warr (1984) measured availability of money through separate indices of income reduction since job loss and number of dependants, finding that both these factors made independent contributions to level of distress, after controlling for age, length of unemployment, and attitudes to job-seeking.

Hobbs *et al.* (1985) developed an index of poverty which was based upon weekly income in relation to number of dependants. This combined index appears more adequate than the separate measures used by Jackson and Warr. However, results were very similar, with a strong association between poverty and overall distress, measured through the General Health Ques-tionnaire. The sample studied by Hobbs and colleagues included both em-ployed and unemployed respondents, so that the independent contribution of low standard of living during unemployment could not itself be assessed. However, D'Arcy and Siddique (1985) presented data separately for un-employed people, showing that those with the lowest levels of income during unemployment exhibited particularly high levels of distress.

In a study of unemployed men in Edinburgh, Platt and Kreitman (1985) observed that parasuicide rates varied between different parts of the city.

Partial regression analyses suggested that level of poverty in an area was of major predictive importance. Interpretation of individual cases was not possible from the aggregate nature of these data, but the authors concluded that their cross-sectional finding was consistent with two possibilities: that both unemployment and parasuicide are jointly influenced by poverty, and that unemployment increases probability of parasuicide through its impact on living standards.

In individual-level research, Ullah *et al.* (1985) examined differences in well-being between unemployed British teenagers who had 'someone to turn to for help with money' and those who had no such source of help. Absence of possible financial assistance was found to be significantly associated with elevated distress, depression and anxiety, both in bivariate analyses and in multiple regression equations to control for other potentially important factors. A similar finding in respect of general distress was reported in Australian research by Finlay-Jones and Eckhardt (1984). Warr and Jackson (1985) extended the cross-sectional findings in a longitudinal study of men aged from 17 to 64, finding that non-availability of financial help was significantly predictive of greater deterioration in affective well-being over nine months of unemployment, after controlling for other variables.

Financial difficulties during unemployment have also been studied in respect of relationships within the family. Attempting to meet family requirements with only limited resources is likely to cause increased strain (e.g. Liker and Elder 1983; Moen *et al.* 1982), and this is often especially the case for the wives of unemployed men. For example, Binns and Mars (1984), McKee and Bell (1985) and Morris (1984a) have described role relationships within the families of unemployed British men. Overall financial management and decisions about how to meet children's needs were found to fall principally to the wife, who also usually sought to make available some personal spending money to her husband, but rarely to herself. In a minority of cases husbands felt threatened by their lack of financial control, with challenges to the wife's decision-making centrality leading to increased tension. McKee and Bell (1985) review some of their findings as follows:

'Making ends meet' was cited as the worst aspect of unemployment for a large percentage of the sample, and many families were living in real financial hardship. Money (and the lack of it) was cited as the source of marital rows in many instances, as divisive between husbands and wives, between parents and children, and between families and their wider kin. Rows broke out over how the money was spent, on whom and what... over whose needs were greatest in the family, men against women, young children against older children, stepchildren against biological offspring .... It was often wives who had to live on their wits, variously hunting down bargains, devising new 'economic' meals, locating borrowing sources, placating hungry children, refusing children spending money or treats, patching and mending clothes, going without food or taking less nutritional meals themselves, and sometimes dealing with the creditors (p. 395).

Physical security

The seventh feature in the present model, physical security, is usually associated with the availability of money. Environments need to protect a person against physical threat, and to provide an adequate level of warmth and space for food preparation, relaxation, and sleeping. As discussed in Chapter 10, there appears to be a general need for some personal and private territory, the presence of which can contribute to a stable self-concept and raised well-being. Physical security is also reflected in an expected permanence, in that occupants can look forward to their continued presence or can predict moving to other adequate settings.

This aspect of the environment is clearly likely to be affected by un-employment, although there appear to be no published investigations which are directly relevant. Reduced income can give rise to loss of adequate accom-modation, or to the chronic threat that this will happen. Individuals may become homeless, and families can be forced into run-down, unsanitory, and overcrowded conditions. Alternatively, an unemployed person and his or her family might remain housed as before, but be unable to afford essential repairs or to pay for fuel for heating and lighting. In other cases, seeking jobs in distant regions of the country can promote physical insecurity with temporary or extended problems of accommodation and a lack of personal territory.

Opportunity for interpersonal contact

Contact with others is essential for reducing feelings of loneliness, for pro-viding emotional support, and for helping individuals to attain goals which cannot readily be achieved alone. We should thus expect that opportunity for interpersonal contact is an important contributor to level of mental health during unemployment. This should be observed in both the types of evidence described at the beginning of the chapter. In terms of general impact, reduced opportunity for interpersonal contact after job loss should on average cause a reduction in mental health; and in terms of differences between individual unemployed people, those with less opportunity should show worse mental health than those with more opportunity.

In respect of the first comparison (employed versus unemployed), several investigations have rather surprisingly suggested that amount of social con-tact is increased rather than decreased after loss of a job. Fröhlich's (1983b) study of German married men included questions about changes in several types of activity since becoming unemployed. Forty per cent of the sample reported visiting friends and neighbours more frequently, with only 6 per cent reporting a decrease. In Warr and Payne's (1983b) study of British men unemployed for between six and eleven months, 32 per cent reported spending more time with friends than when employed, compared to 16 per cent reporting a decrease; comparable figures for 'spending time with neighbours' and 'spending time with the family' were 17 per cent and 5 per cent and 79 per cent and 4 per cent respectively. Very similar values were observed in a separate study by Warr (1984c).

In research with unemployed British women, Martin and Wallace (1985) found that younger members of the sample reported similar amounts of interpersonal contact before and after job loss. However, the large majority of older women (often married with husbands in paid work) reported a reduction in contacts after becoming unemployed, typically spending their days alone at home. This latter group was particularly likely to report that unemployment had led to social isolation and feelings of loneliness.

In a cross-sectional comparison between employed and unemployed British adults (men and women), Stokes and Cochrane (1984b) recorded slightly more social contact outside the home for the unemployed group. However, the difference was not statistically significant, and the measure was rather crude: the number of days per week on which a person had any social contact outside the home. More precise measurement through time diaries completed during the day indicates that unemployed people have only a limited amount of contact with others. For example, in a study of unemployed 25- to 45-year-old men in Northern Ireland, Kilpatrick and Trew (1982) observed that 32 per cent of an average day was spent alone and only 15 per cent spent with people outside the family. Corresponding figures for employed men during the waking day appear likely to be around 20 per cent and 35 per cent respectively (Szalai 1972, p. 309), although procedural and geographical differences between studies make these comparisons somewhat uncertain.

The studies cited so far have all examined interpersonal contact merely in terms of its reported quantity. Miles *et al.* (1984) adopted a different approach, asking to what extent unemployed men and women 'meet a broad range of people in my everyday life'. This measure revealed a significantly broader range of contacts among employed people than among their unemployed counterparts.

It is therefore important to distinguish between the amount of social contact and its diversity, an aspect of environmental feature number four in the present model: perhaps unemployed people tend to have more social contact but with fewer people. We should also seek a more differentiated approach by examining separate types of social encounter. For example, we might investigate changes of four principal kinds: contact with work colleagues, entertainment in social settings, contact with family members, and casual meetings which 'pass the time of day' with friends and neighbours. It seems likely that the first two of these will in general decline in quantity after loss of a job, whereas the other two are likely to increase.

Although unemployed people may still maintain some contact with a limited number of ex-colleagues (e.g. Binns and Mars 1984; Fröhlich 1983b), links with other employees are likely to become fewer during unemployment. This is partly because being at work with other people previously filled so many hours of the day, but it is also the case that many individuals even when employed have no contact with colleagues outside working hours. Entertainment in social settings (visiting clubs, pubs, restaurants, etc.) is also widely described as declining after job loss (e.g. Warr 1984c; Warr and Payne 1984), primarily because of shortage of money. Conversely, amount of contact with both family members and friends and neighbours is reported to increase significantly (see above). The nature of these encounters with friends and neighbours has not usually been specified, but it seems likely that shortage of money and excess of time will prompt conversations of a casual, possibly repetitive, kind. (However, the importance of such contacts for providing information about possible job opportunities should not be overlooked; see for instance Morris 1984b; Warr and Lovatt 1977.)

It may thus be the case that, although in overall terms the amount of interpersonal contact can sometimes increase after a transition into unemployment, the opportunity for encounters which are experienced as pleasant is in fact reduced after job loss. Such a pattern would be associated with changes in the other environmental features described here. As noted above, social contacts during unemployment are likely to be limited in their variety, and they may also be inhibited by an absence of externally generated goals.

What of the second comparison mentioned above, between people all of whom are unemployed but who differ in their amount of social contact? Findings here are as expected from the model, with affective well-being positively associated with greater social contact measured through time diaries (Kilpatrick and Trew 1985). Well-being is also significantly positively associated with reported increases since job loss in time spent with friends, and negatively associated with reported decreases in social entertainment requiring money (e.g. Warr 1984c). A narrow range of social contact during unemployment has been found to be significantly associated with greater distress by Miles *et al.* (1984). With a sample of unemployed British teenagers, Warr *et al.* (1985) observed that reported amount of time spent with friends in the past month was significantly correlated with low scores on measures of general distress, depression, and anxiety. The significant associations were retained in multiple regression analyses which included other aspects of behaviour and labour market attitudes. However, in a longitudinal study of unemployed British men, an aggregate index of amount of contact with friends, previous work colleagues, and relatives other than wife or children was found to be unrelated to degree of deterioration over a nine-month period (Warr and Jackson 1985).

The investigation of teenagers also obtained measures of five qualitative aspects of interpersonal contact, focusing upon potential benefits of the kind identified in Chapter 10 (page 180) as 'social support' (Ullah *et al.* 1985). Members of the sample were asked whether they had someone who could suggest interesting things to do, someone to talk with about day-to-day problems, someone to turn to for cheering up when feeling low, and someone to provide information about jobs and benefits. (Interviewees were also asked about financial help; see the discussion of availability of money on page 219.) The presence of the first of these (someone to suggest interesting things to do) was found to be significantly cross-sectionally associated with lower general distress, depression, and anxiety, but the remaining three features were not related to well-being. Kilpatrick and Trew (1985) indexed social support through the presence of close family members living nearby. They found that this factor was significantly associated with lower levels of general distress.

Social support was examined by Gore (1978) through a mixed scale, which tapped frequency of activity outside the home, as well as perceptions of supportive relations and perceived opportunity to engage in supportive activities. Among those men unemployed a month after closure of their plant, less supported members of the sample were found to report a significantly larger number of illness symptoms than did more supported respondents. However, in another American investigation, Linn *et al.* (1985) found non-significant correlations between social support and separate measures of anxiety, depression, and somatic symptoms; but the correlation with general self-esteem was significant. In the study by Warr and Jackson (1985) of unemployed British men on two occasions separated by nine months, emotional support (in terms of the availability of someone to talk with about problems, to cheer you up, and to help you find interesting things to do) was significantly associated with lower distress in cross-sectional analysis, but it was not predictive of magnitude of deterioration across time.

In overview of this eighth environmental characteristic, the changes in opportunity for interpersonal contact which follow job loss are not yet clearly mapped out. Future research should be based upon more precise measurement of particular types of interaction, measuring in each case reported quality and diversity as well as quantity. Nevertheless, cross-sectional comparisons within unemployed samples suggest that affective well-being is in general better for those reporting higher levels of at least some forms of contact. The causal pattern underlying these correlations is likely to be one of mutual influence, with socially rich environments promoting mental health and more healthy people succeeding in creating or maintaining those environments.

Valued social position

As pointed out in Chapters 1 and 10, many different roles within separate or overlapping structures can be important contributors to mental health.

Among these, there is no doubt that in most societies being employed rather than unemployed is a central source of public and private esteem.

On becoming unemployed a person loses a socially approved role and the positive self-evaluations which go with it. The new position is widely felt to be one of lower prestige, deviant, second-rate, or not providing full membership of society. Even when welfare benefits remove the worst financial hardship, there may be shame attached to receipt of funds from public sources and a seeming failure to provide for one's family. An unemployed British man described aspects of this process as follows:

Socially, not having work is upsetting.... You do lose something of your self-respect in the company of people who are working.... There is a stigma, even where a lot of people are out of work. You're almost an affront to people who are working. They feel guilty because they don't care enough; perhaps you remind them it could happen to them.... There's this division between workers and non-workers. You hear them say 'He gets all that help from Social Security, and we don't get any help because my man's working'. They feel you're getting something for nothing (Seabrook 1982, p. 136).

Societies' attitudes to their unemployed members has long been complex and ambivalent (e.g. Garraty 1978), in part because of a recognition that some people are unable to take employment because of a disability for which they cannot be held responsible. These 'deserving poor' are widely felt to warrant sympathy, but how can society be sure that a given unemployed person is 'deserving' rather than being 'idle' or 'work-shy'? And how can the person demonstrate that he or she is not of the latter kind?

In introducing a book of interviews with employed people, Terkel (1972) draws attention to a Labor Day speech by American President Nixon: 'The work ethic holds that labor is good in itself. A man or woman becomes a better person by virtue of the act of working.' Such a normative framework is widely held in most Western societies, although there is sometimes uncertainty about how far 'work' is viewed as extending beyond paid employment into other kinds of task-oriented activity.

Weber (1905) traced aspects of the same ethic back to seventeenth century ascetic Protestantism. For example, Calvin emphasized that since one's 'salvation' or 'damnation' was predetermined by God, it was a duty of the individual to assume that he or she had been 'chosen' and to demonstrate that fact by living the godly life. The latter involved meeting one's obligations in worldly affairs, in part by working hard within one's calling or vocation, a theme which is also central to the teachings of Luther.

How, then, ought the faithful to employ their time? That first of all they must fulfil their spiritual duties—prayer, attendance at church and sacraments, sabbath observance, and the like—goes without saying. But equally they must work hard in their lawful callings. Hard, methodical, continuous, manual and mental labour in a legitimate calling is required of all: it is God's commandment that they who shall not work shall not eat. Idleness, like time-wasting, is the mark of a reprobate (Marshall 1982, p. 76).

Whether or not a religious basis is invoked, such moral beliefs remain common and underlie the loss of public esteem which often follows unemployment. Unemployed people appear to be widely aware of their stigmatized position, and seek to escape from it.

Nevertheless, there has been little systematic research into this specific feature. An indirect approach might be taken in terms of local unemployment levels. When the local rate is very high, an unemployed person may feel less socially stigmatized and less personally deviant than in areas where unemployment is less common. Mental health among unemployed people is on this basis expected to be worse in areas of low rather than high unemployment. Although evidence for this possibility is so far limited, the pattern been found in respect of a single-item measure of dissatisfaction with self by Cohn (1978), and also in terms of parasuicide levels by Platt and Kreitman (1985).

The same argument applies to variations in unemployment rate across time: in periods of widespread unemployment its impact might be relatively less severe. Such a process is also likely to reduce the relationship between unemployment and mental health which is observed in aggregate time-series investigations: in periods of low unemployment, the psychological impact will be enhanced, and when rates are high the negative effect will be more limited.

An interpretation in terms of the ninth environmental characteristic seems appropriate. People are less likely to attribute their own joblessness to personal failings in times and regions of high unemployment; personal deviance and social stigma will thus be experienced less strongly than in the context of low local unemployment. However, other factors may also tend towards the same result. Stronger support networks may be available in areas of high unemployment (an aspect of the eighth 'vitamin' category), and previous mental health will be more similar among the unemployed and employed populations, since job loss will be more widely and impersonally spread.

Taking a more direct approach to valued social position, Miles *et al.* (1984) assessed the degree to which employed and unemployed people felt that 'society in general respects people like me'. Unemployed men and women reported significantly less social esteem than those in jobs, and among the unemployed groups lower esteem was significantly associated with greater distress measured through the General Health Questionnaire. Unemployed people who feel greater pressure from others to obtain a job may be expected to exhibit lower affective well-being than those experiencing no pressure, and this has been shown to be the case, at least for teenagers (Ullah *et al.* 1985).

Aspects of the work ethic have been tapped through measures of 'employment commitment', including items such as 'if unemployment benefit was really high, I would still prefer to have a job' and 'even if I could find plenty to do when unemployed, I'd prefer to have a job'. Scores on measures of that kind have been found to be significantly associated in unemployed samples with low positive affect and high negative affect (Warr 1978), anxiety (e.g. Ullah *et al.* 1985, Warr *et al.* 1985), depression (e.g. Feather and Barber 1983; Feather and Davenport 1981; Ullah *et al.* 1985; Warr *et al.* 1985), negative self-esteem (e.g. Feather and Bond 1983; Warr and Jackson 1983), and general distress (e.g. Jackson and Warr 1984; Jackson *et al.* 1983; Stafford *et al.* 1980; Ullah *et al.* 1985; Warr and Jackson 1985; Warr *et al.* 1985). The importance of employment commitment is maintained after statistical controls are introduced for other labour market attitudes, age, length of unemployment, time spent out of the house, social contact, financial situation, and other possibly relevant factors (e.g. Jackson and Warr 1984; Shamir 1986; Ullah *et al.* 1985; Warr and Jackson 1985; Warr *et al.* 1985).

These studies make clear that employment commitment is a significant mediator of the impact of the jobless environment on mental health. Consistent with an account in terms of frustrated motivation to obtain a job, unemployed people with higher commitment to paid work exhibit substantially lower well-being than those with lower commitment. However, that value orientation may arise from a range of sources, including negative feelings about other environmental factors during unemployment, such as reduced variety or lack of externally generated goals. Although concern over the stigma of unemployment is likely to be one contributor to the level of a person's employment commitment, it is clearly not the only basis. Quantitative investigations into the importance of valued social position on its own remain to be undertaken.

Five specific applications of the model

The previous section has analysed the environment of unemployed people in general in terms of the nine components of the vitamin model. The account examined each component separately and considered unemployed people as a whole, contrasting the jobless environment with that likely to be found in paid work. Another use of the model is to serve as a lens through which to view the position of particular sub-groups of people. Five specific applications will be made in this section, considering middle-aged men, teenagers, women, the long-term unemployed, and those people who regain a job after being unemployed.

Middle-aged men

Research has consistently pointed to the particularly negative impact of unemployment on the affective well-being of middle-aged men, especially those with families in need of financial support. A significant curvilinear relationship between age and low well-being during unemployment has been observed with a wide range of different samples and measuring instruments (e.g. Daniel 1974; Eisenberg and Lazarsfeld 1938; Hepworth 1980). This pattern is retained despite statistical control of a range of other variables (Jackson and Warr 1984; Warr and Jackson 1984, 1985).

Environmental features numbered 6, 9, and 5 are likely to be especially problematic for the middle-aged group: availability of money, valued social position, and environmental clarity. In the first case, the financial demands upon middle-aged men are likely to be particularly great, as many of them have growing children in need of support. Furthermore, some men in this group suffer a particularly large drop in income, having previously sought overtime work or received bonus payments for raised output on piecework schemes. Middle-aged men's social position is also particularly strongly affected by unemployment, since they lose their valued role as provider for the family in addition to their positions as contributor to a work-group and member of the wider labour-force.

In terms of environmental clarity, middle-aged men's uncertainty about the future is compounded by the fact that their unemployment generates ambiguity which also extends into the lives of all family members; plans can less easily be made and the future is less clearly predictable. In addition, they are at that stage of the life-cycle which is often accompanied by insecurity and self-questioning irrespective of employment status: what does the future offer, what do I want from it, what can I contribute to other people, and how do I feel about my life to date? Job loss and continuing unemployment are likely to make these questions particularly difficult to answer.

Teenagers

The position of unemployed teenagers is rather different. As a group they show significantly less impairment in well-being than do middle-aged people, and this may be interpreted principally in terms of environmental features 6, 7, 8, and 9: availability of money, physical security, opportunity for interpersonal contact, and valued social position. In each case, the environments of unemployed teenagers are likely to be relatively less problematic than those of middle-aged people.

For example, the income differential between having a job and being unemployed may be relatively small, especially for those teenagers with few qualifications. Money and material assistance are often provided by parents, and financial requirements are generally less than for older groups. Associated with that, physical security is often unchanged by the transition from school into unemployment, as many teenagers continue to live within the family accommodation.

They may also have relatively good opportunities for interpersonal contact, as they carry forward from school a network of friends and established patterns of leisure activities. In the male samples studied by Fröhlich (1983b) and Warr (1984c), teenagers reported particularly large increases in social interaction following loss of their job. A similar pattern was suggested in the study of unemployed women described by Martin and Wallace (1985) and in research into recent school-leavers conducted by Stokes (1983).

Although unemployed teenagers experience the lack of valued social position which is common during unemployment at all ages, they may see themselves as members of that large group of unemployed youth who are at the mercy of bad economic conditions (e.g. Gurney 1981). With unemployment so widespread among teenagers in recent years, personal responsibility and social stigma are liable to be less strongly felt (e.g. Miles *et al.* 1984; Roberts *et al.* 1982). Non-employment roles may be adopted which provide their own source of esteem, for example as an active member of a music group or youth club, or through providing care for younger siblings or for invalid parents.

Despite these potentially ameliorating conditions, there is no doubt that unemployment has a significant negative impact upon teenagers' affective well-being (e.g. Banks and Jackson 1982; Doherty and Davies 1984; Donovan and Oddy 1982; Feather and O'Brien 1986; Jackson *et al.* 1983; Patton and Noller 1984; Tiggemann and Winefield 1980, 1984; Warr and Jackson, 1983; Winefield and Tiggemann, 1985). However, it is those components of mental health which explicitly concern behaviour in social roles—autonomy, competence, and aspiration—which appear to be of greatest public and political concern.

Gaining a job is of special significance for adolescents, marking the end of childhood dependence and representing entry into the adult world. Independence is aided through the money which employment provides, and autonomous development can be enhanced by moving into living accommodation away from one's parents. Autonomy is thus liable to be retarded by joblessness after leaving school. The development of competence may also be inhibited, as new skills and knowledge acquired from a job and from adult work colleagues are denied to the school-leaver who fails to obtain paid work. This feature appears central to much public concern, as unemployed teenagers are seen to lead a life lacking in the challenge and novel responsibilities which a job may provide. There are also fears that aspirations will be stunted, as teenagers without paid work may become adjusted to a relatively inactive life and lose their interest in gaining a job.

The latter fears seem to be largely unfounded, since teenagers out of a job for long periods tend in general to retain a strong desire for paid employment, even though they may reduce their job-seeking activity in circumstances where the probability of success is low (e.g. Banks and Ullah 1986; Ullah and Banks 1985; Warr *et al.* 1985). However, the harmful impact of teenage unemployment on autonomy and competence is likely to be substantial. Research in those areas has mainly been of a qualitative kind (e.g. Coffield *et al.* 1983), and additional studies, both qualitative and quantitative, would be valuable.

Women

Introducing the third application of the model in this section, it may be noted that the subjects of unemployment research have typically been men. This is partly because during the 1950s and 1960s labour force participation among married women was in many countries relatively low, but primarily because the distinction between unemployment and non-employment (see page 57) is often more easily made for men. Given that the official definition of unemployment includes wanting paid work as well as lacking it, there is sometimes difficulty in deciding whether certain women are unemployed or non-employed. Although many jobless women have a strong desire for paid work (thus being 'unemployed') and others have no such desire (are 'non-employed'), there also exists a third group which is located somewhere on the boundary between the two categories. Ambivalence may be strong for this third group, and self-definition as either in or out of the labour market depends partly on the availability of suitable jobs.

Despite these problems of definition, it is clearly essential to examine the importance of paid employment or its absence upon the mental health of women as well as men. A first step is to consider research which has been restricted to women who are formally defined as unemployed through their registration with official agencies. For such women, the impact of unemployment on affective well-being is as negative as it is for men, and associations between well-being during unemployment and the environmental features examined here are in general equally strong for the two sexes (e.g. Banks and Jackson 1982; Finlay-Jones and Eckhardt 1984; Jackson *et al.* 1983; Martin and Wallace 1985; Miles *et al.* 1984; Warr and Jackson 1983; Warr *et al.* 1985). Indeed there is no reason to expect any difference in these respects between unemployed women and men.

However, many investigators have failed to distinguish in their samples between women who are unemployed and those who are non-employed. In reviewing studies of these undifferentiated samples, it is helpful to consider separately research into women who are married and studies of those who are single, divorced, or separated. (The category of 'married' women in this research field is usually taken to include women living with a partner whether or not they are legally married.) In very broad terms, it may be expected that married women without a job are more likely to be 'non-employed' than are those who are single, divorced, or separated.

Examining 38 previous investigations, Warr and Parry (1982) recorded that for married women in general there was no significant difference in affective well-being between those with and without paid employment; additional and subsequent investigations supporting that conclusion include those by Aneshensel *et al.* (1981), Ballinger *et al.* (1985), Barnett and Baruch (1985), Cleary and Mechanic (1983), Jougla *et al.* (1983), Parry (1986), Roberts and O'Keefe (1981), Ross *et al.* (1983), and Shehan (1984). However, for unmarried women, who are usually in effect principal wage-earners, paid employment was found to be significantly beneficial. Female principal wage-earners without a job are likely to define themselves as 'unemployed', and among that group in general the impact of joblessness is similar for men and for women.

It is useful to consider possible differences associated with the model's nine environmental features for married and unmarried women with and without a job. For women who are married, the necessary comparison is between their domestic role alone (unemployed or non-employed) and an aggregation of both a domestic role and a job role (employed). The variety of possible combinations of features in the two sets of environments is clearly very great, some implying potential gains from a job and others predicting psychological harm. The net result of a comparison between environments naturally depends in each case upon the quality of both a woman's home environment and her job environment.

In many cases, married women who take a paid job are likely to gain in terms of environmental features 4, 6, and 8 (variety, availability of money, and opportunity for interpersonal contact), and the specific impact of employment versus joblessness will depend upon those comparisons. For example, Parry (1986) has observed that high levels of social support (an aspect of the eighth 'vitamin') are necessary if mothers in chronically difficult life settings are to benefit from a job in terms of fewer psychiatric symptoms. Job features 5 and 7 (environmental clarity and physical security) will be beneficial or harmful according to the nature of the employed role, as described in Chapters 8 and 9: some married women undoubtedly have jobs which are distressing in these respects.

Gains may be expected in terms of opportunity for control and opportunity for skill use (features 1 and 2) for women in skilled and managerial jobs; for others the effect of these elements of the job environment may be neutral or negative. Similarly, esteem from one's social position (feature number 9) does not always increase after a married woman gets a job. This depends both upon the nature of her employed role and upon the attitude taken by important people in her life; her husband's view about appropriate roles is likely to be central here.

The environmental feature which has most often been considered in empirical research into paid employment among married women is number 3 in the present model, externally generated goals. As described in Chapter 7, environments which make very few demands upon a person are liable to impair mental health. Married women whose domestic environments are of this kind might be thought likely to gain from paid employment, since this carries with it specific goals and goal-oriented activities. In contrast, married women whose home environments are already very demanding are likely to suffer from the addition of job-related goals (e.g. Jougla *et al.* 1983).

This factor takes on a variety of concrete forms, depending both upon the job environment and the domestic environment. Part-time jobs make fewer time demands than those which are full-time, and are for that reason particularly attractive to many married women. However, part-time employment may carry with it negative features (limited opportunity for skill use and a low income, for example), which make it of little benefit in certain cases. Domestic demands can themselves be modified by help available from one's husband, and paid employment is more likely to benefit women whose husbands help with childcare and housework than in the case of women whose husbands do not assist in these ways (e.g. Kessler and McRae 1982; Krause and Markides 1985).

Domestic demands are likely to be greater in families with dependent children, and we might expect the presence of children in the home to influence the psychological value of paid work for married women. However, several investigators who have looked for a mediating effect of children within their particular sample have failed to find one (e.g. Kessler and McRae 1982; Krause and Markides 1985; Parry 1986). The burdens of childcare presumably vary between families in a range of ways (for example, whether or not help is received from older children), and more direct assessment of domestic and employment demands would be valuable in future research.

The nine environmental features in employed and home roles are also expected to determine the psychological impact of paid work for non-married women. Those who are single with no family commitments are expected to gain from paid employment in ways described in the preceding section and in Chapters 5 to 10; most jobless women in this non-married group will be formally defined as unemployed rather than non-employed. Divorced and separated women experience a pattern of environmental features which varies according to whether or not they have childcare responsibilities. For example, Krause and Markides (1985) observed that paid employment was detrimental to the affective well-being of this group of women if they had young children at home; as noted above, this factor was not significant in their data from married women, suggesting that paid work in addition to childcare gave rise to particular overload for those who were divorced or separated.

In applying the present model to women's employment, it is thus necessary to compare domestic and domestic-plus-employment roles in terms of the nine features separately for different groups. Future analyses and empirical investigations must distinguish between women of different marital status; and differentiation in terms of number and ages of dependent children is also required.

The long-term unemployed

Next, let us consider the position of people who have been unemployed for a considerable length of time. There has recently been a steady increase in the size of this group. For example, 40 per cent of officially counted unemployed people in Britain in 1986 had been continuously out of paid work for more than a year, some 1.3 million from a total of more than three million; almost 25 per cent (750 000 people) had been continuously unemployed for more than two years.

Research has indicated that the impact of job loss is typically rapid, so that affective well-being is significantly impaired at an early stage. Further deterioration is likely in the period after job loss, until a plateau of particularly poor mental health is reached after between three and six months. This pattern is particularly marked for middle-aged men, and additional deterioration beyond that shown at the time of job loss is less evident among teenagers or men approaching retirement age, at least in the welfare conditions of Australia and the United Kingdom (e.g. Banks and Ullah 1986; Feather and Davenport 1981; Finlay-Jones and Eckhardt 1984; Jackson and Warr 1984; Warr and Jackson 1984, 1985; Warr *et al.* 1982; Warr *et al.* 1985). Men approaching retirement are likely to redefine themselves as no longer members of the labour force; and the specific factors making up the jobless environment for teenagers have been considered above.

Most investigations into duration of unemployment have concerned affective well-being. However, a laboratory study by Baum *et al.* (1986) tapped aspects of behaviour which appear to reflect the competence and aspiration components of mental health. In a cross-sectional comparison, they found that people unemployed for between three and five months persisted less on uncontrollably difficult experimental tasks than did those out of work for shorter periods. The group unemployed for three to five months also showed a decline in excretion of adrenaline and noradrenaline throughout the experimental session, consistent with a reduction in concentration and effort; on the other hand, levels for the short-term unemployed group increased during the tasks. Longitudinal research of this kind would now be particularly valuable.

In respect of the general pattern of findings, two issues are of concern in the present setting. How can the deterioration during early months of unemployment be interpreted within the vitamin model? And how can the subsequent stabilization be accounted for within the same framework? The early deterioration seems likely to arise from rapid decrements in most of the features. Although initial days of unemployment may be experienced as something of a relief from previous uncertainty, availability of money (feature number 6) is in many cases likely to decline quickly, physical security (feature number 7) may be impaired at the same time, and, as jobs become perceived as less attainable, there is often a growing concern about loss of important skills (feature number 2). Inability to predict and plan (feature number 5) may become worrying, and social contact through entertainment requiring money is likely to show a steady decrease. Furthermore, the recognition that one may have to remain in this stigmatized social position (feature number 9) may increasingly colour perceptions and actions.

The observed stabilization at a low level of mental health after three to six months (rather than a continuing decline) seems likely to be attributable mainly to a change in feature number 5: environmental clarity. The early period of unemployment often contains much uncertainty, as a person strives to deal with the complexities of official benefit procedures, learns about job-seeking practices, takes up new patterns of interaction with family members, assesses him or herself in relation to personal values, and experiences unusual pressures from other people.

However, these high levels of uncertainty are likely gradually to decline, as an unemployed person finds that previously new situations have become familiar and the frequency of novel threatening events has diminished. Associated with that, daily and weekly routines become established, expenditure limits become clarified, and behaviour may be shaped to avoid threats from new situations or other people. For example, job-seeking is likely to decline as people accept that the probability of success is low (e.g. Sheppard and Belitsky 1966; Ullah and Banks 1985; Warr and Jackson 1985).

At the same time, unemployed people may come to take up additional role activities, with benefits in respect of opportunity for control, opportunity for skill use, externally generated goals, variety, opportunity for interpersonal contact, and valued social position. It may also happen in a small number of cases that additional sources of income are located, perhaps outside the formal economy. In general, however, the changes seem most appropriately viewed as passive and restricted forms of coping. It must be stressed that overall levels of mental health among the long-term unemployed are particularly low, and that their environments in terms of the nine features examined here remain chronically impoverished.

This interpretation of the course of mental health during continued unemployment is of course speculative. As pointed out at the beginning of the chapter, there has so far been little research into the specific processes by which unemployment has its effects. One aim of the present account is to provide a framework for such enquiries, within the unemployed population as a whole and in respect of specific applications of the kind illustrated in this section. There is now a need to develop more adequate measures of each of the nine components of the model, assessing their stability or change in different settings of unemployment.

The model may also be used in studies which span a number of different countries. At present, the processes and outcomes of unemployment tend to be discussed as though they are the same in all parts of the world. Yet there are almost certainly major variations, associated with cultural differences and differences in the availability of money. For example, welfare benefits continue indefinitely in Australia and the United Kingdom, whereas substantial reductions take place after six or nine months in most parts

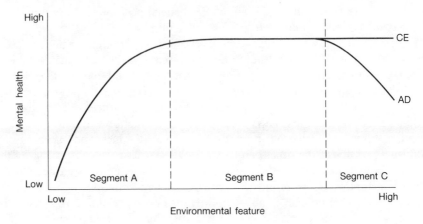

Fig. 12.1   Three principal ranges of environmental values within the vitamin model.

of the United States (e.g. Organization for Economic Co-operation and Development 1984). There is now a need to move towards defining cross-national differences in the mental health of comparable sub-groups (teen-agers, or middle-aged men, for example), using as a basis for interpretation a differentiated model of environmental influences. The present model can serve in this role, being used to characterize particular jobless environments in different countries, and to predict the degree of mental health impairment in each.

Unemployed people who regain a job

Finally in this section, what can the model contribute to an understanding of the process and outcomes of re-entry into paid employment? It is clear that unemployed people who regain a job show a rapid and substantial increase in affective well-being (e.g. Jackson *et al.* 1983; Payne and Jones 1987), and this improvement should be open to interpretation in terms of changes in the nine environmental features of the model. Empirical assessment of that possibility is so far lacking, but the approach appears to be conceptually promising.

The basic assumption of the vitamin model has been presented earlier within Fig. 1.1. That is reproduced here as Fig. 12.1, with an additional emphasis upon the three segments of environmental values which are identified as having differential importance. Segment B covers the broad middle range of the nine environmental categories, within which a constantly beneficial impact is assumed. At lower values, within segment A, harmful effects upon mental health are expected; and this is also the case for the six 'additional decrement' vitamins at extremely high levels, here represented by segment C.

The present argument is that unemployment is usually characterized by low values of all nine environmental features; in the terms of Fig. 12.1, most unemployed people's environments fall within segment A. On regaining a job, the model expects a general shift towards segment B, but the magnitude of environmental improvement will vary considerably between individuals.

For example, most people will move from segment A into segment B in respect of features 8 and 9: opportunity for interpersonal contact and valued social position. But the change in respect of features 1, 4, 6, and 7 may for some people be quite limited, in effect leaving them still within segment A. These features (opportunity for control, variety, availability of money, and physical security) take on very low values in some jobs, so that the transition from unemployment to employment may sometimes give rise to only limited improvements in those respects. On the other hand, many re-employed persons undoubtedly experience major beneficial shifts in these terms.

The transition back into a job can have particularly variable effects for the remaining three factors: opportunity for skill use, externally generated goals, and environmental clarity (numbers 2, 3, and 5). Some employees (those moving into psychologically poor jobs) may experience little or no improvement in these terms, remaining within segment A; others may move into segment B, with consequential gains in mental health. However, some people may find the skill demands, task requirements and/or ambiguity of their job situation particularly great, with a mental health impact of the 'additional decrement' kind in segment C.

The general point is that the vitamin model may be used to characterize in some detail this particular transition (and indeed other transitions; see page 156). The nine features vary widely within the settings of unemployment and within the settings of paid work; and differences between people in the magnitude of mental health changes following the transition between these environments are therefore to be expected. The vitamin model can be used conceptually and empirically to interpret these differential effects. Variations seem likely to be found between types of job and between occupational levels, and analyses need to consider the specific sub-categories which have been described earlier within the nine principal components. Tasks of this kind have yet to be undertaken, but they offer hope of a valuable integration of research into unemployment and that concerned with the characteristics and impact of paid work.

Summary

This chapter has contained two principal sections. The first examined the environments of unemployed people in general from the standpoint of the vitamin model, suggesting that low values of the nine principal environmental features are responsible for the typically negative impact of unemployment. Two kinds of investigation were described, those comparing the environments of employed and unemployed people in the nine respects, and those studying variations within samples of unemployed people alone to explore associations between environmental levels and mental health.

Although research of both kinds is to date rather limited, there was some support for the view that unemployed people tend to be confined to impoverished environments in terms of the model. Significant associations between environmental levels and mental health were also reported, but there remains a need for additional inquiries of quantitative as well as qualitative kinds.

The second part of the chapter described five specific applications of the model. The first three construed the situation of unemployed middle-aged men, teenagers, and several categories of women in terms of the nine suggested 'vitamins'. The position of long-term unemployed people was also viewed from this standpoint, seeking to interpret temporal changes in mental health, including the stabilization at low levels which occurs after several months. The fifth application was in terms of re-entry into a job, where differences between people were interpreted in terms of shifts in the value of nine environmental factors within the non-linear assumption of the vitamin model.

13

Interactions between persons and situations

The vitamin model was introduced at the outset as a framework which was 'situation-centred and enabling' (page 16). Its aim was to define principal categories of the environment and to suggest ways in which those may affect mental health. However, it also recognized that individuals have some power to shape the content of their environment. Personal influence of that kind was viewed as both cognitive, in terms of appraisal and the imposition of meaning, and also behavioural, in terms of activities to create or modify environmental conditions.

All situation-centred models carry with them assumptions about people. These assumptions are usually implicit, but they are crucial in underpinning statements within the model. In effect they assert that there is something about the human make-up which gives rise to the general importance of those situational categories which the model has identified. In the present case, for example, opportunity for control (environmental feature number 1) is considered to be important because people are assumed in general to desire, or perhaps to need, to influence what happens to them. That assumption is in a sense part of the model's view of human nature. Although a situation-centred model, it necessarily presupposes some characteristics of persons.

However, just as environments are recognized to differ, so are variations expected between people. These variations set limits to the empirical confirmation of many situation-centred predictions, and they need to be accommodated within any broad conceptual framework. That is of course widely accepted, and possible interactions between persons and situations have been extensively discussed.

Nevertheless, empirical progress in defining these interactions in real-life settings has not been great. In part this lack of progress derives from the conceptual difficulties of combining models about situations with those about persons, but also from the problems which arise in practice when one seeks to obtain independent measures of situations and of persons. Within experimental research in artificial environments, it is possible to specify and control situational features reasonably well; person–situation interactions can there be studied quite effectively (e.g. Nygard 1981). However, in real-life settings one can less easily manipulate environments, so that controlled comparisons are less possible. Furthermore, people with similar characteristics tend to select themselves into or out of particular settings according to a common preference. As a result, there is often in practice less variation between people within a situation than might in principle be expected. The probability of finding strong person–situation interaction effects is thereby further reduced.

In addition, there are recurrent problems in measuring situations. As described in Chapter 1, conventional forms of environmental measurement tend to rely upon subjective assessment by persons in that environment. One is thus likely to study environments after their measured attributes have already been influenced cognitively by those persons who are the object of study. A form of person–situation interaction has already occurred before situational measures are obtained; once again, it is difficult in practice to separate persons and situations.

Despite these problems, some success has been achieved in the areas covered by this book. Findings will be reviewed within a framework which draws attention to four principal types of personal characteristics. These will first be introduced, and the ways in which individual differences enter into the present situation-centred model will be considered. Some statistical procedures for identifying significant interactions between persons and situations will next be summarized, before a model of processes across time is presented in Fig. 13.1. Empirical findings about individual differences in reactions to jobs and unemployment will then be reviewed in Chapter 14.

Enduring personal characteristics

It is of course possible to describe people and the variations between them in many different ways. The merits and disadvantages of each descriptive framework depend in part upon the purposes to be served, and in the present setting a four-category perspective appears to be helpful. Enduring personal characteristics will be grouped under four broad headings: demographic features, abilities, values, and baseline mental health.

Demographic features, abilities, and values

Within the first category are variables such as age, sex, nationality, or ethnic group membership. Also included, but presenting greater difficulty of measurement, are socio-economic status and life-cycle stage. Variables of these kinds have been widely studied by investigators in many different fields, and research illustrations will be cited later. Demographic features are of interest in their own right, but may sometimes be more helpfully viewed as indicators of other features or processes, standing as 'proxy' measures of the latter.

The other sets of personal characteristics are in a sense more 'psychological', covering differences between people in their styles of perceiving, thinking, valuing, and behaving. These styles can be relatively stable over time and across situations, but they are also liable to change, within limits, in response to situational pressures.

The category of 'abilities' is taken to include all interpersonal, intellectual, and psycho-motor skills. In occupational settings these are sometimes referred to as abilities within the domains respectively of people, data, and things. Although malleable through training and experience, they may also be viewed as relatively stable attributes.

The number and variety of different abilities are clearly very large, and they may be construed in different ways. One approach is to seek higher-order factors such as 'verbal ability', 'numerical ability', or 'manual dexterity'. Another is to identify particular occupational skills, 'operating machine X' or 'leading a discussion group' for example. Whatever approach is taken, it is clear that abilities differ in their specificity of focus. In terms of person–situation interactions in the present setting, we may note that a narrow-scope ability is by definition one with restricted potential impact upon person–situation interactions, whereas a broad-ranging competence may have a much wider influence.

The third category includes all types of dispositional value orientation. Once again, these may be broad in their focus, covering for example moral, religious, or political value systems; or they may be of a more restricted kind, dealing with attitudes and beliefs about specific objects or issues. This category of enduring characteristics is sometimes treated in the language of personality theories, sometimes viewed as motivational pressures for action, and sometimes considered primarily in terms of attitudes. Although there are important differences between these approaches, they may in the present discussion be grouped together, labelling their subject-matter generically as 'values'.

Baseline mental health

However, it appears desirable to separate from within that group of dispositions a number of features which may sometimes more helpfully be viewed as 'baseline mental health'. Consider for instance the content of personality inventories. These often include scales of sociability, orderliness, impulsivity, and similar characteristics, features which will here be placed within the preceding category of 'values'. But they also cover some enduring dispositions which may be better treated as components of mental health. Five features will serve as illustrations of that possibility.

Consider first the personality factor of 'neuroticism'. This has been at the core of several theories, most notably that developed by Eysenck. In the manual of the Eysenck Personality Questionnaire, the typical high scorer on this factor is described as being 'an anxious, worrying individual, moody and frequently depressed. He is likely to sleep badly, and to suffer from various psychosomatic disorders. He is overly emotional, reacting too strongly to all sorts of stimuli, and finds it difficult to get back on an even keel after each emotionally arousing experience.... His main characteristic is a constant preoccupation with things that might go wrong, and a strong emotional reaction of anxiety to these thoughts' (Eysenck and Eysenck 1975, pp. 9–10).

Although that account is presented in terms of a stable personality disposition, it may also be read as a description of low affective well-being. The central element is raised anxiety, but depression is also included. In effect then, the measure of this personality factor might also be viewed as a broad-band index of a person's continuing location on the first dimension of affective well-being (see page 41).

Watson and Clark (1984) have drawn attention to the existence of many personality measures in the area covered by Eysenck's neuroticism scale. Illustrations include scales of trait anxiety, emotional instability, manifest anxiety, and several subscales from broad-ranging inventories such as the California Psychological Inventory and the Minnesota Multiphasic Personality Inventory. Definitional overlap between these concepts is accompanied by strong statistical intercorrelations, and Watson and Clark argue for the existence of a pervasive individual difference factor which is tapped by all the measures. They see this as a general disposition to experience negative affect in any kind of environment.

Scores on this factor are shown by Watson and Clark to be stable over many years (see also Conley 1984, 1985), and to be associated with raised levels of psychosomatic symptoms (see also Costa and McRae 1985) and with current levels of distress (see also Goodchild and Duncan-Jones 1985). Although widely described as a feature of personality, it seems appropriate also to view this enduring disposition as an aspect of baseline mental health: people exhibit consistent differences in their continuing level of affective well-being, irrespective of current environmental conditions.

Let us apply this view to a second aspect of personality. A generalized confidence in oneself and in the outcomes of one's endeavours is tapped by several personality inventories and has been of interest to many investigators. For instance, Antonovsky (1980) has been particularly concerned with factors influencing the course of ill-health, emphasizing among these the importance of 'a global orientation that expresses the extent to which one has a pervasive, enduring though dynamic feeling of confidence that one's internal and external environments are predictable and that there is a high probability that things will work out as well as can reasonably be expected' (p. 123).

Although presented as 'a crucial element in the basic personality structure of an individual' (p. 124), this concept might alternatively be viewed as an aspect of continuing mental health. So might Ben-Sira's (1985) notion of 'potency', which is defined in terms of a person's enduring confidence in his or her own capacities within an ordered society. In the present framework, these forms of self-confidence are captured in high affective well-being on the third axis of Fig. 2.1 (page 27), where feelings about the self are evaluatively positive and take on an active tone. Such feelings are also associated with raised subjective competence, the second component of mental health within the present account.

Third, consider a person's belief that he or she has some control over what happens in life. Kobasa *et al.* (1982) have identified this as a central 'personality disposition' within their concept of 'hardiness'. They suggest that the generalized perception of oneself as having an influence upon events and outcomes is central to people's ability to tolerate aversive conditions (see also Kobasa 1979; Kobasa and Pucetti 1983).

Such a disposition is similar to subjective forms of the third component of mental health introduced in Chapter 2. 'Autonomy' was there described in part as covering the extent to which a person is an independent agent, acting upon the environment and feeling responsible for his or her actions. Although Kobasa, and several other authors, treat this feature as an aspect of personality which moderates the impact of environmental conditions upon mental health, an alternative perspective is to treat it as a reflection of baseline mental health itself.

Kobasa and colleagues also identify within 'hardiness' the personality disposition of 'commitment'. Committed persons are said to have a generalized sense of purpose and to be emotionally involved in their environment. Such characteristics have here been taken to define the aspiration component of mental health (see page 31). It may also be appropriate to include within that component the third hardiness disposition described by Kobasa and colleagues. This is 'challenge', 'expressed as the belief that change rather than stability is normal in life and that the anticipation of changes are [*sic*] interesting incentives to growth rather than threats to security' (Kobasa *et al.* 1982, p. 170).

As a final example, consider research into coping behaviour. This has been described as 'any response to external life-strains that serves to prevent, avoid, or control emotional distress' (Pearlin and Schooler 1978, p. 3). It may be studied as a context-specific activity (e.g. Lazarus and Folkman 1984; Parkes 1984), or viewed as a relatively enduring personal style.

In the latter case one might examine differences between individuals in their characteristic ways of coping with demands or in terms of their overall level of coping effectiveness. Such differences might be viewed as personal dispositions. Within the present framework, they are better treated as continuing aspects of competence, the second component of mental health. In that way coping behaviour in a specific situation would be treated as an index of this form of mental health in the short term, and consistency across time would be considered indicative of enduring competence, an aspect of baseline mental health.

Several factors which are widely described in the literature as personality influences upon the way environmental features affect mental health may thus be viewed instead as enduring aspects of mental health itself. Rather than being additional and separate personality variables, these stable components of mental health represent different baselines from which the environment exerts its effect.

Aversive environmental features have a smaller negative impact on people with better baseline mental health for two reasons. First, because these people start from a position which gives rise to higher scores on measures of the several components; even if an environmental feature exerted a constant effect upon all persons, certain individuals would exhibit better subsequent mental health since they started at a higher level. Secondly, better baseline mental health protects people against negative environmental features because of the transactional nature of mental health itself. The components of competence, autonomy, and aspiration are such that to assert that a person is of good mental health is to indicate that he or she is able to deal effectively with difficulties and demands, and has a positive, self-regulating orientation towards the environment. Negative features of the environment will be better handled by this person than by someone of poorer mental health.

The apparent stability of mental health across time and situations can give rise to methodological problems in the investigation of environmental influences. In cross-sectional research, low mental health scores may in a proportion of cases be more a reflection of chronic poor health than a response to a particular environment (e.g. Depue and Monroe 1986). Longitudinal studies are thus desirable, seeking to identify the extent to which mental health is modified after exposure to a new situation; such research is in practical terms immensely difficult.

In summary of this section, it is proposed to treat enduring personal characteristics under four headings: baseline mental health, demographic features, values, and abilities. In each case the attributes within a category may be broad and relatively abstract, or they may be specific and concrete. To be included, however, they must be relatively stable over a period of time and across a range of situations.

Measuring the impact of personal characteristics

Using that outline categorization, how might we identify and measure the impact of enduring personal characteristics within the present situation-centred model? Two forms of influence require consideration. First is the possibility of a direct effect, irrespective of any environmental features. In investigating this possibility, we would measure an aspect of current mental health (affective well-being, perhaps) and enquire how this is influenced by one or more enduring personal characteristics. At its simplest, this first question would be answered by a correlation coefficient, indicating the extent of association between the outcome variable and an enduring characteristic, for example, age, extraversion, intelligence, or previous affective well-being.

Such an approach parallels that taken in earlier chapters, where features of the environment rather than of the person were examined. As noted there, it is important to move beyond simple correlations between two variables, using also multivariate approaches in order to learn whether one characteristic continues to make an independent contribution to mental health after others have been statistically controlled. In the present setting, we need to examine simultaneously a range of personal attributes, to learn about the impact of each after controlling for the others.

In addition to possible direct effects of personal features, a second type of influence particularly requires examination. This concerns the extent to which personal factors modify the in-general impact of a situational feature. Given that the relationship between an environmental condition and an aspect of mental health is of a certain kind overall, does that relationship differ between individuals in any systematic way? In seeking such a differential pattern, one is inquiring about the presence of a statistical interaction between environmental and personal variables. Such an interaction is sometimes said to demonstrate a 'mediating' effect (in this case, personal variables may 'mediate' the impact of specific environmental conditions on mental health), but other descriptions are in terms of 'moderators', 'modifiers', or 'buffers'.

Statistical procedures

In investigating person–situation interactions of these kinds, one of three statistical procedures is usually adopted. First is sub-group analysis, where the correlation between level of an environmental feature and, say, affective well-being is calculated separately for the sub-groups under investigation. For example, one might ask whether ethnic groups A and B show a significant difference in the association between opportunity for control and job-related well-being. If so, and if level of control opportunity is the same for the two groups, this pattern is presumably due to differential processes of some kind, with opportunity for control having varying personal significance in the two sub-groups.

A second analysis of this possibility is through some form of multiple regression procedure. One might introduce ethnic group membership as a variable within an analysis of data obtained from all members of the study sample. In its simplest two-predictor form, this analysis would include as predictor variables one job characteristic and one personal factor, together with some form of interaction term reflecting the influence of these variables on each other. Most common in this field is a multiplicative interaction term, where values of an environmental variable and a personal variable are multiplied together for each member of the sample. The research question in this form of 'moderated regression' analysis asks whether the interaction term makes a significant independent contribution to the prediction of affective well-being over and above the statistical influence of each of the two separate factors.

A third approach is the use of analysis of variance with two dichotomized variables. This is in several ways formally equivalent to moderated regression, although some information is lost in cases where a range of scores (pertaining to a job characteristic, for example) is collapsed into a single classification. For example, one might divide members of the sample into four groups: first, in terms of high or low scores on the environmental condition (say, above and below the median value); and then, within each of those two groups, in terms of a personal factor, say ethnic group membership A or B. In studying job-related well-being one could in this way ask about the statistical significance of two main effects (associated with high or low levels of the job characteristic, and with ethnic group membership) and also about the interaction term (job characteristic by ethnic group membership). It is the latter which is important in learning about person–situation interactions.

However, these three procedures all set out to test direct effects and interaction terms within the assumption of linear relationships between variables. Central to the vitamin model examined in previous chapters was the belief that elements within the nine environmental categories were associated with mental health in a non-linear manner. A non-linear assumption also appears reasonable in respect of certain enduring characteristics of people. For example, high job demands may have a particularly negative impact for employees in the lowest range of baseline mental health, but a constant, less negative impact upon all other employees. As another illustration, middle-aged men may be more affected by unavailability of money during unemployment than those who are both younger and older; relationships with age would then vary in a curvilinear manner.

It is thus important to examine environmental conditions and personal attributes through finer discriminations than are permitted by dichotomization. At least three sub-groups in each case are necessary for tests of the vitamin model. This classification can be undertaken within analysis of variance designs, given adequately large sample sizes. Possible non-linear patterns may also be examined in regression analyses (for example through use of quadratic terms), but some form of sub-group presentation is also necessary in order to interpret those effects identified as statistically significant.

An overall framework

In practice, there has been relatively little empirical research into interactions between personal and environmental variables in the area of this book. Although the need to incorporate an individual-difference perspective into situation-centred models is widely recognized, few investigators have considered both types of variable within a single study. Those who have examined person–situation interactions have apparently without exception reported results from linear analyses, through standard regression procedures or analysis of variance with merely two sub-groups in respect of each factor. The review presented in the next chapter must therefore be restricted to evidence of that kind.

First, however, the preceding themes may be integrated and extended within Fig. 13.1. This builds upon the vitamin model of nine environmental categories and five aspects of mental health, to suggest how the four categories of enduring personal characteristics might have two kinds of influence.

The basic situation-centred model which has been examined in earlier chapters is here summarized in terms of the relationships between boxes 2 and 4 in the figure. The four types of enduring personal characteristics (baseline mental health, demographic features, values, and abilities) are shown to be potentially important at two locations. First, in the relationship between box 1 and box 2 it is suggested that these personal characteristics have an impact upon the environmental conditions to which an individual is exposed. In some cases this differential exposure is involuntary; in others it is more through choice, giving rise to 'self-selection' of persons into situations. For example, members of lower socio-economic status groups may experience reduced opportunity for control in comparison with those in higher groups; and female employees might be permitted only to enter jobs which in general have lower opportunity for skill use. Self-selection may occur through people moving into jobs which in general meet their interests and do not cause them unacceptable strain. These forms of personal influence upon environmental conditions are of considerable theoretical importance (e.g. Schneider 1983), but they have not been examined systematically within a broad-ranging model of the kind suggested by Fig. 13.1.

The second form of personal influence is located in the relationship between boxes 2, 3, and 4. This covers possible mediating effects of the kind illustrated above, where a particular environmental condition might have different associations with aspects of mental health depending on people's enduring characteristics. The arrows in the diagram may be taken to reflect postulated causal influence. The continuation, in dashed form, of the links between box 2 and box 4 as they pass through box 3 is intended to indicate that the contents of box 3 remain relatively unaltered as they interact with box 2: some limited change may occur, but the major importance of box 3 is in modifying the impact of box 2 on box 4. This contrasts with the arrows from box 1, which terminate at box 2, in order to represent the belief that environmental conditions are themselves likely to be affected by the impact of enduring personal characteristics.

Any acceptable model of processes through time requires the possibility of multiple feedback loops, as later events come to influence the state of variables located earlier in the presentation of a framework. For visual simplicity, only three of these are included in Fig. 13.1, indicated by 'recycle' arrows. Current mental health (box 4) is viewed as having a subsequent influence upon the nature of baseline mental health (box 1A); and in response to environmental conditions both values (3C) and abilities (3D) are thought

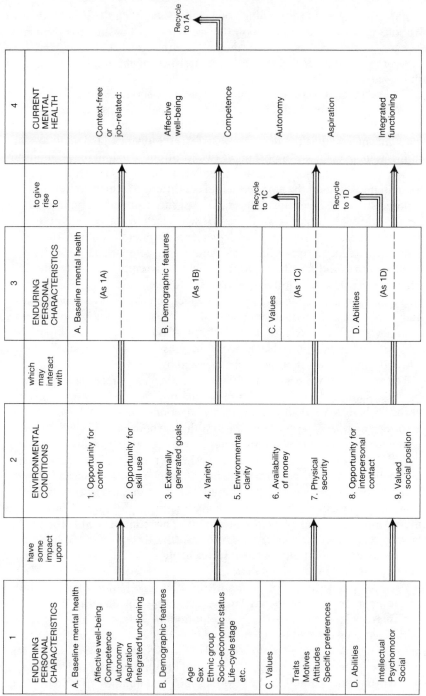

Fig. 13.1 Persons and situations within the vitamin model.

to be open to some change which may be relatively permanent through feedback into boxes 1C and 1D respectively.

One other aspect of Fig. 13.1 deserves comment. It is assumed that multiple influences operate *within* each of the principal groups of factors. This has already been argued for box 2, where the nine environmental features are known to be interdependent in many ways, and in box 4, where the components of mental health are conceptually and statistically interrelated. Similar interconnections are expected within box 1. For example, age and sex may both influence attitudes and other value orientations; and baseline affective well-being may differ as a function of socio-economic status. These interconnections again argue for research designs and adequately large samples which permit assessment of the independent contributions of several individual factors after controlling for the influence of other variables. This issue is taken up again in the next chapter.

Summary

This chapter has built upon the introduction provided in Chapter 1 to consider the importance to the vitamin model of enduring personal characteristics. Four groups of these have been identified, labelled as 'baseline mental health', 'demographic features', 'values', and 'abilities'. The first group is taken to include several features often considered as elements of personality, such as neuroticism, self-confidence, and hardiness. In each case the personal attributes within a category may be broad and abstract, or they may be specific and concrete.

Three principal approaches to the possible mediating impact of personal characteristics have been summarized. These are based upon sub-group analyses, multiple regressions, and analyses of variance. In each case, non-linear interactions have rarely been examined, and the need to do that in future has been emphasized here.

An overall account of possible interactions between people and situations has been set out in Fig. 13.1. This expands the situation-centred model of earlier chapters to illustrate how the four categories of personal variables may have their impact with respect to mental health. The framework identifies several forms of empirical enquiry, and serves as a perspective through which the research literature may be examined.

14

Personal characteristics and mental health in jobs and unemployment

This chapter describes and interprets some findings from research in the settings of both work and unemployment. Particular attention will be paid to investigations which seek to identify the modifying influence of personal factors on the relationship between environmental characteristics and current health. In the terms of Fig. 13.1 (page 246), these studies examine how relations between boxes 2 and 4 might be modified by the contents of box 3.

First, however, some simpler studies will be reviewed, those which examine the relationship between personal factors and mental health, irrespective of environmental characteristics. In terms of elements within Fig. 13.1, these consider possible associations between boxes 1 and 4, irrespective of box 2. The chapter will conclude by extending consideration to the modifying impact of personal characteristics during unemployment.

Individual differences and job-related mental health

Baseline mental health

Several investigators have examined bivariate relationships between enduring personal characteristics and aspects of current job-related well-being. For example, with respect to baseline mental health (box 1A of Fig. 13.1), Kahn et al. (1964) found that continuing levels of neuroticism were significantly predictive of job-related anxiety; however, the correlation with overall job satisfaction was not significant. Cherry (1984a) recorded a significant correlation of neuroticism scores with feelings of job strain measured as many as 16 years later. In a study of unskilled manual employees across 50 consecutive days, Hill (1975) observed that feelings of boredom were significantly more common among those with higher neuroticism scores.

Staw et al. (1986) examined baseline mental health of male employees in terms of what is here described as the first axis of context-free affective well-being. Raters analysed test results, case records and extensive interviews held at five different life periods, between the ages of 12 and 62. 'Affective disposition' was assessed in terms of characteristics such as warmth, hostility, irritability, cheerfulness, etc., and correlations were examined between this context-free assessment and several forms of job attitude, both at the same assessment period and at later times.

Concurrent associations for men in their 40s and late 50s were found to be substantial, and values dropped only a little when predictions were made from 'affective disposition' assessed in earlier years. For example, the synchronous correlation between rated affective disposition and overall job attitude for members of the sample in their 40s was 0.38; predicting this job attitude from context-free affect at age 16 yielded a correlation as high as 0.26. These significant associations were retained despite statistical controls for socio-economic status and job complexity.

With respect to the behavioural components of baseline mental health, subjective autonomy has often been found to be negatively associated with job-related strain. O'Brien (1984b) and Spector (1982) have summarized research using Rotter's locus of control scale (see page 51), in which employees with greater internal control beliefs were found to exhibit lower levels of job strain. This parallels the observation from clinical research that internal locus of control is significantly associated with low anxiety of a context-free kind (e.g. Archer 1979; Lefcourt 1982). Spector's (1982) review suggests that internal control scores are also associated with greater overall job satisfaction, although relationships with some specific satisfactions (in respect of colleagues and supervision) are reported to be non-significant.

One particular form of affective well-being which might sometimes be considered an aspect of baseline mental health is job satisfaction itself. Measures of overall satisfaction and of satisfaction with specific job features have been found to be relatively stable across time. For example, Cook *et al.* (1981) cite test–retest correlations for specific satisfactions across periods up to 16 months which range around a median of 0.62. Staw and Ross (1985) report that, for people remaining with the same employer across two or five years, test–retest correlations for overall job satisfaction were 0.47 and 0.37 respectively. For employees who changed both their occupation and their employer over those periods, correlations remained as high as 0.33 and 0.19 respectively. It seems likely that some people are more liable than others to express satisfaction with whatever job they hold.

Demographic features

In respect of box 1B of Fig. 13.1 (demographic features), several studies have examined current job satisfaction as a function of employee sex. Among a group of American clerical workers, Miller and Terborg (1979) observed that women exhibited significantly higher overall job satisfaction than men, as well as significantly higher satisfaction with the work itself, pay, and fringe benefits. However, it seems certain that research of this kind within specific locations will yield varying patterns of sex differences, depending upon the nature of the male and female jobs under investigation.

Large-sample studies are thus desirable. Analysing data from seven separate representative samples of the American working population, Weaver (1980) has shown that average overall job satisfaction scores are almost identical for men and women (see also Quinn and Staines 1979; Weaver 1978a). This was also found by D'Arcy *et al.* (1984) with Canadian respondents.

Examining more specific forms of well-being, a study with a nationally representative Finnish sample found that career dissatisfaction and job-related exhaustion were significantly greater among women than men; this pattern was retained in separate analyses for blue-collar and white-collar employees (Kauppinen-Toropainen *et al.* 1983). Such differences are likely to arise mainly from differences in job conditions, since women are in general segregated into jobs which are often less attractive in terms of the nine features examined in this book (e.g. Davidson 1987; Form and McMillen 1983; Nieva and Gutek 1981).

However, interpretation is made difficult by a consistently-observed sex difference irrespective of employment status. It is widely found that women report higher levels of distress, anxiety, and depression than men (e.g. Kessler and McRae 1981; Jick and Mitz 1985). That difference might arise from differential exposure to negative environments, differential responsiveness to those environments, or a differential readiness to report symptoms of low well-being. In practice, a combination of influences seems likely to be involved.

One particular form of strain arises from the need to cope with demands both from a job and from domestic or childcare responsibilities. As was described in Chapter 7, this form of low well-being is in general more likely to be experienced by women than by men (see also Zappert and Weinstein 1985).

Another group of studies has investigated the job-related correlates of age differences. A review of this field by Rhodes (1983) makes it clear that overall job satisfaction and satisfaction with the work itself are significantly positively associated with age, at least up to about 60 years. This association is retained, for men and for women, despite controls for income, occupational level, marital status, and other variables (Weaver 1978a). It is also present in multiple regression analyses which include a range of job characteristics and work values (Kalleberg and Loscocco 1983), suggesting that over and above the contribution of these other factors a developmental process of ageing is itself important. However, it appears that some specific forms of job satis-faction, such as satisfaction with colleagues, supervision, and opportunity for promotion, are not always correlated with employee age (Rhodes 1983), although significant associations have been observed within particular organizations (e.g. Lee and Wilbur 1985). Feelings of boredom in unskilled manual jobs have also been found to be more common among young employees (Hill 1975; Smith 1955), although the degree to which that difference is due to self-selection across time into jobs which are personally interesting has not been ascertained.

Other demographic features associated with overall job satisfaction include ethnic group membership. For example, in American surveys black employees consistently yield significantly lower scores than whites (Weaver 1978b, 1980). Whether this discrepancy derives from differences associated with ethnicity or from correlated differences in job content has not been determined. Socio-economic status (often assessed through occupational level) has also frequently been shown to be positively related to overall job satisfaction (e.g. Kalleberg and Loscocco 1983; Weaver, 1978a,b, 1980; and many studies cited in earlier chapters). In addition, job-related anxiety tends to be significantly greater among employees at higher organizational levels (e.g. Cherry 1984a; Jamal 1985; Warr and Payne 1983a); higher-level jobs tend to yield both greater satisfaction and greater anxiety.

Values

Within the third category of enduring personal characteristics, identified earlier as 'values' (box 1C in Fig. 13.1, page 246), we might expect investigators to have examined relationships between personality factors and job-related mental health. In practice, such studies are rare, perhaps because of uncertainty about the possible theoretical basis of any observed association. It is not clear how most aspects of personality, apart from those defined here as components of baseline mental health, would be expected to impinge upon job-related mental health in general terms, irrespective of specific job content. Thus it is not surprising that in the course of their wider investigation of American managers, Kahn *et al.* (1964) found neither extraversion nor general flexibility to be associated with job-related anxiety.

One specific value orientation which might give rise to increased job strain has been considered by Brewin (1980). He observed that managers who seek psychotherapeutic assistance with job-related difficulties are often very exacting in their personal work standards, failing to moderate these in the face of even extremely adverse conditions. This particular form of personal inflexibility contains its own rationale for a negative job-related impact: the behavioural style in question compounds the problems of very high workload.

A related motive system is reflected in the 'type A' behaviour pattern (e.g. Glass 1977; Matthews 1982). This was defined by Friedman and Rosenman (1974) as 'an action-emotion complex that can be observed in any person who is aggressively involved in a chronic, incessant struggle to achieve more and more in less and less time, and, if required to do so, against the opposing efforts of other things or other persons' (p. 67). Strictly speaking, the type A pattern is viewed not as a personality trait but as a set of behaviours elicited from susceptible individuals by a challenging environment. However, individuals show consistency across situations in their tendency to exhibit this type of behaviour, and stable differences between people are widely found. It is of interest here to ask about the association of this enduring characteristic with job-related mental health.

Howard *et al.* (1977) examined differences in overall job satisfaction scores, finding no correlation with Canadian managers' self-reported tendency to type A behaviour. A similar finding was obtained with a sample of British managers by Keenan and McBain (1979); and Howard *et al.* (1986) extended the negative result to separate indices of intrinsic and extrinsic satisfaction. On the other hand, scores on a broad-band index of context-free emotional distress (covering restlessness, agitation, fatigue, depression, and other symptoms) were observed to be significantly greater for managers identified as extreme in respect of type A behaviour (Howard *et al.* 1976).

Turning to the second axis of well-being, van Dijkhuizen (1981) found that Dutch managers with the highest type A behaviour scores were particularly likely to report job-related anxiety; and significant positive associations with job-related and context-free anxiety were reported among American women employees by Kelly and Houston (1985), before and after controlling for occupational level. In Burke and Weir's (1980) research with senior Canadian administrators, type A behaviour was unrelated to overall or facet-specific job satisfaction, but was significantly associated with independent physician ratings of anxiety and muscle tension. Kittel *et al.* (1983) studied a representative sample of Belgian men aged between 40 and 55. They found that type A scores were overall associated with increased feelings of job strain, and that these associations remained significant in multiple regression analyses controlling for employment grade, educational level, marital status, and several physiological indicators.

From the behavioural definition of the type A construct, this pattern of results seems likely to be replicated elsewhere. However, we should be cautious about interpreting raised anxiety levels as indicating low mental health in all situations. As was discussed in Chapter 2 (page 35), job-related or context-free anxiety might be considered appropriate in situations of high challenge and risk-taking, where (for example) individuals are exhibiting high competence, autonomy, and aspiration in the pursuit of difficult goals. Many type A managers could be viewed as high scorers on those behavioural components of mental health, although there are undoubtedly cases where exceptional levels of time-urgency and determined goal-seeking give rise to personal costs which observers may consider to be excessive.

Abilities

Finally in this section, what is known about the relationship between job-related mental health and employees' abilities (box 1D)? It appears that no research into that association has been reported, possibly for the lack of a conceptual rationale mentioned earlier. A context-free approach (looking in general at an ability and an aspect of mental health) seems to have limited value, if no attention is paid to the specific job conditions in which a person's abilities might be employed. It often seems preferable to enquire into the *interactions between* job features and personal characteristics, rather than looking at the latter in isolation. This approach will be adopted in the next section.

Personal modifiers of the impact of job conditions

Several investigators have examined enduring personal characteristics as possible moderators of the impact of the nine environmental features within the vitamin model. In the terms of Fig. 13.1 (page 246), their research looks for the presence of statistically significant interactions between elements in boxes 2 and 3 in relation to current mental health (in box 4). Research designs have been of the three kinds introduced in Chapter 13, although in practice sub-group analyses have been most common, examining environment-outcome correlations obtained from two sub-groups of people in order to ascertain if one correlation is significantly greater than the other.

Matching personal characteristics

Although the number of studies of this kind in employment settings is relatively small, the published evidence is somewhat confusing. In part that is because possible moderating variables appear sometimes to have been selected for study on an arbitrary basis. What is required is an overall framework from which to derive predictions about personal characteristics which may be important in respect of each of the nine environmental features.

Let us think in terms of the presence or absence of 'matching' personal characteristics, and suggest that, for each environmental category, individuals differ in the degree to which they possess a given matching characteristic. Attributes defined as 'matching' may be viewed primarily as constellations of motives and preferences, ranging from very broad systems which might be described in terms of personality dispositions to very localized preferences for particular environmental features. They are thus principally value orientations within boxes 1C and 3C of Fig. 13.1. Such orientations have been described in other settings as attitudes, needs, commitments, ego-involvements, and sensitivities. Persons with a particular value orientation are considered likely to seek out opportunities which match that orientation, to appreciate environmental features which reward it, and to feel badly when those features are not available to them. In addition, however, some characteristics may be deemed to 'match' an environmental feature because they embody particular types and levels of abilities (boxes 1D and 3D of Fig. 13.1); examples will be cited later.

Variations in an environmental feature are expected to have a greater impact on well-being for people who possess each matching characteristic than for those lacking the matching attribute. Consider, for example, persons who have a strong desire for money, perhaps to meet pressing family needs. These people are likely to be more affected by variations in wage level from moderate to low than are employees with limited financial concern. We may thus take this specific value orientation as a 'matching characteristic' in respect of that particular job feature.

The operation of matching characteristics is illustrated in respect of the 'constant effect' form of the vitamin model in Fig. 14.1(a). Within that schematic presentation, the lines for the two sub-groups may sometimes fall in slightly different locations from those shown; in all cases, however, a significant interaction would be evidenced by lines which depart substantially from being parallel in the left-hand part of the diagram.

However, most of the environmental features examined in this book are assumed to be of the vitamin AD type, with an additional decrement in mental health occurring at extremely high levels of the feature. The assumed operation of matching personal characteristics in these cases is shown in Fig. 14.1(b). This indicates that the matching characteristic is again thought to be particularly influential at low levels of an environmental feature of the AD type (as with the CE features). However, at very high levels of an AD job feature it is people *lacking* the matching characteristic who are specially influenced by environmental variation.

Consider the second job factor in the present framework, opportunity for skill use. One matching personal characteristic in that case might be the possession of relevant unused abilities. At low levels of opportunity for skill use, persons with that matching attribute will be more affected by variations in this job factor, as illustrated to the left of Fig. 14.1(b); for example, high-ability people will be particularly frustrated by very low opportunity to use their skill. However, at very high levels of opportunity for skill use, these people will experience a smaller decrement than those who lack the relevant skills, since they will be more able to cope with the pressures of the situation. This reversed expectation is shown to the right of the diagram.

Before moving on to consider which personal attributes might be defined as 'matching characteristics' for each of the nine environmental categories, it is necessary to examine a motivational characteristic which has been referred to as 'growth-need strength' or 'higher-order need strength' (see also page 53). This has served as a possible modifying characteristic in many studies

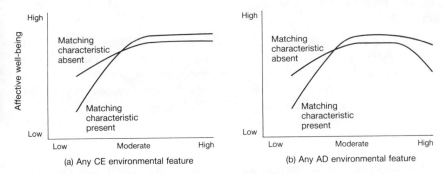

Fig. 14.1 Personal modifiers of environmental conditions: A schematic representation in terms of matching personal characteristics.

of job satisfaction. It was described by Hackman and Oldham (1975, pp. 162–3) as an 'individual difference characteristic' which reflects 'the strength of the respondent's desire to obtain 'growth' satisfaction from his or her work'. The latter is viewed in terms of satisfaction of needs for autonomy, independence, and achievement; and growth-need strength is typically measured through items which tap a person's liking for work which presents challenges and which permits independence, creativity, and personal development. In effect, this attribute is a set of preferences for certain sorts of intrinsic work characteristics. As such it might be viewed as a 'matching' personal characteristic in respect of those particular job features.

Research findings

Table 14.1 (on page 257) contains several groups of personal attributes, those thought to 'match' each environmental feature. As with other aspects of the present conceptual framework, the contents of this table have been drawn up partly on the basis of research evidence and partly as a result of extrapolation from that evidence in the light of issues raised throughout the book.

The list of matching personal characteristics could no doubt be expanded, but it already goes some way beyond published findings. Where empirical support appears to be available, a bracketed 'ES' follows an item. Those cases have all concerned job satisfaction as an outcome variable. They should in principle be differentiated according to the range of an environmental feature which has been examined. Confirmatory evidence could be within the range from low to moderate environmental values in Fig. 14.1, within the range from high to very high, or within both ranges. This differential information is rarely provided in research reports. However, it appears (for example, on the basis of the direction of cited correlations between a job feature and job satisfaction) that almost all those studies giving rise to an entry of 'ES' in Table 14.1 were concerned with low to moderate levels of a job attribute.

1. Opportunity for control   First, what is known about matching personal characteristics in respect of opportunity for control in a job? Wanous (1974) examined correlations between reported opportunity for control and overall job satisfaction among female American telephone operators, considering growth-need strength as a possible moderator. For high growth-need strength employees the correlation was 0.59, but for the low growth-need strength sub-group it was -0.09. Sims and Szilagyi (1976) reported similar findings in respect of satisfaction with the work itself.

Although there have been cases where no difference of this kind was found (e.g. Brief and Aldag 1975), two reviews of results from previous investigations conclude that overall there is clear evidence for a moderating influence of this personal characteristic. Loher *et al.* (1985) examined the data on relationship between opportunity for control in a job and overall job satisfaction, finding median correlations of 0.65 and 0.23 for high and low growth-need strength sub-groups. In terms of the left-hand side of Fig. 14.1(b), the lines for the presence and absence of this matching characteristic both rise from left to right but they depart substantially from being parallel. Spector (1985) investigated specific satisfactions with the work itself, co-workers, and supervision, reporting a significant modifying influence of growth-need strength in each case; however, no difference was present in respect of satisfaction with promotion opportunities.

Growth-need strength may be set within boxes 1C and 3C of Fig. 13.1 (page 246), as a relatively specific matching value orientation. In some circumstances, however, it may be preferable to treat it as a particular form of baseline job-related aspiration, viewed within the account of mental health presented in Chapters 2 and 3 (see page 53). In either case its moderating influence in relation to opportunity for control and job satisfaction is interpretable by noting its characteristic as a specific preference for environmental features which are congruent with that preference.

O'Brien and Dowling (1980) obtained measures of employees' desire for personal control, including this possible modifying characteristic within a multiple regression prediction of overall job satisfaction. They found that the linear interaction between desired control and perceived opportunity for control made no additional contribution to this form of well-being. Sims and Szilagyi (1976) used Rotter's (1966) measure of people's general sense of internal or external control. This might be viewed more as a measure of subjective autonomy within baseline mental health than as a motivational factor. In either case, Sims and Szilagyi found that its modifying impact on the relationship between opportunity for control and satisfaction with the work itself failed to reach statistical significance. In view of these negative findings, it cannot be claimed empirically that high desire for personal control mediates the impact of opportunity for control in a job, but this moderating

Table 14.1 Possible matching personal characteristics for each environmental category

Category	Possible matching characteristics
1. Opportunity for control (AD)	High growth-need strength (ES) High desire for personal control High need for independence (ES) Low authoritarianism (ES) Low neuroticism High relevant ability
2. Opportunity for skill use (AD)	High growth-need strength (ES?) High desire to use/extend skills (ES) Relevant skills which are unused Low neuroticism
3(a) Externally generated goals: Level of demands (AD)	High growth-need strength (ES) High desire for high workload (ES) Type B behaviour High need for achievement Low neuroticism High relevant ability (ES)
3(b) Externally generated goals: Task identity (AD)	High growth-need strength (ES) High desire for task identity
4. Variety (AD)	High growth-need strength (ES) High desire for variety (ES)
5(a) Environmental clarity: Feedback (AD)	High growth-need strength High desire for feedback
5(b) Environmental clarity: Role clarity (AD)	High need for clarity/intolerance of ambiguity (ES) External control beliefs (ES?) Low need for achievement (ES?)
6. Availability of money (CE)	High desire for money
7. Physical security (CE)	High desire for physical security
8. Opportunity for interpersonal contact (AD)	High sociability Lack of contact in other environments High desire for social support
9. Valued social position (CE)	High desire for social esteem

'ES' = empirical support is available for a significant person-situation interaction in respect of job satisfaction.

effect is proposed within Table 14.1 on *a priori* grounds.

Positive results were obtained in Vroom's (1959) investigation of two other personal characteristics. He observed that supervisors' job satisfaction was more closely dependent upon their opportunity to participate in decision-making (feature number 1 in the present framework) if they had personality attributes which matched that opportunity. Correlations were high for employees defined as having a strong need for independence or low authoritarian values (0.55 and 0.53 respectively), but significantly lower for their less independent or more authoritarian counterparts (0.13 and 0.03 respectively) The differences remained significant after controlling statistically for variations in age, education, and occupational level.

One study has suggested that being male rather than female might serve as a matching characteristic in respect of this feature. In multiple regression analyses, Mottaz (1986) examined the predictors of overall job satisfaction separately for men and for women. Holding constant other variables, such as age, education, marital status, income, job tenure, and other job features, he found that opportunity for control made a significantly greater contribution to job satisfaction for men than for women. Additional data suggested that men might have a stronger preference for this job factor, so that desire for control might in fact be the causally important variable in this comparison. Further studies of sex differences relative to specific job attributes and mental health would be useful.

Table 14.1 suggests that low neuroticism and high relevant ability might also serve as matching characteristics in respect of opportunity for control. Their mediating impact may be thought to be especially likely at very high levels of this job feature. The additional decrement is predicted in Fig. 14.1(b) to be greater for people *lacking* matching characteristics, in this case individuals who are *more* neurotic and of *low* relevant ability; such people are less likely to be able to cope with the control requirements which occur in the unusual conditions of this extremely high level. These possibilities appear not to have been examined in empirical research.

2.   Opportunity for skill use   Evidence of person–situation interactions in respect of the second job feature is rather limited. Wanous (1974) included within the study introduced above separate assessments of satisfaction with particular job features. He found that correlations between the amount of opportunity for skill use and satisfaction with that opportunity differed according to employees' growth-need strength (0.68 and 0.32 for high and low scorers respectively), but this difference was significant only by a one-tailed test.

O'Brien and Dowling (1980) obtained clearer results with a specific measure of desired skill utilization. Employees in their sample typically desired more opportunity for skill use than they reported themselves to possess, and the multiplicative interaction of desired and reported skill use was found to make a significant independent contribution to the prediction of overall job satisfaction.

It is important to note that many measures of this second job feature have in practice included personal standards and preferences within what purports to be an assessment of the environment. Opportunity for skill use is widely measured in terms of, for example, the 'chance to use your abilities' (Kornhauser 1965) or the 'chance to do the things you do best' (Caplan *et al.* 1975), with a clear implication that absence of these chances is undesirable. Recorded low opportunities are thus often indications that a person is unable to use his or her skills as much as is desired. The measure has thus in practice itself become one of congruence between the environment and the person, rather than being an index of an environmental feature alone.

Measures of opportunity for skill use are therefore likely to overlap with indicators of what appears as a matching personal characteristic in Table 14.1: possession of relevant skills which are unused. It is desirable in future research to seek to separate these two factors, identifying and separating the characteristics of an environment and a person.

This approach has been taken by Quinn and Mandilovitch (1980) in respect of the education level required by a job and the education level attained by job-holders. Required educational level was measured in several ways (through estimates by employees and through job dictionary assessments, for instance), and overall job satisfaction was consistently found to be associated with the match between required level and attained level. Particularly low job satisfaction was observed among workers who had been educated substantially beyond the level required for their job (see also Mottaz 1984).

3. *Externally generated goals* The third environmental feature has been separated in Table 14.1 into two elements as described in Chapter 7: level of demands, and task identity.

In respect of low to moderate levels of the first subcategory, Wanous (1974) found that the moderating impact of growth-need strength upon satisfaction with that specific feature was again statistically significant. A specific preference for reduced job demands was examined by O'Brien and Dowling (1980). They found that the degree to which employees desired a reduced workload significantly modified the negative correlation between reported high demands and overall job satisfaction.

Caplan and Jones (1975) studied a change from very high workload to moderately high load, and observed that corresponding changes in anxiety were greater for people defined as type A than for those identified as type B. This may be interpreted within the definition of this characteristic given earlier (page 251), when it was pointed out that type A people are viewed as particularly responsive to environmental challenges. In the terms of Fig. 14.1(b) (page 255), the effect described by Caplan and Jones occurred in the right-hand sector of the environmental feature. At these high levels, a stronger association is said to be expected when a matching personal characteristic is absent rather than present. Type A persons are usually the focus of investigation in this environmental range, and for these people it is *type B* behaviour which is *absent*. Table 14.1 therefore identifies type B behaviour (rather than type A) as a possible matching characteristic for level of work demands.

A general conclusion about the interaction of demands and type A or type B behaviour is however made difficult by negative findings in the cross-sectional study by Keenan and McBain (1979). They analysed separately data about job overload and about role conflict (another form of high job demands examined in Chapter 7). In neither case was a significant interaction observed with type A behaviour in respect of overall job satisfaction or job-related anxiety. Chesney and Rosenman (1980) have argued that differences between type A and type B persons are likely to be observed only in settings of high workload, so that a mediating effect should be predicted only at high levels of demands (the right-hand sector of the present Fig. 1.1 and Fig. 14.1). They briefly describe some findings which appear to support that suggestion. However, the difficulties of research into this interaction, and the limited evidence for it, have been emphasized by Ivancevich and Matteson (1984).

Section 3(a) in Table 14.1 (page 257) also suggests that neuroticism may modify the impact of very high job demands. The expectation is that high scorers on measures of neuroticism will be affected negatively to a greater degree than low scorers by job demands which reach very high levels. However, when Kahn *et al.* (1964) examined this possibility in respect of role conflict and context-free tension, no evidence of an interaction was found: high scorers on their measure of neuroticism exhibited constantly greater tension irrespective of the level of this job characteristic.

We should also consider ability level as a possible moderator of the impact of varying job demands. At low demand levels, employees of higher relevant ability might be expected to experience more adverse consequences than those of lower ability; the former group would tend to feel frustrated by the non-use of their potential. As represented to the left of Fig. 14.1(b), high (rather than low) ability would thus be defined as a matching personal characteristic.

However, at very high levels of job demand (in situations of considerable role conflict, for example), it is people of lower ability who would be particularly negatively affected, since they would be less able to cope with the high demands. Abdel-Halim (1981) examined this possibility through an index of self-reported ability in relation to one's job. This variable was found to have a significant moderating impact upon the relationship between role conflict and intrinsic job satisfaction, of the kind illustrated to the right of Fig. 14.1(b). (Recall that *high* relevant ability is here defined as the matching characteristic; low ability is thus represented in the figure by absence of the characteristic.) Task identity (3b in Table 14.1) was introduced in Chapter 7 as the degree to which a job contains 'whole' elements and gives rise to clearly identifiable results. The possible modifying effect of high growth-need strength on the association between job satisfaction and low to moderate levels of this feature has been studied by several researchers. Results from individual studies typically fail to yield significant person-job interactions (e.g. Brief and Aldag 1975; Sims and Szilagyi 1976; Wanous 1974), but reviews by Loher *et al.* (1985) and Spector (1985) indicate that the general pattern is one of stronger associations for employees with higher growth-need strength. Loher and colleagues recorded median correlations with overall job satisfaction of 0.44 and 0.25 for high and low scorers respectively; and a significant difference between average correlations was cited by Spector in respect of overall and co-worker satisfaction, but not in relation to intrinsic satisfaction or satisfaction with pay or promotion opportunities.

4. Variety Growth-need strength has also been found to interact with the fourth job feature under investigation here. Stronger correlations between level of variety and job satisfaction are usually found for employees with higher growth-need strength (e.g. Sims and Szilagyi 1976; Wanous 1974). As was pointed out in Chapter 5, studies using the Job Diagnostic Survey's scale of 'skill variety' are best discounted, since that measure taps level of skill as well as job variety.

A specific measure of preference for variety within one's job was observed to be a significant moderator by O'Brien and Dowling (1980). In a multiple regression analysis they found that preferred-times-reported variety contributed independently to the prediction of overall job satisfaction.

5. Environmental clarity Less consistent findings are observed for feedback, an aspect of environmental clarity (5a in Table 14.1, page 255). Brief and Aldag (1975), Sims and Szilagyi (1976) and others report no evidence of person–situation interaction, but the review by Loher *et al.* (1985) includes a median correlation between feedback and overall job satisfaction of 0.64 for employees high on growth-need strength and one of 0.34 for their low-scoring counterparts. However, Spector's (1985) meta-analysis revealed a significant interaction effect only in respect of satisfaction with supervision and promotion opportunities; growth-need strength was not found to moderate the association with overall satisfaction and other specific satisfactions.

The second aspect of environmental clarity shown in Table 14.1 is clarity in respect of role demands (5b in the table). This is usually measured negatively in terms of degree of ambiguity, with 'high' ambiguity corresponding to 'low' clarity. Significant interactions have been reported in respect of one specific matching personal characteristic, need for certainty or inability to tolerate ambiguity. For example, Kahn *et al.* (1964) found that this characteristic mediated the relationship between role ambiguity and context-free tension: the correlation was greater for managers who had a stronger need for clarity. In a study of American nurses, Lyons (1971) obtained a similar finding in respect of overall job satisfaction, with significantly different correlations between clarity and satisfaction for high scorers and low scorers on the measure of need (0.54 and 0.20 respectively); however, the difference between sub-group correlations for job-related tension (-0.69 and -0.40 respectively) was not significant. The same pattern was found (with different measures) in Keenan and McBain's (1979) study of British managers.

Morse (1975) adopted a somewhat different approach to the interaction between environmental clarity and need for certainty. Employees at clerical and similar levels of two American organizations were placed into jobs rated as relatively 'certain' or relatively 'uncertain', within a design where jobs matched personal need for certainty in some cases but were incongruent with that need in others. Staff in a comparison group were placed into jobs without regard to the degree of match between this aspect of their personality and their job.

A measure of subjective job-related competence was derived from a projective test at the time of placement into these jobs and also eight months later. The study's hypothesis was that employees in matched jobs (high personal need with high job certainty, or low need with low job certainty) would exhibit a greater increase in subjective competence between the two measurement occasions than would employees assigned to jobs without consideration of their need for certainty. The two groups were found to be very similar in levels of subjective competence at the initial point of measurement, and the predicted pattern of change was observed: significantly greater increases occurred in the matched group, and a resultant significant cross-sectional difference was present at follow-up. This personal characteristic appears to be an important mediator of the impact of low to moderate levels of job clarity.

Keenan and McBain (1979) found that managers with relatively external locus of control scores showed a stronger positive correlation between role clarity and low job-related tension than those whose scores were more internal; however, no difference was found in respect of overall job satisfaction. Contrary to the latter result, external scorers in Abdel-Halim's (1980) study of American managers exhibited a significantly larger positive correlation between role clarity and intrinsic job satisfaction than did more internal scorers. Abdel-Halim also observed a significant moderating effect of need for achievement, with a stronger positive correlation between clarity and intrinsic satisfaction for low rather than high scorers; low need for achievement yielded a steeper curve of the kind illustrated in the left-hand section of Fig. 14.1(b) (page 255) than did high need for achievement.

6 to 9. Other job features The remaining four environmental features can be reviewed more briefly, since very few studies of their modification by personal characteristics have been reported. No information appears to be available for features 6 and 7, availability of money and physical security, although specific motives in each area seem likely to mediate their impact.

These postulated matching characteristics are indicated in Table 14.1 as 'high desire for' money and physical security respectively. Feature number 9 is similarly indicated to be liable to the mediating impact of high desire for social esteem.

The impact of low to moderate opportunity for interpersonal contact (feature number 8) is likely to be modified by level of employee's sociability. A lack of social contact in non-job environments (experienced, for instance, by a single person living alone at home) might also yield a greater impact of this job feature. However, no evidence about those possibilities has been located.

One study has enquired into the moderating role of growth-need strength, finding this important in respect of low to moderate friendship opportunities at work and the degree to which an employee is required to deal with other people. In both cases correlations with satisfaction with work content were significantly stronger for employees exhibiting higher growth-need strength (Sims and Szilagyi 1976). However, locus of control score did not moderate those associations.

Mottaz's (1986) examination of the correlates of overall job satisfaction suggested that support from supervisor is more important for women than for men. Holding constant other variables (see the description in respect of opportunity for control), supervisor support made a significantly greater independent contribution for female employees; however, there were no differences in respect of co-worker support. Consistent with an interpretation in terms of value differences, women were found to rate supervisor support as significantly more important than did men, but no difference was present in the value attached to co-worker support.

As described in Chapter 10, one approach to valued social position (feature number 9) has been through the 'task significance' sub-scale of the Job Diagnostic Survey. Scores on this measure are found to be significantly associated with high overall job satisfaction. Reviewing the moderating impact of growth-need strength on this relationship, Loher *et al.* (1985) found that correlations were typically higher (a median of 0.53) for employees with high growth-need strength than for those with lower scores (a median of 0.29).

It is not entirely clear why growth-need strength should be expected to modify the impact of this job feature. Indeed, researchers' frequent use of that measure of need raises an important methodological difficulty. The studies reviewed above have all treated job features singly, in isolation from others. Yet we know that several of the features tend to covary within jobs (see, for example, page 101). It thus remains possible that particular patterns in relation to one job feature are, at least in part, reflections of a process arising from another, correlated, feature. Although employee growth-need strength appears to modify the impact of, say, task significance, in reality its importance may be in respect of other correlated job features. This general problem has been discussed at several points throughout the book, emphasizing in each case that multivariate analyses are required in order better to learn about the independent contributions of specific environmental features.

Within research into possible modifying effects of enduring personal characteristics, the same problem arises in respect of measures of personal factors. Where one personal value orientation emerges as a moderator, this will almost always be correlated with other individual characteristics. The latter may in practice be causally more important. A more systematic formulation of extended sets of matching attributes for each of the nine job features would now be very helpful, in order better to understand and predict multivariate patterns of modifying effects.

Overall job complexity   As was pointed out in Chapter 6, the 'complexity' of a job has often been assessed in terms of the 'motivating potential score' of the Job Diagnostic Survey. This combines several intrinsic job features, and is strongly predictive of employees' job satisfaction. In view of the interest shown by researchers in growth-need strength, it is not surprising that this personal characteristic has been examined as a possible moderator of the impact of 'motivating potential'. Despite some negative findings (e.g. Brief and Aldag 1975; Oldham *et al.* 1976), the general pattern is of a significant modifying effect. For example, Loher *et al.* (1985) concluded from their meta-analysis that the average correlation (after correction for measurement unreliability) with overall job satisfaction was 0.68 for high growth-need strength employees and 0.38 for those obtaining lower scores. A similar conclusion was reached by Spector (1985), who also reported significantly larger correlations for high (versus low) scorers in respect of satisfaction with work content, co-workers, pay, and opportunities for personal growth and for promotion.

Jackson *et al.* (1981) expressed concern that research in this field has typically involved simultaneous measurement of all variables—predictors, outcomes, and potential moderators. In order to rule out the operation of response consistency bias, they included in their analyses growth-need strength scores obtained several months previously. Despite that control a significant moderator effect was found, with correlations between job complexity (an aggregate of intrinsic characteristic values) and overall job satisfaction of 0.68 and 0.35 for high and low scorers respectively.

Cherrington and England (1980) based their study on the fact that possible moderator variables can differ in their degree of specificity. For example, broad value orientations about the importance of certain types of work may be contrasted with very specific preferences for a certain kind of job feature. They argued that more focused personal values are likely to yield a stronger modifying contribution than those which are general in scope. This was illustrated by including a direct measure of desire for increased job discretion among broader indices of work values. This specific preference emerged as the only significant moderator of the relationship between job complexity (the presence of intrinsic characteristics) and overall job satisfaction; correlations were 0.41 and 0.21 for high and low scorers respectively.

The importance of specific preferences as instances of matching personal characteristics appears to have been conclusively demonstrated in the studies summarized here. However, the research tradition giving rise to these findings is unsatisfactory from the standpoint of this book. The emphasis on measures of job-related well-being, especially in terms of job satisfaction, is too narrow. Research of the kind described above needs to be extended into other aspects of mental health, particularly components which are context-free. This is important both in its own right, and also to examine the possibility that different personal characteristics act as mediators in respect of different components of mental health.

One final complication should be considered. The model of person–situation interactions summarized in Fig. 14.1 and Table 14.1 has assumed that matching personal attributes may be influential (in opposite directions) at both extremes of the range of an environmental characteristic of the vitamin AD kind. For example, high desire for high workload has been suggested to be particularly associated with job satisfaction from low to moderate levels of job demands. Conversely, low desire for a high workload ('absence of a matching characteristic' in the terms of Fig. 14.1(b)) has been indicated to accompany a stronger correlation between demands and satisfaction at very high levels of demand.

However, it may be the case that some personal characteristics moderate the impact of an environmental characteristic at only one pole of the horizontal axis in Fig. 14.1(b). For example, level of neuroticism seems likely to be particularly important at extremely high levels of environmental demand, but its significance in conditions of low demand is less clear. Brewin's (1980) study of managers with very exacting personal work standards was described earlier in the chapter; obsessive concern for excellence may also be a mediating personal characteristic only at high, but not at low, levels of externally generated goals.

Preference models of person–environment fit

The general theme, supported above, that employees' preferences are important in influencing responses to job content, has been explored through a second research tradition. In the terms of Chapter 1, this tends to be 'person-centred' rather than 'situation-centred', and starts with a focus upon employees' needs, interests or values. The approach sets out to identify principal forms of preference (creating a 'categorical' model of people; see page 1), and to examine the degree to which each preference is met in specific jobs or groups of jobs. By describing people and environments in parallel terms, it becomes possible to investigate how congruence between a person and an environment may be predictive of responses to that environment. Congruence is usually measured in terms of needs or preferences, by subtracting a person's need score from the degree to which an environment is considered to meet that need.

This approach may be illustrated through three sets of investigations. These cover the related areas of vocational interests, need and 'press', and 'work adjustment'. Thereafter, a more microscopic approach to 'person–environment fit' will be introduced.

Vocational interests are usually defined in terms of a consistent preference for certain types of job. For example, Holland (1976) has drawn attention to six categories of vocational preference, labelled as Realistic, Investigative, Social, Conventional, Enterprising, and Artistic. It is assumed, and widely observed, that having a job which is broadly congruent with one's interests is associated with higher job satisfaction and context-free well-being (e.g. Furnham and Schaeffer 1984; Wiggins *et al.* 1983). This general finding presumably arises from the fact that an 'interest' falls within the same family of constructs as 'satisfaction' and other forms of well-being; interests that are fulfilled are by definition reflected in satisfaction.

A related perspective has been taken by Stern (1970), who built upon Murray's theory of personality. From the latter Stern created measures to assess 30 different personal needs, such as those for achievement, affiliation, deference, and order. Environments were construed in the same terms, through 30 different types of 'press'. This was described as the 'external situational counterpart to the internalized personality needs' (Stern 1970, p. 7), and the pattern of presses within an organization was taken to constitute its climate or atmosphere. (Stern's research mainly concerned teaching institutions.)

Following Murray (1938), press was viewed both in objective terms ('alpha press') and through a person's self-reports ('beta press'); and an index of needs (in the individual) and of press (in the environment) was developed, using the same 30 dimensions of each. Factor analysis was used to reduce the number of variables to five second-order factors (in terms of expressive, intellectual, protective, vocational, and collegiate needs), and comparisons were made between the needs of different groups of individuals and between patterns of press in different institutions. The possibility of developing subtractive measures of congruence between person and environment was raised (e.g. Stern 1970; p. 201), but this theme was not developed in a manner which connects usefully with the present framework.

Dawis and Lofquist's (e.g. 1984) theory of 'work adjustment' comes closer to the present account, and serves as the third example of a person-centred preference model. The authors describe individual differences in 'work personality' in terms of six basic values, derived through factor analysis from 20 'work-related needs'. These values concern achievement, comfort, status, altruism, safety, and autonomy. Job environments are construed in parallel terms, yielding profiles of 'occupational reinforcers' in different job settings. The degree to which environmental features meet employees' needs is assumed to determine the level of their job satisfaction, and a significant association between overall congruence and satisfaction is demonstrated empirically.

The theory developed by Dawis and Loftquist has many other elements, concerning employee ability and job tenure, for example. These do not bear directly upon the present discussion, and will not be described further. Of importance here is the fact that their preference model, and the two others mentioned above, view person-job congruence across a broad range of characteristics; jobs and people are described in parallel terms, and differences are summarized *across all the variables*. This global form of congruence is typically found to be correlated (through a total score, or by multiple or canonical correlation) with job satisfaction, but the analysis is at too high a level of generality to contribute further to the vitamin model, which is built around nine specific characteristics of the environment.

A much more microscopic approach to job characteristics and individual preferences has been taken by certain other forms of 'person–environment fit' models. These, like the present account, have examined particular environmental features, but they differ in their suggestion that information about each job attribute should be complemented by reports from an employee about what level of that attribute he or she would prefer. When the preferred level and the actual level (or, more usually, the level as subjectively rated) coincide, 'perfect fit' is said to be present in respect of that feature, and job-related affective well-being is expected to be at its highest level. Deviations from perfect fit can take two forms: an employee may wish to have more of a feature than is present (reporting a deficiency, relative to what is desired), or he or she may prefer less than is present (reporting an excess of a job feature).

Caplan *et al.* (1975) and French *et al.* (1982) describe procedures whereby data about both the person and the environment are recorded on identical scales in respect of every job feature considered to be of interest. They advocate that the degree of 'person–environment fit' (or 'P–E fit') should be measured for each separate feature through the subtraction of the level preferred by the person (P) from the level reported as present in the environment (E). As indicated above, this calculation may yield evidence of a deficiency (E-minus-P takes on a negative value) or an excess (E-minus-P is positive). In a third calculation, ignoring the sign of E-minus-P yields an index of absolute discrepancy, referred to as 'poor fit' (in either direction).

French *et al.* (1982) have examined how far these three subtractive indices of specific preferences improve the prediction of job-related well-being over and above the contribution of a job feature or employees' preference alone.

It is clear that in some cases prediction is significantly improved, but results are generally inconsistent.

Consider their findings in respect of overall job complexity. Reported environmental level (E) was found to correlate -0.31 with job dissatisfaction. However, the absolute value of E-minus-P ('poor fit') yielded a larger correlation, 0.47, with that outcome measure. Corresponding pairs of correlation values for job-related anxiety, depression and somatic symptoms were 0.00 and 0.21, -0.09 and 0.22, and -0.11 and 0.16. Analyses of their data in respect of two other job features considered in this book, workload demands and role ambiguity, suggested that information about the degree of 'poor fit' increased the predictability of job dissatisfaction, but that job-related anxiety, depression, and somatic symptoms were in general at least as well predicted by the environmental values on their own. In other cases, scores of either excess fit or deficiency fit were sometimes found to increase predictability of job-related well-being, but no overarching principles were identified which could account for the varying pattern of relative importance of the two types of score.

In research with a different sample, French *et al.* (1983) also found evidence that subtractive measures of specific P–E fit could sometimes increase predictability, but the particular kind of fit which was important again varied in an apparently unsystematic manner between the variables. O'Brien and Dowling (1980) examined only the index of 'poor fit' (the absolute discrepancy between reported and preferred values), finding that this added significantly to the prediction of job satisfaction (beyond the reported environmental levels alone) in the case of only three out of five job attributes. They concluded that the subtractive preference measure accounted overall for less than 3 per cent of the variance in job satisfaction, compared to up to 38 per cent in the case of job attributes themselves.

A rather similar figure (a median of 3.1 per cent) is quoted by French *et al.* (1982, p. 52) for additional variance accounted for by subtractive information about fit. However, that figure appears to derive only from the cases where the contribution of fit is itself significant; if all other cases were included, the median contribution would presumably be reduced. This point applies also to the similar conclusion reached by French *et al.* (1983, p. 93).

As French and colleagues point out in both publications, there are methodological problems attached to their approach. For example, strong intercorrelations are sometimes present between values of E, P and E-minus-P, suggesting that multicollinearity can distort the pattern of multiple regression weights. The use of difference scores has itself been criticized, for example because of a consequential increase in unreliability of data (Cronbach and Furby 1970; Johns 1981; Wall and Payne 1973). Furthermore, if the variance in E scores differs considerably from that in P scores, P-E fit values will be determined substantially by the set with the larger variance. In addition, it is not clear whether one should calculate difference scores for individual items within a scale (for example, of job variety) or merely in respect of scale totals. Another difficulty arises from the central importance of the distribution of observed scores around the level of 'perfect fit'. A small change in that distribution can markedly affect the importance which will be afforded to excess, deficiency, or good fit interpretations.

This last point draws attention to the fact that different results are often to be expected from different samples of employees. The data of French *et al.* (1982) were those previously gathered by Caplan *et al.* (1975), which covered a wide range of occupations and revealed widespread differences between occupational levels. For example, unskilled blue-collar employees in the sample had very low opportunity for skill use, but professional employees had high levels of this job feature; the opposite pattern was present for workload demands. It seems clear that measures of P–E fit in respect of those job features would yield different associations with job-related well-being for the two employee groups. Parallel differences are to be expected across other samples and research settings.

Despite such difficulties, this particular approach to people's specific preferences will no doubt continue to find a place within the research area of this book. How might it be linked with the vitamin model under consideration here? In distinguishing between deficiency fit and excess fit, the P–E fit approach has some similarity with the non-linear assumptions built into the vitamin AD model. However, the present model's plateau of constant moderate impact suggests that subtractive P–E misfit values may be of unequal importance according to the current value of E. This may be illustrated in the manner suggested in Fig. 14.2

Environmental levels have there been divided into three segments, as was done in relation to the transition from unemployment to paid work described in Chapter 12. In segment A, where the six AD features take on low values, people are likely to report a deficiency: P values (preferences) are likely to be generally above E (environmental) values. Because any difference within this range of E values is viewed as having a strong impact on mental health (represented by the steepness of the curve), these subtractive deficiency scores are expected to be strongly associated with mental health. The same point applies, but in reverse, within segment C, where people are expected generally to report an excess of each feature. However, misfits within segment B are assumed to have little effect upon mental health, since environmental variations merely involve shifts within the plateau of constantly beneficial impact. A P–E discrepancy of a given size within this segment is thus predicted to have a smaller impact on mental health than a discrepancy of the same size within either segment A or segment B.

That pattern of differential importance is the one expected on conceptual grounds. However, in statistical terms the contribution of misfit scores may in practice be rather small even within the two outer segments. This is because the P values are likely to be consistently above the E values in segment

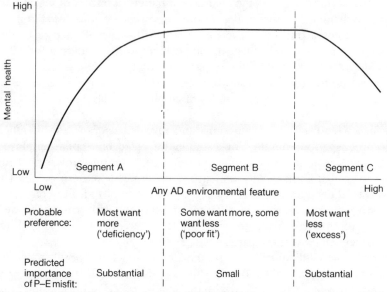

Fig. 14.2   Schematic representation of the likely importance of P-E misfit within three ranges of environmental values.

A, and consistently below them in segment C. Within the limitations of measurement these differences will tend to emerge as constant effects, changing E by a standard amount, so that the correlates of E-minus-P will be very similar to the correlates of E alone.

The more that research data extend across the three segments of an environmental feature, the more we might expect 'poor fit' scores in relation to a specific feature to make an additional contribution beyond E values on their own. In general, however, it seems unlikely from the data and reasoning of this section that this type of analysis will account for substantial proportions of variance in well-being.

Overview

The account provided here of 'matching' personal characteristics has provided a framework within which to interpret empirical research into the personal modifiers of job conditions. There is substantial evidence that specific values or preferences in relation to a job feature are important mediators of the impact of that feature. However, it is necessary to go beyond merely the identification of preferences (a relevant 'high desire', in the terms of Table 14.1) to consider other personal attributes.

The presentation above has introduced as possible matching characteristics neuroticism, authoritarianism, type B behaviour, and ability in specific cases. Further analysis of these possibilities is now required, coupled with research attention to a wider range of mental health measures; the recent emphasis upon job satisfaction is too restrictive. Furthermore, progress towards more extensive evidence for personal modifiers requires the development and testing of model-based predictions within different ranges of each environmental feature.

Among those investigations which have included personal characteristics, significant mediating effects are observed relatively infrequently. As was argued in Chapter 13, this may be partly explained by processes of self-selection or self-exclusion over time. Although there are undoubtedly cases where an individual's values and abilities are extremely incongruent with the characteristics of his or her job, levels of incongruence are likely to be limited by the tendency for people to move, or to be moved, out of jobs which are sharply inconsistent with their own attributes.

Evidence for person–situation interactions in respect of a specific job characteristic appears to require a wide range of scores on the personal variable in question. The fact that this is often absent, coupled with a substantial direct effect of the job feature selected for study, seems likely to reduce the probability of finding that this direct effect is substantially modified by the personal attribute. Nevertheless, it seems certain that more person–situation interactions in job settings will be observed, beyond those which have been demonstrated so far.

Individual differences and unemployment

Towards the book's objective of embracing both jobs and unemployment within the same nine-category account, it would now be desirable to examine personal modifiers of the impact of each of those features during unemployment. Unfortunately, there has been no research of that detailed kind, so that empirical data about personal moderators of each feature cannot be reviewed.

However, a few studies have looked at individual differences in the impact of unemployment itself, without differentiation into specific components of the unemployed person's environment. Such research may be viewed within the terms of Fig. 13.1 (page 246) as considering the direct effects of enduring personal characteristics (box 1) upon current mental health (box 4). It does not address person–situation interactions of the kind reviewed in the previous sections, since no variations in environmental conditions (box 2) are measured within the research design.

Let us consider in turn the four categories of enduring personal characteristics identified in Fig. 13.1: baseline mental health, demographic features, values, and abilities.

The first of these is likely to be reflected in current mental health during unemployment for the two reasons cited in the previous chapter. Some people start from a position of better mental health than others, so that (for example) a constant negative effect of aversive conditions would result in their remaining healthier than their counterparts who started from a lower baseline.

Furthermore, the transactional nature of mental health ensures that those who are initially higher on competence, autonomy, and aspiration are likely to deal more effectively than others with the problems of unemployment. They are thus expected to show a smaller decrement than people initially less healthy in those respects.

To examine the influence of baseline mental health on the impact of un-employment, we need to take measures of health prior to loss of a job. In line with the general lack of longitudinal research in this area, studies of that kind have not been reported. However, Liker and Elder's (1983) longitudinal study of income loss during the 1930s is relevant. This extended beyond merely unemployment (with some people remaining in jobs but at lower rates of pay), but findings in respect of emotional instability are of interest in this section. Interviewer ratings of instability and tenseness were made in 1930 and also between 1933 and 1935. It was found that men initially defined as relatively unstable became even less stable as a result of economic stress, whereas no significant change occurred among the more stable members of the sample.

Some findings described by White (1985) touch upon this issue. In a longitudinal study of continuously unemployed British men and women, information was gathered about the occurrence of 'new or worse health problems'. It was found that these were more common among people who had experienced ill-health in the three years before becoming unemployed. Warr and Jackson (1985) obtained a similar finding in a multiple regression analysis of factors predicting deterioration during continuous unem-ployment. The reported presence of a chronic health impairment at initial interview was associated with greater subsequent decrement in general health, after controlling for other possibly relevant variables. These results concern primarily physical health, but the notion that prior vulnerability gives rise to greater subsequent decrement might be extrapolated to changes in mental health after loss of a job.

Aggregate time-series investigations into community unemployment level and mental hospital admission rate may also be considered. Findings were interpreted in Chapter 11 in terms of raised unemployment either 'provoking' new cases of mental illness or 'uncovering' previously established illness among people who have not sought medical help (see page 200). However, the 'uncovering' explanation may itself be interpreted in terms of differential vulnerability: people with poor baseline mental health, who have for some time been on the borderline of obtaining medical treatment, may find that this is more needed in difficult economic times.

Differential vulnerability may also give rise to a process of 'reprovocation'. Increased demand on medical facilities during periods of high unemployment may arise primarily from those people who previously but not currently have been defined as ill. Difficult economic conditions may be more likely to 'reprovoke' illness in these people than to bring about illness for the first time in people always previously below the threshold of medical caseness. Evidence about this possibility has yet to be gathered.

Turning to box 1B in Fig. 13.1 (page 246), the impact of certain demographic factors during unemployment has already been examined in Chapter 12. At that point, age and sex differences were considered, and the importance of an unemployed women's marital and parental status was reviewed. Ethnic group differences might also be expected to be important, but little evidence is available from studies which control for other factors such as age or occupational level (cf. Warr *et al.* 1985).

Also included within box 1B is socio-economic status, and predictions about the differential impact of unemployment on middle-class and working-class people have frequently been offered. These sometimes suggest that middle-class people will suffer more, because of the greater social stigma attached to their unemployment (feature number 9 in the present model). Alternatively, middle-class people might be thought to suffer less, since they have greater access to money (feature number 6). It is difficult to test these predictions in the absence of prior information about mental health during employment, and without controls for age, duration of unemployment, and so on. The limited evidence available suggests that unemployment may have a homogenizing influence, with variance in affective well-being tending to be reduced, so that socio-economic status fails to have its customary impact (Payne *et al.* 1984). However, more information is required before this possibility may be firmly accepted.

Box 1C of Fig. 13.1 draws attention to the potential importance of value orientations such as traits, motives, attitudes, and specific preferences. These have formed the basis of most of the 'matching' personal characteristics suggested in Table 14.1 to modify the impact of particular job conditions. In the present context, research reviewed in Chapter 12 has made clear the general importance of 'employment commitment'. Unemployed people who are more strongly committed to having paid employment are likely to experience lower well-being than those with a less strong commitment (see page 226).

The importance of this form of value orientation has been documented in a different manner among married women by Ross *et al.* (1983). Levels of depression among American wives were found to be unrelated to whether or not they had a job. However, a significant interaction was observed with women's preference for paid employment or housework. Among wives who preferred housework, having a job was associated with greater depression; but among those who preferred a job, employment was associated with lower depression. Other studies obtaining that result have been described by Warr and Parry (1982). In terms of the distinction made in Chapters 11 and 12, 'unemployed' women are expected to suffer from lack of a job, but 'non-employed' women are not.

A different type of value orientation which might affect the influence of unemployment is concerned with continuing levels of activity. Some people exhibit a stronger preference than others for purposive activity, associated with the establishment of personal goals, the search for stimulating environments, and the perception of opportunities which are unrecognized by others. It might be expected that 'proactive' people of that kind would be harmed less by unemployment, since they would create for themselves environments which are relatively rich in terms of most of the nine features in the present model.

Fryer and Payne (1984) have illustrated how people who exhibit this enduring personal characteristic can locate themselves during unemployment in settings which contain high levels of opportunity for control and for skill use, externally generated goals, variety, opportunity for interpersonal contact, and a valued social position. Their sample contained unemployed men and women who adopted roles in community, religious or political organizations, which permitted them to be active and personally satisfied despite the absence of payment for their work. Mental health was not formally measured in this study, but affective well-being, competence, autonomy, and aspiration appear from the researchers' account all to have been high. The sample had exhibited stable levels of proactivity over many preceding years; they brought to their unemployment a value system which strongly determined its impact.

The fourth category of enduring personal characteristics introduced in Fig. 13.1 is that of abilities. It might be expected that people who possess particular skills are likely to be able to employ them to personal advantage during unemployment. This might be seen through hobby activities or through assistance (paid or unpaid) to friends and neighbours. However, this possibility appears to have received no research attention. It would be appropriate now to develop more concrete hypotheses about specific forms of ability and their likely importance during unemployment.

Finally, several themes from this and earlier chapters can be brought together to ask a fundamental question. Can particular characteristics of jobs make certain workers exceptionally vulnerable to mental ill-health during subsequent unemployment? The argument for this possibility centres upon what are here defined as components two, three, and four of mental health: competence, autonomy, and aspiration.

Research reviewed throughout the book has suggested that continued exposure to job conditions which are clearly adverse in terms of the nine principal factors will impair a worker's competence, autonomy, and aspiration. The evidence for this conclusion is less strong than in respect of the affective well-being component of mental health, but it is gradually accumulating. Employees in jobs with very low opportunity for control or for skill use, and with other attributes shown in earlier chapters to be harmful, are expected to develop or retain poor mental health of these kinds. As a result they may lose, or be prevented from acquiring, those very characteristics which help them to cope with adversity during unemployment or in other chronically difficult situations.

Such a possibility, bridging the two environments of this book, is implied by many writers but is rarely made explicit (cf. O'Brien 1985). It deserves urgent and sustained research attention.

Summary

This chapter has covered three groups of issues. In the first section, research was described which examined bivariate relationships between enduring personal characteristics and aspects of current job-related well-being. As introduced in Chapter 13, four types of personal characteristics were considered: baseline mental health, demographic features, values, and abilities. It was shown that job-related well-being can be predicted from several personal variables of this kind, such as neuroticism, age, and a preference for very high work standards.

However, within the present framework the interaction between personal characteristics and job features was emphasized as of primary importance. Research in that area was summarized in the second section of the chapter. The empirical review presented there was preceded by an account in terms of possible 'matching' personal characteristics. These included several values and preferences, but extended also into particular abilities and broader personality traits thought to be relevant to individual job features.

Table 14.1 (page 257) summarized empirical support for particular combinations of job features and personal attributes, and identified a number of additional personal characteristics suggested as 'matching' but so far not demonstrated as such. The need to extend research beyond merely job satisfaction into other elements of mental health has been stressed throughout the chapter.

Also within the second section was an account of preference models of 'person–environment fit'. Three person-centred approaches were described, covering vocational interests, need and press, and work adjustment. These were seen to be of limited relevance to the vitamin model, since they do not differentiate between individual job features. A fourth preference model, in terms of separate subtractions of environmental (E) and preference (P) scores for each job characteristic, was examined, and a possible extension in terms of the vitamin AD model was proposed.

The final section examined individual differences in the impact of unemployment. Few studies have been reported in that area, with none at all investigating the interaction between particular environmental and personal characteristics. However, some tentative conclusions were reached in respect of prior emotional stability, other forms of health-related vulnerability, age, sex, socio-economic status, employment commitment, and continuing levels of activity.

The chapter ended by raising a question which is fundamental both within the present model and in its societal implications. Can continued exposure to negative job characteristics impair workers' ability to cope with the problems of subsequent unemployment? Such a process of downward adaptation appears to be implied by the context-free impact of certain job features, but so far it has remained unexplored.

15

The vitamin model: appraisal and application

This final chapter aims to bring together and extend themes which have been introduced throughout the book. The principal characteristics of the vitamin model will be summarized, and some strengths and weaknesses will be identified. Attention will then turn to a more practical question: what can be done to change jobs and unemployment, in order to reduce their negative impact upon mental health? Progress is likely to be slow in both cases, but it is important to develop new policies and to initiate change wherever possible.

The notion of mental health

First, however, we should review the book's principal outcome variable. Mental health has been presented as a characteristic of people which is both relatively stable and also open to change. A distinction has been drawn between mental health which is context-free and that which is specific to a restricted range of situations. In the latter case, it is *job-related* mental health which has been of interest in this presentation.

Chapters 2 and 3 developed an account of context-free and job-related mental health in terms of five principal components. These seem to embody the central themes in Western writing, and it was emphasized that somewhat different accounts would be required in different cultural settings. For example, most Western commentators place a greater value on independence relative to interdependence than do Eastern writers.

It is clear that mental health is a value-laden concept, and that definitions and assessments can vary between times and between cultures. However, within a particular setting we need a descriptive framework within which to characterize differences between people, whether or not they are identified as 'ill' in a medical sense. The present account has been directed to the population at large, seeking to describe differences in mental health between people almost all of whom are to some degree 'healthy'. In its emphasis upon people who are not currently defined as 'ill', the account has dealt with issues falling within the area sometimes referred to as covering 'positive mental health' (e.g. Jahoda 1958).

The five principal components have been described as affective well-being, competence, autonomy, aspiration, and integrated functioning; and attention has mainly been directed at the first four of these. The fifth component, covering issues of balance within a person and relatedness between the other components, has been little discussed. Occupational research evidence is almost completely lacking, primarily because assessment requires detailed clinical enquiries of a kind not usually conducted within the domain of the book.

Affective well-being is viewed in terms of two independent dimensions of 'pleasure' and 'arousal' (see Fig. 2.1, page 27). Three primary axes of measurement have been suggested: from discontented to contented, from anxious to comfortable, and from depressed to actively pleased (see Fig. 3.1, page 41). Context-free assessments of these three kinds were illustrated respectively in terms of general distress symptoms, anxiety, and depression; and the need for more systematic assessment of positive forms of each was emphasized. In job-related terms, the three axes of affective well-being have been assessed through measures of, for example, job satisfaction, job-related tension, and job-related depression (see Table 3.1, page 47).

It seems appropriate that affective well-being has most often been measured through self-reports from a focal person, since it is inherently subjective in nature. However, the validity of these self-reports has often been demonstrated in behavioural terms. For example, higher levels of reported psychosomatic symptoms are significantly associated with greater use of medication and more frequent visits to the doctor (e.g. Frese 1985). Raised levels of job-related tension are accompanied by greater cigarette consumption (Conway *et al.* 1981), and chronic job-related tension is associated with a higher probability of death in the subsequent ten years (House *et al.* 1986). Ratings by friends, colleagues, or spouses of a focal person's level of positive or negative affect closely parallel the reports obtained directly from that person (e.g. Conley 1985; Diener 1984; Watson and Clark 1984). Husbands' accounts of job-related emotional exhaustion coincide with wives indicating that their spouse comes home tense and that he has difficulty sleeping at night (Jackson and Maslach 1982). In clinical settings, there is substantial evidence that scores on self-completion inventories of distress and other forms of low well-being are significantly associated with independent psychiatric assessments (e.g. Mellinger *et al.* 1983).

The components of mental health identified as competence, autonomy, and aspiration represent more directly a person's transactions with the environment. In addition to a distinction in each case between context-free and job-related forms, separate treatment of 'subjective' and 'objective' aspects was recommended. Statements about the former (about 'subjective competence', for example) refer to a person's own view, whereas measures of 'objective competence' derive from assessments by one or more observers.

'Competence' itself refers to a person's ability to cope with problems, and has been examined in other settings under labels such as effective coping, environmental mastery, self-efficacy, and effectance motivation. Statements about autonomy, the third component, cover two features. First is the extent to which a person is an independent agent, acting upon the environment and feeling responsible for his or her actions; second is the degree to which the person successfully interacts with other people, contributing to their interests as well as to his or her own. It is the balance between independence and interdependence which forms the basis of assessment of a person's autonomy. Finally, aspiration concerns the degree to which a person establishes realistic goals and makes active efforts to attain them; the converse is apathy and acceptance of a situation, no matter how unsatisfactory.

Research into the mental health of both employed and unemployed people has been heavily concentrated upon affective well-being. A small number of studies have examined subjective competence, autonomy or aspiration, but the lack of systematic enquiries into those behavioural aspects of mental health (especially their 'objective' forms) is much to be deplored. For example, long periods of work in jobs lacking opportunity for control and opportunity for skill use may be expected to have a substantial negative effect upon levels of job-related and context-free forms of competence, autonomy and aspiration. Limited evidence of that kind has been obtained (see for instance Table 6.1, page 107), but more information is sorely needed.

The three behavioural components of mental health (competence, autonomy, and aspiration) are usually in practice positively associated with level of affective well-being. For example, high job-related competence tends to be accompanied by high positive affect. However, there are circumstances in which affective well-being does not map closely onto other forms of mental health. This possibility can be illustrated through job-related anxiety (the second axis of well-being) and the behavioural component of job-related aspiration. Although high levels of anxiety usually permit the inference of low mental health, high anxiety which is associated with high aspiration is more difficult to assess. This combination may, for example, be found in highly motivated managers, who seek out challenges and take risks in a way that raises their anxiety level.

Observers may conclude that anxiety is sometimes appropriate within the behavioural requirements of the manager's role, and that accompanying evidence of high competence, autonomy, and aspiration should be taken to indicate good mental health despite raised levels of job-related anxiety. An index of the latter is in these circumstances on its own misleading as evidence about mental health more broadly defined.

It was emphasized in Chapters 2 and 3 that assessments of mental health require consideration of the environment in which a person is located, and that judgements of emotions and behaviours in terms of degree of health were strongly tinged by cultural expectations about what was desirable or appropriate in a given setting. This general point is sometimes overlooked in studies of employed and unemployed people, when scores on measures of affective well-being are taken on their own as indicating level of mental health. A more complex approach would clearly be helpful.

The vitamin model

The framework which has been addressed throughout the book was introduced in Chapter 1 as both a 'categorical' and a 'process' model, using terms suggested by McGuire (1983). In the former case, nine principal categories of environmental attributes were identified. These were suggested to be major determinants of mental health in any setting, and each was viewed as comprising several subcategories.

Within the process model there are two interrelated elements. First is the vitamin analogy, in which the pattern of relationship between an environmental feature and an aspect of mental health is assumed to be non-linear, in the manner of the impact of vitamins upon aspects of physical health. Second, some suggestions have been made about the detailed ways in which mental health may be affected by different levels of each environmental feature within the categorical model.

The overall framework has been introduced as 'situation-centred' rather than 'person-centred', in that its primary focus is upon features of the environment. However, processes of personal influence upon the environment are also recognized, in the form of an 'enabling' model (Gergen and Gergen 1982). People are seen to influence their environment in both cognitive and behavioural terms. In the former case, through processes of appraisal and the imposition of personal meaning, 'objective' environmental features are amended in different ways by different perceivers. And, in behavioural terms, people not only select themselves into or out of certain types of environment but they also initiate events and processes which contribute to later states of that environment.

The vitamin model as a whole may thus be examined in respect of three principal parts. First, we should assess the value and limitations of the suggested categorization and subcategorization of the environment. Second, the process model, containing a non-linear assumption and specific accounts of processes, should be appraised. And third, the perspective on person–situation interactions should be evaluated. The next three sections attempt to make these appraisals.

Categorization of the environment

It has been suggested that mental health is responsive to nine principal environmental characteristics. These have been identified as facilitating or constraining personally-important processes and activities. The orientation was likened in Chapter 1 to Gibson's (1979) use of the concept of 'affordances'. He developed this notion within an 'ecological approach to visual perception', and a similar treatment in respect of large-scale social planning has been advocated by Emery (1985):

Social plans...have to be formulated in ecological terms; the plans have to specify what it is that that species *requires* of its environment and what that environment *affords* to that species. The term 'ecological' is appropriate to this level of descriptors because we are not simply referring to the physical properties of things and their atoms as described by physical scientists. An ecological description refers to the properties that an environment has *relative* to the capabilities and requirements of a particular species and, vice versa, the effectiveness of that species in respect of that environment. In the ecological context we can speak of environmental things and events as having meaning and value to a species because of what they *afford* to that species. Planning in terms of meanings and values (affordances and requirements) is planning in terms of the potential and probable adaptive behaviours of that species (Emery 1985, p. 1014; italics in original).

The present categorization should be viewed in these ecological terms, with intended reference to any kind of environment. The account has concentrated upon jobs and unemployment, and a summary of the categories and sub-categories suggested for job settings is provided in Table 15.1

The features described there have been examined throughout Chapters 5 to 10, with the settings of unemployment considered in Chapter 12. We may now reflect on the material in those chapters to ask: how appropriate is this overall categorization? Three main criteria may be suggested for evaluating a categorical model. First is the question of its inclusiveness: are all principal features covered, with no substantial omissions? Second is the question of empirical validity in respect of suggested outcome variables: how far does research evidence confirm the assumed importance of the features? And third, we should consider a model's heuristic value: how well does it lend itself to application and development?

Inclusiveness   The present model has been devised in the light of considerable previous research into both jobs and unemployment. It sets out to be wider in its coverage than perspectives which are restricted merely to intrinsic features of jobs. For example, the Job Characteristics Model of Hackman and Oldham (1975, 1980) assigns principal importance to five 'core job dimensions'. These are skill variety, task identity, task significance, autonomy, and feedback, features which are included respectively within categories 4, 3, 9, 1, and 5 of the present account (see, for example, Table 15.1). In addition, however, the present model identifies a number of other environmental features which need to be considered. The same point may be made of Jahoda's (1981, 1982) 'latent functions' model of employment and unemployment. She emphasized the importance of time structure, social contact, goals and purposes, personal status, and enforced activity (with financial gain as the 'manifest function'). These appear respectively within

Table 15.1   Environmental categories and subcategories within the vitamin model, in its application to job settings

---

1. Opportunity for control
   Opportunity for intrinsic control, over job content and procedures
   Level and type of pacing
   Opportunity for extrinsic control, over employment conditions and company policies
   Control over other environmental features within the model

2. Opportunity for skill use
   Opportunity to use current skills
   Opportunity to acquire new skills

3. Externally generated goals
   Intrinsic job demands: level and pattern
   Conflicts between demands
   Task identity
   Traction and flow
   Time demands: level and pattern

4. Variety
   Intrinsic variety, within job tasks
   Length of cycle time
   Extrinsic variety, in respect of job contexts

5. Environmental clarity
   Information about the consequences of actions (feedback)
   Information about future developments (job future ambiguity versus clarity)
   Information about role requirements and performance standards (role ambiguity versus clarity)

6. Availability of money
   Income relative to need (deprivation/adequacy)
   Income relative to other people (inequity/fairness)

7. Physical security
   Temperature, noise, illumination, vibration
   Absence of danger
   Good equipment design

8. Opportunity for interpersonal contact
   Amount of interaction which is possible (level of contact)
   Quality of available interaction (friendship opportunities, social support)
   Privacy and personal territory

9. Valued social position
   Esteem from roles
   Personal meaningfulness of job

---

categories 3, 8, 3, 9, 3, and 6 of the present model, with five additional features covered by the remaining elements.

The vitamin model also seeks to avoid the limitations of perspectives in terms of environmental 'stress'. Aspects of job or other settings have sometimes been approached from the standpoint that they may be defined as stressful, giving rise to feelings of strain. This perspective can accommodate many types of investigation, but it is limited by its emphasis upon the negative aspects of environments. Furthermore, the notions of stress and resulting strain are liable to become over-inclusive. For example, the former has been extended to include water pollution (Evans 1982) and the latter to cover job dissatisfaction and even obesity (Caplan *et al.* 1975).

The categorical approach taken here recognizes that a given feature can both promote and impair mental health, depending on its level and duration. The nine features may be used to interpret findings and to make predictions within areas covered by the Job Characteristics Model and the Latent Functions Model, and also by stress researchers; furthermore, 'extrinsic' features are accommodated in addition to those which are intrinsic to the work itself.

Empirical support   Research findings described throughout the book make it clear that the characteristics listed in Table 15.1 are significantly associated with several aspects of job-related and context-free mental health. As indicated in previous chapters, the evidence is of varying strength, and it is particularly important to expand the range of outcome variables beyond merely measuring job-related well-being.

It has been pointed out in Chapters 6 and 12 (pages 113 and 211) that there are considerable difficulties in identifying specific causal agents in everyday settings. Even when a particular environmental feature has been shown to be significantly correlated with an aspect of mental health, we cannot readily determine whether it is that factor itself or some correlated but unmeasured variable which has major explanatory significance. At the very least we need multivariate analyses, identifying the independent contribution of several factors in the context of each other.

Enquiries of that kind may permit us to exclude certain variables from a model, but they cannot circumvent the difficulties of inferring causal direction from cross-sectional data. As has been observed on many occasions, we now need increased numbers of longitudinal investigations, in order to specify causal relationships within what is almost certainly a cyclical process across time.

The evidence for the proposed nine factors is as convincing as that for other environmental models, primarily since the same findings and their limitations are applicable to each. However, in addition to problems raised in the previous paragraphs, three general deficiencies may be mentioned. First, there is a need to specify possible differences in importance of a given feature, according to which aspect of mental health is under consideration. Leaving aside for now the question of the pattern of an association (for example, its non-linear nature; see the next section), we still might expect varying strengths of association between an environmental feature and different forms of mental health, for example, job-related affective well-being versus context-free competence. This possibility has rarely been considered, and now requires further conceptual and empirical examination.

Second, more attention must also be paid to the likely mode of combination of different environmental features. This issue was considered in Chapter 7, through the example of workload demands in settings of different levels of opportunity for control. It appeared likely that job features combined additively or subtractively rather than synergistically, although different weights might be accorded to certain factors. For example, differences in variety may be thought to be less influential than differences in opportunity for control. In addition, particular features are likely to be more important in combination when they are in the 'threatening' ranges of Fig. 1.1 than when they fall within the 'benign' middle plateau (see page 10). It is also possible that the mode of combination of environmental features varies according to which aspect of mental health is being examined. Research has so far not approached the complexity which is needed to settle issues of that kind.

A third development required in order to strengthen empirical tests of the model concerns the measurement of each environmental feature. Recognizing that advances often come from an iterative process between conceptualization and operationalization, it is apparent that no comprehensive measurement procedure exists to tap the categories and subcategories of the present model.

A number of self-report indices of environmental features are of course available, but these tend to be concentrated upon job features that are intrinsic, and they often have a content which cuts across several of the characteristics examined here. For example, Karasek's (1979) index of 'job decision latitude' appears from its title to cover opportunity for control (feature number 1), but in fact it also covers skill level, variety, and the need for creativity (see page 84).

It may be concluded that the present categorical model is as well supported empirically as any similar general perspective. However, additional evidence is still required, and this needs to be based upon developments of both a conceptual and an operational kind.

Heuristic value   The third set of issues to be examined in this appraisal of the book's categorical model concerns its potential for application and development. The fact that it covers all kinds of environments appears to be a particular strength, and extensions to cover other settings and to analyse transitions and 'culture shock' now seem desirable.

The focus within this book has been upon the environments of jobs and joblessness. For example, a standard language has been suggested through which all job environments can be described and compared. The framework may also be used to map out changes in jobs across time, and to characterize people's movements between jobs or from jobs to unemployment or into retirement. Comparisons in these terms can also be made between industrial sectors, or between similar job titles in different companies or countries. Furthermore, the model appears useful in clarifying the factors which need to be modified in order to improve the nature of oppressive environments. The framework is thus open to 'development' as well as 'research', within the sense of the term 'research and development'.

Particular categories and subcategories may also be explored in greater detail than has been undertaken in this general treatment. For example, many jobs involving work with computer-based equipment place high demands upon a worker, but these may be of a cognitive rather than a physical kind. Within those settings, category 3 (externally generated goals) has to be focused upon specific kinds of cognitive task requirements; particular concepts and associated measuring instruments then become necessary. Incidentally, in elaborating this category to embrace cognitive demands one should also consider the remaining eight features of the model, since the impact of a job derives from the full range of characteristics.

The division of the environment into nine principal categories (rather than, say, 20) appears to be appropriately precise for most purposes. However, it is a matter of judgement whether fewer or more categories would be preferable, and this assessment will partly depend upon the applications which a judge has in mind. The number of features probably cannot be reduced below two (covering intrinsic and extrinsic attributes), but the upper limit could be very much above the nine suggested. In practice, however, the several subcategories of the nine suggested elements yield a larger set within the present framework, so that the fineness of categorization can be adjusted to meet a user's need. Models are always simplifications of reality, and the present simplification appears to lend itself conveniently to practical and theoretical application, with an appropriately manageable complexity. However, neither this model nor any other can be defined as 'correct' in respect of the number of primary categories it proposes.

A general attribute of categorical models should be noted here. The strength of the approach comes through analysing and differentiating between elements, but that strength through separation of parts is in some respects a weakness. By their very nature, categorical models cannot do justice to configural or idiographic perspectives on the world. That limitation is associated with a tendency for categorical models to be most often addressed through research methods which are quantitative rather than qualitative. For some researchers this approach is unsatisfying; they prefer to examine patterns and dynamic processes in a more qualitative manner. That is of course also valuable in some settings, and its relevance to the overall vitamin model will be further stressed below. In general, however, although categorical models are no more 'correct' than configural perspectives, they tend to have a more substantial base of research findings and methods on which to stand.

Another characteristic of the categorical component of the present model is that it does not seek to account for the development of an environment up to the present time. No aetiological description or interpretation is provided; instead the model starts with a current situation and asks about its consequences. Studies of aetiology and development are themselves of great interest, but they fall outside the scope of the present framework.

Processes within the vitamin model

Let us turn next to the ways in which the nine principal categories are thought to affect mental health. As noted previously, two issues need to be considered, the vitamin analogy and the operation of specific processes in respect of each environmental feature.

The vitamin analogy   At the heart of the present model is a postulated pattern of association between level of an environmental feature and level of mental health. This is thought to be segmented in the manner shown in Fig. 1.1 (page 10), where each feature is suggested to be particularly harmful at low values, but to have a constantly beneficial effect across a wide range beyond a certain threshold. This pattern corresponds to that representing the influence of vitamins upon physical health, and it is from that similarity that the present model is overall termed the 'vitamin model'.

Several vitamins are toxic in very large doses, so that the association between increased vitamin intake and physical health becomes negative after a broad range of moderate amounts. This has been included in the present account by distinguishing between 'vitamin AD' relationships (those with an 'additional decrement' at very high levels) and 'vitamin CE' patterns (those with a constant effect at all values beyond the desirable minimum). It has been suggested that three environmental features are likely to fit the 'constant effect' pattern (availability of money, physical security, and valued social position; numbers 6, 7, and 9 respectively), with the remainder being of the 'additional decrement' kind.

It seems clear from their nature and from everyday experience that the nine features proposed in the categorical model cannot be linearly associated with mental health; this point was developed in Chapter 1 (see page 13). Given that a non-linear pattern is probable, there is heuristic value in proposing a central plateau of constantly beneficial effect rather than a smooth curve with a steadily changing direction. Empirical research is in practice unlikely to be able to discriminate between a plateau and a curve of varying slope, and there is conceptual and practical merit in viewing environments and their attributes as falling within two distinct classes. First are those which are to some degree threatening, requiring both individual action and also research attention. Second are those (in the middle range of the horizontal axis of Fig. 1.1) which are constantly benign despite changes in the environment.

Several conceptual bases for postulating such a plateau were suggested in Chapter 1 (see page 11), and we may now enquire retrospectively about empirical evidence in the area of this book. It is clear from the reviews of research presented in earlier chapters that relevant data remain extremely scarce. Three studies (those by Champoux 1980, Karasek 1979, and van Dijkhuizen 1980) have been cited as broadly supportive, but the vast majority of investigations have relied on linear statistical procedures; as a result they give no support to any non-linear pattern, neither the vitamin model nor any other.

This absence of evidence has been recorded throughout the book, but it would be a poor reason to abandon the model. On the contrary, what is needed now are research designs which permit the assumption to be tested in a more direct way than previously.

One conceptual refinement may be needed in respect of relationships with different aspects of mental health. The vitamin analogy seems particularly appropriate for context-free rather than context-specific mental health. This point was developed in Chapter 6 (page 112), where it was observed that job-related mental health may have a shorter plateau within Fig. 1.1 than context-free mental health. This point needs empirical examination, as well as further conceptual specification.

It is in the nature of analogies in general that they have aspects which fail to correspond to the reality under examination; if that were not so, then the account would aim to be a description or a direct explanation rather than an analogy (e.g. Warr 1980). By using analogies we import an interpretative framework into a clearly different conceptual setting, in order to exploit the similarities and to learn from our understanding of the initial domain. The hope is that we can gain from the partial correspondence which exists between the settings, but the overlap is of course recognized as incomplete. In the present case four points may be noted, where non-correspondence suggests particular caution in interpretation.

First is the fact that vitamin compounds are more disparate in their nature and effects than are many of the environmental features examined here. The compounds are all required for normal metabolic functioning, but otherwise they have very little in common with each other. For example, vitamin D has its own chemical nature and works to assist bone development; vitamin A has a quite different composition and acts upon the visual system (e.g. Barker and Bender 1980, 1982). On the other hand, several of the proposed environmental analogues of vitamins are likely to combine together to influence mental health, by adding to the impact of others or compensating for their deficiency. Similarly, their impact upon separate aspects of mental health appears to be rather less differentiated than is the case for chemical vitamins. This difference in specificity between physical and psychological processes is also seen in other research fields. For example, epidemiologists in physical medicine are forced more often than their colleagues in psychological medicine to develop accounts which are disease-specific, holding quite different sets of factors responsible for each type of illness.

A second respect in which overlap is incomplete lies in the fact that people continuously influence the nature of their environments, and thus the psychological impact of those environments. In effect they act to modify the availability of situational 'vitamins', whereas in respect of physical health the naturally occurring substances usually have their effects without people engaging in purposeful activity. Any importation of physical analogies into a model of relationships between people and their environment will face this limitation, since motivation is present in people but not in things.

However, there are circumstances in which people take positive steps through dietary adjustment to restore a deficiency of chemical vitamins. This is particularly the case since the development of vitamin tablets. Just as people may seek out certain environmental characteristics through their own purposeful activity, so may they decide that they wish to alter their intake of a certain vitamin and bring this about by a change in diet or through tablet consumption.

A third aspect of the analogy to be noted here concerns the reason for the importance of chemical and environmental vitamins. Vitamin deficiency harms people because in some sense the body needs that particular chemical compound (within a certain range of quantities) for effective functioning. By the same token, within the 'ecological' perspective described earlier, people are assumed to need the environmental vitamins; it is human characteristics which cause the environmental features to be important.

This suggests that each of the nine features should correspond to a fundamental human need. In developing that possibility in more detail, one would move more into a 'person-centred' model, away from the present 'situation-centred' emphasis. That is not appropriate at this stage, but it may be observed that, whereas most of the nine features do seem to correspond to a basic need, the sixth category (availability of money) appears to be of a different character. The psychological importance of this component is within contemporary society, where money is essential for attainment of the other features. The sixth feature may thus be viewed as culture-specific, rather than as something which is universally needed in the manner of chemical vitamins.

A fourth respect in which the vitamin account is an incomplete analogy arises from the fact that people have a wide range of different kinds of dietary requirements. Vitamins are merely one group of important elements among several such groups. Food and drink must also provide proteins, carbohydrates, fats, water, and certain mineral substances. Vitamins are thus necessary but not sufficient for good physical health; they fall far short of comprising a 'balanced diet'.

However, the nine enviromental features of this book are more comprehensive in their impact. As a group they appear to be more important to mental health. The analogy is thus primarily attractive within the book's process model, suggesting non-linear relationships of the AD and CE kinds. It is less persuasive within the categorical account, where, relative to other types of factor, the contributions to physical and mental health respectively of true vitamins and the proposed analogue vitamins are recognized to be of unequal weight.

Despite these four areas of limited correspondence, there appears to be sufficient overlap between chemical and environmental 'vitamins' for us to seek to build upon the analogy. Research in the general area of this book has been dominated by models and statistical procedures which assume linear relationships between environmental and psychological features. It is now time to press forward with alternative assumptions, and the vitamin analogy provides a good basis for that change of direction.

Specific processes   Let us turn next to specific processes in respect of each environmental category and subcategory. How adequate is the present account of these? Some consideration has been given in earlier chapters to the ways in which each feature has its effect. For example, the insidious influence of chronic poverty was illustrated in Chapter 1 and Chapter 12, processes of 'flow' within work and other tasks were reviewed in Chapter 7, and the manner in which physical injury may impair mental health was considered in Chapter 9. Nevertheless, the book's concern to set out a general framework and its emphasis upon quantitative evidence have somewhat reduced the attention given to specific processes and their interdependent modes of operation.

Quantitative studies have tended to focus upon environmental features and psychological outcomes, with less consideration of the intervening processes. The development of a process model requires in addition more qualitative enquiries into dynamic interactions and mutual interdependencies across time. Some research of that kind has been carried out, more by sociologists than psychologists, and it would be valuable if that could be integrated and extended in respect of the present nine-category account.

Specifically with regard to the vitamin analogy, we need to know about the pattern of processes which may give rise to the non-linear relationship assumed in Fig. 1.1. For example, the processes bringing about impairment at high levels of an environmental feature are expected to differ from those which are important at low levels; this difference deserves exploration.

The basis of the central plateau warrants particular attention. Two principal reasons have been suggested for the assumption that mental health remains stable within an unproblematic middle range of each environmental factor. First, the processes contributing habitually to a person's level of baseline mental health are likely to inhibit change unless environmental pressures become severe, that is, outside the middle range. Second, mental health is conditioned by an accumulation of environmental features, and other elements may combine with the single factor in question to yield a moderate impact, constraining variation in mental health despite changes in one aspect of the environment. (Three supplementary arguments in terms of perception and adaptation were also developed in Chapter 1; see page 12.)

Combinational processes also require examination. Chapter 7 drew attention to the need to consider the manner in which workload and opportunity for control have their joint consequences. Two broad possibilities were suggested, a compensatory reaction and a process of mutual influence (see page 131). More descriptive and interpretative research is now required, which can elucidate the processes whereby particular sets of environmental features work together to have their aggregate effects.

This may at first sight appear to require investigation of a huge number of possible combinations of variables, but in practice the number of combinations within actual environments is limited. For example, work which is rapidly machine-paced tends also to provide low opportunity for control, to contain little variety, and to generate high levels of job demand. Since certain variables tend to co-exist, we could seek out those combinations which are most common, and explore in qualitative terms how the nine features have their impact in interaction with each other. Particularly attractive here would be studies of combination within the three separate segments of the vitamin AD model, seeking to identify communalities and contrasts between the segments.

Interactions between persons and situations

The third part of the overall vitamin model concerns personal influences within a framework which has been devised as 'situation-centred' and 'enabling'. A classification of enduring personal characteristics has been proposed in Chapter 13, which identifies as important four groups of attributes: baseline mental health, demographic features, values, and abilities. A perspective in terms of 'matching characteristics' was then developed, and research findings viewed from that perspective were summarized in Chapter 14. Fig. 13.1 (page 246) set out the ways in which persons and situations are thought to be mutually interactive within the framework of the overall vitamin model; and Fig. 14.1 (page 255) illustrated how different patterns of relationships between environmental features and mental health are expected for people with different enduring characteristics.

The previous chapters have emphasized the conceptual and practical difficulties associated with research into person–situation interactions, and some suggestions have been made for future studies. The present account of moderating personal variables is probably as well supported empirically as other accounts, since it is substantially based upon findings from earlier investigations. However, there is clearly a long way to go before details of matching characteristics in respect of each environmental category have been defined.

The research summarized in Chapter 14 was largely quantitative, examining interactions in a statistical sense. In addition to extending that type of enquiry, it is also essential that we study interactions defined in a processual sense, seeking to deepen understanding of the modes of person–situation interaction across time. Persons affect situations, and situations affect persons; the process is a reciprocal one. We now need more qualitative investigations, to fill out the details and to interpret these processes of mutual influence. The vitamin model of environmental categories and matching personal characteristics provides one overall perspective from which to develop that research.

Good and bad jobs and good and bad unemployment

Mental health aspects of unemployment were examined in Chapter 11, where a generally negative impact was clearly documented. However, it was emphasized in that chapter, and more extensively in Chapter 12, that the environments of unemployed people vary considerably between themselves.

Between-environment differences were also described in the previous chapters, when the vitamin model was applied to jobs. We may now return to the theme introduced in Chapter 1, that the environments of both employment and unemployment can be characterized in the same nine terms. In general, jobless environments are more adverse in these terms than employment settings, but there is likely to be a degree of overlap: some people's jobs are worse in terms of environmental 'vitamins' than are some settings of unemployment.

Consider a 55-year-old unemployed man, whose previous job was highly stressful, who now has a regular income (from an occupational pension or elsewhere), and who is active in managerial roles in several clubs and societies. The environment of this person, in terms of the nine factors of the vitamin model, is likely to be one which enhances mental health, perhaps beyond the level attained in previous employment. We may thus think of the circumstances of unemployed people as ranging from psychologically 'bad' (the most common case) through to those which are reasonably 'good'. In the same way, jobs may also be construed along that continuum: from those which are psychologically 'good' (the typical situation) through to others which are psychologically 'bad'.

It now becomes important to consider ways in which both jobs and joblessness can be moved from the psychologically 'bad' end of this dimension towards conditions which are relatively 'good'. Shifts of that kind are extremely complex, deserving book-length examination in their own right. However, some principal issues may be identified here. Let us first consider changes which might be made in respect of jobs.

Changing the work environment

It has been emphasized throughout the book that the majority of job settings are likely to fall within the benign mid-range plateau of the vitamin assumption. Research evidence of several kinds supports this assertion. For example, average levels of expressed satisfaction with jobs are high, and average job-related tension is low. This is important to indicate that, whereas practical steps are required in order to improve some work environments, these are likely to concern only a minority of cases.

There are three kinds of reason for instituting change in those settings. First is the moral argument. Given that there are significant causal effects of the nine principal job factors on mental health, outside as well as inside the workplace, we have a moral responsibility to act upon that knowledge. Second is a research-oriented argument. Investigations have very often been cross-sectional, assessing both job conditions and mental health at one point in time. There is now an urgent need to carry out longitudinal studies, monitoring across periods of time the psychological consequences of changes at the workplace. Such intervention studies can both contribute to greater understanding and also provide benefits to employees within the organization in question.

Mental health and work performance   A third reason for changing job characteristics known to impair mental health is a practical one: several forms of better mental health are likely to be associated with better work performance. This expectation arises for three reasons. First is the fact that poor mental health at the left-hand extreme of Fig. 1.1 tends to be a response to perceived job characteristics which themselves fail to stimulate good performance. Second, in relation to the six AD vitamins poor mental health in the right-hand segment of Fig. 1.1 often reflects a person's inability to cope with job requirements. And, third, better mental health (in the middle segment) may be exhibited in raised aspiration and high-arousal forms of affective well-being. These associations between job content, mental health, and job performance are no doubt circular in causal terms, as each set of factors operates to influence the others across time.

In considering performance, it is important to think beyond simple indices of individual output. Although in some jobs output is almost entirely determined by single employees on their own, there are many cases where it derives from the contributions of an interdependent group of people, such that individual output cannot be separately assessed. In other cases, work is undertaken by a complex system of people and machines, and a worker's effectiveness may be primarily a question of motivation and competence in anticipating likely system errors and correcting them before they can occur; sustained levels of output-oriented effort are here rather limited contributors to overall system performance.

In practice, most studies of work performance have been based upon ratings by superiors or peers. These tend to be rather crude, and may be subject to a number of biases. For example, employees who frequently raise problems and complaints may be rated by managers as less effective than their colleagues who take care not to engage the attention of their supervisor. Furthermore, the range in performance ratings is usually very limited, since obviously poor performers have previously been excluded or have chosen to leave. Recognizing these limitations, we should ask what is known about the relationship between rated work performance and the components of mental health which have been addressed throughout the book.

Consider first the three principal axes of affective well-being, from discontented to contented, from anxious to comfortable, and from depressed to actively pleased (see Fig. 3.1, page 41). The first of these is illustrated by responses in terms of job satisfaction, and two meta-analyses of satisfaction-performance correlations have recently been published. Iaffaldano and Muchinsky (1985) examined 217 correlations from previous studies, correcting for sampling error and measurement unreliability. The mean corrected coefficient between rated performance and overall job satisfaction was 0.29, and that for intrinsic satisfaction was 0.23. A similar analysis of an overlapping set of recent data reported by Petty *et al.* (1984) yielded mean corrected values of 0.31 and 0.27 respectively.

Both investigations suggested that some specific facet satisfactions were less likely to be correlated with performance, in ways which seem conceptually plausible. For example, Iaffaldano and Muchinsky cite corrected mean values in respect of satisfaction with pay and satisfaction with colleagues of only 0.06 and 0.12 respectively.

The links between overall satisfaction and rated performance are stronger among professional and managerial samples than among blue-collar workers; corrected mean values of 0.41 and 0.20 respectively were cited by Petty and colleagues. This difference seems likely to arise from different performance-reward contingencies in the two types of job, but further clarification of that point is required. Another factor moderating the relationship was investigated by Norris and Niebuhr (1984). In a study of American technical employees, they observed a significantly stronger association between satisfaction and supervisory ranking of overall performance for those higher on Rotter's (1966) measure of internal control. This difference was interpreted in terms of internal scorers' tendency to attribute job success to personal causes, reflecting aspects of their own competence, rather than to external or chance factors.

A more specific form of job behaviour was studied by Rosse and Hulin (1985). They were interested in employees' attempts to make positive changes in their job activities and conditions. Tendency to attempt such changes was measured through self-reports (for example, 'discussing with your superior ways to improve your job'), and significant positive correlations with specific job satisfaction scores were observed (median r = 0.35). As in other cases, the causal pattern is likely to be reciprocal, with higher well-being arising from successful attempts to change conditions and also encouraging further attempts.

All these analyses have concerned the first axis of affective well-being measured in *job-related* terms. No studies have been located which examine the relationship between job performance and *context-free* measures of this dimension. That is also the case for context-free measures of dimensions two and three.

Job-related well-being along the second dimension (from anxious to comfortable) has been studied in Canadian samples by Jamal (1984, 1985). In one study (Jamal 1984) supervisors' ratings of nurses' work quality, motivation and interest in patient care were found to be significantly associated with lower levels of job-related tension (median r = -0.35). The second investigation covered managers and blue-collar workers, with ratings being obtained from supervisors of each person's work quantity and quality, and effort exerted in the job. The correlations were again statistically significant, but of smaller magnitude (median r = -0.14).

The impact of this form of well-being upon performance seems likely to arise mainly from people with low well-being, who are experiencing high levels of job-related anxiety. Such anxiety is expected not only to arise from but also to contribute to problems in coping with job demands. At higher levels of this form of well-being (in the range of 'comfortable' feelings; see Fig. 3.1, page 41), performance is less likely to be associated with affect, since that sector of the axis taps low arousal of kinds which are likely to suppress motivated activity.

The third axis of job-related affective well-being is expected to be particularly correlated with performance among samples with moderate to high well-being. This axis covers feelings from depressed to actively pleased, and variations within the latter sector seem likely to derive from as well as contribute to raised performance levels. However, empirical evidence for or against this possibility appears to be lacking.

There is also a paucity of research into the association with performance of other components of mental health: competence, autonomy, and aspiration. From their content one would expect that job-related forms of each of these would be significantly related to job behaviour. Morse (1976) has shown that subjective job-related competence is significantly predictive of managers' subsequent performance, as rated by superiors, peers and subordinates; and Gardell (1982) has described how increased subjective competence is associated with greater work activity and personal initiative. Otherwise the empirical literature appears to be empty in respect of this question.

In general terms, it seems probable that the contribution of mental health to job performance will arise primarily at very low or very high levels of the former. For employees with moderate mental health scores, other determinants of performance (for example, intrinsic and extrinsic incentives, group pressures, structural features of the task) appear likely to be particularly salient. In focusing upon mental health with a view to improving job performance, we should thus concentrate attention upon workers who are likely to have poor mental health (especially in job-related forms), in order to identify local environmental features which might be acted upon.

This conclusion brings us back to the point which opened this section: the majority of jobs are expected to fall within the benign mid-range plateau of the vitamin assumption, so that attempts to enhance job quality are required in only a minority of cases. Focusing on that minority, we may now ask about the steps which need to be taken at the level of an employing organization.

There is a general requirement for management and trade unions to formulate a long-term strategy in the area of this book. In doing this, conflicts between the mental health needs of employees and the productivity requirements of management will often become clear. However, given that only a minority of jobs within an organization are likely to be problematic in mental health terms, energy can be directed to reforming this limited number. The first step is thus to scan all jobs within an organization, forming an outline assessment of each in respect of the categories and subcategories of the vitamin model (see Table 15.1, page 282). This initial screening can be undertaken fairly rapidly, but should be followed by more detailed examination of possibly problematic cases, to identify specific features which research suggests are harmful at the levels observed.

The account in this book has intentionally been at an abstract level, seeking to bring within its scope jobs of all kinds. The nine principal features will take different specific forms within different types of organization, and users of the model will no doubt adapt its basic features and terminology to meet the requirements of their own situation. In that respect, it would be unwise in some practical settings to use the category labels introduced here. Those were devised to cover environments of all kinds within a non-linear account in respect of mental health. In practical applications in job settings it will often be better to use more focused and informal terms. Some examples are suggested in Table 15.2, but other labels may be preferred, especially if particular subcategories are to be emphasized.

Working with computers   In applying the model to job environments, particular attention might be paid to work requiring interaction with computer-based equipment. Such work is expanding rapidly, and managers, trade union officials and equipment designers currently have considerable scope through their decision-making to affect employee mental health.

Extensive consideration has been given in respect of these jobs to the first two features of the present model, in terms of possible 'deskilling' which may

Table 15.2   Category labels which may be appropriate in theoretical and practical settings

Theoretical term within the vitamin model	Illustrative label for use in job settings
1. Opportunity for control	Employee discretion
2. Opportunity for skill use	Required skills
3. Externally generated goals	Work demands
4. Variety	Work variety
5. Environmental clarity	Level of uncertainty
6. Availability of money	Pay
7. Physical security	Health and safety
8. Opportunity for interpersonal contact	Communication and contacts
9. Valued social position	Self-respect from the job

accompany the introduction of 'information technology' work. Recognizing that managements are often concerned to maximize their own control over operators' freedom of action (see Chapter 5), it has sometimes been argued that technological change will encourage managerial decisions which constrain the opportunity for control and for skill use by lower-level employees. The negative mental health consequences of such a process (in relation to the first two categories of the present model) have been one focus of the book, but wider concerns in respect of the distribution of power within organizations and within society at large have also been expressed (e.g. Braverman 1974). In job content terms, it may be thought that managerial attempts to centralize control during the introduction of computer-based equipment might yield a polarization of opportunities for skill use, with managers and technical and professional staff enhancing their skills whereas the skill content of shop-floor work becomes impoverished.

In practice, however, case study research has indicated that 'deskilling' at lower levels is a far from inevitable consequence of information technology (e.g. Buchanan and Boddy 1983; Sorge *et al.* 1983; Wall 1987). This is important. Not only does it demonstrate that conditions conducive to good employee mental health can be built into new technology jobs, but also the research indicates that it is often possible to design computer-based jobs where workers are sufficiently skilled and motivated to anticipate system malfunctioning and to initiate corrective action before serious problems arise.

In terms of the third feature of the present model, task demands can often be very high in computer-based jobs, since there is an organizational need for raised productivity to recoup the capital costs of expensive equipment. Demands may also be of a changed character, requiring cognitive rather than physical work, in ways which are initially unpredictable by designers and users alike. An additional pressure on workers sometimes arises from the fact that operators' activity is to be recorded on a central computer for observation and appraisal by management.

Variety (the fourth environmental 'vitamin') is often reduced in new technology jobs, as both task activities and work location become more fixed; this factor may require particular attention. Environmental clarity (feature number 5) can be affected by the introduction of computer-based equipment in a number of ways, depending on the nature of the equipment in question. In certain cases there may be a marked loss of job feedback. For example, in some sales jobs a pile of written orders can provide clear evidence about one's achievement during a period of work; after computerization, where orders are entered directly into a computer, no such record may be available in material form. In other settings, however, feedback from one's actions and decisions may be enhanced, in terms of a prompt system response immediately after an input message.

Another aspect of environmental clarity which has particular importance for information technology jobs concerns the degree to which operators can understand the pattern and rationale of their computer's behaviour. Without a relatively clear conceptual model, their ability to diagnose faults and avoid errors will be severely limited. These issues of 'cognitive ergonomics' must be addressed in terms of the software programs underlying computer activity, seeking to create sensible allocations of tasks between the user or the program, with the former having a sound cognitive representation of the latter (e.g. Corbett 1985; Long 1987).

Aspects of physical security, in terms of safety and working conditions, have been illustrated in respect of visual display units in Chapter 9 (page 172). The implementation of new technology appears likely to have varying consequences for the remaining three environmental features, depending upon the equipment and tasks in question. In general, however, we might expect a slight overall reduction in opportunity for interpersonal contact, and a slight overall increase in availability of money and enhanced social position. Within those general expectations, specific enquiries are of course needed in particular organizational settings

Change procedures   Returning to a consideration of jobs more generally, interventions to improve employee mental health can be of two kinds. Some are directed primarily at changing the job or organization, whereas others are aimed to assist individual people without directly modifying their environment. Attempts of the former kind can sometimes be viewed under the heading of 'job design'. Design specifications may be created and applied (for example, in terms of the environmental categories described here), in order to build jobs in a systematic manner, rather than letting them develop haphazardly in the absence of an overall plan.

Early approaches were sometimes referred to as 'job enrichment', a term closely associated with Herzberg's theorizing (e.g. 1966), with 'enrichment' aiming to enhance the intrinsic content of work. Employees in very simple jobs may be given additional tasks to perform, particularly those which involve greater responsibility and require more skilled work. Another procedure is in terms of 'job rotation', where employees change jobs with others in the same wage grade, either within a period of work or between periods. This can increase variety, but is unlikely to be of great advantage if rotation is between jobs which are all equally poor; there needs also to be some increment in the other characteristics identified here. (See also Chapter 5, page 98.)

More recent procedures of job design tend to emphasize the interdependence between tasks undertaken by different employees and groups of employees. It is now seen as desirable to examine and if necessary change the content of jobs undertaken by groups of employees as well as by single individuals (e.g. Wall *et al.* 1986). The need to treat extrinsic as well as intrinsic features has also become accepted. For example, redesigning jobs to increase opportunity for control or opportunity for skill use requires consideration of wage levels, since the new tasks may have shifted their location in a job evaluation framework. Financial savings may of course be expected elsewhere, and many instances of job redesign have occurred within pay and productivity agreements (e.g. Kelly 1982).

It is often necessary to extend change attempts beyond the level of a particular job or one set of jobs, directing attention also to broader aspects of the organization or a specific part of it. Interventions to change organizations are inevitably complex and are likely to require considerable resources of time and expertise. In general terms, the primary focus might be of three kinds: seeking to modify structural features and relationships between roles, influencing employees through training and counselling, or explicitly analysing and using power vested in individuals and groups. These approaches are sometimes referred to as 'structural', 'human resources', and 'political' respectively.

The literature on job design and organizational change is enormous. It is not appropriate to seek to review it comprehensively at this stage of the book; the issues are raised here in order to make the point that the vitamin model can provide a useful basis for determining the goals of intervention at the level of both the job and the organization.

A second type of programme to enhance employee mental health was identified earlier in this section as being aimed to assist individual people without directly modifying their job environment. Counselling or psychotherapeutic assistance may be provided, without seeking to change directly the nature of required tasks. For example, some organizations have introduced 'stress management' programmes, providing training which aims to help employees to relax and cope better with job stressors (e.g. West *et al.* 1984). Psychotherapy from clinical psychologists or psychiatrists is also available to clients with job-related problems (e.g. Firth and Shapiro 1986), and offers considerable potential in this area.

Changing unemployment

Finally, let us examine possible approaches to improving the position of unemployed people. Two broad perspectives have been adopted, the first in terms of reducing unemployment levels themselves (and thereby shortening the amount of time people spend unemployed), and the second in terms of modifying principal environmental features.

Reducing unemployment levels Within the first general perspective, three themes have received attention. First is the creation of additional jobs, drawing into these people who would otherwise be unemployed. Several possibilities have been suggested for action at government level; for example, funding useful work on public facilities, encouraging new construction projects, supporting companies against international competition, or providing temporary jobs for unemployed people. There have also been attempts to expand self-employment and to create new companies, on the basis that small organizations can grow more rapidly than many large ones, thus taking on greater numbers of people overall.

Attention has also been directed at the possible contributions to be made by successfully established companies. For example, many large employers appear to be acknowledging some responsibility for the welfare of local communities. Associated with this they are making available resources in terms of low-cost premises or seconding staff to provide managerial expertise to newly founded companies; additional young trainees may be taken on, work may be sub-contracted to new local firms, and spare equipment may be loaned to starting companies at minimal cost.

The second group of attempts to reduce overall levels of unemployment sets out to restrict the total duration of a 'working life'. Governments in several countries have recently extended periods of youth training, in effect delaying the age of entry into the labour market, and thus the number of people who might become unemployed. At the other end of the range, attempts have been made to lower the retirement age, in order that more vacancies will become available for people currently seeking jobs.

Third, there have been several suggestions about ways to reduce the number of hours spent in paid employment, at least by some employees. If that were achieved, it is assumed that other people would be drawn in to fill the gaps so created.

Steps which might be taken in this area include a reduction in overtime working or in the standard working week, or an expansion in holiday allowances. Alternatively, employees might be asked to work for a smaller number of weeks per year, 40 instead of 52, for example, with holidays taken from within that number (e.g. Handy 1984). Such people could draw unemployment benefit for their period outside employment. Associated with that is the possibility of more part-time jobs, or various forms of 'work-sharing', whereby two people are employed in some combination of part-time contracts to meet a full-time need (e.g. Rathkey 1985).

However, it appears that most men, especially those with family responsibilities, are unwilling to undertake paid work for less than what is conventionally viewed as 'full-time'. There may be scope for more part-time employment of teenagers or men approaching retirement, but in general it is women who appear to be more attracted to jobs of that kind.

Modifying the environment   The other broad approach to improving the position of unemployed people is to seek to modify the environmental features which impinge upon them. Such steps are often advocated on the grounds that high levels of unemployment are likely to persist for the foreseeable future, at least within certain geographical regions.

Chapters 11 and 12 emphasized that most unemployed people are likely to experience low levels of the nine environmental 'vitamins'. However, differences between individual situations are to be expected, and these may be particularly marked in cross-national comparisons. For example, in respect of availability of money (feature number 6), some governments provide benefits of unlimited duration for unemployed people, whereas others set limits of, say, six or twelve months. Amount of benefit also varies considerably, with 80 or 90 per cent of previous income payable in some countries, but less than 50 per cent in others.

Associated differences are expected in physical security (feature number 7). Among unemployed people these may be reflected in varying levels of adequacy of housing, sanitation, and heating. Security of these kinds is widely threatened by an extended period of unemployment.

In seeking to improve the environment of unemployed people, action in respect of these two features may warrant primary consideration in many countries. A second group of environmental factors is made up of categories 1 to 4 within the present model. Unemployed people's lives are often diminished through limited opportunities for personal control and for skill utilization, the absence of externally generated goals, and a restricted variety of settings and activities. Recognizing that these features are to some extent open to influence through the agency of individuals themselves (e.g. Fryer and Payne 1984), there is nevertheless a general need to seek to modify unemployed people's environments in these respects.

The principal requirement appears to be for additional or expanded formal or informal institutions in areas of high local unemployment. It is through roles within institutions that these four environmental 'vitamins' may become more available to unemployed people. Traditional concerns of churches, clubs, and societies could be expanded to draw in people who lack paid jobs, and new forms of institution might be created. Among the possibilities here are centres for unemployed people themselves (e.g. Forrester and Ward 1986), easily accessible training establishments with flexible and attractive programmes, and resource networks or skills exchanges (e.g. Senior and Naylor 1984). Local authorities might provide subsidized leisure facilities for unemployed people (e.g. Glyptis 1983), and voluntary agencies could expand their role to provide more unpaid work for unemployed people.

Developments of these kinds would be likely also to generate increased opportunity for interpersonal contact (feature number 8), as well as to reduce the public and private stigma attached to being unemployed (feature number 9). There would also be the possibility of increasing environmental clarity (the fifth characteristic), in that role requirements can become more explicit through regular commitments to other people, and future events can be better predicted and planned in the light of those commitments.

Attempts of these kinds to improve the environment of unemployed people are being made in many communities. They often involve the development of some intermediate roles, between full-time paid work and full-time un-employment. Payment for working part of the week or year may be encouraged (see the previous section), as may temporary periods of non-employment, outside the labour market and not seeking a job.

However, progress in this area has been limited by the fact that few countries have an overall national policy in respect of unemployment and part-employment. There is often an absence of agreed public concern to change the jobless environment. Recognizing a need to help unemployed people in these terms is sometimes seen as an admission of defeat in respect of the first broad approach, reducing the rate of unemployment itself. In reality, the two approaches are surely more complementary than contradictory.

Summary

This chapter has looked back upon the framework developed in earlier pages, and has identified some of its strengths and weaknesses. After a summary of the book's account of mental health, the overall vitamin model was characterized as having three main constituents: a categorical model, a process model, and a model of person–situation interactions.

Categorization of the environment has been in terms of nine principal features. This part of the overall framework was assessed favourably in terms of its inclusiveness and basic empirical support. However, certain questions required more systematic examination, especially in relation to possible differences in the importance of single features and in relation to their modes of combination. The need for more refined measurement of the suggested categories and subcategories was also stressed. The heuristic value of the categorical model was deemed to be good, but a general inadequacy of such approaches in handling dynamic or idiographic perspectives was noted.

Turning to the process model, two issues were considered: the vitamin analogy and the operation of specific processes in respect of each environmental feature. The conceptual and heuristic bases of the segmented association proposed through the vitamin analogy were summarized, and the scarcity of empirical evidence was noted. Recognizing that all analogies are by their nature incomplete in some respects, four areas of limited overlap in the present case were described. Specific processes of environmental impact were next considered, at which point additional qualitative research into particular features was advocated.

In terms of person–situation interactions, the model has been based upon the identification of 'matching personal characteristics' for each environmental category. This seems conceptually appropriate, but the chapter noted a lack of sophisticated empirical research and a continuing need for more qualitative as well as quantitative investigations.

The second part of the chapter has brought together the book's treatment of jobs and unemployment, to observe that the two environments can usefully be construed in terms of the same nine categories. Some jobs are in their content and outcomes psychologically worse than some settings of unemployment, although the average difference is clearly in favour of paid work.

It was recommended that management and trade unions seek to formulate a long-term strategy in the area of this book, and that all jobs be examined for their probable impact on employee mental health. The majority of jobs were viewed as likely to fall within the benign mid-range plateau of the vitamin model, with only a minority requiring attention. Work with computer-based equipment was suggested to deserve particularly close scrutiny. Possible approaches to enhancing mental health through job design, organizational change, and individual counselling were briefly introduced.

Approaches to improving the position of unemployed people were considered in the final section. Two broad strategies were described: reducing overall levels of unemployment, and improving the position of those who remain unemployed. Examples of each approach were presented, and it was argued that the two should be treated as complementary rather than contradictory.

References

Abdel-Halim, A. A. (1980). Effects of person–job compatibility on managerial reactions to role ambiguity. *Organizational Behavior and Human Performance* **26**, 193–211.

Abdel-Halim, A. A. (1981). A re-examination of ability as a moderator of role perceptions—satisfaction relationship. *Personnel Psychology* **34**, 549–61.

Abdel-Halim, A. A. (1982). Social support and managerial affective responses to job stress. *Journal of Occupational Behaviour* **3**, 281–95.

Abraham, K. (1950). Observations on Ferenczi's paper on Sunday neuroses. (First published in 1918.) In R. Fliess (ed.), *The psycho-analytic reader*. London: Hogarth Press.

Adams, J. S. (1963). Toward an understanding of inequity. *Journal of Abnormal and Social Psychology* **67**, 422–36.

Adams, J.S. and Freedman, S. (1976). Equity theory revisited: Comments and annotated bibliography. In L. Berkowitz and E. Walster (eds), *Advances in experimental social psychology* (vol. 9). New York: Academic Press.

Ahr, P. R., Gorodezky, M. J., and Cho, D. W. (1981). Measuring the relationship of public psychiatric admissions to rising unemployment. *Hospital and Community Psychiatry* **32**, 398–401.

Aiken, M. and Hage, J. (1966). Organizational alienation: A comparative analysis. *American Sociological Review* **31**, 497–507.

Akerstedt, T. (1984). Work schedules and sleep. *Experientia* **40**, 417–22.

Alban-Metcalfe, B. and Nicholson, N. (1984). *The career development of British managers*. London: British Institute of Management.

Aldag, R. J., Barr, S. H., and Brief, A. P. (1981). The measurement of perceived task characteristics. *Psychological Bulletin* **90**, 415–31.

Alfredsson, L. and Theorell, T. (1983). Job characteristics of occupations and myocardial infarction risk: Effect of possible confounding factors. *Social Science and Medicine* **17**, 1497–503.

Alfredsson, L., Karasek, R., and Theorell, T. (1982). Myocardial infarction risk and psychosocial work environment: An analysis of the male Swedish working force. *Social Science and Medicine* **16**, 463–7.

Algera, J. A. (1983). Objective and perceived task characteristics as a determinant of reactions by task performers. *Journal of Occupational Psychology* **56**, 95–107.

Alloy, L. B. and Abramson, L. Y. (1979). Judgment of contingency in depressed and non-depressed students: Sadder but wiser? *Journal of Experimental Psychology: General* **108**, 441–85.

Altman, I. (1975). *The environment and social behavior.* Monterey: Brooks Cole.

Altman, I. and Chemers, M. (1980). *Culture and environment.* Monterey: Brooks Cole.

Altman, I., Taylor, D. A., and Wheeler, L. (1971). Ecological aspects of group behavior in social isolation. *Journal of Applied Social Psychology* **1**, 76–100.

American Psychiatric Association (1981). *Diagnostic and statistical manual of mental disorders.* 3rd edn. Washington: American Psychiatric Association.

Anderson, N. (1974). *Man's work and leisure.* Leiden: E. J. Brill.

Andrews, F. M. and Withey, S. B. (1974). Developing measures of perceived life quality: Results from several national surveys. *Social Indicators Research* **1**, 1–26.

Andrisani, P. J. and Nestel, G. (1976). Internal–external control as a contributor to and outcome of work experience. *Journal of Applied Psychology* **61**, 156–65.

Aneshensel, C. S., Frerichs, R. R., and Clark, V. A. (1981). Family roles and sex differences in depression. *Journal of Health and Social Behavior* **22**, 379–93.

Aneshensel, C. S., Frerichs, R. R., and Huba, G. J. (1984). Depression and physical illness: A multiwave, nonrecursive model. *Journal of Health and Social Behavior* **25**, 350–71.

Angyal, A. (1965). *Neurosis and treatment: A holistic theory.* New York: Wiley.

Anon, (1983a). Social habits and health. In *Social trends.* London: HMSO.

Anon (1983b). Pattern of household spending in 1982. *Employment Gazette* **91**, 517–23.

Antonovsky, A. (1980). *Health, stress and coping.* San Francisco: Jossey-Bass.

Apter, M. J. (1984). Reversal theory and personality: A review. *Journal of Research in Personality* **18**, 265–88.

Archer, R. P. (1979). Relationships between locus of control and anxiety. *Journal of Personality Assessment* **43**, 617–26.

Armor, D. J., Polich, J. M., and Stambul, H. B. (1978). *Alcoholism and treatment.* New York: Wiley.

Aro, S. and Hanninen, V. (1984). Life events or life processes as determinants of mental strain? A five-year follow-up study. *Social Science and Medicine* **18**, 1037–44.

Ashley, P. (1983). *The money problems of the poor.* London: Heinemann.

Ayoub, M. M. (1973). Work place design and posture. *Human Factors* **15**, 265–8.

Bachman, J. G., O'Malley, P. M., and Johnston, L. D. (1984). Drug use among young adults: The impacts of role status and social environment. *Journal of Personality and Social Psychology* **47**, 629–45.

Baldamus, W. (1961). *Efficiency and effort: An analysis of industrial administration.* London: Tavistock Publications.

Ballinger, C. B., Smith, A. H. W., and Hobbs, P. R. (1985). Factors associated with psychiatric morbidity in women: A general practice survey. *Acta Psychiatrica Scandinavica* **71**, 272–80.

Bandura, A. (1977). Self-efficacy: Toward a unifying theory of behavioral change. *Psychological Review* **84**, 191–215.

Banks, M. H. and Jackson, P. R. (1982). Unemployment and risk of minor psychiatric disorder in young people: Cross-sectional and longitudinal evidence. *Psychological Medicine* **12**, 789–98.

Banks, M. H. and Ullah, P. (1986). Unemployment and less qualified urban youth. *Employment Gazette* **94**, 205–10.

Barker, B. M. and Bender, D. A. (eds) (1980). *Vitamins in medicine* (4th edn, vol. 1). London: Heinemann.

Barker, B. M. and Bender, D. A. (eds) (1982). *Vitamins in medicine* (4th edn, vol. 2). London: Heinemann.

Barling, P. W. and Handal, P. J. (1980). Incidence of utilization of public mental health facilities as a function of short-term economic decline. *American Journal of Community Psychology* **8**, 31–9.

Barnett, R. C. and Baruch, G. K. (1985). Women's involvement in multiple roles and psychological distress. *Journal of Personality and Social Psychology* **49**, 135–45.

Barron, F. (1953). An ego-strength scale which predicts response to psychotherapy. *Journal of Consulting Psychology* **17**, 327–33.

Baum, A., Fleming, R., and Reddy, D. M. (1986). Unemployment stress: Loss of control, reactance and learned helplessness. *Social Science and Medicine* **22**, 509–16.

Baum, A., Grunberg, N. E., and Singer, J. E. (1982). The use of psychological and neuroendocrinological measurements in the study of stress. *Health Psychology* **1**, 217–36.

Beale, N. and Nethercott, S. (1985). Job loss and family morbidity: A study of a factory closure. *Journal of the Royal College of General Practitioners* **35**, 510–14.

Bebbington, P., Hurry, J., Tennant, C., Sturt, E., and Wing, J. K. (1981). Epidemiology of mental disorders in Camberwell. *Psychological Medicine* **11**, 561–80.

Bech, P., Gram, L. F., Reisby, N., and Rafaelson, O. J. (1980). The WHO depression scale: Relationship to the Newcastle scales. *Acta Psychiatrica Scandinavica* **62**, 140–53.

Bechtold, S. E., Sims, H. P., and Szilagyi, A. D. (1981). Job scope relationships: A three-wave longitudinal analysis. *Journal of Occupational Behaviour* **2**, 189–202.

Beck, A. T., Ward, C. H., Mendelson, M., Mock, J., and Erbaugh, J. (1961). An inventory for measuring depression. *Archives of General Psychiatry* **4**, 561–71.

Beckman, L. J. (1981). Effects of social interaction and children's relative inputs on older women's psychological well-being. *Journal of Personality and Social Psychology* **41**, 1075–86.

Beiser, M. (1974). Components and correlates of mental well-being. *Journal of Health and Social Behavior* **15**, 320–27.

Ben-Sira, Z. (1985). Potency: A stress-buffering link in the coping-stress-disease relationship. *Social Science and Medicine* **21**, 397–406.

Berger-Gross, V. and Kraut, A. I. (1984). Great expectations: A no-conflict explanation of role conflict. *Journal of Applied Psychology* **69**, 261–71.

Berndt, D. J., Berndt, S. M., and Kaiser, C. F. (1984). Multidimensional assessment of depression. *Journal of Personality Assessment* **48**, 489–94.

Berndt, D. J., Petzel, T. P., and Kaiser, C. F. (1983). Evaluation of a short form of the Multiscore Depression Inventory. *Journal of Consulting and Clinical Psychology* **51**, 790–1.

Biddle, B. J. (1979). *Role theory.* New York: Academic Press.

Billings, A. G. and Moos, R. H. (1982). Work stress and the stress-buffering roles of work and family resources. *Journal of Occupational Behaviour* **3**, 215–32.

Binns, D. and Mars, G. (1984). Family, community and unemployment: A study in change. *Sociological Review* **32**, 662–95.

Binswanger, L. (1963). *Being-in-the-world.* New York: Basic Books.

Birchall, D. and Wild, R. (1977). Job characteristics and the attitudes of female manual workers: A research note. *Human Relations* **30**, 355–42.

Birren, J. E. and Renner, V. J. (1981). Concepts and criteria of mental health and aging. *American Journal of Orthopsychiatry* **51**, 242–54.

Blatt, S. J., D'Affliti, J. P., and Quinlan, D. M. (1976). Experiences of depression in normal young adults. *Journal of Abnormal Psychology* **85**, 383–9.

Blatt, S. J., Quinlan, D. M., Chevron, E. S., McDonald, C., and Zuroff, D. (1982). Dependency and self-criticism: Psychological dimensions of depression. *Journal of Consulting and Clinical Psychology* **50**, 113–24.

Blau, G. (1981). An empirical investigation of job stress, social support, service length, and job strain. *Organizational Behavior and Human Performance* **27**, 279–302.

Blauner, R. (1964). *Alienation and freedom.* Chicago: University of Chicago Press.

Boucher, J. and Osgood, C. E. (1969). The Polyanna hypothesis. *Journal of Verbal Learning and Verbal Behavior* **8**, 1–8.

Boyle, G. J. (1985). Self-report measures of depression: Some psychometric considerations. *British Journal of Clinical Psychology* **24**, 45–59.

Bradburn, N. M. (1969). *The structure of psychological well-being.* Chicago: Aldine.

Bradburn, N. M. and Caplovitz, D. (1965). *Reports on happiness.* Chicago: Aldine.

Bradshaw, J., Cooke, K., and Godfrey, C. (1983). The impact of unemployment on the living standards of families. *Journal of Social Policy* **12**, 433–52.

Braunstein, W. B., Powell, B. J., McGowan, J. F., and Thoreson, R. W. (1983). Employment factors in outpatient recovery of alcoholics: A multivariate study. *Addictive Behaviors* **8**, 345–51.

Braverman, H. (1974). *Labor and monopoly capital: The degradation of work in the twentieth century.* New York: Monthly Review Press.

Breaugh, J. A. (1985). The measurement of work autonomy. *Human Relations* **38**, 551–70.

Brenner B. (1975). Quality of affect and self-evaluated happiness. *Social Indicators Research* **2**, 315–31.

Brenner, M. H. (1971). Economic changes and heart disease mortality. *American Journal of Public Health* **61**, 606–11.

Brenner, M. H. (1973a). *Mental illness and the economy*. Cambridge: Harvard University Press.

Brenner, M. H. (1973b). Fetal, infant, and maternal mortality during periods of economic instability. *International Journal of Health Services* **3**, 145–59.

Brenner, M. H. (1979). Mortality and the national economy: A review, and the experience of England and Wales. *The Lancet* **2**, 568–73.

Brenner, M. H. (1980a). Industrialization and economic growth: Estimates of their effects on the health of populations. In M. H. Brenner, A. Mooney, and T. J. Nagy (eds), *Assessing the contributions of the social sciences to health*. Washington: American Academy for the Advancement of Science.

Brenner, M. H. (1980b). Importance of the economy to the nation's health. In L. Eisenberg and A. Kleinman (eds), *The relevance of social science for medicine*. New York: Reidel.

Brenner, M. H. (1983). Mortality and economic instability: Detailed analyses for Britain and comparative analyses for selected industrialized countries. *International Journal of Health Services* **13**, 563–620.

Brenner, M. H. and Mooney, A. (1982). Economic change and sex-specific cardiovascular mortality in Britain 1955–1976. *Social Science and Medicine* **16**, 431–42.

Brenner, M. H. and Mooney, A. (1983). Unemployment and health in the context of economic change. *Social Science and Medicine* **17**, 1125–38.

Brett, J. M. (1980). The effect of job transfer on employees and their families. In C. L. Cooper and R. L. Payne (eds), *Current concerns in occupational stress*. London: Wiley.

Brett, J. M. (1982). Job transfer and well-being. *Journal of Applied Psychology* **67**, 450–63.

Brewin, C. R. (1980). Work-role transitions and stress in managers: Illustrations from the clinic. *Personnel Review* **9**(3), 27–30.

Brief, A. P. and Aldag, R. J. (1975). Employee reactions to job characteristics: A constructive replication. *Journal of Applied Psychology* **60**, 182–6.

Brief, A. P. and Aldag, R. J. (1976). Correlates of role indices. *Journal of Applied Psychology* **61**, 468–72.

Brief, A. P. and Aldag, R. J. (1978). The job characteristics inventory: An examination. *Academy of Management Journal* **21**, 659–70.

Brinkmann, C. (1984). Financial, psychosocial and health problems associated with unemployment. In G. Fragnière (ed.), *The future of work*. Assen: Van Gorcum.

Broadbent, D. E. (1981). Chronic effects from the physical nature of work. In B. Gardell and G. Johansson (eds), *Working life*. Chichester: Wiley.

Broadbent, D. E. (1985). The clinical impact of job design. *British Journal of Clinical Psychology* **24**, 33–44.

Broadbent, D. E. and Gath, D. (1981). Symptom levels in assembly-line workers. In G. Salvendy and M. J. Smith (eds), *Machine pacing and occupational stress*. London: Taylor and Francis.

Broadbent, D. E. and Little, F. A. J. (1960). Effects of noise reduction in a work situation. *Occupational Psychology* **34**, 133–40.

Broadbent, D. E., Cooper, P. F., FitzGerald, P. and Parkes, K. R. (1982) The Cognitive Failures Questionnaire (CFQ) and its correlates. *British Journal of Clinical Psychology* **21**, 1–16.

Brookes, M. J. and Kaplan, A. (1972). The office environment: Space planning and affective behavior. *Human Factors* **14**, 373–91.

Brousseau, K. R. (1978). Personality and job experience. *Organizational Behavior and Human Performance* **22**, 235–52.

Brousseau, K. R. and Prince, J. B. (1981). Job-person dynamics: An extension of longitudinal research. *Journal of Applied Psychology* **66**, 59–62.

Bruggemann, A., Groskurth, P., and Ulich, E. (1975). *Arbeitszufriedenheit*. Bern: Huber.

Bryant, F. B. and Veroff, J. (1982). The structure of psychological well-being: A sociohistorical analysis. *Journal of Personality and Social Psychology* **43**, 653–73.

Bryant, F. B. and Veroff, J. (1984). Dimensions of subjective mental health in American men and women. *Journal of Health and Social Behavior* **25**, 116–35.

Buchanan, D. A. and Boddy, D. (1983). Advanced technology and the quality of working life: The effects of computerized controls on biscuit-making operators. *Journal of Occupational Psychology* **56**, 109–19.

Buck, V. E. (1972). *Working under pressure*. London: Staples Press.

Burke, R. J. and Weir, T. (1980). The type A experience: Occupational and life demands, satisfaction and well-being. *Journal of Human Stress* **6**, 28–38.

Burke, R. J., Weir, T., and Duncan, G. (1976). Informal helping relationships in work organizations. *Academy of Management Journal* **19**, 370–7.

Burke, R. J., Weir, T., and DuWors, R. E. (1980). Work demands on administrators and spouse well-being. *Human Relations* **33**, 253–78.

Buss, T. F. and Redburn, F. S. (1983). *Mass unemployment: Plant closings and community mental health*. Beverly Hills: Sage.

Campbell, A., Converse, P. E., and Rodgers, W. L. (1976). *The quality of American life*. New York: Russell Sage Foundation.

Campbell, D. J. (1982). Determinants of choice of goal difficulty level: A review of situational and personality influences. *Journal of Occupational Psychology* **55**, 79–95.

Campion, M. A. and Thayer, P. W. (1985). Development and field evaluation of an interdisciplinary measure of job design. *Journal of Applied Psychology* **70**, 29–43.

Caplan, R. D. and Jones, K. W. (1975). Effects of work load, role ambiguity, and type A personality on anxiety, depression and heart-rate. *Journal of Applied Psychology* **60**, 713–19.

Caplan, R. D., Cobb, S., French, J. R. P., Van Harrison, R., and Pinneau, S. R. (1975). *Job demands and worker health*. Washington: US Department of Health, Education and Welfare.

Carruthers, M. E. (1977). The chemical anatomy of stress. In P. Kielholz (ed.), *Beta-blockers and the central nervous system*. Berne: Huber.

Catalano, R. A. and Dooley, C. D. (1977). Economic predictors of depressed mood and stressful life events in a metropolitan community. *Journal of Health and Social Behavior* **18,** 292–307.

Catalano, R. A. and Dooley, C. D. (1979). Does economic change provoke or uncover behavioral disorder? A preliminary test. In L. Ferman and J. Gordus (eds), *Mental health and the economy.* Kalamazoo, Michigan: Upjohn Foundation.

Catalano, R. A. and Dooley, C. D. (1983). Health effects of economic instability: A test of economic stress hypothesis. *Journal of Health and Social Behavior* **24,** 46–60.

Catalano, R. A., Dooley, C. D., and Jackson, R. L. (1981). Economic predictors of admissions to mental health facilities in a nonmetropolitan community. *Journal of Health and Social Behavior* **22,** 284–97.

Catalano, R. A., Dooley, C. D., and Jackson, R. L. (1985). Economic antecedents of help seeking: Reformulation of time-series tests. *Journal of Health and Social Behavior* **26,** 141–52.

Champoux, J. E. (1978). A preliminary examination of some complex job scope—growth need strength interactions. *Academy of Management Proceedings,* 59–63.

Champoux, J. E. (1980). A three-sample test of some extensions to the job characteristics model of work motivation. *Academy of Management Journal* **23,** 466–78.

Chapanis, A. (1976). Engineering psychology. In M. D. Dunnette (ed.), *Handbook of industrial and organizational psychology.* New York: Wiley.

Cherlin, A. and Reeder, L. G. (1975). The dimensions of psychological well-being: A critical review. *Sociological Methods and Research* **4,** 189–214.

Cherrington, D. J. and England, J. L. (1980). The desire for an enriched job as a moderator of the enrichment-satisfaction relationship. *Organizational Behavior and Human Performance* **25,** 139–59.

Cherry, N. (1984a). Nervous strain, anxiety and symptoms amongst 32-year-old men at work in Britain. *Journal of Occupational Psychology* **57,** 95–105.

Cherry, N. (1984b). Women and work stress: Evidence from the 1946 birth cohort. *Ergonomics* **27,** 519–26.

Chesney, M. A. and Rosenman, R. H. (1980). Type A behaviour in the work setting. In C. L. Cooper and R. L. Payne (eds), *Current concerns in occupational stress.* Chichester: Wiley.

Cleary, P. D. and Mechanic, D. (1983). Sex differences in psychological distress among married people. *Journal of Health and Social Behavior* **24,** 111–21.

Clegg, C. W. (1984). The derivation of job designs. *Journal of Occupational Behaviour* **5,** 131–46.

Cobb, S. and Kasl, S. V. (1977). *Termination: The consequences of job loss.* Cincinatti: US Department of Health, Education and Welfare.

Cobb, S. and Rose, R. M. (1973). Hypertension, peptic ulcer, and diabetes in air traffic controllers. *Journal of the American Medical Association* **224,** 489–92.

Coburn, D. (1978). Work and general psychological and physical well-being. *International Journal of Health Services* **8,** 415–35.

Cochrane, R. and Stopes-Roe, M. (1980). Factors affecting the distribution of psychological symptoms in urban areas of England. *Acta Psychiatrica Scandinavica* **61,** 445–60.

Cochrane, R. and Stopes-Roe, M. (1981). Women, marriage, employment and mental health. *British Journal of Psychiatry* **139,** 373–81.

Coffield, F., Borrill, C., and Marshall, S. (1983). How young people try to survive being unemployed. *New Society* **64,** 1072, 332–4.

Cohen, A. (1976). The influence of a company hearing conservation program on extra-auditory problems in workers. *Journal of Safety Research* **8,** 146–62.

Cohen, S. (1980). Aftereffects of stress on human performance and social behavior: A review of research and theory. *Psychological Bulletin* **88,** 82–108.

Cohen, S. and Weinstein, N. (1982). Nonauditory effects of noise on behavior and health. In G. W. Evans (ed.), *Environmental stress.* Cambridge: Cambridge University Press.

Cohen, S., Kamarck, T., and Mermelstein, R. (1983). A global measure of perceived stress. *Journal of Health and Social Behavior* **24,** 385–96.

Cohn, R. M. (1978). The effect of employment status change on self-attitudes. *Social Psychology* **41,** 81–93.

Colligan, M. J. and Murphy, L. R. (1979). Mass psychogenic illness in organizations: An overview. *Journal of Occupational Psychology* **52,** 77–90.

Colligan, M. J., Pennebaker, J. W., and Murphy, L. R. (eds) (1982). *Mass psychogenic illness: A social psychological analysis.* Hillsdale: Erlbaum.

Colligan, M. J., Smith, M. J., and Hurrell, J. J. (1977). Occupational incidence rates of mental health disorders. *Journal of Human Stress* **3,** 34–9.

Conley, J. J. (1984). Longitudinal consistency of adult personality: Self-reported psychological characteristics across 45 years. *Journal of Personality and Social Psychology* **47,** 1325–33.

Conley, J. J. (1985). Longitudinal stability of personality traits: A multitrait-multimethod-multioccasion analysis. *Journal of Personality and Social Psychology* **49,** 1266–82.

Conway, T. L., Vickers, R. R., Ward, H. W., and Rahe, R. H. (1981). Occupational stress and variation in cigarette, coffee, and alcohol consumption. *Journal of Health and Social Behavior* **22,** 155–65.

Cook, D. G., Cummins, R. O., Bartley, M. J., and Shaper, A. G. (1982). Health of unemployed middle-aged men in Great Britain. *The Lancet* 5 June, 1290–4.

Cook, J. D., Hepworth, S. J., Wall, T. D., and Warr, P. B. (1981). *The experience of work.* London: Academic Press.

Cooke, R. A. and Rousseau, D. M. (1984). Stress and strain from family roles and work-role expectations. *Journal of Applied Psychology* **69,** 252–60.

Cooper, C. L. and Davidson, M. (1982). *High pressure: Working lives of women managers.* London: Fontana.

Cooper, R. (1973). Task characteristics and intrinsic motivation. *Human Relations* **26,** 387–413.

Corbett, J. M. (1985). Prospective work design of a human-centred CNC lathe. *Behaviour and Information Technology* **4,** 201–14.

Costa, P. T. and McRae, R. R. (1980). Influence of extraversion and neuroticism on subjective well-being: Happy and unhappy people. *Journal of
Personality and Social Psychology* **38**, 668–78.

Costa, P. T. and McRae, R. R. (1985). Hypochondriasis, neuroticism, and
aging. *American Psychologist* **40**, 19–28.

Crawford, A., Plant, M. A., Kreitman, N., and Latcham, R. W. (1987).
Unemployment and drinking behaviour: Some data from a general population survey of alcohol use. *British Journal of Addiction,* in press.

Creigh, S., Roberts, C., Gorman, A., and Sawyer, P. (1986). Self-employment
in Britain. *Employment Gazette* **94**, 183–94.

Cronbach, L. J. and Furby, L. (1970). How should we measure 'change'—or
should we? *Psychological Bulletin* **74**, 68–80.

Crown, S. and Crisp, A. H. (1966). A short clinical diagnostic self-rating
scale for psychoneurotic patients. *British Journal of Psychiatry* **112**,
917–23.

Csikszentmihalyi, M. (1975). *Beyond boredom and anxiety.* San Francisco:
Jossey-Bass.

Dainoff, M. J., Hurrell, J. J., and Happ, A. (1981). A taxonomic framework
for the description and evaluation of paced work. In G. Salvendy and M. J.
Smith (eds), *Machine pacing and occupational stress.* London: Taylor and
Francis.

Dalton, M. (1959). *Men who manage.* New York: Wiley.

Daniel, W. W. (1974). *A national survey of the unemployed.* London: Political
and Economic Planning Institute.

D'Arcy, C. and Siddique, C. M. (1985). Unemployment and health: An analysis
of Canada Health Survey data. *International Journal of Health Services* **15**,
609–35.

D'Arcy, C., Syrotuik, J., and Siddique, C. M. (1984). Perceived job attributes,
job satisfaction, and psychological distress: A comparison of working men
and women. *Human Relations* **37**, 603–11.

Davidson, M. (1987). Women and employment. In P.B. Warr (ed.), *Psychology
at work* (3rd edn.). Harmondsworth: Penguin.

Davidson, M. and Cooper, C. L. (1983). *Stress and the woman manager.*
Oxford: Martin Robertson.

Davies, R., Hamill, L., Moylan, S., and Smee, C. H. (1982). Incomes in and
out of work. *Employment Gazette* **90**, 237–43.

Dawis, R. V. and Lofquist, L. H. (1984). *A psychological theory of work
adjustment.* Minneapolis: University of Minnesota Press.

Dean, J. W. and Brass, D. J. (1985). Social interaction and the perception of
job characteristics in an organization. *Human Relations* **38**, 571–82.

Delmonte, M. M. and Ryan, G. M. (1983). The Cognitive–Somatic Anxiety
Questionnaire (CSAQ): A factor analysis. *British Journal of Clinical Psychology* **22**, 209–12.

Dempsey, P. (1964). A unidimensional depression scale for the MMPI. *Journal
of Consulting Psychology* **28**, 364–70.

Depue, R. A. and Monroe, S. M. (1986). Conceptualization and measurement
of human disorder in life stress research: The problem of chronic disturbance.
Psychological Bulletin **99**, 36–51.

Derogatis, L. R. and Melisaratos, N. (1983). The Brief Symptom Inventory: An introductory report. *Psychological Medicine* **13**, 595–605.

Derogatis, L. R., Lipman, R. S., Rickels, K., Uhlenhuth, E. H., and Covi, L. (1974). The Hopkins Symptom Checklist: A self-report symptom inventory. *Behavioral Science* **19**, 1–15.

Diener, E. (1984). Subjective well-being. *Psychological Bulletin* **95**, 542–75.

Diener, E. and Emmons, R. A. (1985). The independence of positive and negative affect. *Journal of Personality and Social Psychology* **47**, 1105–17.

Dijkhuizen, N. Van (1980). *From stressors to strains*. Lisse: Swets and Zeitlinger.

Dijkhuizen, N. Van (1981). Measurement and impact of organizational stress. In J. Siegrist and M.J. Halhuber (eds), *Myocardial infarction and psychosocial risks*. Berlin: Springer.

Dobson, K. S. (1985). The relationship between anxiety and depression. *Clinical Psychology Review* **5**, 307–24.

Doherty, J. and Davies, C. (1984). The psychological effects of unemployment on a group of adolescents. *Educational Review* **36**, 217–28.

Dohrenwend, B. P., Shrout, P. E., Egri, C., and Mendelsohn, F. S. (1980). Nonspecific psychological distress and other dimensions of psychopathology: Measures for use in the general population. *Archives of General Psychiatry* **37**, 1229–38.

Donaldson, L. (1975). Job enlargement: A multidimensional process. *Human Relations* **28**, 593–610.

Donovan, A. and Oddy, M. (1982). Psychological aspects of unemployment: An investigation into the emotional and social adjustment of school leavers. *Journal of Adolescence* **5**, 15–30.

Dooley, C. D. and Catalano, R. A. (1984a). Why the economy predicts help-seeking: A test of competing explanations. *Journal of Health and Social Behavior* **25**, 160–76.

Dooley, C. D. and Catalano, R. A. (1984b). The epidemiology of economic stress. *American Journal of Community Psychology* **12**, 387–409.

Dooley, C. D., Catalano, R. A., Jackson, R., and Brownell, A. (1981). Economic, life, and symptom changes in a non-metropolitan community. *Journal of Health and Social Behavior* **22**, 144–54.

Dougherty, T. W. and Pritchard, R. D. (1985). The measurement of role variables: Exploratory examination of a new approach. *Organizational Behavior and Human Decision Processes* **35**, 141–55.

Drenth, P. J. D., Hoolwerf, G., and Thierry, H. (1976). Psychological aspects of shift work. In P. B. Warr (ed.), *Personal goals and work design*. Chichester: Wiley.

Drury C. G. (1985). Stress and quality control inspection. In C. L. Cooper and M. J. Smith (eds.), *Job stress and blue collar work*. Chichester: Wiley.

Dunham, R. B. (1976). The measurement and dimensionality of job characteristics. *Journal of Applied Psychology* **61**, 404–9.

Dunham, R. B. (1977). Relationships of perceived job design characteristics to job ability requirements and job value. *Journal of Applied Psychology* **62,** 760–3.

Dyer, L. and Theriault, R. (1976). The determinants of pay satisfaction. *Journal of Applied Psychology* **61,** 596–604.

Eaton, W. W. and Kessler, L. G. (eds) (1985). *Epidemiologic field methods in psychiatry: The NIMH Epidemiological Catchment Area Program.* Orlando: Academic Press.

Eden, D. (1982). Critical job events, acute stress, and strain: A multiple interrupted time series. *Organizational Behavior and Human Performance* **30,** 312–29.

Eisenberg, P. and Lazarsfeld, P. F. (1938). The psychological effects of unemployment. *Psychological Bulletin* **35,** 358–90.

Emery, F. (1985). Public policies for healthy workplaces. *Human Relations* **38,** 1013–22.

Erikson, E. H. (1950). *Childhood and society.* New York: Norton.

Erikssen, J., Rognum, T., and Jervell, J. (1979). Unemployment and health. *The Lancet* no. 1, 1189.

Estes, R. J. and Wilensky, H. L. (1978). Life cycle squeeze and the morale curve. *Social Problems* **25,** 277–92.

Etzion, D. (1984). Moderating effect of social support on the stress–burnout relationship. *Journal of Applied Psychology* **69,** 615–22.

Evans, G. W. (ed.) (1982). *Environmental stress.* Cambridge: Cambridge University Press.

Evans, P. and Bartolome, F. (1980). *Must success cost so much?* London: Grant McIntyre.

Eyer, J. (1977). Does unemployment cause the death rate peak in each business cycle? *International Journal of Health Services* **7,** 625–62.

Eysenck, H. J. and Eysenck, S. B. G. (1975). *Manual of the Eysenck Personality Questionnaire.* London: Hodder and Stoughton.

Fagin, L. and Little, M. (1984). *The forsaken families: The effects of unemployment on family life.* Harmondsworth: Penguin.

Feather, N. T. (1982). Unemployment and its psychological correlates: A study of depressive symptoms, self-esteem, Protestant ethic values, attributional style, and apathy. *Australian Journal of Psychology* **34,** 309–23.

Feather, N. T. and Barber, J. G. (1983). Depressive reactions and unemployment. *Journal of Abnormal Psychology* **92,** 185–95.

Feather, N. T. and Bond, M. J. (1983). Time structure and purposeful activity among employed and unemployed university graduates. *Journal of Occupational Psychology* **56,** 241–54.

Feather, N. T. and Davenport, P. R. (1981). Unemployment and depressive affect: A motivational analysis. *Journal of Personality and Social Psychology* **41,** 422–36.

Feather, N. T. and O'Brien, G. E. (1986). A longitudinal study of the effects of employment and unemployment on school-leavers. *Journal of Occupational Psychology* **59,** 121–44.

Feldman, D. C. and Brett, J. M. (1983). Coping with new jobs: A comparative study of new hires and job changers. *Academy of Management Journal* **26,** 258–72.

Ferenczi, S. (1926). Sunday neuroses. (First published in 1918.) In *Further contributions to the theory and technique of psycho-analysis*. London: Hogarth Press.

Festinger, L. (1954). A theory of social comparison processes. *Human Relations* **7**, 117–40.

Fimian, M. J. (1984). The development of an instrument to measure occupational stress in teachers. *Journal of Occupational Psychology* **57**, 277–93.

Fineman, S. (1983). *White collar unemployment*. Chichester: Wiley.

Finlay-Jones, R. A. and Eckhardt, B. (1981). Psychiatric disorder among the young unemployed. *Australian and New Zealand Journal of Psychiatry* **15**, 265–70.

Finlay-Jones, R. A. and Eckhardt, B. (1984). A social and psychiatric survey of unemployment among young people. *Australian and New Zealand Journal of Psychiatry* **18**, 135–43.

Firth, J. (1983). Experiencing uncertainty: A case from the clinic. *Personnel Review* **12**(2), 11–15.

Firth, J. (1985). Personal meanings of occupational stress. *Journal of Occupational Psychology* **58**, 139–48.

Firth, J. and Shapiro, D. A. (1986). An evaluation of psychotherapy for job-related distress. *Journal of Occupational Psychology* **59**, 111–19.

Fisher, C. D. and Gitelson, R. (1983). A meta-analysis of the correlates of role conflict and ambiguity. *Journal of Applied Psychology* **68**, 320–33.

Fleming, R., Baum, A., and Singer, J. E. (1984). Toward an integrative approach to the study of stress. *Journal of Personality and Social Psychology* **46**, 939–49.

Fleming, R., Baum, A., Reddy, D., and Gatchel, R. J. (1984). Behavioral and biochemical effects of job loss and unemployment stress. *Journal of Human Stress* **10**, 12–17.

Folkard, S. and Monk, T. H. (eds) (1985). *Hours of work: Temporal factors in work-scheduling*. Chichester: Wiley.

Forbes, J. F. and McGregor, A. (1984). Unemployment and mortality in post-war Scotland. *Journal of Health Economics* **3**, 239–57.

Fordyce, M. W. (1985). The psychap inventory: A multi-scale test to measure happiness and its concomitants. *Social Indicators Research* **18**, 1–33.

Form, W. and McMillen, D. B. (1983). Women, men, and machines. *Work and Occupations* **10**, 147–78.

Forrester, K. and Ward, K. (1986). Organising the unemployed? The TUC and the unemployed workers centres. *Industrial Relations Journal* **17**, 46–56.

Fox, A. J. and Goldblatt, P. O. (1982). *Longitudinal study: Socio-demographic mortality differentials*. London: HMSO.

Fox, J. G. (1983). Industrial music. In D. J. Oborne and M. M. Gruneberg (eds), *The physical environment at work*. Chichester: Wiley.

Frank, J. A. (1981). Economic change and mental health in an uncontaminated setting. *American Journal of Community Psychology* **9**, 395–410.

Frankenhaeuser, M. (1981). Coping with job stress: A psychological approach. In B. Gardell and G. Johansson (eds), *Working life: A social science contribution to work reform*. Chichester: Wiley.

Frankenhaeuser, M. and Johansson, G. (1976). Task demand as reflected in catecholamine excretion and heart rate. *Journal of Human Stress* **2**, 15–23.

Frankenhaeuser, M. and Johansson, G. (1981). On the psychophysiological consequences of understimulation and overstimulation. In L. Levi (ed.), *Society, stress and disease* (vol. 4). Oxford: Oxford University Press.

Fraser, R. (1947). *The incidence of neurosis among factory workers.* London: HMSO.

Fraser, R. (1968). *Work: Twenty personal accounts.* Harmondsworth: Penguin.

Fraser, R. (1969). *Work: Twenty personal accounts* (vol. 2). Harmondsworth: Penguin.

French, J. R. P., Caplan, R. D., and Van Harrison, R. (1982). *The mechanisms of job stress and strain.* New York: Wiley.

French, J. R. P., Doehrman, S. R., Davis-Sacks, M. L., and Vinokur, A. (1983). *Career change in midlife: Stress, social support, and adjustment.* Michigan: Institute for Social Research.

Frese, M. (1979). Arbeitslosigkeit, Depressivität und Kontrolle: Eine Studie mit Wiederholungsmessung. In T. Kieselbach and H. Offe (eds), *Arbeitslosigkeit.* Darmstadt: Steinkopff.

Frese, M. (1984). Transitions in jobs, occupational socialization and strain. In V. Allen and E. van de Vliert (eds), *Role transitions.* New York: Plenum.

Frese, M. (1985). Stress at work and psychosomatic complaints: A causal interpretation. *Journal of Applied Psychology* **70**, 314–28.

Frese, M. and Harwich, C. (1984). Shiftwork and the length and quality of sleep. *Journal of Occupational Medicine* **26**, 561–6.

Frese, M. and Sabini, J. (eds) (1985). *Goal-directed behavior: The concept of action in psychology.* Hillsdale: Erlbaum.

Freud, S. (1930). *Civilization and its discontents.* London: Hogarth Press.

Fried, Y., Rowland, K. M., and Ferris, G. R. (1984). The physiological measurement of work stress: A critique. *Personnel Psychology* **37**, 583–615.

Friedman, A. L. (1977). *Industry and labour: Class struggle at work and monopoly capitalism.* London: Macmillan.

Friedman, M. and Rosenman, R. (1974). *Type A behavior and your heart.* New York: Knopf.

Fröhlich, D. (1983a). Economic deprivation, work orientation and health: Conceptual ideas and some empirical findings. In J. John, D. Schwefel, and H. Zöllner (eds), *Influence of economic instability on health.* Berlin: Springer.

Fröhlich, D. (1983b). *The use of time during unemployment.* Assen: Van Gorcum.

Fruensgaard, K., Benjaminsen, S., Joensen, S., and Helstrup, K. (1983). Psychosocial characteristics of a group of unemployed patients consecutively admitted to a psychiatric emergency department. *Social Psychiatry* **18**, 137–44.

Fryer, D. M. and McKenna, S. (1987). The laying off of hands. In S. Fineman (ed.), *Unemployment: Personal and social consequences.* London: Tavistock.

Fryer, D. M. and Payne, R. L. (1983). Book borrowing and unemployment. *Library Review* **32**, 196–206.

Fryer, D. M. and Payne, R. L. (1984). Proactivity in unemployment: Findings and implications. *Leisure Studies* **3**, 273–95.

Fryer, D. M. and Payne, R. L. (1986). Being unemployed: A review of the literature on the psychological experience of unemployment. In C. L. Cooper and I. Robertson (eds), *Review of industrial and organizational psychology*. Chichester: Wiley.

Fryer, D. M. and Warr, P. B. (1984). Unemployment and cognitive difficulties. *British Journal of Clinical Psychology* **23**, 67–8.

Furnham, A. and Schaeffer, R. (1984). Person–environment fit, job satisfaction and mental health. *Journal of Occupational Psychology* **57**, 295–307.

Gadbois, C. (1978). Les conditions de travail et leurs formes d'emprise sur la vie hors travail. *Cahiers de Psychologie* **21**, 245–68.

Ganster, D. C., Fusilier, M. R., and Mayes, B. T. (1986). Role of social support in the experience of stress at work. *Journal of Applied Psychology* **71**, 102–10.

Gardell, B. (1971). Alienation and mental health in the modern industrial environment. In L. Levi (ed.), *Society stress and disease* (vol. 1). Oxford: Oxford University Press.

Gardell, B. (1982). Worker participation and autonomy: A multilevel approach to democracy at the workplace. *International Journal of Health Services* **12**, 527–58.

Garfield, S. L. (1978). Research on client variables in psychotherapy. In S. L. Garfield and A. E. Bergin (eds), *Handbook of psychotherapy and behavior change: An empirical analysis* (2nd edn). New York: Wiley.

Garraty, J. A. (1978). *Unemployment in history*. New York: Harper and Row.

Gaskell, G. and Smith, P. (1981). 'Alienated' black youth: An investigation of 'conventional wisdom' explanations. *New Community* **9**, 182–93.

Gavin, J. F. and Axelrod, W. L. (1977). Managerial stress and strain in a mining organization. *Journal of Vocational Behavior* **11**, 66–74.

Gergen, K. J. and Gergen, M. M. (1982). Explaining human conduct: Form and function. In P. Secord (ed.), *Explaining human behavior: Consciousness, human action, and social structure*. Beverly Hills: Sage.

Gibson, J. J. (1979). *The ecological approach to visual perception*. Boston: Houghton Mifflin.

Gil, D. (1971). Violence against children. *Journal of Marriage and the Family* **33**, 637–57.

Gilleard, C. J., Willmott, M., and Vaddadi, K. S. (1981). Self-report measures of mood and morale in elderly depressives. *British Journal of Psychiatry* **138**, 230–5.

Glass, D. C. (1977). *Behavior patterns, stress, and coronary disease*. Hillsdale: Erlbaum.

Glass, D. C. (1981). Type A behavior: Mechanisms linking behavioral and pathophysiologic processes. In J. Siegrist and M. J. Halhuber (eds), *Myocardial infarction and psychosocial risks*. Berlin: Springer.

Glyptis, S. (1983). Business as usual? Leisure provision for the unemployed. *Leisure Studies* **2**, 287–300.

Goldberg, D. P. (1972). *The detection of psychiatric illness by questionnaire*. Oxford: Oxford University Press.

Goldberg, D. P. (1978). *Manual for the General Health Questionnaire*. Windsor: National Foundation for Educational Research.

Goldberg, D. P. and Hillier, V. F. (1979). A scaled version of the General Health Questionnaire. *Psychological Medicine* **9**, 139–45.

Goodchild, M. E. and Duncan-Jones, P. (1985). Chronicity and the General Health Questionnaire. *British Journal of Psychiatry* **146**, 55–61.

Goodman, P. S. (1974). An examination of referents used in the evaluation of pay. *Organizational Behavior and Human Performance* **12**, 170–95.

Goodwin, L. (1972). *Do the poor want to work?* Washington: The Brookings Institution.

Gore, S. (1978). The effect of social support in moderating the health consequences of unemployment. *Journal of Health and Social Behavior* **19**, 157–65.

Gorz, A. (ed.) (1976). *The division of labour: The labour process and class-struggle in modern capitalism.* Brighton: The Harvester Press.

Gough, H. G. (1975). *Manual for the California Psychological Inventory.* Palo Alto: Consulting Psychologists Press.

Grandjean, E. (1980). Ergonomics of VDUs: Review of present knowledge. In E. Grandjean and E. Vigliani (eds), *Ergonomic aspects of visual display terminals.* London: Taylor and Francis.

Grandjean, E. (ed.) (1984). *Ergonomics and health in modern offices.* London: Taylor and Francis.

Gravelle, H. S. E., Hutchinson, G., and Stern, J. (1981). Mortality and unemployment: A critique of Brenner's time-series analysis. *The Lancet* **2**, 675–9.

Grayson, D. (1984). Payment systems for the future. *Employment Gazette* **92**, 121–5.

Grayson, J. P. (1985). The closure of a factory and its impact on health. *International Journal of Health Services* **15**, 69–93.

Greenberger, D. B. and Strasser, S. (1986). Development and application of a model of personal control in organizations. *Academy of Management Review* **11**, 164–77.

Greenhalgh, L. and Rosenblatt, Z. (1984). Job insecurity: Toward conceptual clarity. *Academy of Management Review* **9**, 438–48.

Greenhaus, J. H. and Beutel, N. J. (1985). Sources of conflict between work and family roles. *Academy of Management Review* **10**, 76–88.

Griffeth, R. W. (1985). Moderation of the effects of job enrichment by participation: A longitudinal field experiment. *Organizational Behavior and Human Decision Processes* **35**, 73–93.

Groen, J. J. (1981). Work and peptic ulcer. In L. Levi (ed.), *Society, stress and disease* (vol. 4). Oxford: Oxford University Press.

Gurney, R. M. (1981). Leaving school, facing unemployment, and making attributions about the causes of unemployment. *Journal of Vocational Behavior* **18**, 79–91.

Hacker, W. (1985). Activity: A fruitful concept in industrial psychology. In M. Frese and J. Sabini (eds), *Goal-directed behavior: The concept of action in psychology.* Hillsdale: Erlbaum.

Hackman, J. R. and Lawler, E. E. (1971). Employee reactions to job characteristics. *Journal of Applied Psychology* **55**, 259–86.

Hackman, J. R. and Oldham, G. R. (1975). Development of the Job Diagnostic Survey. *Journal of Applied Psychology* **60,** 159–70.

Hackman, J. R. and Oldham, G. R. (1980). *Work redesign.* Reading, Massachusetts: Addison-Wesley.

Hackman, J. R., Pearce, J. L., and Wolfe, J. C. (1978). Effects of changes in job characteristics on work attitudes and behaviors: A naturally occurring quasi-experiment. *Organizational Behavior and Human Performance* **21,** 289–304.

Hage, J. (1982). Theory-building. In N. Nicholson and T. D. Wall (eds), *The theory and practice of organizational psychology.* London: Academic Press.

Hall, D. T. and Hall, F. S. (1980). Stress and the two-career couple. In C. L. Cooper and R. L. Payne (eds), *Current concerns in occupational stress.* Chichester: Wiley.

Hall, D. T. and Schneider, B. (1973). *Organizational climates and careers: The work lives of priests.* New York: Seminar Press.

Handy, C. (1984). *The future of work.* Oxford: Blackwell.

Harrison, G. A., Palmer, C. D., Jenner, D. A., and Reynolds, V. (1981). Associations between rates of urinary catecholamine excretion and aspects of lifestyle among adult women in some Oxfordshire villages. *Human Biology* **53,** 617–33.

Hawton, K. and Rose, N. (1986). Unemployment and attempted suicide among men in Oxford. *Health Trends* **18,** 29–32.

Headey, B., Holstrom, E., and Wearing, A. (1984). Well-being and ill-being: Different dimensions? *Social Indicators Research* **14,** 115–39.

Health and Safety Executive (1983). *Visual display units.* London: HMSO.

Heller, F. A. and Wilpert, B. (1981). *Competence and power in managerial decision-making.* Chichester: Wiley.

Henderson, M. and Argyle, M. (1985). Social support by four categories of work colleagues. *Journal of Occupational Behaviour* **6,** 229–39.

Henderson, S., Byrne, D. G., and Duncan-Jones, P. (1981). *Neurosis and the social environment.* Sydney: Academic Press.

Hendrie, H. C. (1981). Depression in the course of physical illness. In G. Salvendy and M. J. Smith (eds), *Machine pacing and occupational stress.* London: Taylor and Francis.

Hendrix, W. H., Ovalle, N. K., and Troxler, R. G. (1985). Behavioral and physiological consequences of stress and its antecedent factors. *Journal of Applied Psychology* **70,** 188–201.

Henry, J. P. (1982). The relation of social to biological processes in disease. *Social Science and Medicine* **16,** 369–80.

Heppner, P. P. and Petersen, C. H. (1982). The development and implications of a personal problem-solving inventory. *Journal of Counseling Psychology* **29,** 66–75.

Hepworth, S. J. (1980). Moderating factors of the psychological impact of unemployment. *Journal of Occupational Psychology* **53,** 139–45.

Herold, D. M. and Parsons, C. K. (1985). Assessing the feedback environment in work organizations: Development of the job feedback survey. *Journal of Applied Psychology* **70,** 290–305.

Herzberg, F. (1966). *Work and the nature of man.* Chicago: World Publishing Company.

Herzog, A. R., Rodgers, W. L., and Woodworth, J. (1982). *Subjective well-being among different age groups.* Ann Arbor, Michigan: Institute for Social Research.

Hickson, D. J. (1961). Motives of workpeople who restrict their output. *Occupational Psychology* **35,** 111–21.

Hill, A. B. (1975). Work variety and individual differences in occupational boredom. *Journal of Applied Psychology* **60,** 128–31.

Hobbs, P. R., Ballinger, C. B., McLure, A., Martin, B., and Greenwood, C. (1985). Factors associated with psychiatric morbidity in men: A general practice survey. *Acta Psychiatrica Scandinavica* **71,** 281–6.

Holland, J. L. (1976). Vocational preferences. In M. D. Dunnette (ed.), *Handbook of industrial and organizational psychology.* Chicago: Rand McNally.

Homans, G. C. (1961). *Social behavior: Its elementary forms.* New York: Harcourt Brace.

House, J. S. (1981). *Work stress and social support.* Reading, Massachusetts: Addison-Wesley.

House, J. S., Strecher, V., Metzner, H. L., and Robbins, C. A. (1986). Occupational stress and health among men and women in the Tecumseh Community Health Study. *Journal of Health and Social Behavior* **27,** 62–77.

House, J. S., McMichael, A. J., Wells, A. J., Kaplan, B. H., and Landerman, L. R. (1979). Occupational stress and health among factory workers. *Journal of Health and Social Behavior* **20,** 139–60.

House, R. J. and Rizzo, J. R. (1972). Role conflict and ambiguity as critical variables in a model of organizational behavior. *Organizational Behavior and Human Performance* **7,** 467–505.

House, R. J., Schuler, R. S., and Levanoni, E. (1983). Role conflict and ambiguity scales: Reality or artefacts? *Journal of Applied Psychology* **68,** 334–7.

Howard, J. H., Cunningham, D. A., and Rechnitzer, P. A. (1976). Health patterns associated with type A behavior: A managerial population. *Journal of Human Stress* **2,** 24–31.

Howard, J. H., Cunningham, D. A., and Rechnitzer, P. A. (1977). Work patterns associated with type A behavior: A managerial population. *Human Relations* **30,** 825–36.

Howard, J. H., Cunningham, D. A., and Rechnitzer, P. A. (1986). Role ambiguity, type A behavior, and job satisfaction: Moderating effects on cardiovascular and biochemical responses associated with coronary risks. *Journal of Applied Psychology* **71,** 95–101.

Howarth, E. and Schokman-Gates, K. (1981). Self-report multiple mood instruments. *British Journal of Psychology* **72,** 421–41.

Hurrell, J. J. (1985). Machine-paced work and the Type-A behaviour pattern. *Journal of Occupational Psychology* **58,** 15–25.

Iaffaldano, M. T. and Muchinsky, P. M. (1985). Job satisfaction and job performance: A meta-analysis. *Psychological Bulletin* **97,** 251–73.

Idzikowski, C. and Baddeley, A. D. (1983). Fear and dangerous environments. In G. R. J. Hockey (ed.), *Stress and fatigue in human performance*. Chichester: Wiley.

Ilgen, D. R., Fisher, C. D., and Taylor, M. S. (1979). Consequences of individual feedback on behavior in organizations. *Journal of Applied Psychology* **64**, 349–71.

Ivancevich, J. M. and Matteson, M. T. (1984). The type A-B person—work environment interaction model for examining occupational stress and consequences. *Human Relations* **37**, 491–513.

Iversen, L. and Klausen, H. (1986). Alcohol consumption among laid-off workers before and after closure of a Danish shipyard. *Social Science and Medicine* **22**, 107–9.

Jackson, P. R. and Warr, P. B. (1984). Unemployment and psychological ill-health: The moderating role of duration and age. *Psychological Medicine* **14**, 605–14.

Jackson, P. R., Paul, L. J., and Wall, T. D. (1981). Individual differences as moderators of reactions to job characteristics. *Journal of Occupational Psychology* **54**, 1–8.

Jackson, P. R., Stafford, E. M., Banks, M. H., and Warr, P. B. (1983). Unemployment and psychological distress in young people: The moderating role of employment commitment. *Journal of Applied Psychology* **68**, 525–35.

Jackson, S. E. (1983). Participation in decision making as a strategy for reducing job-related strain. *Journal of Applied Psychology* **68**, 3–19.

Jackson, S. E. and Maslach, C. (1982). After-effects of job-related stress: Families as victims. *Journal of Occupational Behaviour* **3**, 63–77.

Jackson, S. E. and Schuler, R. S. (1985). A meta-analysis and conceptual critique of research on role ambiguity and role conflict in work settings. *Organizational Behaviour and Human Decision Processes* **36**, 16–78.

Jaco, E. G. (1960). *The social epidemiology of mental disorders*. New York: Russell Sage Foundation.

Jahoda, M. (1958). *Current concepts of positive mental health*. New York: Basic Books.

Jahoda, M. (1981). Work, employment, and unemployment: Values, theories, and approaches in social research. *American Psychologist* **36**, 184–91.

Jahoda, M. (1982). *Employment and unemployment: A social-psychological analysis*. Cambridge: Cambridge University Press.

Jahoda, M., Lazarsfeld, P. F., and Zeisel, H. (1933). *Marienthal: The sociography of an unemployed community*. (English translation, 1971, by Aldine-Atherton, New York.)

Jamal, M. (1984). Job stress and job performance controversy: An empirical assessment. *Organizational Behavior and Human Performance* **33**, 1–21.

Jamal, M. (1985). Relationship of job stress to job performance. *Human Relations* **38**, 409–24.

James, L. R. and Tetrick, L. E. (1986). Confirmatory analytic tests of three causal models relating job perceptions to job satisfaction. *Journal of Applied Psychology* **71**, 77–82.

Jayaratne, S. and Chess, W. A. (1984). The effects of emotional support on perceived job stress and strain. *Journal of Applied Behavioral Science* **20**, 141–53.

Jenner, D. A., Reynolds, V., and Harrison, G. A. (1980). Catecholamine excretion rates and occupation. *Ergonomics* **23**, 237–46.

Jick, T. D. and Mitz, L. F. (1985). Sex differences in work stress. *Academy of Management Review* **10**, 408–20.

Johansson, G. and Aronsson, G. (1984). Stress reactions in computerized administrative work. *Journal of Occupational Behaviour* **5**, 159–81.

Johansson, G., Aronsson, G., and Lindstrom, B. O. (1978). Social psychological and neuroendocrine stress reactions in highly mechanised work. *Ergonomics* **21**, 583–99.

John, J. (1983). Economic instability and mortality in the Federal Republic of Germany. In J. John, D. Schwefel, and H. Zöllner (eds), *Influence of economic instability on health*. Berlin: Springer.

John, J. (1985). Economic instability and health: Infant mortality and suicide reconsidered. In G. Westcott, P. G. Svensson, and H. F. K. Zöllner (eds), *Health policy implications of unemployment*. Copenhagen: World Health Organization.

Johns, G. (1981). Difference score measures of organizational behavior variables: A critique. *Organizational Behavior and Human Performance* **27**, 443–63.

Jones, D. M. (1983). Noise. In G. R. J. Hockey (ed.), *Stress and fatigue in human performance*. Chichester: Wiley.

Jones, G. R. (1986). Socialization tactics, self-efficacy, and newcomers' adjustments to organizations. *Academy of Management Journal* **29**, 262–79.

Jougla, E., Bouvier-Colle, M. H., Maguin, P., Diaz-Valdes, R., and Minvielle, D. (1983). Health and employment of a female population in an urban area. *International Journal of Epidemiology* **12**, 67–76.

Kabanoff, B. (1980). Work and non-work: A review of models, methods and findings. *Psychological Bulletin* **88**, 60–77.

Kabanoff, B. and O'Brien, G. E. (1980). Work and leisure: A task attributes analysis. *Journal of Applied Psychology* **65**, 596–609.

Kabanoff, B. and O'Brien, G. E. (1982). Relationships between work and leisure attributes across occupational and sex groups in Australia. *Australian Journal of Psychology* **34**, 165–82.

Kahn, R. L. (1981). *Work and health*. New York: Wiley.

Kahn, R. L., Wolfe, D. M., Quinn, R. P., and Snoek, J. D. (1964). *Organizational stress: Studies in role conflict and ambiguity*. New York: Wiley.

Kalleberg, A. L. and Loscocco, K. A. (1983). Aging, values and rewards: Explaining age differences in job satisfaction. *American Sociological Review* **48**, 78–90.

Kammann, R. and Flett, R. (1983). Affectometer 2: A scale to measure current level of general happiness. *Australian Journal of Psychology* **35**, 259–65.

Kammann, R., Christie, D., Irwin, R., and Dixon, G. (1979). Properties of an inventory to measure happiness (and psychological health). *New Zealand Psychologist* **8**, 1–12.

Kanter, R. M. (1977). *Work and family in the United States: A critical review and agenda for research and policy.* New York: Russell Sage Foundation.

Kantowitz, B. H. and Sorkin, R. D. (1983). *Human factors: Understanding people–system relationships.* New York: Wiley.

Kanungo, R. N. (1979). The concepts of alienation and involvement revisited. *Psychological Bulletin* **86,** 119–38.

Kaplan, E. M. and Cowen, E. L. (1981). Interpersonal helping behavior of industrial foremen. *Journal of Applied Psychology* **66,** 633–8.

Karasek, R. A. (1979). Job demands, job decision latitude, and mental strain: Implications for job redesign. *Administrative Science Quarterly* **24,** 285–308.

Karasek, R. A. (1981). Job socialization and job strain: The implications of two related psychosocial mechanisms for job design. In B. Gardell and G. Johansson (eds), *Working life.* Chichester: Wiley.

Karasek, R. A., Russell, R. S., and Theorell, T. (1982). Physiology of stress and regeneration in job-related cardiovascular illness. *Journal of Human Stress* **8,** 29–42.

Karasek, R. A., Triantis, K. P., and Chaudhry, S. S. (1982). Coworker and supervisor support as moderators of associations between task characteristics and mental strain. *Journal of Occupational Behaviour* **3,** 181–200.

Karasek, R. A., Baker, D., Marxer, F., Ahlbom, A., and Theorell, T. (1981). Job decision latitude, job demands, and cardiovascular disease: A prospective study of Swedish men. *American Journal of Public Health* **71,** 694–705.

Kasl, S. V. (1979a). Changes in mental health status associated with job loss and retirement. In R. M. Rose and G. L. Klerman (eds), *Stress and mental disorder.* New York: Raven Press.

Kasl, S. V. (1979b). Mortality and the business cycle: Some questions about research strategies when utilizing macro-social and ecological data. *American Journal of Public Health* **69,** 784–8.

Kasl, S. V. (1982). Strategies of research on economic instability and health. *Psychological Medicine* **12,** 637–49.

Kasl, S. V. and Cobb, S. (1980). The experience of losing a job: Some effects on cardiovascular functioning. *Psychotherapy and Psychosomatics* **34,** 88–109.

Kasl, S. V. and Wells, J. A. (1985). Social support and health in the middle years: Work and the family. In S. Cohen and S. L. Syme (eds), *Social support and health.* Orlando: Academic Press.

Kasl, S. V., Gore, S., and Cobb, S. (1975). The experience of losing a job: Reported changes in health, symptoms and illness behavior. *Psychosomatic Medicine* **37,** 106–22.

Kauppinen-Toropainen, K., Kandolin, I., and Mutanen, P. (1983). Job dissatisfaction and work-related exhaustion in male and female work. *Journal of Occupational Behaviour* **4,** 193–207.

Kavanagh, M. J., Hurst, M. W., and Rose, R. (1981). The relationship between job satisfaction and psychiatric health symptoms for air traffic controllers. *Personnel Psychology* **34,** 691–707.

Keenan, A. and McBain, G. D. M. (1979). Effects of type A behaviour, intolerance of ambiguity, and locus of control on the relationship between role stress and work-related outcomes. *Journal of Occupational Psychology* **52,** 277–85.

Keith, P. M. and Schafer, R. B. (1980). Role strain and depression in two-job families. *Family Relations* **29,** 483–8.

Kellner, R. and Sheffield, B. F. (1973). A self-rating scale of distress. *Psychological Medicine* **3,** 88–100.

Kelly, J. E. (1982). *Scientific management, job redesign and work performance.* London: Academic Press.

Kelly, K. E. and Houston, B. K. (1985). Type A behaviour in employed women: Relation to work, marital and leisure variables, social support, stress, tension, and health. *Journal of Personality and Social Psychology* **48,** 1067–79.

Kemp, N. J., Wall, T. D., Clegg, C. W., and Cordery, J. L. (1983). Autonomous work groups in a greenfield site: A comparative study. *Journal of Occupational Psychology* **56,** 271–88.

Kendell, R. E. (1975). *The role of diagnosis in psychiatry.* Oxford: Blackwell.

Kessler, R. C. and Cleary, P. D. (1980). Social class and psychological distress. *American Sociological Review* **45,** 463–78.

Kessler, R. C. and McRae, J. A. (1981). Trends in the relationship between sex and psychological distress. *American Sociological Review* **46,** 443–52.

Kessler, R. C. and McRae, J. A. (1982). The effect of wives' employment on the mental health of married men and women. *American Sociological Review* **47,** 216–27.

Kiev, A. and Kohn, V. (1979). *Executive stress.* New York: AMACOM.

Kiggundu, M. N. (1980). An empirical test of the theory of job design using multiple job ratings. *Human Relations* **33,** 339–51.

Kilpatrick, R. and Trew, K. (1982). What unemployed men do: A Belfast sample. Paper presented to *Understanding Unemployment* Conference, Belfast.

Kilpatrick, R. and Trew, K. (1985). Life-styles and psychological well-being among unemployed men in Northern Ireland. *Journal of Occupational Psychology* **58,** 207–16.

Kiresuk, T. J. and Sherman, R. E. (1968). Goal attainment scaling: A method for evaluating comprehensive community mental health programs. *Community Mental Health Journal* **4,** 443–53.

Kirjonen, J. and Hanninen, V. (1986). Getting a better job: Antecedents and effects. *Human Relations* **39,** 503–16.

Kittel, F., Kornitzer, M., Backer, G. de, Dramaix, M., Sobolski, J., Degre, S., and Denolin, H. (1983). Type A in relation to job stress, social and bioclinical variables. *Journal of Human Stress* **9,** 37–45.

Klausen, H. and Iversen, L. (1981). *The closing of the Nordhavn shipyard.* Copenhagen: Institute for Social Medicine.

Knulst, W. and Schoonderwoerd, L. (1983). *Waar blijft de Tijd.* Rijswijk: Sociaal en Cultureel Planbureau.

Kobasa, S. C. (1979). Stressful life events, personality and health: An inquiry into hardiness. *Journal of Personality and Social Psychology* **37,** 1–11.

Kobasa, S. C. and Pucetti, M. C. (1983). Personality and social resources in stress resistance. *Journal of Personality and Social Psychology* **45,** 839–50.

Kobasa, S. C., Maddi, S. R., and Kahn, S. (1982). Hardiness and health: A prospective study. *Journal of Personality and Social Psychology* **42**, 168–77.

Kobrick, J. L. and Fine, B. J. (1983). Climate and human performance. In D. J. Oborne and M. M. Gruneberg (eds), *The physical environment at work*. Chichester: Wiley.

Koch, J. L. and Steers, R. M. (1978). Job attachment, satisfaction and turnover among public sector employees. *Journal of Vocational Behavior* **12**, 119–28.

Kohn, M. L. and Schooler, C. (1973). Occupational experience and psychological functioning: An assessment of reciprocal effects. *American Sociological Review* **38**, 97–118.

Kohn, M. L. and Schooler, C. (1978). The reciprocal effects of the substantive complexity of work and intellectual flexibility: A longitudinal assessment. *American Journal of Sociology* **84**, 24–52.

Kohn, M. L. and Schooler, C. (1982). Job conditions and personality: A longitudinal assessment of their reciprocal effects. *American Journal of Sociology* **87**, 1257–86.

Kohn, M. L. and Schooler, C. (1983). *Work and personality: An inquiry into the impact of social stratification*. Norwood, New Jersey: Ablex Publishing Corporation.

Komarovsky, M. (1940). *The unemployed man and his family*. New York: Dryden Press. (Reprinted by Arno Press, 1971.)

Kopelman, R. E., Greenhaus, J. H., and Connolly, T. F. (1983). A model of work, family, and interrole conflict: A construct validation study. *Organizational Behavior and Human Performance* **32**, 198–215.

Kornhauser, A. W. (1965). *Mental health of the industrial worker: A Detroit study*. New York: Wiley.

Krantz, D. S. and Manuck, S. B. (1984). Acute psychophysiologic reactivity and risk of cardiovascular disease: A review and methodologic critique. *Psychological Bulletin* **96**, 435–64.

Krause, N. and Markides, K. S. (1985). Employment and psychological well-being in Mexican American women. *Journal of Health and Social Behavior* **26**, 15–26.

Kreitman, N. and Platt, S. (1984). Suicide, unemployment, and domestic gas detoxification in Britain. *Journal of Epidemiology and Community Health* **38**, 1–6.

Kroemer, K. H. E. (1983). Engineering anthropometry: Work space and equipment to fit the user. In D. J. Oborne and M. M. Gruneberg (eds), *The physical environment at work*. Chichester: Wiley.

Kroes, W. (1981). Psychological job stress and worker health: A programmatic effort. In L. Levi (ed.), *Society, stress and disease* (vol. 4). Oxford: Oxford University Press.

Kyriacou, C. and Sutcliffe, J. (1978). Teacher stress: Prevalence, sources and symptoms. *British Journal of Educational Psychology* **48**, 159–67.

Lambert, M. J., Christensen, E. R., and DeJulio, S. S. (eds) (1983). *The assessment of psychotherapy outcome*. New York: Wiley.

Langer, E. J. (1983). *The psychology of control*. Beverly Hills: Sage.

Langner, T. S. (1962). A twenty-two item screening score of psychiatric symptoms indicating impairment. *Journal of Health and Social Behavior* **3**, 269–76.

LaRocco, J. M. and Jones, A. P. (1978). Co-worker and leader support as moderators of stress–strain relationships in work situations. *Journal of Applied Psychology* **63**, 629–34.

LaRocco, J. M., House, J. S., and French, J. R. P. (1980). Social support, occupational stress, and health. *Journal of Health and Social Behavior* **21**, 202–18.

Larsen, R. J., Diener, E., and Emmons, R. A. (1985). An evaluation of subjective well-being measures. *Social Indicators Research* **14**, 1–18.

Latack, J. C. (1984). Career transitions within organizations: An exploratory study of work, nonwork, and coping strategies. *Organizational Behavior and Human Performance* **34**, 296–322.

Laubli, T., Hunting, W., and Grandjean, E. (1980). Visual impairments in VDU operators related to environmental conditions. In E. Grandjean and E. Vigliani (eds), *Ergonomic aspects of visual display terminals*. London: Taylor and Francis.

Lauer, R. H. and Thomas, R. (1976). A comparative analysis of the psychological consequences of change. *Human Relations* **29**, 239–48.

Lawler, E. E. (1965). Managers' perceptions of their subordinates' pay and of their supervisors' pay. *Personnel Psychology* **18**, 413–22.

Lawler, E. E. (1971). *Pay and organizational effectiveness*. New York: McGraw-Hill.

Lawlis, G. F. (1971). Motivational factors reflecting employment instability. *Journal of Social Psychology* **84**, 215–23.

Layton, C. (1985). Change-scores on the GHQ and derived sub-scales for male school-leavers with subsequent differing work status. *Personality and Individual Differences* **7**, 419–22.

Layton, C. (1986). Employment, unemployment, and response to the General Health Questionnaire. *Psychological Reports* **58**, 807–10.

Lazarus, R. S. (1975). The healthy personality: A review of conceptualizations and research. In L. Levi (ed.), *Society, stress and disease* (vol. 2). Oxford: Oxford University Press.

Lazarus, R. S. and Folkman, S. (1984). *Stress, appraisal, and coping*. New York: Springer.

Lee, R. and Wilbur, E. R. (1985). Age, education, job tenure, salary, job characteristics, and job satisfaction: A multivariate analysis. *Human Relations* **38**, 781–91.

Lefcourt, H. M. (1982). *Locus of control: Current trends in theory and research* (2nd edn). Hillsdale: Erlbaum.

Lefkowitz, J. and Brigando, L. (1980). The redundancy of work alienation and job satisfaction: Some evidence of convergent and discriminant validity. *Journal of Vocational Behavior* **16**, 115–31.

Leventman, P. G. (1981). *Professionals out of work*. New York: Free Press.

Levi, L., Brenner, S. O., Hall, E. M., Hjelm, R., Salovaara, H., Arnetz, B., and Pettersson, I. L. (1984). The psychological, social, and biochemical impacts of unemployment in Sweden. *International Journal of Mental Health* **13**, 18–34.

Levinson, H. (1964). *Emotional health in the world of work.* New York: Harper and Row.

Lewin, K., Dembo, T., Festinger, L., and Sears, P. S. (1944). Level of aspiration. In J. McV. Hunt (ed.), *Personality and behavior disorders.* New York: Ronald Press.

Lewis, A. (1967). *The state of psychiatry: Essays and addresses.* London: Routledge and Kegan Paul.

Liem, R. and Liem, J. (1978). Social class and mental illness reconsidered: The role of economic stress and social support. *Journal of Health and Social Behavior* **19**, 139–56.

Liff, S. (1981). Mental health of women factory workers. *Journal of Occupational Behaviour* **2**, 139–46.

Liker, J. K. and Elder, G. H. (1983). Economic hardship and marital relations in the 1930s. *American Sociological Review* **48**, 343–59.

Liles, D. H., Deivanayagam, S., Ayoub, M. M., and Mahajan, P. (1984). A job severity index for the evaluation and control of lifting injury. *Human Factors* **26**, 683–93.

Lin, N. and Ensel, W. M. (1984). Depression-mobility and its social etiology: The role of life-events and social support. *Journal of Health and Social Behavior* **25**, 176–88.

Linn, M. W., Sandifer, R., and Stein, S. (1985). Effects of unemployment on mental and physical health. *American Journal of Public Health* **75**, 502–6.

Locke, E. A., Shaw, K. N., Saari, L. M., and Latham, G. P. (1981). Goal setting and task performance: 1969–1980. *Psychological Bulletin* **90**, 125–52.

Lodahl, T. and Kejner, M. (1965). The definition and measurement of job involvement. *Journal of Applied Psychology* **49**, 24–33.

Loevinger, J. (1980). *Ego development: Conceptions and theories.* San Francisco: Jossey-Bass.

Loher, B. T., Noe, R. A., Moeller, N. L., and Fitzgerald, M. P. (1985). A meta-analysis of the relation of job characteristics to job satisfaction. *Journal of Applied Psychology* **70**, 280–9.

Long, J. (1987). Cognitive ergonomics and human-computer interaction. In P. B. Warr (ed.), *Psychology at work* (3rd edn). Harmondsworth: Penguin.

Lott, A. J. and Lott, B. E. (1965). Group cohesiveness as interpersonal attraction. *Psychological Bulletin* **64**, 259–309.

Louis, M. R. (1980a). Surprise and sense-making: What newcomers experience in entering unfamiliar organizational settings. *Administrative Science Quarterly* **25**, 226–51.

Louis, M. R. (1980b). Career transitions: Varieties and commonalities. *Academy of Management Review* **5**, 329–40.

Louis, M. R. (1982). Career transitions: A missing link in career development. *Organizational Dynamics* **10**, 68–77.

Lubin, B. (1965). Adjective checklists for the measurement of depression. *Archives of General Psychiatry* **12**, 57–62.

Lundberg, U. and Frankenhaeuser, M. (1980). Pituitary–adrenal and sympathetic–adrenal correlates of distress and effort. *Journal of Psychosomatic Research* **24**, 125–30.

Lupton, T. (1963). *On the shop floor*. Oxford: Pergamon Press.

Lyons, T. F. (1971). Role clarity, need for clarity, satisfaction, tension, and withdrawal. *Organizational Behavior and Human Performance* **6**, 99–110.

Mackay, C. J. (1980). The measurement of mood and psychophysiological activity using self-report techniques. In I. Martin and P. H. Venables (eds), *Techniques in psychopharmacology*. Chichester: Wiley.

Madge, N. (1983). Unemployment and its effects on children. *Journal of Child Psychology and Psychiatry* **24**, 311–19.

Manpower Services Commission (1984). *Labour Market Quarterly Report, February 1984*. Sheffield: MSC.

Mansfield, R. (1972). The initiation of graduates in industry. *Human Relations* **25**, 77–86.

Margolis, L. H. and Farran, D. C. (1984). Unemployment and children. *International Journal of Mental Health* **13**, 107–24.

Markham, S. E. (1985). An investigation of the relationship between unemployment and absenteeism: A multi-level approach. *Academy of Management Journal* **28**, 228–34.

Marshall, G. (1982). *In search of the spirit of capitalism: An essay on Max Weber's Protestant ethic thesis*. London: Hutchinson.

Marshall, J. R. and Funch, D. P. (1979). 'Mental Illness and the Economy': A critique and partial replication. *Journal of Health and Social Behavior* **20**, 282–9.

Marshall, J. R. and Funch, D. P. (1980). (Reply to Ratcliff.) *Journal of Health and Social Behavior* **21**, 391–3.

Martin, J. and Roberts, C. (1984). *Women and employment: A lifetime perspective*. London: HMSO.

Martin, R. and Wallace, J. (1985). Women and unemployment: Activities and social contact. In B. Roberts, R. Finnegan, and D. Gallie (eds), *New approaches to economic life*. Manchester: Manchester University Press.

Martin, T. N. (1984). Role stress and inability to leave as predictors of mental health. *Human Relations* **37**, 969–83.

Maslach, C. and Jackson, S. E. (1981). The measurement of experienced burnout. *Journal of Occupational Behaviour* **2**, 99–113.

Maslach, C. and Jackson, S. E. (1984). Burnout in organizational settings. In S. Oskamp (ed.), *Applied social psychology annual* (vol. 5). Beverly Hills: Sage.

Maslow, A. H. (1943). A theory of human motivation. *Psychological Review* **50**, 370–96.

Maslow, A. H. (1973). *The farther reaches of human nature*. Harmondsworth: Penguin.

Matthews, K. A. (1982). Psychological perspectives on the type A behavior pattern. *Psychological Bulletin* **91**, 293–323.

May, R. (1967). *Psychology and the human dilemma*. Princeton: Van Nostrand.

McDougall, W. (1932). *The energies of man*. London: Methuen.

McDowell, I. and Praught, E. (1982). On the measurement of happiness. *American Journal of Epidemiology* **116,** 949–58.

McEnrue, M. P. (1984). Perceived competence as a moderator of the relationship between role clarity and job performance: A test of two hypotheses. *Organizational Behavior and Human Performance* **34,** 379–86.

McGehee, W. and Tullar, W. L. (1979). Single-question measures of overall job satisfaction: A comment on Quinn, Staines, and McCullough. *Journal of Vocational Behavior* **14,** 112–17.

McGuire, W. J. (1983). A contextualist theory of knowledge: Its implications for innovation and reform in psychological research. In L. Berkowitz (ed.), *Advances in experimental social psychology* (vol. 16). New York: Academic Press.

McKee, L. and Bell, C. (1985). Marital and family relations in times of male unemployment. In B. Roberts, R. Finnegan, and D. Gallie (eds), *New approaches to economic life*. Manchester: Manchester University Press.

McLean, A. (1981). Therapeutic and preventive occupational mental health activities in industrialized societies. In L. Levi (ed.), *Society, stress and disease* (vol. 4). Oxford: Oxford University Press.

McPherson, A. and Hall, W. (1983). Psychiatric impairment, physical health and work values among unemployed and apprenticed young men. *Australian and New Zealand Journal of Psychiatry* **17,** 335–40.

Megaw, E. D. and Bellamy, L. J. (1983). Illumination at work. In D. J. Oborne and M. M. Gruneberg (eds), *The physical environment at work*. Chichester: Wiley.

Meier, S. T. (1984). The construct validity of burnout. *Journal of Occupational Psychology* **57,** 211–19.

Mellinger, G. D., Balter, M. B., Uhlenhuth, E. H., Cisin, I. H., Manheimer, D. I., and Rickels, K. (1983). Evaluating a household measure of psychic distress. *Psychological Medicine* **13,** 607–21.

Melville, D. I., Hope, D., Bennison, D., and Barraclough, B. (1985). Depression among men made involuntarily redundant. *Psychological Medicine* **15,** 789–93.

Merton, R. (1957). *Social theory and social structure*. Glencoe: Free Press.

Michael, P. L. and Bienvenue, G. R. (1983). Industrial noise and man. In D. J. Oborne and M. M. Gruneberg (eds), *The physical environment at work*. Chichester: Wiley.

Miles, I. (1983). Adaptation to unemployment? University of Sussex, Science Policy Research Unit Report.

Miles, I., Howard, J., and Henwood, F. (1984). Dependence, interdependence and changing work roles. University of Sussex, Science Policy Research Unit Report.

Miles, R. H. (1975). An empirical test of causal inference between role perceptions of conflict and ambiguity and various personal outcomes. *Journal of Applied Psychology* **60,** 334–9.

Miller, G. A., Galanter, E., and Pribram, K. H. (1960). *Plans and the structure of behavior*. New York: Holt, Rinehart and Winston.

Miller, H. E. and Terborg, J. R. (1979). Job attitudes of part-time and full-time employees. *Journal of Applied Psychology* **64,** 380–6.

Miller, J., Schooler, C., Kohn, M. L., and Miller, K. A. (1979). Women and work: The psychological effects of occupational conditions. *American Journal of Sociology* **85**, 66–94.

Miller, S. M. (1981). Predictability and human stress. In L. Berkowitz (ed.), *Advances in experimental social psychology* (vol. 14). New York: Academic Press.

Millward, N. (1972). Piecework earnings and workers' controls. *Human Relations* **25**, 351–76.

Moch, M. (1980). Job involvement, internal motivation, and employees' integration into networks of work relationships. *Organizational Behavior and Human Performance* **25**, 15–31.

Moen, P. (1979). Family impacts of the 1975 depression: Duration of unemployment. *Journal of Marriage and the Family* **41**, 561–72.

Moen, P., Kain, E. L., and Elder, G. H. (1982). Economic conditions and family life: Contemporary and historical perspectives. In R. R. Nelson and F. Skidmore (eds), *American families and the economy*. Washington: National Academy Press.

Morris, L. D. (1984a). Redundancy and patterns of household finance. *Sociological Review* **32**, 492–523.

Morris, L. D. (1984b). Patterns of social activity and post-redundancy labour-market experience. *Sociology* **18**, 339–52.

Morse, J. J. (1975). Person–job congruence and individual adjustment and development. *Human Relations* **28**, 841–61.

Morse, J. J. (1976). Sense of competence and individual managerial performance. *Psychological Reports* **38**, 1195–8.

Mortimer, J. T. and Finch, M. D. (1986). The development of self-esteem in the early work career. *Work and Occupations* **13**, 217–39.

Mortimer, J. T. and Lorence, J. (1979). Occupational experience and the self-concept: A longitudinal study. *Social Psychology Quarterly* **42**, 307–23.

Moser, K. A., Fox, A. J., and Jones, D. R. (1984). Unemployment and mortality in the OPCS longitudinal study. *The Lancet* **2**, 1324–9.

Moser, K. A., Fox, A. J., Jones, D. R., and Goldblatt, P. O. (1986). Unemployment and mortality: Further evidence from the OPCS longitudinal study. *The Lancet* **1**, 365–7.

Mostow, E. and Newberry, P. (1975). Work role and depression in women: A comparison of workers and housewives in treatment. *American Journal of Orthopsychiatry* **45**, 538–48.

Mottaz, C. J. (1981). Some determinants of work alienation. *Sociological Quarterly* **22**, 515–29.

Mottaz, C. J. (1984). Education and work satisfaction. *Human Relations* **37**, 985–1004.

Mottaz, C. J. (1986). Gender differences in work satisfaction, work-related rewards and values, and the determinants of work satisfaction. *Human Relations* **39**, 359–78.

Mowday, R. T., Steers, R. M., and Porter, L. W. (1979). The measurement of organizational commitment. *Journal of Vocational Behavior* **14**, 224–47.

Murgatroyd, S. and Apter, M. J. (1984). Eclectic psychotherapy: A structural–phenomenological approach. In W. Dryden (ed.), *Individual therapy in Britain*. London: Harper and Row.

Murray, H. (1938). *Explorations in personality*. Oxford: Oxford University Press.

Myers, C. S. (1920). *Mind and work*. London: University of London Press.

Myers, J. K., Lindenthal, J. J., Pepper, M. P., and Ostrander, D. R. (1972). Life events and mental status: A longitudinal study. *Journal of Health and Social Behavior* **13**, 398–406.

Narendranathan, W., Nickell, S., and Metcalf, D. (1982). *An investigation into the incidence and dynamic structure of sickness and unemployment in Britain, 1965–1975*. London: Centre for Labour Economics.

Near, J. P., Rice, R. W., and Hunt, R. G. (1980). The relationship between work and non-work domains: A review of empirical research. *Academy of Management Review* **5**, 415–29.

Nerell, G. and Wahlund, I. (1981). Stressors and strain in white-collar workers. In L. Levi (ed.), *Society, stress and disease* (vol. 4). Oxford: Oxford University Press.

Nezu, A. M. (1985). Differences in psychological distress between effective and ineffective problem solvers. *Journal of Counseling Psychology* **32**, 135–8.

Nicholson, N. (1976). The role of the shop steward: An empirical case study. *Industrial Relations Journal* **7**(1), 15–26.

Nicholson, N. (1984). A theory of work–role transitions. *Administrative Science Quarterly* **29**, 172–91.

Nieva, V. F. and Gutek, B. A. (1981). *Women and work*. New York: Praeger.

Norris, D. R. and Niebuhr, R. E. (1984). Attributional influences on the job performance–job satisfaction relationship. *Academy of Management Journal* **27**, 424–31.

Nygard, R. (1981). Toward an interactional psychology: Models from achievement motivation research. *Journal of Personality* **49**, 363–87.

Oborne, D. J. (1983). Vibration at work. In D. J. Oborne and M. M. Gruneberg (eds), *The physical environment at work*. Chichester: Wiley.

O'Brien, G. E. (1980). The centrality of skill-utilization for job design. In K. D. Duncan, M. M. Gruneberg, and D. Wallis (eds), *Changes in working life*. Chichester: Wiley.

O'Brien, G. E. (1982a). Evaluation of the job characteristics theory of work attitudes and performance. *Australian Journal of Psychology* **34**, 383–401.

O'Brien, G. E. (1982b). The relative contribution of perceived skill-utilization and other perceived job attributes to the prediction of job satisfaction: A cross-validation study. *Human Relations* **35**, 219–37.

O'Brien, G. E. (1983). Skill-utilization, skill-variety and the job characteristics model. *Australian Journal of Psychology* **35**, 461–8.

O'Brien, G. E. (1984a). Reciprocal effects between locus of control and job attributes. *Australian Journal of Psychology* **36**, 57–74.

O'Brien, G. E. (1984b). Locus of control, work and retirement. In H. Lefcourt (ed.), *Research with the locus of control construct* (vol. 3). New York: Academic Press.

O'Brien, G. E. (1985). Distortion in unemployment research: The early studies of Bakke and their implications for current research on employment and unemployment. *Human Relations* **38**, 877–94.

O'Brien, G. E. and Dowling, P. (1980). The effects of congruency between perceived and desired job attributes upon job satisfaction. *Journal of Occupational Psychology* **53**, 121–30.

O'Brien, G. E. and Kabanoff, B. (1979). Comparison of unemployed and employed workers on work values, locus of control, and health variables. *Australian Psychologist* **14**, 143–54.

Oldham, G. R. and Brass, D. J. (1979). Employee reactions to an open-plan office: A naturally occurring quasi-experiment. *Administrative Science Quarterly* **24**, 267–84.

Oldham, G. R. and Rotchford, N. L. (1983). Relationships between office characteristics and employee reactions: A study of the physical environment. *Administrative Science Quarterly* **28**, 542–56.

Oldham, G. R., Hackman, J. R., and Pearce, J. L. (1976). Conditions under which employees respond positively to enriched work. *Journal of Applied Psychology* **61**, 395–403.

Oldham, G. R., Hackman, J. R., and Stepina, L. P. (1978). *Norms for the Job Diagnostic Survey*. New Haven: Yale University School of Organization and Management.

Organization for Economic Co-operation and Development (1984). *OECD employment outlook*. Paris: OECD.

Organization for Economic Co-operation and Development (1985). *The integration of women into the economy*. Paris: OECD.

Ormel, J. (1983). Neuroticism and well-being inventories: Measuring traits or states? *Psychological Medicine* **13**, 165–76.

Overall, J. E. and Zisook, S. (1980). Diagnosis and phenomenology of depressive disorders. *Journal of Consulting and Clinical Psychology* **48**, 626–34.

Pahl, R. E. (1984). *Divisions of labour*. Oxford: Blackwell.

Parker, D. F. and DeCotiis, T. A. (1983). Organizational determinants of job stress. *Organizational Behavior and Human Performance* **32**, 160–77.

Parker, S. (1983). *Leisure and work*. London: Allen and Unwin.

Parkes, K. R. (1982). Occupational stress among student nurses: A natural experiment. *Journal of Applied Psychology* **67**, 784–96.

Parkes, K. R. (1984). Locus of control, cognitive appraisal, and coping in stressful episodes. *Journal of Personality and Social Psychology* **46**, 655–68.

Parry, G. (1986). Paid employment, life events, social support and mental health in working-class mothers. *Journal of Health and Social Behavior* **27**, 193–208.

Parry, G. and Warr, P. B. (1980). The measurement of mothers' work attitudes. *Journal of Occupational Psychology* **53**, 245–52.

Patton, M. J., Connor, G. E., and Scott, K. J. (1982). Kohut's psychology of the self: Theory and measures of counseling outcome. *Journal of Counseling Psychology* **29**, 268–82.

Patton, W. and Noller, P. (1984). Unemployment and youth: A longitudinal study. *Australian Journal of Psychology* **36**, 399–413.

Payne, R. L. and Fletcher, B. C. (1983). Job demands, supports and constraints as predictors of psychological strain among schoolteachers. *Journal of Vocational Behavior* **22**, 136–47.

Payne, R. L. and Jones, J. G. (1986). Measurement and methodological issues in social support. In S. Kasl and C. L. Cooper (eds), *Stress and health.* Chichester: Wiley.

Payne, R. L. and Jones, J. G. (1987). Social class and re-employment: Change in health and perceived financial circumstances. *Journal of Occupational Behaviour,* in press.

Payne, R. L. and Rick, J. T. (1985). Psychobiological markers of stress in surgeons and anaesthetists. In T. D. Dembrowski, T. H. Schmidt, and C. Blumschen (eds), *Biobehavioural factors in coronary heart disease.* Basel: Karger.

Payne, R. L., Warr, P. B., and Hartley, J. (1984). Social class and psychological ill-health during unemployment. *Sociology of Health and Illness* **6**, 152–74.

Pearlin, L. I. and Lieberman, M. A. (1979). Social sources of emotional distress. *Research in Community and Mental Health* **1**, 217–48.

Pearlin, L. I. and Schooler, C. (1978). The structure of coping. *Journal of Health and Social Behavior* **19**, 2–21.

Pearlin, L. I., Menaghan, E. G., Lieberman, M. A., and Mullan, J. T. (1981). The stress process. *Journal of Health and Social Behavior* **22**, 337–56.

Petty, M. M., McGee, G. W., and Cavender, J. W. (1984). A meta-analysis of the relationships between individual job satisfaction and individual performance. *Academy of Management Review* **9**, 712–21.

Phares, E. J. (1976). *Locus of control in personality.* Morristown: General Learning Press.

Pichot, P. and Olivier-Martin, R. (eds) (1974). *Psychological measurements in psychopharmacology.* Basel: Karger.

Pierce, J. L. and Dunham, R. B. (1978). The measurement of perceived job characteristics: The Job Diagnostic Survey versus the Job Characteristics Inventory. *Academy of Management Journal* **21**, 123–8.

Pinder, C. C. (1981). The role of transfers and mobility experiences in employee motivation and control. In H. Meltzer and W. R. Nord (eds), *Making organizations humane and productive.* New York: Wiley.

Pines, A. M. and Kafry, D. (1981). Tedium in the life and work of professional women as compared with men. *Sex Roles* **7**, 963–77.

Pines, A. M., Aronson, E., and Kafry, D. (1981). *Burnout: From tedium to personal growth.* New York: Free Press.

Piotrkowski, C. S. (1978). *Work and the family system.* New York: The Free Press.

Plant, M. A., Peck, D. F., and Samuel, E. (1985). *Alchohol, drugs, and school-leavers.* London: Tavistock.

Platt, S. (1984). Unemployment and suicidal behaviour: A review of the literature. *Social Science and Medicine* **19**, 93–115.

Platt, S. and Kreitman, N. (1985). Parasuicide and unemployment among men in Edinburgh 1968–1982. *Psychological Medicine* **15**, 113–23.

Pleck, J. H., Staines, G. L., and Lang, L. (1980). Conflicts between work and family life. *Monthly Labor Review* **103**(3), 29–32.

Poulton, E. C. (1978). Blue-collar stressors. In C. L. Cooper and R. L. Payne (eds), *Stress at work*. Chichester: Wiley.

Privette, G. (1983). Peak experience, peak performance, and flow: A comparative analysis of positive human experiences. *Journal of Personality and Social Psychology* **45**, 1361–8.

Quinn, R. P. and Mandilovitch, M. S. B. (1980). Education and job satisfaction, 1962–1977. *Vocational Guidance Quarterly* **29**, 100–11.

Quinn, R. P. and Shepard, L. J. (1974). *The 1972–73 quality of employment survey*. Ann Arbor, Michigan: Institute for Social Research.

Quinn, R. P. and Staines, G. L. (1979). *The 1977 quality of employment survey*. Ann Arbor, Michigan: Institute for Social Research.

Radloff, L. S. (1975). Sex differences in depression: The effects of occupation and marital status. *Sex Roles* **1**, 249–65.

Radloff, L. S. (1977). The CES-D Scale: A self-report depression scale for research in the general population. *Applied Psychological Measurement* **1**, 385–401.

Rainwater, L. (1974). *What money buys: Inequality and the social meanings of income*. New York: Basic Books.

Ramsey, J. D. (1983). Heat and cold. In G. R. J. Hockey (ed.), *Stress and fatigue in human performance*. Chichester: Wiley.

Rapoport, R. and Rapoport, R. (1978). *Working couples*. London: Routledge and Kegan Paul.

Ratcliff, K. S. (1980). On Marshall and Funch's critique of 'Mental illness and the economy'. *Journal of Health and Social Behavior* **21**, 389–91.

Rathkey, P. (1985). Work sharing: Flawed fallacy or rational response? In G. Fragnière (ed.), *The future of work*. Assen: Van Gorcum.

Renshaw, J. R. (1976). An exploration of the dynamics of the overlapping worlds of work and family. *Family Process* **15**, 143–65.

Reynolds, V., Jenner, D. A., Palmer, C. D., and Harrison, G. A. (1981). Catecholamine excretion rates in relation to life-styles in the male population of Otmoor, Oxfordshire. *Annals of Human Biology* **8**, 197–209.

Rhodes, S. R. (1983). Age-related differences in work attitudes and behavior: A review and conceptual analysis. *Psychological Bulletin* **93**, 328–67.

Rice, R. W. (1984). Organizational work and the overall quality of life. In S. Oskamp (ed.), *Applied social psychology annual* (vol. 5). Beverly Hills: Sage.

Rizzo, J. R., House, R. J., and Lirtzman, S. I. (1970). Role conflict and ambiguity in complex organizations. *Administrative Science Quarterly* **15**, 150–63.

Roberts, K. H. and Glick, W. (1981). The job characteristics approach to task design: A critical review. *Journal of Applied Psychology* **66**, 193–217.

Roberts, K., Duggan, J., and Noble, M. (1982). Out-of-school youth in high unemployment areas: An empirical investigation. *British Journal of Guidance and Counselling* **10**, 1–11.

Roberts, R. E. and O'Keefe, S. J. (1981). Sex differences in depression re-examined. *Journal of Health and Social Behavior* **22**, 394–400.

Rosenberg, M. (1965). *Society and the adolescent self-image*. Princeton: Princeton University Press.

Ross, C. E. and Huber, J. (1985). Hardship and depression. *Journal of Health and Social Behavior* **26,** 312–27.

Ross, C. E., Mirowsky, J., and Huber, J. (1983). Dividing work, sharing work, and in-between: Marriage patterns and depression. *American Sociological Review* **48,** 809–23.

Rosse, J. G. and Hulin, C. L. (1985). Adaptation to work: An analysis of employee health, withdrawal and change. *Organizational Behavior and Human Decision Processes* **36,** 324–47.

Rotter, J. B. (1966). Generalized expectancies for internal versus external control of reinforcement. *Psychological Monographs* **80,** 1–28.

Roy, A. (1981). Vulnerability factors and depression in men. *British Journal of Psychiatry* **138,** 75–7.

Roy, D. F. (1952). Quota restriction and goldbricking in a machine shop. *American Journal of Sociology* **67,** 427–42.

Roy, D. F. (1960). 'Banana time', job satisfaction and informal interaction. *Human Organization* **18,** 158–68.

Russell, J. A. (1979). Affective space is bipolar. *Journal of Personality and Social Psychology* **37,** 345–56.

Russell, J. A. (1980). A circumplex model of affect. *Journal of Personality and Social Psychology* **39,** 1161–78.

Russell, J. A. (1983). Pancultural aspects of the human conceptual organization of emotions. *Journal of Personality and Social Psychology* **45,** 1281–8.

Russell, J. A. and Ridgeway, D. (1983). Dimensions underlying children's emotion concepts. *Developmental Psychology* **19,** 795–804.

Salvendy, G. (1981). Classification and characteristics of paced work. In G. Salvendy and M. J. Smith (eds), *Machine pacing and occupational stress.* London: Taylor and Francis.

Schlozman, K. L. and Verba, S. (1979). *Injury to insult: Class and political response.* Cambridge, Massachusetts: Harvard University Press.

Schneider, B. (1983). Interactional psychology and organizational behavior. In L. L. Cummings and B. M. Staw (eds), *Research in organizational behavior* (vol. 5). Greenwich, Connecticut: JAI Press.

Schriesheim, C. A. and Murphy, C. J. (1976). Relationships between leader behavior and subordinate satisfaction and performance: A test of some situational moderators. *Journal of Applied Psychology* **61,** 634–41.

Schuler, R. S., Aldag, R. J., and Brief, A. P. (1977). Role conflict and ambiguity: A scale analysis. *Organizational Behavior and Human Performance* **20,** 111–28.

Schwab, D. P. and Wallace, M. J. (1974). Correlates of employee satisfaction with pay. *Industrial Relations* **13,** 78–89.

Schwefel, D., John, J., Potthof, P., and Hechler, A. (1984). Unemployment and mental health: Perspectives from the Federal Republic of Germany. *International Journal of Mental Health* **13,** 35–50.

Seabrook, J. (1982). *Unemployment.* London: Quartet Books.

Seeman, M. (1959). On the meaning of alienation. *American Sociological Review* **24,** 783–91.

Seeman, M. and Anderson, C. S. (1983). Alienation and alcohol: The role of work, mastery, and community in drinking behavior. *American Sociological Review* **48**, 60–77.

Seers, A., McGee, G. W., Serey, T. T., and Graen, G. B. (1983). The interaction of job stress and social support: A strong inference investigation. *Academy of Management Journal* **26**, 273–84.

Sekaran, U. (1985). The paths to mental health: An exploratory study of husbands and wives in dual-career families. *Journal of Occupational Psychology* **58**, 129–37.

Seligman, M. E. P. (1975). *Helplessness: On depression, development, and death.* San Francisco: Freeman.

Senior, B. and Naylor, J. B. (1984). A skills exchange for unemployed people. *Human Relations* **37**, 589–602.

Shackleton, V. J. (1981). Boredom and repetitive work: A review. *Personnel Review* **10**(4), 30–6.

Shamir, B. (1983). Some antecedents of work-nonwork conflict. *Journal of Vocational Behavior* **23**, 98–111.

Shamir, B. (1986). Protestant work ethic, work involvement and the psychological impact of unemployment. *Journal of Occupational Behaviour* **7**, 25–38.

Shapiro, D. A., Parry, G., and Brewin, C. R. (1979). Stress, coping and psychotherapy: The foundations of a clinical approach. In C. Mackay and T. Cox (eds), *Response to stress: Occupational aspects.* Guildford: International Publishing Corporation.

Shaw, J. B. and Riskind, J. H. (1983). Predicting job stress using data from the Position Analysis Questionnaire. *Journal of Applied Psychology* **68**, 253–61.

Shehan, C. L. (1984). Wives' work and psychological well-being: An extension of Gove's social role theory of depression. *Sex Roles* **11**, 881–99.

Shepard, J. M. (1972). Alienation as a process: Work as a case in point. *The Sociological Quarterly* **13**, 161–73.

Shepherd, D. M. and Barraclough, B. M. (1980). Work and suicide: An empirical investigation. *British Journal of Psychiatry* **136**, 469–78.

Sheppard, H. L. and Belitsky, A. H. (1966). *The job hunt: Job-seeking behavior of unemployed workers in a local economy.* Baltimore: Johns Hopkins Press.

Shostrom, E. L. (1964). An inventory for the measurement of self-actualization. *Educational and Psychological Measurement* **24**, 207–18.

Sims, H. P. and Szilagyi, A. D. (1976). Job characteristic relationships: Individual and structural moderators. *Organizational Behavior and Human Performance* **17**, 211–30.

Sims, H. P., Szilagyi, A. D., and Keller, R. T. (1976). The measurement of job characteristics. *Academy of Management Journal* **19**, 195–212.

Smart, R. G. (1979). Drinking problems among employed, unemployed and shift workers. *Journal of Occupational Medicine* **11**, 731–6.

Smith, D. J. (1980). How unemployment makes the poor poorer. *Policy Studies* **1**, 20–6.

Smith, F. J. (1976). Index of Organizational Reactions, (IOR). *JSAS Catalog of Selected Documents in Psychology* 6, 54, No. 1265.

Smith, M. B. (1968). Competence and 'mental health': Problems in conceptualizing human effectiveness. In S. B. Sells (ed.), *The definition and measurement of mental health*. Washington: Department of Health, Education and Welfare.

Smith, M. J. (1985). Machine-paced work and stress. In C. L. Cooper and M. J. Smith (eds), *Job stress and blue-collar work*. Chichester: Wiley.

Smith, M. J., Cohen, B. G. F., Stammerjohn, L. W., and Happ, A. (1981). An investigation of health complaints and job stress in video display operators. *Human Factors* **23**, 387–400.

Smith, P. C. (1955). The prediction of individual differences in susceptibility to industrial monotony. *Journal of Applied Psychology* **39**, 322–9.

Smith, P. C. and Lem, C. (1955). Positive aspects of motivation in repetitive work: Effects of lot size upon spacing of voluntary work stoppages. *Journal of Applied Psychology* **39**, 330–3.

Smith, P. C., Kendall, L. M., and Hulin, C. L. (1969). *The measurement of satisfaction in work and retirement*. Chicago: Rand-McNally.

Snaith, R. R., Bridge, G. W. K., and Hamilton, M. (1976). The Leeds scales for the self-assessment of anxiety and depression. *British Journal of Psychiatry* **128**, 156–65.

Sorensen, G., Pirie, P., Folsom, A., Luepker, R., Jacobs, D., and Gillum, R. (1985). Sex differences in the relationship between work and health: The Minnesota Heart Survey. *Journal of Health and Social Behavior* **26**, 379–94.

Sorge, A., Hartmann, G., Warner, M., and Nicholas, I. J. (1983). *Micro-electronics and manpower in manufacturing*. Aldershot: Gower.

South, S. J. (1985). Economic conditions and the divorce rate: A time-series analysis of the post-war United States. *Journal of Marriage and the Family* **47**, 31–41.

Spector, P. E. (1982). Behavior in organizations as a function of employee's locus of control. *Psychological Bulletin* **91**, 482–97.

Spector, P. E. (1985). Higher-order need strength as a moderator of the job scope–employee outcome relationship: A meta-analysis. *Journal of Occupational Psychology* **58**, 119–27.

Spielberger, C. D., Gorsuch, R. L., and Lushene, R. E. (1970). *Manual for the State-Trait Anxiety Inventory*. Palo Alto, California: Consulting Psychologists Press.

Spruit, I. P. (1982). Unemployment and health in macro-social analysis. *Social Science and Medicine* **16**, 1903–17.

Spruit, I. P., Bastiaansen, J., Verkley, H., van Niewenhuijzen, M. G., and Stolk, J. (1985). *Experiencing unemployment, financial constraints and health*. Leiden: Institute of Social Medicine.

Stack, S. (1981). Divorce and suicide: A time-series analysis, 1933–1970. *Journal of Family Issues* **2**, 77–90.

Stack, S. and Haas, A. (1984). The effect of unemployment duration on national suicide rates: A time series analysis, 1948–1982. *Sociological Focus* **17**, 17–29.

Stafford, E. M., Jackson, P. R., and Banks, M. H. (1980). Employment, work involvement and mental health in less qualified young people. *Journal of Occupational Psychology* **53**, 291–304.

Staines, G. L. (1980). Spillover versus compensation: A review of the literature on the relationship between work and nonwork. *Human Relations* **33**, 111–29.

Staines, G. L. and Pleck, J. H. (1983). *The impact of work schedules on the family.* Ann Arbor: Institute for Social Research.

Staines, G. L. and Pleck, J. H. (1984). Nonstandard work schedules and family life. *Journal of Applied Psychology* **69**, 515–23.

Staw, B. M. and Ross, J. (1985). Stability in the midst of change: A dispositional approach to job attitudes. *Journal of Applied Psychology* **70**, 469–80.

Staw, B. M., Bell, N. E., and Clausen, J. A. (1986). The dispositional approach to job attitudes: A lifetime longitudinal test. *Administrative Science Quarterly* **31**, 56–77.

Steinberg, L. D., Catalano, R., and Dooley, D. (1981). Economic antecedents of child abuse and neglect. *Child Development* **52**, 975–85.

Stern, G. G. (1970). *People in context: Measuring person–environment congruence in education and industry.* New York: Wiley.

Stogdill, R. M. (1963). *Manual for the Leader Behavior Description Questionnaire, Form 12.* Columbus: Ohio State University.

Stokes, G. (1983). Work, unemployment and leisure. *Leisure Studies* **2**, 269–86.

Stokes, G. and Cochrane, R. (1984a). The relationship between national levels of unemployment and the rate of admission to mental hospitals in England and Wales, 1950–1976. *Social Psychiatry* **19**, 117–25.

Stokes, G. and Cochrane, R. (1984b). A study of the psychological effects of redundancy and unemployment. *Journal of Occupational Psychology,* **57**, 309–22.

Stone, E. F. and Gueutal, H. G. (1985). An empirical derivation of the dimensions along which characteristics of jobs are perceived. *Academy of Management Journal* **28**, 376–96.

Stone, E. F. and Porter, L. W. (1975). Job characteristics and job attitudes: A multivariate study. *Journal of Applied Psychology* **60**, 57–64.

Strupp, H. H. and Hadley, S. W. (1977). A tripartite model of mental health and therapeutic outcomes. *American Psychologist* **32**, 187–96.

Sutton, R. I. (1984). Job stress among primary and secondary schoolteachers. *Work and Occupations* **11**, 7–28.

Swinburne, P. (1981). The psychological impact of unemployment on managers and professional staff. *Journal of Occupational Psychology* **54**, 47–64.

Sykes, A. J. M. (1976). Overtime, false returns, and restrictive practices: The perception of an industrial pay system. *Human Relations* **29**, 1083–101.

Szalai, A. (ed.) (1972). *The use of time: Daily activities of urban and suburban populations in twelve countries.* The Hague: Mouton.

Szasz, T. S. (1961). *The myth of mental illness.* New York: Harper and Row.

Szasz, T. S. (1983). Mental illness as strategy. In P. Bean (ed.), *Mental illness: Changes and trends.* Chichester: Wiley.

Szilagyi, A. D. and Holland, W. E. (1980). Changes in social density: Relationships with functional interaction and perceptions of job characteristics, role stress, and work satisfaction. *Journal of Applied Psychology* **65**, 28–33.

Taber, T. D., Beehr, T. A., and Walsh, J. T. (1985). Relationships between job evaluation ratings and self-ratings of job characteristics. *Organizational Behavior and Human Decision Processes* **35**, 27–45.

Terkel, S. (1972). *Working: People talk about what they feel about what they do*. New York: Pantheon Books.

Tharenou, P. (1979). Employee self-esteem: A review of the literature. *Journal of Vocational Behavior* **15**, 316–46.

Tharenou, P. and Harker, P. (1982). Organizational correlates of employee self-esteem. *Journal of Applied Psychology* **67**, 797–805.

Tharenou, P. and Harker, P. (1984). Moderating influence of self-esteem on relationships between job complexity, performance, and satisfaction. *Journal of Applied Psychology* **69**, 622–32.

Theorell, T. and Akerstedt, T. (1976). Day and night work: Changes in cholesterol, uric acid, glucose and potassium in serum and in circadian patterns of urinary catecholamine excretion. *Acta Medica Scandinavica* **200**, 47–53.

Theorell, T. and Floderus-Myrhed, B. (1977). 'Workload' and risk of myocardial infarction: A prospective psychosocial analysis. *International Journal of Epidemiology* **6**, 17–21.

Thierry, H. and Jansen, B. (1984). Work and working time. In P. J. D. Drenth, H. Thierry, P. J. Willems, and C. J. de Wolff (eds), *Handbook of work and organizational psychology*. Chichester: Wiley.

Thoits, P. A. (1982). Conceptual, methodological, and theoretical problems in studying social support as a buffer against life stress. *Journal of Health and Social Behavior* **23**, 145–59.

Thoits, P. A. (1983). Multiple identities and psychological well-being: A reformulation and test of the social isolation hypothesis. *American Sociological Review* **48**, 174–87.

Thoits, P. A. and Hannan, M. (1979). Income and psychological distress: The impact of an income-maintenance experiment. *Journal of Health and Social Behavior* **20**, 120–38.

Thomas, L. E., McCabe, E., and Berry, J. E. (1980). Unemployment and family stress: A reassessment. *Family Relations* **29**, 517–24.

Thompson, P. (1983). *The nature of work*. London: Macmillan.

Tiffany, D. W., Cowan, J. R., and Tiffany, P. M. (1970). *The unemployed: A social–psychological portrait*. Englewood Cliffs: Prentice-Hall.

Tiggemann, M. and Winefield, A. H. (1980). Some psychological effects of unemployment in school-leavers. *Australian Journal of Social Issues* **15**, 269–76.

Tiggemann, M. and Winefield, A. H. (1984). The effects of unemployment on the mood, self-esteem, locus of control, and depressive affect of school-leavers. *Journal of Occupational Psychology* **57**, 33–42.

Tilley, A. J., Wilkinson, R. T., Warren, P. S. G., Watson, B., and Drud, M. (1982). The sleep and performance of shift workers. *Human Factors* **24**, 629–41.

Tosi, D. J. and Lindamood, C. A. (1975). The measurement of self-actualization: A critical review of the Personal Orientation Inventory. *Journal of Personality Assessment* **39**, 215–24.

Townsend, P. (1974). Poverty as relative deprivation. In D. Wedderburn (ed.), *Poverty, inequality and class structure*. Cambridge: Cambridge University Press.

Turner, A. N. and Miclette, A. L. (1962). Sources of satisfaction in repetitive work. *Occupational Psychology* **36,** 215–31.

Ullah, P. and Banks, M. H. (1985). Youth unemployment and labour market withdrawal. *Journal of Economic Psychology* **6,** 51–64.

Ullah, P., Banks, M. H., and Warr, P. B. (1985). Social support, social pressures and psychological distress during unemployment. *Psychological Medicine* **15,** 283–95.

Upmeyer, A. (1981). Perceptual and judgmental processes in social contexts. In L. Berkowitz (ed.), *Advances in experimental social psychology* (vol. 14). New York: Academic Press.

Vaillant, G. E. (1975). Natural history of male psychological health. III, Empirical dimensions of mental health. *Archives of General Psychiatry* **32,** 420–8.

Vaillant, G. E. (1977). *Adaptation to life.* Boston: Little, Brown.

Vaillant, G. E. and Vaillant, C. O. (1981). Natural history of male psychological health: Work as a predictor of positive mental health. *American Journal of Psychiatry* **138,** 1433–40.

Vecchio, R. P. (1980). The function and meaning of work and the job. *Academy of Management Journal* **23,** 361–7.

Veenhoven, R. and Jonkers, T. (1984). *Data-book of happiness.* Dordrecht: Reidel.

Veit, C. T. and Ware, J. E. (1983). The structure of psychological distress and well-being in general populations. *Journal of Consulting and Clinical Psychology* **51,** 730–42.

Veith-Flanigan, J. and Sandman, C. A. (1985). Neuroendocrine relationships with stress. In S. R. Burchfield (ed.), *Stress: Psychological and physiological interactions.* Washington: Hemisphere.

Verbrugge, L. M. (1983). Multiple roles and physical health of women and men. *Journal of Health and Social Behavior* **24,** 16–30.

Viney, L. L. (1985). 'They call you a dole bludger': Some experiences of unemployment. *Journal of Community Psychology* **13,** 31–45.

Von Hofsten, C. (1985). Perception and action. In M. Frese and J. Sabini (eds), *Goal-directed behavior: The concept of action in psychology.* Hillsdale: Erlbaum.

Vredenburgh, D. J. and Trinkaus, R. J. (1983). An analysis of role stress among hospital nurses. *Journal of Vocational Behavior* **23,** 82–95.

Vroom, V. H. (1959). Some personality determinants of the effects of participation. *Journal of Abnormal and Social Psychology* **59,** 322–7.

Wachtel, P. J. (1967). Conceptions of broad and narrow attention. *Psychological Bulletin* **68,** 417–29.

Wadsworth, M. and Ford, D. H. (1983). Assessment of personal goal hierarchies. *Journal of Counseling Psychology* **30,** 514–26.

Wagner, F. R. and Morse, J. J. (1975). A measure of individual sense of competence. *Psychological Reports* **36,** 451–9.

Walker, C. R. and Guest, R. H. (1952). *The man on the assembly line.* Cambridge, Massachusetts: Harvard University Press.

Wall, T. D. (1987). New technology and job design. In P. B. Warr (ed.), *Psychology at work* (3rd edn). Harmondsworth: Penguin.

Wall, T. D. and Clegg, C. W. (1981a). A longitudinal field study of group work redesign. *Journal of Occupational Behaviour* **2**, 31–49.

Wall, T. D. and Clegg, C. W. (1981b). Individual strain and organizational functioning. *British Journal of Clinical Psychology* **20**, 135–6.

Wall, T. D. and Payne, R. L. (1973). Are deficiency scores deficient? *Journal of Applied Psychology* **58**, 322–6.

Wall, T. D., Clegg, C. W., and Jackson, P. R. (1978). An evaluation of the job characteristics model. *Journal of Occupational Psychology* **51**, 183–96.

Wall, T. D., Kemp, N. J., Jackson, P. R., and Clegg, C. W. (1986). Outcomes of autonomous workgroups: A long-term field experiment. *Academy of Management Journal* **29**, 280–304.

Wanous, J. P. (1974). Individual differences and reactions to job characteristics. *Journal of Applied Psychology* **59**, 616–22.

Wanous, J. P. (1977). Organizational entry: Newcomers moving from outside to inside. *Psychological Bulletin* **84**, 601–18.

Warr, P. B. (1978). A study of psychological well-being. *British Journal of Psychology* **69**, 111–21.

Warr, P. B. (1980). An introduction to models in psychological research. In A. Chapman and D. Jones (eds), *Models of man*. Leicester: British Psychological Society.

Warr, P. B. (1982). A national study of non-financial employment commitment. *Journal of Occupational Psychology* **55**, 297–312.

Warr, P. B. (1984a). Job loss, unemployment and psychological well-being. In V. Allen and E. van de Vliert (eds), *Role transitions*. New York: Plenum Press.

Warr, P. B. (1984b). Work and unemployment. In P. J. D. Drenth, H. Thierry, P. J. Willems, and C. J. de Wolff (eds), *Handbook of work and organization psychology*. Chichester: Wiley.

Warr, P. B. (1984c). Reported behaviour changes after job loss. *British Journal of Social Psychology* **23**, 271–5.

Warr, P. B. (1985). Twelve questions about unemployment and health. In B. Roberts, R. Finnegan, and D. Gallie (eds), *New approaches to economic life*. Manchester: Manchester University Press.

Warr, P. B. and Jackson, P. R. (1983). Self-esteem and unemployment among young workers. *Le Travail Humain* **46**, 355–66.

Warr, P. B. and Jackson, P. R. (1984). Men without jobs: Some correlates of age and length of unemployment. *Journal of Occupational Psychology* **57**, 77–85.

Warr, P. B. and Jackson, P. R. (1985). Factors influencing the psychological impact of prolonged unemployment and of re-employment. *Psychological Medicine* **15**, 795–807.

Warr, P. B. and Lovatt, D. J. (1977). Retraining and others factors associated with job finding after redundancy. *Journal of Occupational Psychology* **50**, 67–84.

Warr, P. B. and Parry, G. (1982). Paid employment and women's psychological well-being. *Psychological Bulletin* **91**, 498–516.

Warr, P. B. and Payne, R. L. (1982). Experiences of strain and pleasure among British adults. *Social Science and Medicine* **16**, 1691–7.

Warr, P. B. and Payne, R. L. (1983a). Affective outcomes of paid employment in a random sample of British workers. *Journal of Occupational Behaviour* **4,** 91–104.

Warr, P. B. and Payne, R. L. (1983b). Social class and reported changes in behavior after job loss. *Journal of Applied Social Psychology* **13,** 206–22.

Warr, P. B. and Routledge, T. (1969). An opinion scale for the study of managers' job satisfaction. *Occupational Psychology* **43,** 95–109.

Warr, P. B. and Wall, T. D. (1975). *Work and well-being.* Harmondsworth: Penguin.

Warr, P. B., Banks, M. H., and Ullah, P. (1985). The experience of unemployment among black and white urban teenagers. *British Journal of Psychology* **76,** 75–87.

Warr, P. B., Barter, J., and Brownbridge, G. (1983). On the independence of positive and negative affect. *Journal of Personality and Social Psychology* **44,** 644–51.

Warr, P. B., Cook, J., and Wall, T. D. (1979). Scales for the measurement of some work attitudes and aspects of psychological well-being. *Journal of Occupational Psychology* **52,** 129–48.

Warr, P. B., Jackson, P. R., and Banks, M. H. (1982). Duration of unemployment and psychological well-being in young men and women. *Current Psychological Research* **2,** 207–14.

Warr, P. B., Fineman, S., Nicholson, N., and Payne, R. L. (1978). *Developing employee relations.* Farnborough: Saxon House.

Watson, D. and Clark, L. A. (1984). Negative affectivity: The disposition to experience aversive emotional states. *Psychological Bulletin* **96,** 465–90.

Watson, D. and Tellegen, A. (1985). Toward a consensual structure of mood. *Psychological Bulletin* **98,** 219–35.

Weaver, C. N. (1978a). Sex differences in the determinants of job satisfaction. *Academy of Management Journal* **21,** 265–74.

Weaver, C. N. (1978b). Black–white correlates of job satisfaction. *Journal of Applied Psychology* **63,** 255–8.

Weaver, C. N. (1980). Job satisfaction in the United States in the 1970s. *Journal of Applied Psychology* **65,** 364–7.

Weber, M. (1905). *The protestant ethic and the spirit of capitalism.* London: Unwin (1971 edn).

Weiner, H. J., Akabas, S. H., and Sommer, J. J. (1973). *Mental health care in the world of work.* New York: Association Press.

Weiss, R. S. and Kahn, R. L. (1960). Definitions of work and occupation. *Social Problems* **8,** 142–51.

Weissman, M. M. and Bothwell, S. (1976). Assessment of social adjustment by patient self-report. *Archives of General Psychiatry* **33,** 1111–15.

Weissman, M. M., Paykel, E. S., Siegel, R., and Klerman, G. L. (1971). The social role performance of depressed women: A comparison with a normal sample. *American Journal of Orthopsychiatry* **41,** 390–405.

Wells, J. A. (1982). Objective job conditions, social support and perceived stress among blue-collar workers. *Journal of Occupational Behaviour* **3,** 79–94.

Werbel, J. D. (1983). Job change: A study of an acute job stressor. *Journal of Vocational Behavior* **23**, 242–50.

Wessman, A. E. and Ricks, D. F. (1966). *Mood and personality*. New York: Holt, Rinehart and Winston.

West, D. J., Horan, J. J., and Games, P. A. (1984). Component analysis of occupational stress inoculation applied to registered nurses in an acute care hospital setting. *Journal of Counseling Psychology* **31**, 209–18.

Westcott, G. (1985). The effect of unemployment on the health of workers in a UK steel town: Preliminary results. In G. Westcott, P. G. Svensson, and H. F. K. Zöllner (eds), *Health policy implications of unemployment*. Copenhagen: World Health Organization.

Weyer, G. and Hodapp, V. (1979). Job stress and essential hypertension. In I. G. Sarason and C. D. Spielberger (eds), *Stress and anxiety* (vol. 6). New York: Wiley.

White, M. (1983). *Long-term unemployment and labour markets*. London: Policy Studies Institute.

White, M. (1985). Life stress in long-term unemployment. *Policy Studies* **5**, 31–49.

White, R. W. (1959). Motivation reconsidered: The concept of competence. *Psychological Review* **66**, 297–333.

Whyte, W. F. (1948). *Human relations in the restaurant industry*. New York: McGraw-Hill.

Wicker, A. W. (1981). Nature and assessment of behavior settings. In P. McReynolds (ed.), *Advances in psychological assessment* (vol. 5). San Francisco: Jossey-Bass.

Wiener, Y., Vardi, Y., and Muczyk, J. (1981). Antecedents of employees' mental health: The role of career and work satisfaction. *Journal of Vocational Behavior* **19**, 50–60.

Wiggins, J. D., Lederer, D. A., Salkowe, A., and Rys, G. S. (1983). Job satisfaction related to tested congruence and differentiation. *Journal of Vocational Behavior* **23**, 112–21.

Wilder, C. S. (1980). *Selected health characteristics by occupation, United States 1975–76*. Hyattsville, Maryland: US Department of Health and Human Services.

Wilkes, B., Stammerjohn, L., and Lalich, N. (1981). Job demands and worker health in machine-paced poultry inspection. *Scandinavian Journal of Work and Environmental Health* **7**(4), 12–19.

Williams, A. W., Ware, J. E., and Donald, C. A. (1981). A model of mental health, life events, and social supports, applicable to general populations. *Journal of Health and Social Behavior* **22**, 324–36.

Williams, D. G. (1981). Personality and mood: State–trait relationships. *Personality and Individual Differences* **2**, 303–9.

Williams, T. A. (1985). Visual display technology, worker disablement and work organization. *Human Relations* **38**, 1065–84.

Wills, T. A. (1985). Supportive functions of interpersonal relationships. In S. Cohen and S. L. Syme (eds), *Social support and health*. Orlando: Academic Press.

Wilson, H. and Herbert, G. W. (1978). *Parents and children in the inner city.* London: Routledge and Kegan Paul.

Winefield, A. H. and Tiggemann, M. (1985). Psychological correlates of employment and unemployment: Effects, predisposing factors, and sex differences. *Journal of Occupational Psychology* **58**, 229–42.

Wineman, J. D. (1982). The office environment as a source of stress. In G. W. Evans (ed.), *Environmental stress.* Cambridge: Cambridge University Press.

Wing, J. K., Cooper, J. E., and Sartorius, N. (1974). *The measurement and classification of psychiatric symptoms.* Cambridge: Cambridge University Press.

Winnubst, J. A. M., Marcelissen, F. H. G., and Kleber, R. J. (1982). Effects of social support in the stressor–strain relationship: A Dutch sample. *Social Science and Medicine* **16**, 475–82.

Winter, J. M. (1983). Unemployment, nutrition and infant mortality in Britain 1920–1950. In J. John, D. Schwefel, and H. Zöllner (eds), *Influence of economic instability on health.* Berlin: Springer.

Wittenborn, J. R. (1984). Observer ratings. In M. Hersen and L. Michelson (eds), *Issues in psychotherapy research.* New York: Plenum Press.

Wyatt, S., Fraser, J. A., and Stock, F. G. L. (1928). *The comparative effects of variety and uniformity in work.* (Industrial Fatigue Research Board Report No. 52.) London: HMSO.

Yankelovich, D. (1982). *New rules: Searching for self-fulfilment in a world turned upside down.* New York: Bantam Books.

Yoshitake, H. (1978). Three characteristic patterns of subjective fatigue symptoms. *Ergonomics* **21**, 231–3.

Young, M. and Willmott, P. (1973). *The symmetrical family: A study of work and leisure in the London region.* London: Routledge and Kegan Paul.

Zappert, L. T. and Weinstein, H. M. (1985). Sex differences in the impact of work on physical and psychological health. *American Journal of Psychiatry* **142**, 1174–8.

Zevon, M. A. and Tellegen, A. (1982). The structure of mood change: An idiographic/nomothetic analysis. *Journal of Personality and Social Psychology* **43**, 111–22.

Zung, W. W. K. (1965). A self-rating depression scale. *Archives of General Psychiatry* **12**, 63–70.

Zung, W. W. K. (1971). A rating instrument for anxiety disorders. *Psychosomatics* **12**, 371–9.

Subject index

The book is organised in terms of the impact of environmental conditions on five components and many sub-components of mental health. Throughout several chapters, large numbers of research findings are cited in respect of each element. Inclusion of all those separate observations about mental health would distort the Subject index, and reduce its value as a pointer to more salient themes. Individual research findings linking context-free and job-related mental health to specific environmental features have therefore been excluded from the listing below.

abilities 8, 19, 90, 93, 213, 239, 246, 253, 254, 257, 258, 259, 260, 274, 290
accidents 58, 67, 170, 171
achievement need 257, 262
action theory 5
activity 42, 214, 281
adaptation 61, 154
additional decrement 10, 13–15, 78, 93, 98, 100, 117, 127, 132, 148, 153, 160, 186–8, 212, 235, 254, 265, 269, 286–7, 289–90, 292
additive combinations 130–1, 133, 185, 284
adrenaline 45, 62–3, 66, 96, 118, 123, 142, 198, 232
affect, negative 30, 42, 44, 47, 168, 240
affect, positive 44, 47
affective well-being 30, 34–5, 38, 51, 107–8, 127, 159, 240, 279
    concept of 26–9
    measurement of 40–9
    see also axes of well-being, duration of well-being
affordances 3, 17, 281
age 34, 42, 60, 61, 86, 90, 203, 226–8, 238, 246, 250–1, 273
aggregate time-series
    investigations 199–202, 204–6, 272
alcohol 72, 104, 203–4
alienation 47, 80, 108, 138, 190
ambiguity, *see* environmental clarity, role ambiguity *vs.* clarity
ambivalence 58–9, 194, 229
analogies 14, 285, 287–9
anticipatory socialization 154
anxiety 12, 28, 29, 32, 42, 44, 47, 70, 199, 218, 252, 272, 278
appraisal 16, 79, 112, 237, 280
arousal 26–8, 36, 40, 42, 48, 63, 82, 278

aspiration 28, 38, 48, 70, 88, 106, 107–8, 149, 159, 179, 198, 228, 232, 242, 256, 274, 279
    concept of 26, 31–4, 103
    measurement of 52–3
attempted suicide, *see* parasuicide
attention 12, 13, 137
authoritarianism 96, 104, 257, 258
automatization 99
autonomy in jobs, *see* opportunity for control
autonomy in mental health 13, 28, 38, 106, 107–8, 159, 197, 228, 241, 242, 274, 279, 281
    concept of 26, 30–1
    measurement of 51–2
availability of money 2, 6–7, 14, 88, 150, 162–8, 169, 192, 211, 214, 217–19, 222, 227, 230, 232, 246, 257, 273, 282, 288, 296, 297, 300
axes of well-being 41–9, 51, 61–2, 84, 105, 145, 159, 278, 279, 293

banana time 97
baseline mental health 19, 76, 239–42, 246, 248–9, 271–3, 289–90
batch size 136
blood pressure 45, 122, 125
boredom 47, 63, 97, 248
building design 179, 186–8
    see also physical security
burnout 47, 48, 50

capitalism 79, 89
cardiac functioning, *see* blood pressure, heart disease, heart-rate
carry-over from jobs 72–6, 139, 140, 168–9
catecholamines 45, 62–3, 142

categorical model 1–9, 17, 20, 109, 138, 265, 271, 280–6
causal attributions 12, 18
causality, cyclical 114–15, 158, 190, 210–11, 245–7, 283, 291, 292, 294
central plateau 11–13, 21, 105, 112, 157, 160, 174, 212, 284, 286–7, 292, 295
  see also non-linear assumption
changing job environments 9, 21, 297
changing unemployment 9, 21, 299–301
children 21, 48, 58, 139, 141, 206–7, 217, 219, 227, 231, 250
cigarettes 65, 122, 142, 203, 278
clarity, *see* environmental clarity, role ambiguity *vs.* clarity
climate 266
cognitive demands 285, 296–7
cognitive ergonomics 297
cognitive failures questionnaire 49
combined effects 113–14, 128–34, 174, 178, 185, 210–11, 243, 263, 283, 290
common-method variance 18, 110–12
competence 28, 38, 106–8, 148, 159, 196–7, 228, 232, 242, 274, 279, 284, 294
  concept of 26, 29–30
  measurement of 49–51
  see also subjective competence
computers 20, 136, 148, 172–3, 285, 295–7
configural models 285–6
constant effect 10–11, 14, 167–8, 174, 254, 286–7, 289
context-free *vs.* job-related mental health 40, 49, 75–6, 106, 112, 184, 277, 287
control, *see* opportunity for control
controlling models 15
coping 13, 16, 19, 29, 45, 49, 54, 169, 241, 279
  see also baseline mental health
cortisol 45, 123, 149
cycle time 96, 99–100, 282
cyclical causal processes 114–15, 158, 190, 210–11, 245–7, 283, 291, 292, 294

danger 67, 171, 173, 282
decision latitude, *see* opportunity for control
demands
  cognitive 285, 296–7
  extrinsic 118, 138–43
  intrinsic 118–28, 282
  job 62, 64, 67–8, 70, 98, 117, 174, 257, 259, 268, 290, 296
  time 70, 138–43, 282
  see also externally generated goals, norms, obligations, overload, roles, traction
demographic features 19, 238, 246, 249–51, 273, 290

depression 28, 29, 42, 44, 47–8, 68, 70, 199, 278
discretion, *see* opportunity for control
distress 32, 34, 42, 47, 252, 278
divorce 206
domestic work 20, 48, 57, 58, 69, 139, 141, 215, 230, 231, 250, 273
drinking 72, 104, 203–4
duration of unemployment 202, 232–3, 273
duration of well-being 28, 34–5, 127, 160–1, 169, 283

ecological models 281
effectance motivation 29
employment as therapy 70–1
employment commitment 60, 225–6, 228, 273
enabling models 15, 115, 237, 280
environment, measurement of, *see* independent measures, ratings of environments
environmental clarity 2, 6, 14, 87, 117, 145–61, 178, 211, 215–16, 227, 230, 246, 257, 261–2, 282, 296, 297, 301
equipment design 172–3, 282, 295
equity 163, 165–6, 282
ergonomics, cognitive 297
esteem, *see* self-esteem, social esteem
ethnic group 61, 244, 251, 273
external control beliefs, *see* internal *vs.* external control beliefs
externally generated goals 2, 5–6, 13, 87, 98, 117–43, 150, 211, 213–15, 222, 230, 246, 257, 259–61, 274, 282, 296, 297, 300
  see also job demands, obligations, roles
extraversion 251
extrinsic characteristics 173, 283, 285
extrinsic control 80, 87–90, 93
extrinsic demands 118, 138–43
extrinsic satisfaction 47
extrinsic variety 94, 282

facet-specific satisfaction 46, 47, 81, 95, 264
family 20, 65, 74–5, 139–41, 163, 181, 202, 206–7, 217, 219, 221, 229–31
fatigue 48, 74, 171
feedback 6, 70, 102, 134, 137, 146–9, 159, 178, 179, 257, 281, 282, 297
fit, measures of 267–8
flexitime 142
flow 136–8, 213
friendship opportunities 8, 177, 220, 282
future ambiguity 149–50, 158–9, 169, 216, 282

gender differences 56, 58, 60, 61, 62, 83, 121, 123, 141, 204, 229, 238, 247, 249–50, 258, 263, 273
general health questionnaire 42, 43, 83, 103, 134, 166, 191, 196, 218, 225
gestalt tasks 134
goals, *see* externally generated goals
growth-need strength 53, 254–5, 256, 261, 263, 264

happiness 27, 41–2, 47, 63
hardiness 241
heart disease 67–8, 85, 97, 123–4, 128–9
heart-rate 29, 45, 122
higher-order need strength 53, 254–5, 256, 261, 263, 264
hospital admissions 66, 200, 202, 272
hours of work 139–43
housework 20, 48, 57, 58, 69, 139, 141, 215, 230, 231, 250, 273

ideational flexibility 84, 96, 104
identity 33
illumination 94, 171, 282
income 46, 83, 147–8, 215, 227, 232, 272, 282, 296
    see also availability of money
independence, *see* autonomy
independent measures of the environment 17, 79, 81, 96, 102, 103, 110–12, 121, 151
individual differences 18–19, 61, 128, 237–42, 245–7, 248–75, 291, 300
    see also person-situation interactions
industrial fatigue research board 94
information about consequences of behaviour 146–9, 158–9, 282
    see also future ambiguity
information about the future 149–51, 158–9, 211, 215–16, 282
    see also future ambiguity
information about required behaviour 151–3, 158–9, 178, 282
    see also role clarity *vs.* ambiguity
information after a transition 153–7, 158–9
information technology 136, 148, 172–3, 285, 295–7
inner-directedness 52
institutions 5, 8, 57, 300
integrated functioning 26, 33–4, 38, 53–4, 106–8, 159
interaction between factors 113–14, 128–34, 174, 178, 185, 210–11, 243, 263, 283, 290
interdependence 30–1, 51, 52, 277, 298
internal *vs.* external control beliefs 30, 51, 68, 91, 249, 256, 257, 262, 293
    see also autonomy in mental health

intrinsic characterisitcs 102, 285
intrinsic control 80–7, 93, 282
intrinsic demands 118–28, 282
intrinsic motivation 53
intrinsic rewards 102, 138
intrinsic satisfaction 47, 293
intrinsic variety 94, 282
isolation 178–9, 221

job characteristics inventory 81, 95, 173, 177
job characteristics model 281, 283
job complexity 100–5, 107, 264–5
job creation 299
job decision latitude 84, 105, 130, 284
    see also opportunity for control
job, definition of 56
job demands 62, 64, 67–8, 70, 98, 117–43, 174, 257, 259, 268, 290, 296
job design 83, 297
job diagnostic survey 81, 95, 105, 110, 111, 146, 173, 179, 191, 261, 264
job insecurity 149–51
job involvement 47, 48–9
job level 60, 61, 62, 63, 64–5, 66, 68, 78, 92–3, 104, 120, 140, 164, 250, 251, 269, 293
    see also socio-economic status
job-related anxiety 47–8, 61–2, 64, 66, 107, 262, 278, 279, 294
job-related depression 48, 66, 107, 294
job-related exhaustion 48, 64, 68, 73, 278
job-related tension 47–8, 61–2, 64, 66, 107, 262, 278, 279, 294
job-related *vs.* context-free mental health 40, 49, 75–6, 106, 112, 184, 277, 287
job rotation 88, 98, 298
job satisfaction 46–7, 61, 63, 72, 107, 249, 265, 278, 293–4
job-seeking 213, 228

labour costs 103
    see also work performance
latent functions model 211, 281, 283
leisure 52, 73, 75, 118, 139, 227, 301
life satisfaction 41–2, 47, 72, 90
living standards, *see* availability of money
local unemployment rate 225
locus of control beliefs 30, 51, 68, 91, 249, 256, 257, 262, 293
    see also autonomy in mental health
long-term unemployment 231–4

machine-pacing 85–7, 99, 282, 290
mass psychogenic illness 188

matching personal characteristics 253–65, 273, 290–1
meaningfulness of job 191–2, 282
measurement of environments, *see* independent measures, ratings of environments
measurement of mental health, *see* affective well-being, aspiration, autonomy, competence, mental health
mental health
  concept of 24–39, 277–80
  measurement of 38, 40–55
  value base 24, 30, 32–5, 36–8, 277, 279–80
meta-analysis 81, 102, 134, 146, 191, 261, 264, 293
middle-aged men and unemployment 20, 226–7
mid-range plateau 11–13, 21, 105, 112, 157, 160, 174, 212, 269, 284, 286–7, 292, 295
  see also non-linear assumption
model
  categorical 1–9, 17, 20, 109, 138, 265, 271, 280–6
  job characteristics 281, 283
  latent functions 211, 281, 283
  matching characteristics 253–65, 273, 290–1
  person-situation interaction 1, 15–19, 238–42, 245–7, 248–75, 290–1
  process 1, 9–15, 17, 20, 109, 131–2, 138, 280, 286–90
  vitamin 9–15, 19–21, 84–5, 92, 105, 112–13, 117, 127, 188, 234–5, 269–70, 280–91
models
  analogical 14, 285, 287–9
  configural 285–6
  controlling 15
  ecological 281
  enabling 15, 115, 237, 280
  person-centred 15, 265, 266, 280, 288
  person-environment fit 265–70
  situation-centred 15–19, 115, 237, 265, 280, 288
moderator variables 19, 243–4, 253–65, 270–1, 290
money, *see* availability of money
morale 47, 49, 181
mortality rates 109, 203, 204–5, 278
motivating potential score 101–2, 105, 110, 264
motivation 4, 8, 32, 36, 51, 176, 292
movement between jobs 68–9, 82, 85, 104–5, 147, 153–7, 285
  see also transitions
multivariate analyses 113–14, 210–11, 243–4, 268, 283
music 94, 97

need for achievement 257, 262
needs 8, 177, 253, 262, 266
negative affect 30, 42, 44, 47, 168, 240
neuroticism 44, 47, 239–40, 248, 257, 260, 265
new technology 20, 136, 148, 172–3, 285, 295–7
noise 67, 94, 170–1, 282
non-employment 57, 58, 194, 228, 229, 273
non-linear assumption 9–15, 20, 21, 78, 84–5, 92, 105, 112–13, 127, 128–34, 153, 156, 158, 160, 164, 211–12, 234, 244, 269–70, 286–7, 289, 295
noradrenaline 45, 62–3, 96, 123, 198, 232

obligations 5, 8, 57, 58, 71
occupational level 60, 61, 62, 63, 64–5, 66, 68, 78, 92–3, 104, 120, 140, 164, 250, 251, 269, 293
  see also socio-economic status
opportunity for control 2, 3–4, 14, 79–90, 91, 93, 98, 99, 101, 107–9, 128–34, 150, 154, 160, 174, 178, 192, 212, 230, 246, 256–8, 274, 282, 284, 290, 296, 297
opportunity for interpersonal contact 2, 7–8, 14, 150, 176–88, 216, 220–3, 227, 230, 246, 257, 274, 282, 296, 297, 301
opportunity for skill use 2, 4–5, 14, 87, 88, 90–4, 98, 99, 101, 107–9, 150, 154, 160, 212–13, 216, 230, 246, 254, 257, 258–9, 274, 282, 296, 297
output restriction 86, 167
overcrowding 14
  see also privacy, social density
overload 6, 13, 64, 67, 74, 118, 119, 120, 126, 230–1
overtime 67, 83, 140, 299

pacing 85–7, 99, 282, 290
parasuicide 205–6, 218–19
part-employment 301
part-time jobs 56–7, 58, 62, 139, 231, 300
pay 46, 83, 147–8, 215, 227, 232, 272, 282, 296
  see also availability of money
payment by results 166–7
perceptual discrimination 12–13
performance 33, 137, 168, 171, 188, 292–5, 296
person-centred models 15, 265, 266, 280, 288
person–environment fit models 265–70
person-situation interactions 1, 15-15–19, 237–42, 245–7, 253–75, 290–1
personal agency 6, 32, 214, 274, 300
personal territory 186–8, 282

physical ill-health 168–9, 170, 195, 202–6, 207, 272
physical security 2, 7, 14, 150, 168–74, 216, 220, 227, 230, 246, 257, 282, 296, 297, 300
piecework 147–8, 166–7
plans 5, 97–8, 149, 215, 232
plant closure 149, 202–3
positive affect 44, 47
positive mental health 31, 277
potency 240
poverty 7, 36, 164, 217, 218
see also availability of money
power, *see* opportunity for control
powerlessness 52, 80, 81, 296
predictability, *see* environmental clarity, role ambiguity *vs.* clarity
press 266
privacy 7, 186–8, 282
proactivity 6, 32, 214, 274, 300
process model 1, 9–15, 17, 109, 131–2, 138, 280, 286–90
proxy measures 113, 185, 210, 238, 263
psychiatric assessments 25, 38, 42, 122, 198, 199, 278
psychosomatic symptoms 29, 43, 45–6, 62, 64, 66, 67, 123, 199, 278
psychotherapy 69–70, 251, 298–9

qualitative research 64, 109, 112, 138, 228, 285, 289

rate of change 6, 145
ratings
of employees 51, 293–5
of environments 18, 79, 110–12, 114, 238
of mental health 33, 36–8, 45, 51, 53
reciprocal causality 114–15, 158, 190, 210–11, 245–7, 283, 291, 292, 294
re-employment 157, 196, 234–5
repetition, *see* cycle time, variety
resource networks 301
restriction of output 89, 167
retirement 20, 154, 232, 285, 299
reversal theory 28–9
risk-taking 14, 36, 119, 148, 252, 279
role ambiguity *vs.* clarity 151–3, 159, 179, 257, 261–2, 268, 282
role conflict 124–6, 179, 260, 282
roles 5, 6, 8, 17, 37, 57, 154, 189, 228, 230, 232, 233, 300

safety, *see* physical security
satisfaction
facet-specific 46, 47, 81, 95, 264

job 46–7, 61, 63, 72, 107, 249, 265, 278, 293–4
life 41–2, 47, 72, 90
self-confidence 88, 199, 241
see also subjective competence
self-denigration 45, 47, 104
self-efficacy 29, 50, 279
self-employment 56, 299
self-esteem 9, 26, 28, 30, 45, 88, 90, 122, 224–5
self-realization 32
self-regulation, *see* autonomy
self-selection into environments 16, 61, 68, 71, 142, 195, 207, 238, 245, 271, 288, 293
sensory deprivation 118
sex differences 56, 58, 60, 61, 62, 83, 121, 123, 141, 204, 229, 238, 247, 249–50, 258, 263, 273
shift-working 141–2
situation-centred models 15–19, 115, 237, 265, 280, 288
skill acquisition 4, 31, 213, 257, 282, 295
skill utilization, *see* opportunity for skill use
skills exchanges 301
sleep problems 29, 42, 48, 62, 65, 142, 149, 199, 278
smoking 65, 122, 142, 203, 278
sociability 257, 263
social adjustment scale 50
social class 20, 75–6, 88, 89–90, 189–90, 204, 238, 246, 251, 273
see also job level
social comparison 8, 9
social contact 178–80, 188, 218, 282
social density 179, 186–8
see also overcrowding, privacy
social esteem 8–9, 188–92, 224–5, 227, 230, 257, 282
social relationships, *see* opportunity for interpersonal contact
social support 8, 67, 180–6, 219, 223, 257, 282
socio-economic status 20, 75–6, 88, 89–90, 189–90, 204, 238, 246, 251, 273
see also job level
spill-over from jobs 72–6, 139, 140, 168–9
stability across time 240, 242, 249, 274
standard of living, *see* availability of money
status, *see* valued social position
stigma 191, 224, 228, 273
stress 75, 120, 171, 185, 272, 283, 298
subjective assessment
of employees 51, 293–5
of environments 18, 79, 110–12, 114, 238
of mental health 33, 36–8, 45, 51, 53
subjective competence 26, 28, 29, 34, 49–50, 65, 82, 85, 107, 137, 152, 181, 196, 278

suicide 205
  see also parasuicide
Sunday neurosis 71–2
syndrome 25

task demands, *see* externally generated
    goals, job demands, overload, traction,
    underload
task identity 102, 134–5, 257, 260, 281, 282
task significance 102, 191–2, 263, 281
teenagers and unemployment 20, 60, 196,
    227–8, 299
temperature 7, 168, 170, 282
time demands 70, 138–43, 282
time structure 97, 213–15, 281
traction 5, 9, 98, 99, 135–6, 138, 148, 213,
    282
trade unions 64, 80, 87, 88, 93, 178, 295
tranquillizers 62, 123, 278
transitions 9, 20, 153–7, 199, 222, 234–5, 284
  see also movements between jobs
type A behaviour 251–2, 257, 260

ulcers 58, 66, 123
uncertainty, *see* environmental clarity, role
    ambiguity *vs.* clarity
uncontrollability, *see* opportunity for control
underload 67, 74, 118
underutilization of skills, *see* opportunity for
    skill use
unemployment
    changing 21, 299–301
    concept of 57, 194, 299
    duration of 202, 232–3, 273
    long-term 231–4
    rate 57, 194–5, 200–1, 225
    research 59–60, 195–207, 210–35, 271–5
    youth 20, 60, 195, 196, 198, 204, 227–8,
        232, 299, 300

valued social position 2, 8–9, 14, 150,
    188–92, 211, 216, 223–6, 227, 230, 232,
    246, 257, 263, 274, 282, 296, 297

values 19, 239, 246, 251–2, 270, 281, 290
values and the assessment of mental
    health 24, 30, 32–5, 36–8, 277, 279–80
variety 2, 6, 13, 73, 87, 91, 94–100, 101,
    107–9, 150, 178, 215, 246, 257, 261, 274,
    282, 290, 300
vibration 171, 174, 282
visual display units 66, 136, 148, 172–3, 297
vitamin analogy 9–15, 19–21, 84–5, 92, 105,
    112–13, 117, 127, 188, 234–5, 269–70,
    286–9
  see also additional decrement, constant
    effect, non-linear assumption
vocational interests 266
voluntary work 20, 57

wages 46, 83, 147–8, 215, 227, 232, 272, 282,
    296
  see also availability of money
welfare benefits 212, 223, 224, 300
well-being, *see* affective well-being
women
    in employment 56–7, 58, 65, 70, 74, 139,
        141, 166
    in unemployment 215, 229–31, 273
  see also gender differences
work adjustment theory 266–7
work, concept of 57–8
work demands, *see* externally generated
    goals, job demands, overload, traction,
    underload
work ethic 224
work performance 50, 168, 171, 188, 292–5,
    296
workaholic behaviour 33
working conditions 46, 67, 168–74, 282, 297
working time 138–43
  see also overtime
workload, *see* externally generated goals,
    job demands, overload, traction,
    underload

youth unemployment 60, 195, 196, 198, 204,
    227–8, 232, 299, 300

Research findings about aspects of mental health in relation to environmental influences are excluded from the above listing. Please see the note at the beginning of this Subject index.

Author index

Abdel-Halim, A.A. 181, 182, 183, 185, 260, 262
Abraham, K. 71
Abramson, L.Y. 18, 71
Adams, J.S. 165
Ahlbom, A. *85, 123, 128, 130*
Ahr, P.R. 200
Aiken, M. 47
Akabas, S.H. *71*
Akerstedt, T. 142
Alban-Metcalfe, B. 156
Aldag, R.J. 95, 110, 125, *125*, 152, *152*, 256, 261, 264
Alfredsson, L. 97, 124, 130, 142
Algera, J.A. 103, 110, 111
Alloy, L.B. 18
Altman, I. 14, 186, 187, 188
American Psychiatric Association 25
Anderson, C.S. 103, 111
Anderson, N. 57
Andrews, F.M. 41, 42
Andrisani, P.J. 68
Aneshensel, C.S. 169, 229
Angyal, A. 30
Antonovsky, A. 240
Apter, M.J. 29
Archer, R.P. *51*, 249
Argyle, M. 177
Armor, D.J. 204
Arnetz, B. *149*
Aro, S. 68
Aronson, E. *42, 82, 122*
Aronsson, G. 66, 67, 96, *111*, 123, *123*, 136, 148
Ashley, P. 7
Axelrod, W.L. 121, 150, 185
Ayoub, M.M. *171*, 172

Bachman, J.G. 204
Backer, G. de, *252*
Baddeley, A.D. 171
Baker, D. *85, 123, 128, 130*
Baldamus, W. 135, 136, 138
Ballinger, C.B. *209, 218*, 229
Balter, M.B. *43, 278*
Bandura, A. 29

Banks, M.H. 60, *60, 196*, 209, *209, 214, 215,* *219, 222, 223, 225, 226*, 228, *228*, 229, *229*, 232, *232*, 233, *234, 273*
Barber, J.G. 226
Barker, B.M. 10, 287
Barling, P.W. 200
Barnett, R.C. 229
Barr, S.H. *110*
Barraclough, B.H. 205, *209*
Barron, F. 54
Barter, J. *44*
Bartley, M.J. *202, 203*
Bartolome, F. 74, 75, 140, 141, 149
Baruch, G.K. 229
Bastiaansen, J. *195, 208, 209*
Baum, A. *16*, 46, 198, *198*, 232
Beale, N. 202
Bebbington, P. 199
Bech, P. 45
Bechtold, S.E. 81, 96, 102, 134, 146
Beck, A.T. 42
Beckman, L.J. 42
Beehr, T.A. *110, 173*
Beiser, M. 44
Belitsky, A.H. 233
Bell, C. 206, 219
Bell, N.E. *248*
Bellamy, L.J. 171
Bender, D.A. 10, 287
Benjaminsen, S. *199, 204*
Bennison, D. *209*
Ben-Sira, Z. 240
Berger-Gross, V. 120, 126, 150, 152
Berndt, D.J. 43
Berndt, S.M. *43*
Berry, J.E. *206*
Beutel, N.J. 142
Biddle, B.J. 5
Bienvenue, G.R. 170
Billings, A.G. 73, 82, 122, 152, 182, 183
Binns, D. 198, 206, 219, 222
Binswanger, L. 8
Birchall, D. 99
Birren, J.E. 34
Blatt, S.J. 43, 45
Blau, G. 181, 182, 185
Blauner, R. 80, 120, 138, 168, 190

Boddy, D. 296
Bond, M.J. 209, 214, 226
Borrill, C. *228*
Bothwell, S. 50
Boucher, J. 176
Bouvier-Colle, M.H. *229*, *230*
Boyle, G.J. 42
Bradburn, N.M. 29, 41, 44, 190, 208, 209
Bradshaw, J. 203, 217
Brass, D.J. 110, 147, 177, 187
Braunstein, W.B. 70
Braverman, H. 89, 296
Breaugh, J.A. 81
Brenner, B. 41
Brenner, M.H. 200, 204, 205
Brenner, S.O. *149*
Brett, J.M. 69, 154, 155
Brewin, C.R. *69*, 70, 251, 265
Bridge, G.W.K. *43*
Brief, A.P. 95, *110*, 125, *125*, 152, *152*, 256, 261, 264
Brigando, L. 47
Brinkmann, C. 209, 217
Broadbent, D.E. 49, 86, 95, 98, 99, 170
Brookes, M.J. 187
Brousseau, K.R. 105, 135, 146, 147
Brownbridge, G. *44*
Brownell, A. *201*
Bruggemann, A. 48
Bryant, F.B. 41, 49
Buchanan, D.A. 296
Buck, V.E. 48, 120, 122
Burke, R.J. 124, 126, 145, 152, 177, 252
Buss, T.F. 149
Byrne, D.G. *149*

Campbell, A. 42, 208
Campbell, D.J. 119
Campion, M.A. 103, 174
Caplan, R.D. 48, 66, *66*, 86, 91, *91*, 120, *120*, 121, 122, 125, 149, 152, 163, 166, 181, 182, 259, 267, *267*, *268*, 269, *269*, 283
Caplovitz, D. 41, 208
Carruthers, M.E. 45
Catalano, R.A. 200, 201, *201*, 202, *206*
Cavender, J.W. *293*
Champoux, J.E. 105, 112, 287
Chapanis, A. 172
Chaudhry, S.S. *124*, *183*, *185*
Chemers, M. 14, 186, 188
Cherlin, A. 44
Cherrington, D.J. 264
Cherry, N. 62, 68, 121, 142, 248, 251
Chesney, M.A. 260
Chess, W.A. 183, 185
Chevron, E.S. *43*, *45*

Cho, D.W. *200*
Christensen, E.R. *43*, *50*
Christie, D. *41*
Cisin, I.H. *43*, *278*
Clark, L.A. 43, 240, 278
Clark, V.A. *229*
Clausen, J.A. *248*
Cleary, P.D. 190, 229
Clegg, C.W. *81*, 83, 88, 89, *102*, *103*, *146*, 150, *191*
Cobb, S. 48, *66*, *86*, *91*, *120*, 121, 123, *125*, 134, 149, *149*, *152*, *163*, *166*, *181*, *182*, 196, 202, *202*, 209, *259*, *267*, *269*, *283*, *298*
Coburn, D. 81, 95
Cochrane, R. 200, 206, 209, 221
Coffield, F. 228
Cohen, A. 171
Cohen, B.G.F. *172*
Cohen, S. 49, 131, 170
Cohn, R.M. 196, 208, 225
Colligan, M.J. 66, 188
Conley, J.J. 19, 240, 278
Connolly, T.F. *139*
Connor, G.E. *54*
Converse, P.E. *42*, *208*
Conway, T.L. 122, 278
Cook, D.G. 202, 203
Cook, J.D. *42*, 46, *53*, *61*, 173, 249
Cooke, K. *203*, *217*
Cooke, R.A. 48, 120, 121, 123, 139
Cooper, C.L. 62, 65, 67, 120
Cooper, J.E. *45*
Cooper, P.F. *49*
Cooper, R. 95, 134
Corbett, J.M. 297
Cordery, J.L. *102*
Costa, P.T. 19, 44, 240
Covi, L. *43*
Cowan, J.R. *195*
Cowen, E.L. 177
Crawford, A. 204
Creigh, S. 56
Crisp, A.H. 43
Cronbach, L.J. 126, 268
Crown, S. 43
Csikszentmihalyi, M. 31, 136, 137, 138
Cummins, R.O. *202*, *203*
Cunningham, D.A. *252*

D'Affliti, J.P. *43*
Dainoff, M.J. 86
Dalton, M. 64
Daniel, W.W. 218, 226
D'Arcy, C. 202, 208, 209, 218, 250
Davenport, P.R. 226, 232
Davidson, M. 62, 65, 67, 120, 141, 250

Davies, C. 209, 228
Davies, R. 217
Davis-Sacks, M.L. *91, 181, 182, 183, 185, 268*
Dawis, R.V. 266
Dean, J.W. 110
DeCotiis, T.A. 48, 125, 182
Degre, S. *252*
Deivanayagam, S. *171*
DeJulio, S.S. *43, 50*
Delmonte, M.M. 43
Dembo, T. *119*
Dempsey, P. 42
Denolin, H. *252*
Depue, R. 19, 242
Derogatis, L.R. 43
Diaz-Valdes, R. *229, 230*
Diener, E. 41, *42*, 44, 45, 162, 163, 278
Dijkhuizen, N. van 48, 85, 92, 112, 123, 127, 149, 153, 158, 180, 182, 183, 252, 287
Dixon, G. *41*
Dobson, K.S. 43
Doehrman, S.R. *91, 181, 182, 183, 185, 268*
Doherty, J. 209, 228
Dohrenwend, B.P. 42
Donald, C.A. 19, *44*
Donaldson, L. 91, 95
Donovan, A. 208, 209, 228
Dooley, C.D. 200, *200*, 201, 202, *206*
Dougherty, T.W. 126, 152
Dowling, P. 256, 258, 259, 261, 268
Dramaix, M. *252*
Drenth, P.J.D. 142
Drud, M. 142
Drury, C.G. 87
Duggan, J. *228*
Duncan, G. *126, 177*
Duncan-Jones, P. *149*, 240
Dunham, R.B. 95, 102, 110
DuWors, R.E. *124, 126, 145, 152*
Dyer, L. 163

Eaton, W.W. 45
Eckhardt, B. 199, 209, 217, 218, 219, 229, 232
Eden, D. *122*
Egri, C. *42*
Eisenberg, P. 226
Elder, G.H. 206, 219, *219*, 272
Emery, F. 281
Emmons, R.A. *42*, 45
England, J.L. 264
Ensel, W.M. 180
Erbaugh, J. *42*
Erikson, E.H. 33
Erikssen, J. 149
Estes, R.J. 209, 218

Etzion, D. 122, 180, 185
Evans, G.W. 283
Evans, P. 74, 75, 140, 141, 149
Eyer, J. 205
Eysenck, H.J. 240
Eysenck, S.B.G. 240

Fagin, L. 198, 206, 214
Farran, D.C. 206, 209
Feather, N.T. 195, 197, 198, 208, 209, 214, 226, 228, 232
Feldman, D.C. 154
Ferenczi, S. 71
Ferris, G.R. *46*
Festinger, L. 8, *119*
Fimian, M.J. 120, 121
Finch, M.D. 83, 105
Fine, B.J. 170
Fineman, S. 88, 209
Finlay-Jones, R.A. 199, 209, 217, 218, 219, 229, 232
Firth, J. 69, 155, 299
Fisher, C.D. 125, *148*, 152, 158
Fitzgerald, M.P. *81, 102, 134, 146, 191, 256, 261, 263, 264*
FitzGerald, P. *49*
Fleming, R. 16, 198, *232*
Fletcher, B.C. 82, 113, 122, 123, 130
Flett, R. 41
Floderus-Myrhed, B. 67
Folkard, S. 142
Folkman, S. 16, 231
Folsom, A. *122, 140, 156*
Forbes, J.F. 205
Ford, D.H. 52
Fordyce, M.W. 41
Form, W. 250
Forrester, K. 301
Fox, A.J. 203, *203*
Fox, J.G. 97
Frank, J.A. 200
Frankenhaeuser, M. 45, 46, 67, 118, 122, 123
Fraser, J.A. *94*
Fraser, R. 59, 98, 119, 122, 191
Freedman, S. 165
French, J.R.P. 48, 66, *66*, *86*, 91, *91*, 92, 120, 121, *122*, 125, *149*, 152, 163, *166*, 181, *181*, 182, *182*, 183, *183*, 185, *185*, 259, 267, *267*, 268, 269, *269*, *283*
Frerichs, R.R. *169, 229*
Frese, M. 5, 67, 110, 111, 142, 153, 154, 209, 278
Freud, S. 71
Fried, Y. 46
Friedman, A.L. 89
Friedman, M. 251

Fröhlich, D. 199, 214, 218, 220, 222, 227
Fruensgaard, K. 199, 204
Fryer, D.M. 197, 213, 214, 216, 274, 300
Funch, D.P. 200
Furby, L. 126, 268
Furnham, A. 266
Fusilier, M.R. *181, 182, 183, 185*

Gadbois, C. 73
Galanter, E. *5*
Games, P.A. *298*
Ganster, D.C. 181, 182, 183, 185
Gardell, B. 53, 78, 82, 88, 102, 111, 164,
    179, 294
Garfield, S.L. 54
Garraty, J.A. 56, 194, 224
Gaskell, G. 208
Gatchel, R.J. *198*
Gath, D. 86, 95, 99
Gavin, J.F. 121, 150, 185
Gergen, K.J. 15, 280
Gergen, M.M. 15, 280
Gibson, J.J. 3, 17, 281
Gil, D. 206
Gilleard, C.J. 42
Gillum, R. *122, 140, 156*
Gitelson, R. 125, 152, 158
Glass, D.C. 124, 251
Glick, W. 110
Glyptis, S. 301
Godfrey, C. *203*, 217
Goldberg, D.P. 42, 43
Goldblatt, P.O. 203, *203*
Goodchild, M.E. 240
Goodman, P.S. 163, 165, 166
Goodwin, L. 194
Gore, S. *202*, 223
Gorman, A. *56*
Gorodezky, M.J. *200*
Gorsuch, R.L. *42, 44*
Gorz, A. 89
Gough, H.G. 42
Graen, G.B. *181, 182, 185*
Gram, L.F. *45*
Grandjean, E. 171, 172, *172*
Gravelle, H.S.E. 205
Grayson, D. 167
Grayson, J.P. 206, 209
Greenberger, D.B. 79
Greenhalgh, L. 150
Greenhaus, J.H. *139*, 142
Greenwood, C. *209*, *218*
Griffeth, R.W. 102
Groen, J.J. 66
Groskurth, P. *48*
Grunberg, N.E. *46*, *198*
Guest, R.H. 94

Gueutal, H.G. 173
Gurney, R.M. 228
Gutek, B.A. 250

Haas, A. 205
Hacker, W. 82
Hackman, J.R. 53, 80, 81, *95*, 102, *102*, 110,
    110, 134, *134*, 146, *146*, 177, 179, *179*,
    191, *191*, 255, *264*, 281
Hadley, S.W. 36, 39
Hage, J. 21, 47
Hall, E.M. *149*
Hall, D.T. 91, 141
Hall, F.S. 141
Hall, W. 209
Hamill, L. *217*
Hamilton, M. *43*
Handal, P.J. 200
Handy, C. 57, 300
Hannan, M. 209
Hanninen, V. 68, 102, 104, 173
Happ, A. *86, 172*
Harker, P. 102
Harrison, G.A. *62*, *123*
Harrison, R. van *48, 66, 86, 91, 120, 121,
    125, 149, 152, 163, 166, 181, 182, 259,
    267, 268, 269, 283*
Hartley, J. *199, 216, 217, 218, 273*
Hartmann, G. *296*
Harwich, C. 142
Hawton, K. 205
Headey, B. 42
Health and Safety Executive 172
Hechler, A. *199, 205*
Heller, F.A. 91
Helstrup, K. *199, 204*
Henderson, M. 177
Henderson, S. 149
Hendrie, H.C. 169
Hendrix, W.H. 180
Henry, J.P. 46
Henwood, F. *214, 221, 222, 225, 228, 229*
Heppner, P.P. 50
Hepworth, S.J. *46*, *173*, 196, 208, 209, 214,
    226, *249*
Herbert, G.W. 7
Herold, D.M. 148
Herzberg, F. 31, *298*
Herzog, A.R. 42
Hickson, D.J. 167
Hill, A.B. 248, 251
Hillier, V.F. 43
Hjelm, R. *149*
Hobbs, P.R. 209, 218, *229*
Hodapp, V. 123
Holland, J.L. 266
Holland, W.E. 179

Holstrom, E. *42*
Homans, G.C. 165
Hoolwerf, G. *142*
Hope, D. *209*
Horan, J.J. *298*
House, J.S. *91*, 102, 109, 122, *122*, 123, 125,
    139, 180, 181, *181*, 182, *182*, *183*, 185,
    185, 278
House, R.J. 48, *92*, 125, *125*, *151*, 152
Houston, B.K. 252
Howard, J. *214*, *221*, *222*, *225*, *228*, *229*
Howard, J.H. 252
Howarth, E. 44
Huba, G.J. *169*
Huber, J. 163, *229*, *273*
Hulin, C.L. *46*, *163*, 293
Hunt, R.G. 72
Hunting, W. *172*
Hurrell, J.J. *86*
Hurry, J. *199*
Hurst, M.W. *72*
Hutchinson, G. *205*

Iaffaldano, M.T. 293
Idzikowski, C. 171
Ilgen, D.R. 148
Irwin, R. *41*
Ivancevich, J.M. 260
Iversen, L. 199, 204

Jackson, P.R. 45, 60, *81*, *102*, *103*, *146*, *191*,
    196, 199, 209, 217, 218, 219, 222, 223,
    226, *226*, 227, 228, 229, 232, *232*, 233,
    234, 264, 272, *298*
Jackson, R.L. *200*, *201*
Jackson, S.E. 48, 50, 73, 82, 121, 125, 146,
    152, 180, 278
Jaco, E.G. 199
Jacobs, D. *122*, *140*, *156*
Jahoda, M. 29, 33, 57, 198, 211, 277, 281
Jamal, M. 68, 251, 294
James, L.R. 115
Jansen, B. 142
Jayaratne, S. 183, 185
Jenner, D.A. 62, *63*, *123*
Jervell, J. *149*
Jick, T.D. 250
Joensen, S. *199*, *204*
Johansson, G. 45, 66, 67, 96, 111, 118, 122,
    123, 136, 148
John, J. *199*, 205, *205*
Johns, G. 268
Johnston, L.D. *204*
Jones, A.P. 181, 182, 183, 185
Jones, D.M. 170
Jones, D.R. *203*

Jones, G.R. 50
Jones, J.G. 180, 196, 234
Jones, K.W. 122, 152, 259
Jonkers, T. 41, 72, 162, 190
Jougla, E. 229, 230

Kabanoff, B. 57, 72, 73, 197
Kafry, D. *42*, 82, *82*, *122*, 180
Kahn, R.L. 57, 61, 64, 120, 124, 126, 151,
    248, 251, 260, 261
Kahn, S. *241*
Kain, E.L. *219*
Kaiser, C.F. *43*
Kalleberg, A.L. 250, 251
Kamarck, T. *49*
Kammann, R. 41
Kandolin, I. *81*, *121*, *130*, *250*
Kanter, R.M. 142
Kantowitz, B.H. 170, 171, 172
Kanungo, R.N. 52
Kaplan, A. 187
Kaplan, B.H. *102*, *122*, *123*, *125*, *139*
Kaplan, E.M. 177
Karasek, R.A. 45, 68, 73, 84, 85, *97*, 105,
    112, 120, 122, 123, 124, *124*, 127, 128,
    129, 130, *130*, 131, 132, 133, 137, *142*,
    168, 183, 185, 284, 287
Kasl, S.V. 149, 186, 196, 202, 205, 209
Kauppinen-Toropainen, K. 81, 121, 130,
    250
Kavanagh, M.J. 72
Keenan, A. 252, 260, 262
Keith, P.M. 139
Kejner, M. 48
Keller, R.T. *81*, *95*, *134*
Kellner, R. 42
Kelly, J.E. 252, 298
Kemp, N.J. 102, *103*, *298*
Kendall, L.M. *46*, *163*
Kendell, R.E. 25
Kessler, L.G. 45
Kessler, R.C. 190, 231, 250
Kiev, A. 67, 120, 149
Kiggundu, M.N. 111
Kilpatrick, R. 214, 221, 222, 223
Kiresuk, T.J. 50
Kirjonen, J. 102, 104, 173
Kittel, F. 252
Klausen, H. 199, 204
Kleber, R.J. *182*, *183*
Klerman, G.L. 50
Knulst, W. 58, 214
Kobasa, S.C. 181, 183, 185, 241
Kobrick, J.L. 170
Koch, J.L. 47
Kohn, M.L. 45, 52, 78, *83*, 96, *96*, 104, *104*,
    115, 119, 122, 149, 165, 189

Kohn, V. 67, 120, 149
Komarovsky, M. 215
Kopelman, R.E. 139
Kornhauser, A.W. 31, 64, 65, 72, 86, 90, 93,
   95, 99, 164, 259
Kornitzer, M. *252*
Krantz, D.S. 16, 46, 124
Krause, N. 231
Kraut, A.I. 120, 126, 150, 152
Kreitman, N. *204*, *205*, *218*, *225*
Kroemer, K.H.E. 172
Kroes, W. 66, 91
Kyriacou, C. 66, 120

Lalich, N. *91*
Lambert, M.J. 43, 50
Landerman, L.R. *102*, *122*, *123*, *125*, *139*
Lang, L. *139*
Langer, E.J. 4, 12, 80
Langner, T.S. 42
LaRocco, J.M. 91, 92, 122, 181, 182, 183,
   185
Larsen, R.J. 42
Latack, J.C. 155
Latcham, R.W. *204*
Latham, G.P. *119*
Laubli, T. 172
Lauer, R.H. 145
Lawler, E.E. 53, 110, 166, 177
Lawlis, G.F. 209
Layton, C. 196, 209
Lazarsfeld, P.F. *198*, 226
Lazarus, R.S. 16, 30, 34, 54, 241
Lederer, D.A. *266*
Lee, R. 251
Lefcourt, M. 30, 51, 150, 249
Lefkowitz, J. 47
Lem, C. 136
Levanoni, E. *125*, *152*
Leventman, P.G. 206
Levi, L. 149
Levinson, H. 155
Lewin, K. 119
Lewis, A. 25
Lieberman, M.A. *51*, 209
Liem, J. 190
Liem, R. 190
Liff, S. 166
Liker, J.K. 206, 219, 272
Liles, D.H. 171
Lin, N. 180
Lindamood, C.A. 52
Lindenthal, J.J. *145*
Lindstrom, B.O. *66*, *96*, *111*, *123*
Linn, M.W. 196, 198, 202, 209, 223
Lipman, R.S. *43*
Lirtzman, S.I. *125*, *151*

Little, F.A.J. 170
Little, M. 198, 206, 214
Locke, E.A. 119
Lodahl, T. 48
Loevinger, J. 30
Lofquist, L.H. 266
Loher, B.T. 81, 102, 134, 146, 191, 256, 261,
   263, 264
Long, J. 297
Lorence, J. 82, 105
Loscocco, K.A. 250, 251
Lott, A.J. 177
Lott, B.E. 177
Louis, M.R. 153, 154
Lovatt, D.J. 222
Lubin, B. 42
Luepker, R. *122*, *140*, *156*
Lundberg, U. 46
Lupton, T. 89, 167
Lushene, R.E. *42*, *44*
Lyons, T.F. 261

McBain, G.D.M. 252, 260, 262
McCabe, E. *206*
McDonald, C. *43*, *45*
McDougall, W. 8, 176
McDowell, I. 44
McEnrue, M.P. 50
McGee, G.W. *181*, *182*, *185*, *293*
McGehee, W. 46
McGowan, J.F. *70*
McGregor, A. 205
McGuire, W.J. 1, 280
MacKay, C.J. 27, 44
McKee, L. 206, 219
McKenna, S. 216
McLean, A. 69
McLure, A. *209*, *218*
McMichael, A.J. *102*, *122*, *123*, *125*, *139*
McMillen, D.B. 250
McPherson, A. 209
McRae, J.A. 231
McRae, R.R. 19, 44, 240, 250
Maddi, S.R. *241*
Madge, N. 206
Maguin, P. *229*, *230*
Mahajan, P. *171*
Mandilovitch, M.S.B. 259
Manheimer, D.I. *43*, *278*
Mansfield, R. 155
Manuck, S.B. 16, 46, 124
Marcelissen, F.H.G. *182*, *183*
Margolis, L.H. 206, 209
Markham, S.E. 201
Markides, K.S. 231
Mars, G. 198, 206, 219, 222
Marshall, G. 224
Marshall, J.R. 200

Marshall, S. *228*
Martin, B. *209, 218*
Martin, J. 141, 166
Martin, R. 215, 221, 228, 229
Martin, T.N. 122
Marxer, F. *85, 123, 128, 130*
Maslach, C. 48, 50, 73, 121, 146, 152, 278
Maslow, A.H. 32
Matteson, M.T. 260
Matthews, K.A. 251
May, R. 8
Mayes, B.T. *181, 182, 183, 185*
Mechanic, D. 229
Megaw, E.D. 171
Meier, S.T. 48
Melisaratos, N. 43
Mellinger, G.D. 43, 278
Melville, D.I. 209
Menaghan, E.G. *51*
Mendelsohn, F.S. *42*
Mendelson, M. *42*
Mermelstein, R. 49
Merton, R. 154
Metcalf, D. *203*
Metzner, H.L. *109, 278*
Michael, P.L. 170
Miclette, A.L. 98, 135, 148, 167
Miles, I. 208, 209, 214, 221, 222, 225, 228, 229
Miles, R.H. 125, 152, 153
Miller, G.A. 5
Miller, H.E. 249
Miller, J. 83, 96, 104
Miller, K.A. *83, 96, 104*
Miller, S.M. 149, 150
Millward, N. 167
Minvielle, D. *229, 230*
Mirowsky, J. *229, 273*
Mitz, L.F. 250
Moch, M. 178, 191
Mock, J. *42*
Moeller, N.L. *81, 102, 134, 146, 191, 256, 261, 263, 264*
Moen, P. 206, 219
Monk, T.H. 142
Monroe, S.M. 19, 242
Mooney, A. 205
Moos, R.H. 73, 82, 122, 152, 182, 183
Morris, L.D. 219, 222
Morse, J.J. 50, 102, 262, 294
Mortimer, J.T. 82, 83, 105
Moser, K.A. 203
Mostow, E. 70
Mottaz, C.J. 81, 181, 182, 258, 259, 263
Mowday, R.T. 47
Moylan, S. *217*
Muchinsky, P.M. 293
Muczyk, J. *102*

Mullan, J.T. *51*
Murgatroyd, S. 29
Murphy, C.J. 48
Murphy, L.R. 188, *188*
Murray, H. 8, 176, 266
Mutanen, P. *81, 121, 130, 250*
Myers, C.S. 167
Myers, J.K. 89, 145

Narendranathan, W. 203
Naylor, J.B. 301
Near, J.P. 72
Nerell, G. 61, 66, 82, 121, 123, 168
Nestel, G. 68
Nethercott, S. 202
Newberry, P. 70
Nezu, A.M. 50
Nicholas, I.J. *296*
Nicholson, N. 64, 88, 125, 153, 154, 156
Nickell, S. *203*
Niebuhr, R.E. 293
Nieva, V.F. 250
Niewenhuijzen, M.G. van *195, 208, 209*
Noble, M. *228*
Noe, R.A. *81, 102, 134, 146, 191, 256, 261, 263, 264*
Noller, P. 198, 209, 228
Norris, D.R. 293
Nygard, R. 237

Oborne, D.J. 171
O'Brien, G.E. 73, 81, 91, 92, 93, 95, 120, 164, 195, 197, 198, 208, 209, 228, 249, 256, 258, 259, 261, 268, 275
Oddy, M. 208, 209, 228
O'Keefe, S.J. 229
Oldham, G.R. 53, 80, 81, 95, 102, 110, 134, 146, 147, 177, 179, 186, 187, 191, 255, 264, 281
Olivier-Martin, R. 43
O'Malley, P.M. *204*
Organization for Economic Co-operation and Development 57, 217, 234
Ormel, J. 19
Osgood, C.E. 177
Ostrander, D.R. *145*
Ovalle, N.K. *180*
Overall, J.E. 43

Pahl, R.E. 58
Palmer, C.D. *63, 123*
Parker, D.F. 48, 125, 182
Parker, S. 57
Parkes, K.R. *49, 85*, 181, 241
Parry, G. 48, *69*, 139, 229, 230, 231, 273

Parsons, C.K. 148
Patton, M.J. 54
Patton, W. 198, 209, 228
Paul, L.J. *264*
Paykel, E.S. 50
Payne, R.L. 48, 58, 62, 63, 82, *88*, 113, 122,
    123, 126, 130, 180, 196, 199, 203, 204,
    208, 209, 213, 214, 216, 217, 218, 220,
    222, 234, 251, 268, 273, 274, 300
Pearce, J.L. *81, 102, 110, 146, 191, 264*
Pearlin, L.I. 45, 51, 209, 241
Peck, D.F. *204*
Pennebaker, J.W. *188*
Pepper, M.P. *145*
Petersen, C.H. 50
Pettersson, I.L. *149*
Petty, M.M. 293
Petzel, T.P. *43*
Phares, E.J. *51*
Pichot, P. 43
Pierce, J.L. 95
Pinder, C.C. 155
Pines, A.M. 42, 82, 122, 180
Pinneau, S.R. *48, 66, 86, 91, 120, 121, 125,*
    149, 152, 163, 166, 181, 182, 259, 267,
    269, 283
Piotrkowski, C.S. 65, 74
Pirie, P. *122, 140, 156*
Plant, M.A. 204, *204*
Platt, S. 205, 206, 218, 225
Pleck, J.H. 139, 141, 142
Polich, J.M. *204*
Porter, L.W. *47*, 110, 177
Potthof, P. *199, 205*
Poulton, E.C. 170
Powell, B.J. *70*
Praught, E. 44
Pribram, K.H. *5*
Prince, J.B. 135, 147
Pritchard, R.D. 126, 152
Privette, G. 137
Pucetti, M.C. 181, 183, 185, 241

Quinlan, D.M. *43, 45*
Quinn, R.P. 48, 50, 60, 61, 63, *64*, 93, 120,
    120, 124, 126, 139, *151, 248*, 250, *251,*
    259, *260, 261*

Radloff, L.S. 42, 209
Rafaelson, O.J. *45*
Rahe, R.H. *122, 278*
Rainwater, L. 7, 162, 189
Ramsey, J.D. 170
Rapoport, R. 141
Ratcliff, K.S. 200
Rathkey, P. 300

Rechnitzer, P.A. *252*
Redburn, F.S. 149
Reddy, D.M. *198, 232*
Reeder, L.G. 44
Reisby, N. *45*
Renner, V.J. 34
Renshaw, J.R. 140, 155
Reynolds, V. *62, 63*, 123
Rhodes, S.R. 250
Rice, R.W. *72*
Rick, J.T. 123
Rickels, K. *43, 278*
Ricks, D.F. 28
Ridgeway, D. 27
Riskind, J.H. 81, 92, 96, 111, 121
Rizzo, J.R. 48, 125, 151, 152
Robbins, C.A. *109, 278*
Roberts, C. *56*, 141, 166
Roberts, K. 228
Roberts, K.H. 110
Roberts, R.E. 229
Rodgers, W.L. *42, 208*
Rognum, T. *149*
Rose, N. 205
Rose, R. *72*
Rose, R.M. 123
Rosenberg, M. 45
Rosenblatt, Z. 150
Rosenman, R. 251, 260
Ross, C.E. 163, 229, 273
Ross, J. 249
Rosse, J.G. 293
Rotchford, N.L. 81, 134, 186
Rotter, J.B. 30, *51*, 68, 91, 256, 293
Rousseau, D.M. 48, 120, 121, 123, 139
Routledge, T. 46
Rowland, K.M. *46*
Roy, A. 199
Roy, D.F. 89, 97, 167
Russell, J.A. 27
Russell, R.S. *45, 131*
Ryan, G.M. 43
Rys, G.S. *266*

Saari, L.M. *119*
Sabini, J. *5*
Salkowe, A. *266*
Salovaara, H. *149*
Salvendy, G. 86
Samuel, E. *204*
Sandifer, R. *196, 198, 202, 209, 223*
Sandman, C.A. 46
Sartorius, N. *45*
Sawyer, P. *56*
Schaeffer, R. *266*
Schafer, R.B. 139
Schlozman, K.L. 206, 208

Schneider, B. 91, 245
Schokman-Gates, K. 44
Schooler, C. 45, 52, 78, *83, 96, 96,* 104, *104,* 115, 119, *120,* 122, 149, 165, 189, 241
Schoonderwoerd, L. 58, 214
Schriesheim, C.A. 48
Schuler, R.S. 125, *125,* 152, *152*
Schwab, D.P. 163
Schwefel, D. 199, 205
Scott, K.J. *54*
Seabrook, J. 59, 198, 217, 224
Sears, P.S. *119*
Seeman, M. 52, 103, 111
Seers, A. 181, 182, 185
Sekaran, U. 139, 141
Seligman, M.E.P. 4, 30
Senior, B. 301
Serey, T.T. *181, 182, 185*
Shackelton, V.J. 97
Shamir, B. 139, 141, 226
Shaper, A.G. *202, 203*
Shapiro, D.A. 69, 299
Shaw, J.B. 81, 92, 96, 111, 121
Shaw, K.N. *119*
Sheffield, B.F. 42
Shehan, C.L. 229
Shepard, J.M. 52
Shepard, L.J. 48, 50, 61
Shepherd, D.M. 205
Sheppard, H.L. 233
Sherman, R.E. 50
Shostrom, E.L. 52
Shrout, P.E. *42*
Siddique, C.M. 202, 208, 209, 218, *250*
Siegel, R. 50
Sims, H.P. *45,* 81, *81,* 95, *96, 102,* 134, *134, 146,* 177, 179, 256, 261, 263
Singer, J.E. *16, 46, 198*
Smart, R.G. 204
Smee, C.H. *217*
Smith, A.H.W. *229*
Smith, D.J. 217, 218
Smith, F.J. 46
Smith, M.B. 29
Smith, M.J. 172
Smith, P. 208
Smith, P.C. 46, 136, 163, 251
Snaith, R.R. 43
Snoek, J.D. *64, 120, 124, 126, 151, 248, 251, 260, 261*
Sobolski, J. *252*
Sommer, J.J. *71*
Sorensen, G. 122, 140, 156
Sorge, A. 296
Sorkin, R.D. 170, 171, 172
South, S.J. 206
Spector, P.E. 102, 249, 256, 261, 264
Spielberger, C.D. 42, 44

Spruit, I.P. 195, 205, 208, 209
Stack, S. 205
Stafford, E.M. *60, 196, 209,* 226, *226, 228, 229, 234*
Staines, G.L. 60, 61, 63, 72, 73, 93, 120, 139, *139,* 141, 142, 250
Stambul, H.B. *204*
Stammerjohn, L.W. *91, 172*
Staw, B.M. 248, 249
Steers, R.M. 47, *47*
Stein, S. *196, 198, 202, 209, 223*
Steinberg, L.D. 206
Stepina, L.P. *95, 102, 134, 146, 179, 191*
Stern, G.G. 266
Stern, J. *205*
Stock, F.G.L. *94*
Stogdill, R.M. 182
Stokes, G. 200, 209, 213, 221, 228
Stolk, J. *195, 208, 209*
Stone, E.F. 110, 173, 177
Stopes-Roe, M. 206, 209
Strasser, S. 79
Stretcher, V. *109, 278*
Strupp, H.H. 36, 39
Sturt, E. *199*
Sutcliffe, J. 66, 120
Sutton, R.I. 120, 121, 123, *123,* 139, 152
Swinburne, P. 59
Sykes, A.J.M. 167
Syrotuik, J. *250*
Szalai, A. 56, 221
Szasz, T.S. 34
Szilagyi, A.D. *45,* 81, *81,* 95, *96, 102, 134, 146,* 177, 179, 256, 261, 263

Taber, T.D. 110, 173
Taylor, D.A. *187*
Taylor, M.S. *148*
Tellegen, A. 27
Tennant, C. *199*
Terborg, J.R. 249
Terkel, S. 58, 101, 191, 224
Tetrick, L.E. 115
Tharenou, P. 45, 102
Thayer, P.W. 103, 174
Theorell, T. *45,* 67, *85,* 97, *97, 123, 124, 128,* 130, *130, 131,* 142, *142*
Theriault, R. 163
Thierry, H. 142, *142*
Thoits, P.A. 8, 180, 189, 209
Thomas, L.E. 206
Thomas, R. 145
Thompson, P. 78
Thoreson, R.W. *70*
Tiffany, D.W. 195
Tiffany, P.M. *195*
Tiggemann, M. 196, 198, 208, 209, 228

Tilley, A.J. 142
Tosi, D.J. 52
Townsend, P. 7
Trew, K. 214, 221, 222, 223
Triantis, K.P. *124*, *183*, *185*
Trinkaus, R.J. 121
Troxler, R.G. *180*
Tuller, W.L. 46
Turner, A.N. 98, 135, 148, 167

Uhlenhuth, E.H. *43*, *278*
Ulich, E. *48*
Ullah, P. *214*, *215*, 219, *222*, 223, 225, 226, *226*, 228, *228*, *229*, 232, *232*, 233, *273*
Upmeyer, A. 12

Vaddadi, K.S. *42*
Vaillant, C.O. 195
Vaillant, G.E. 29, 33, 50, 54, 195
van Dijkhuizen, N. 48, 85, 92, 112, 123, 127, 149, 153, 158, 180, 182, 183, 252, 287
van Harrison, R. *48*, *66*, *86*, *91*, *120*, *121*, *125*, *149*, *152*, *163*, *166*, *181*, *182*, *259*, *267*, *268*, *269*, *283*
van Niewenhuijzen, M.G. *195*, *208*, *209*
Vardi, Y. *102*
Vecchio, R.P. 60
Veenhoven, R. 41, 72, 162, 190
Veit, C.T. *43*
Veith-Flanigan, J. 46
Verba, S. 206, 208
Verbrugge, L.M. 202
Verkley, H. *195*, *208*, *209*
Veroff, J. 41, 49
Vickers, R.R. *122*, 278
Viney, L.L. 209
Vinokur, A. *91*, *181*, *182*, *183*, *185*, *268*
Von Hofsten, C. 3
Vredenburgh, D.J. 121
Vroom, V.H. 258

Wachtel, P.J. 12
Wadsworth, M. 52
Wagner, F.R. 50, 102
Wahlund, I. 61, 66, 82, 121, 123, 168
Walker, C.R. 94
Wall, T.D. *42*, *46*, *53*, *61*, 81, 83, 88, 102, *102*, 103, 125, 126, 134, 146, 150, *173*, 191, *249*, *264*, 268, 296, 298
Wallace, J. 215, 221, 228, 229
Wallace, M.J. 163
Walsh, J.T. *110*, *173*
Wanous, J.P. 154, 256, 258, 259, 261
Ward, C.H. *42*
Ward, H.W. *122*, *278*

Ward, K. 301
Ware, J.E. 19, 43, *44*
Warner, M. *296*
Warr, P.B. 2, 42, 44, 45, 46, *46*, 48, 53, 58, 60, *60*, 61, 62, 63, 88, 125, 139, *173*, 195, 196, *196*, 197, 199, *199*, 203, 204, 205, 208, 209, *209*, 214, 215, 216, *216*, 217, *217*, 218, *218*, 219, *219*, 220, 221, 222, 223, *223*, *225*, 226, *226*, 227, 228, *228*, 229, *229*, 232, 233, *234*, *249*, 251, 272, 273, *273*, 287
Warren, P.S.G. 142
Watson, B. 142
Watson, D. 27, 43, 240, 278
Wearing, A. *42*
Weaver, C.N. 61, 81, 250, 251
Weber, M. 224
Weiner, H.J. 71
Weinstein, H.M. 250
Weinstein, N. 170
Weir, T. *124*, *126*, *145*, *152*, *177*, 252
Weiss, R.S. 57
Weissman, M.M. 50
Wells, A.J. *102*, *122*, *123*, *125*, *139*, 167
Wells, J.A. 186
Werbel, J.D. 155
Wessman, A.E. 28
West, D.J. 298
Westcott, G. 203, 209
Weyer, G. 123
Wheeler, L. *187*
White, M. 195, 218, 272
White, R.W. 29
Whyte, W.F. 64
Wicker, A.W. 17
Wiener, Y. 102
Wiggins, J.D. 266
Wilbur, E.R. 251
Wild, R. 99
Wilder, C.S. 202
Wilensky, H.L. 209, 218
Wilkes, B. 91
Wilkinson, R.T. 142
Williams, A.W. 19
Williams, D.G. 44
Williams, T.A. 172
Willmott, M. *42*
Willmott, P. 58, 61, 140
Wills, T.A. 8, 183
Wilpert, B. 91
Wilson, H. 7
Winefield, A.H. 196, 198, 208, 209, 228
Wineman, J.D. 187
Wing, J.K. 45, *199*
Winnubst, J.A.M. 182, 183
Winter, J.M. 205
Withey, S.B. 41, 42
Wittenborn, J.R. 45

Wolfe, D.M. *64, 120, 124, 126, 151, 248, 251, 260, 261*
Wolfe, J.C. *81, 102, 146, 191*
Woodworth, J. *42*
Wyatt, S. *94*

Yankelovich, D. 34
Yoshitake, H. 48

Young, M. 58, 61, 140

Zappert, L.T. 250
Zeisel, H. *198*
Zevon, M.A. 27
Zisook, S. 43
Zung, W.W.K. 42, 45
Zuroff, D. *43, 45*